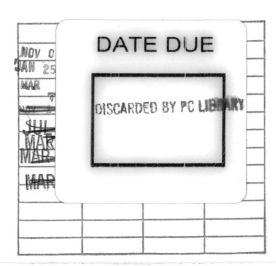

STATE OF THE
WORLD
1991

Other Norton/Worldwatch Books

Lester R. Brown et al.

State of the World 1984

State of the World 1985

State of the World 1986

State of the World 1987

State of the World 1988

State of the World 1989

State of the World 1990

STATE OF THE WORLD
1991

A Worldwatch Institute Report on Progress Toward a Sustainable Society

PROJECT DIRECTOR
Lester R. Brown

ASSOCIATE PROJECT
DIRECTORS
Christopher Flavin
Sandra Postel

EDITOR
Linda Starke

SENIOR RESEARCHERS
Lester R. Brown
Alan Durning

Christopher Flavin
Hilary F. French
Jodi Jacobson
Marcia D. Lowe
Sandra Postel
Michael Renner

RESEARCH ASSOCIATES
Nicholas Lenssen
John C. Ryan
John E. Young

W·W·NORTON & COMPANY

NEW YORK   LONDON

The text of this book is composed in Baskerville, with the display set in Caslon.
Composition and manufacturing by the Haddon Craftsmen, Inc.

First Edition

ISBN 0-393-02934-4
ISBN 0-393-30733-6 (pbk.)

W. W. Norton & Company, Inc., 500 Fifth Avenue, New York, N.Y. 10110
W. W. Norton & Company Ltd., 10 Coptic Street, London WC1A 1PU

1 2 3 4 5 6 7 8 9 0

 This book is printed on recycled paper

HC 59
.5733

Acknowledgments

On the face of it, *State of the World* is a presumptuous endeavor: a handful of office-bound researchers in Washington, D.C., attempt first to describe the intricate currents and countercurrents of humanity's interaction with the global environment, and then proceed to recommend how to shift the currents in other directions.

Whatever success we achieve in this undertaking is in large measure a tribute to the work of people whose names do not appear under chapter titles. We cannot thank them enough. First and foremost, Worldwatch is blessed with an insightful Board of Directors, ably guided by Chairman Orville Freeman. The Institute's talented team of administrative and communications professionals show not only uncommon dedication and skill, but also uncommon grace and wit—which help keep the Institute's human environment healthy. They are, in alphabetical order, Mark Cheater, Carole Douglis, Guy Gorman, James Gorman, Gloria Grant, Barbara Granzen, Blondeen Gravely, Joseph Gravely, Geni Hamilton, Heather Hanford, Millicent Johnson, Reah Janise Kauffman, Steven Kaufman, Denise Byers Thomma, and Howard Youth. Though Stephen Dujack left for new endeavors since our last edition, he deserves special thanks for his contribution to Worldwatch.

Research assistants dedicate long hours to the nuts and bolts work of assembling *State of the World*. Holly Brough contributed extraordinarily to Chapter 9

and helped too with Chapter 8, while Erik Hagerman did double duty on Chapters 5 and 6. Ann Misch took over for departing staffer Meri McCoy-Thompson on Chapters 7 and 8. Marnie Stetson assisted both authors of Chapter 10, on top of her efforts for Chapter 2, and Peter Weber toiled long and hard on Chapter 1.

Worldwatch owes its existence to the largesse of a number of organizations that have supported our work over the years. Core funding for the *State of the World* series comes from the Rockefeller Brothers Fund and the Winthrop Rockefeller Trust. Research funding comes from the Geraldine R. Dodge, George Gund, William and Flora Hewlett, W. Alton Jones, William D. and Catherine T. MacArthur, Andrew W. Mellon, Curtis and Edith Munson, Edward John Noble, Public Welfare, Surdna, and Rockefeller foundations, and the United Nations Population Fund.

Returning senior researcher Lori Heise surveyed the entire manuscript at a critical juncture, and a bevy of experts outside the institute looked over various chapter drafts for errors of fact or analysis, often on very short notice. The authors gratefully acknowledge Frederik van Bolhuis, Robert Buschbacher, Martin Calhoun, Carroll Carter, Herman Cesar, William U. Chandler, Scott Chaplin, W.W. Charters, Karen Christensen, Maheshwar Dayal, Elizabeth Deakin, Jean Durning, Duncan Fisher, Adrienne Germaine, David Goldstein, Robert

Goodland, Robert Gough, Michael Grubb, Stanley Henshaw, H.M. Hubbard, Nada Johanisová, Ron Kilcoyne, Eliza Klose, Stanislav Kolar, Skip Laitner, David Lewis, Richard Liroff, Arjun Makhijani, Norman Myers, Sigismund Niebel, R.K. Pachauri, David Perry, D.J. Peterson, Steven Polasky, Michael Replogle, Bruce M. Rich, Elliott Sclar, Roger Sedjo, Kristen Suokko, Thomas H. Tietenberg, János Vargha, Philip Warburg, Carl Weinberg, Carl-Jochen Winter, and Edward Wolf. Of course, any remaining errors are the sole responsibility of the authors.

In the course of one month, miracle-working editor Linda Starke turns our 10 disparate chapter drafts into a unified whole, attending both to detail and to structure. Likewise, Bart Brown makes quick work of the index, giving the volume far greater power as a reference tool. And, running the anchor leg in our relay team, Iva Ashner and Andy Marasia at W.W. Norton & Company in New York provide us with books printed flawlessly—on recycled paper—at a full sprint.

Each year, the work of numerous researchers, analysts, and thinkers outside Worldwatch help shape *State of the World*. This year, we would like to specially acknowledge Herman Daly, senior economist at the World Bank, for tirelessly providing intellectual leadership on the most pressing issues of our time—how to reconcile economic activity with the dictates of environmental sustainability. As economist, philosopher, and author, Herman Daly has expanded the frontiers of economic thought and international development. His work inspires us each year, but it greatly influenced the thinking and analysis embodied in several chapters in this volume in particular. We give Herman our deepest thanks and appreciation.

Lester R. Brown, Christopher Flavin, and Sandra Postel

Contents

List of Tables and Figures

LIST OF TABLES

LIST OF FIGURES

Foreword

This eighth annual assessment is being released at a time when the world has become painfully aware of the full extent of air, water, and soil pollution in Eastern Europe and the Soviet Union. As the political curtain that had shielded this region from full view has risen, unprecedented environmental horror stories are coming out. In some cities in Eastern Europe, pollution is so severe that it has reduced life expectancy several years below that in surrounding areas. Respiratory disease, soaring cancer rates, allergies, nervous system malfunctions, and birth deformities are among the litany of environmental ills plaguing these societies.

Although *State of the World* typically deals exclusively with global issues, this year we have departed from that tradition by devoting an entire chapter to one geographic region, namely Eastern Europe and the Soviet Union. We last did this six years ago, in *State of the World 1985*, when we published a chapter on reversing Africa's decline.

Our final chapter logically follows the last chapter in *State of the World 1990*, in which we sketched the basic outline of an environmentally sustainable global economy. This year, Chapter 10 focuses on the means of achieving that goal, ranging from World Bank reform to the restructuring of tax systems. Only by redesigning the incentives that shape private decisions and the priorities that guide international development can the global economy be transformed from a self-destructing one into a sustainable one.

This past year saw continuing growth in the translation of *State of the World* into other languages. With 20 editions of *State of the World 1990* available, it can now be read in more languages than the *Reader's Digest*. In addition to appearing in all the major languages—English, Spanish, Portuguese, Arabic, Chinese, Japanese, Indonesian, German, Italian, French, and Russian, *State of the World* is also available in Norwegian, Dutch, Thai, Malay, and Korean. We are particularly pleased that in Eastern Europe, *State of the World* is now appearing in Czech and Bulgarian as well as Polish and Romanian. And the German edition is being marketed in all of Germany. This year, we expect to add Danish, Finnish, Turkish, and possibly Greek.

Growth in sales of *State of the World* continues unabated. The first printing in English for the 1984 volume was 16,000. The first printing of *State of the World 1991* is 102,000 copies. In addition to the North American edition, there are now separate English language editions for India, Australia, and the United Kingdom, which includes the remainder of the Commonwealth countries.

One reason for this enormous growth is that *State of the World* is acquiring a semi-official character, largely by default. Various specialized U.N. agencies produce "state of" reports in agriculture, population, environment, and the global economy, to cite a few. But the

United Nations does not produce an integrated state of the world report. Thus national governments, U.N. agencies themselves, and the international development community rely heavily on the analysis and information in *State of the World*.

Another encouraging development has been the growing interest of the academic community in ecological literacy. More and more university leaders are recognizing the need to produce graduates who are well grounded in environmental issues if they are to be prepared for life in the late twentieth and early twenty-first centuries.

Among the leaders in this field is Tufts University President Jean Mayer, who went so far as to convene an international meeting of university presidents on this subject at Tufts' conference center in Talloires, France. Western New England College in Massachusetts, with an enrollment of 2,100, wants all their graduates to read at least one *State of the World* report in some course along the way. University of Georgia President Charles Knapp announced in 1989 the goal of giving every graduate an educated awareness of the environment.

This interest in ecological literacy is translating into strong growth in college classroom use of *State of the World*, where it is widely ordered as the primary or a supplemental text. *State of the World 1989* was adopted for use in 1,106 courses in some 584 U.S. colleges and universities. Partial returns for *State of the World 1990* indicate even more extensive adoption. California, for example, had some 63 campuses using the 1989 report in 131 courses.

At the international level, groups have started to spring up spontaneously to help market and distribute Worldwatch publications. The first of these, Worldwatch Institute Japan, undertook the translation of *State of the World* into Japanese and more recently launched their own version of our magazine, *World Watch*.

In the Nordic countries, the establishment of Worldwatch Institute Norden under the leadership of Magnar Norderhaug has dramatically increased the use of Worldwatch research products, including *State of the World*, in these countries. With sales of 9,000 for the Norwegian edition, per capita availability is higher in Norway than in any other country.

Worldwatch Institute Europe is being organized by Gunter Pauli. Among other things, Pauli has arranged for the European editions to be launched by an address to the European Parliament's Environmental Commission, which consists of some 50 members of parliament. The first meeting, in Brussels in February 1990, was so successful that a launch meeting for *State of the World 1991* has been scheduled in Strasbourg in mid-February.

Another rewarding phenomenon for the Institute is the increasing number of individuals who take it upon themselves to distribute copies of *State of the World* to key decision makers. Ted Turner, for example, in each of the last several years has purchased 1,000 copies to hand out to Fortune 500 CEOs and members of Congress, and some 400 copies for the senior editors and reporters at his Cable News Network. William Bryant, a member of the Michigan House of Representatives, regularly buys 150 copies for distribution to his colleagues.

Outside the United States, Raymond Rooth, a Norwegian industrial executive and a member of the board of Worldwatch Institute Norden, purchased 900 copies for key people in his own country. Bjorn Stigson, a corporate executive from Sweden and a director of ASEA-Brown Boveri-Flakt, bought 500 copies of the Swedish edition for distribution to members of parliament and provincial governments in Sweden.

For the Institute, 1990 was an exciting and demanding year. In addition to Earth Day 1990 in April, with all the attendant public and media interest in issues of concern to Worldwatch, the fall brought the premiere of RACE TO SAVE THE PLANET. This 10-hour film series, produced by public television station WGBH in Boston, was inspired by our *State of the World* reports. Underlining its importance, the Public Broadcasting Service in the United States aired the series twice in the fall of 1990.

We take some satisfaction in this rising level of concern about the future of the planet. We believe that this will be the environmental decade, the time when the issues we analyze will belatedly get the attention they deserve. And we thank you, our readers, for helping make it so.

Lester R. Brown
  Project Director

Christopher Flavin
Sandra Postel
  Associate Project Directors

Worldwatch Institute
1776 Massachusetts Ave., N.W.
Washington, DC 20036

December 1990

STATE OF THE
WORLD
1991

1

The New World Order

Lester R. Brown

As the nineties begin, the world is on the edge of a new age. The cold war that dominated international affairs for four decades and led to an unprecedented militarization of the world economy is over. With its end comes an end to the world order it spawned.

The East-West ideological conflict was so intense that it dictated the shape of the world order for more than a generation. It provided a clear organizing principle for the foreign policies of the two superpowers and, to a lesser degree, of other governments as well. But with old priorities and military alliances becoming irrelevant, we are now at one of those rare points in history—a time of great change, a time when change is as unpredictable as it is inevitable.[1]

No one can say with certainty what the new order will look like. But if we are to fashion a promising future for the next generation, then the enormous effort required to reverse the environmental degradation of the planet will dominate world affairs for decades to come. In effect, the battle to save the planet will replace the battle over ideology as the organizing theme of the new world order.

As the dust from the cold war settles, both the extent of the environmental damage to the planet and the inadequacy of efforts to cope with it are becoming all too apparent. During the 20 years since the first Earth Day, in 1970, the world lost nearly 200 million hectares of tree cover, an area roughly the size of the United States east of the Mississippi River. Deserts expanded by some 120 million hectares, claiming more land than is currently planted to crops in China. Thousands of plant and animal species with which we shared the planet in 1970 no longer exist. Over two decades, some 1.6 billion people were added to the world's population—more than inhabited the planet in 1900. And the world's farmers lost an estimated 480 billion tons of topsoil, roughly equivalent to the amount on India's cropland.[2]

This planetary degradation proceeded despite the environmental protection efforts of national governments over the past 20 years. During this time nearly all countries created environmental agencies. National legislatures passed thousands of laws to protect the environment. Tens of thousands of grassroots environmental groups sprung up in response to locally destructive activities. Membership in national environmental

Units of measure are metric unless common usage dictates otherwise.

organizations soared. But as Earth Day 1990 chairman Denis Hayes asks, "How could we have fought so hard, and won so many battles, only to find ourselves now on the verge of losing the war?"[3]

One reason for this failure is that although governments have professed concern with environmental deterioration, few have been willing to make the basic changes needed to reverse it. Stabilizing climate, for example, depends on restructuring national energy economies. Getting the brakes on population growth requires massive changes in human reproductive behavior. But public understanding of the consequences of continuously rising global temperatures or rapid population growth is not yet sufficient to support effective policy responses.

The goal of the cold war was to get others to change their values and behavior, but winning the battle to save the planet depends on changing our own values and behavior.

The battle to save the earth's environmental support systems will differ from the battle for ideological supremacy in some important ways. The cold war was largely an abstraction, a campaign waged by strategic planners. Except for bearing the economic costs, which were very real, most people in the United States and the Soviet Union did not directly take part. In the new struggle, however, people everywhere will need to be involved: individuals trying to recycle their garbage, couples trying to decide whether to have a second child, and energy ministers trying to fashion an environmentally sustainable energy system. The goal of the cold war was to get others to change their values and behavior, but winning the battle to save the planet

depends on changing our own values and behavior.

The parallel with the recent stunningly rapid changes in Eastern Europe is instructive. At some point, it became clear to nearly everyone that centrally planned economies were not only not working, but that they are inherently unworkable. Empty shelves in shops and long lines outside them demonstrated all too convincingly that a centrally controlled socialist economy could not even satisfy basic needs, much less deliver the abundance it promised. Once enough people, including Mikhail Gorbachev, realized that socialist planners could not resolve this contradiction within the existing system, reform became inevitable.

Likewise, the contradiction between the indicators that measure the health of the global economy and those that gauge the health of its environmental support systems is becoming more visible. This inherent conflict affects all economic systems today: the industrialized economies of the West, the reforming economies of the East, and the developing economies of the Third World. As with the contradictions in Eastern Europe, those between economic and environmental indicators can be resolved only by economic reform, in effect by reshaping the world economy so that it is environmentally sustainable. (See Chapter 10.)

TWO VIEWS OF THE WORLD

Anyone who regularly reads the financial papers or business weeklies would conclude that the world is in reasonably good shape and that long-term economic trends are promising. Obviously there are still problems—the U.S. budget deficit, Third World debt, and the unsettling effect of rising oil prices—but to an economist, things appear manageable. Even those predicting a severe global recession in 1991 are bullish about the longer term economic prospects for the nineties.

Yet on the environmental front, the situation could hardly be worse. Anyone who regularly reads scientific journals has to be concerned with the earth's changing physical condition. Every major indicator shows a deterioration in natural systems: forests are shrinking, deserts are expanding, croplands are losing topsoil, the stratospheric ozone layer continues to thin, greenhouse gases are accumulating, the number of plant and animal species is diminishing, air pollution has reached health-threatening levels in hundreds of cities, and damage from acid rain can be seen on every continent.

These contrasting views of the state of the world have their roots in economics and ecology—two disciplines with intellectual frameworks so different that their practitioners often have difficulty talking to each other. Economists interpret and analyze trends in terms of savings, investment, and growth. They are guided largely by economic theory and indicators, seeing the future more or less as an extrapolation of the recent past. From their vantage point, there is little reason to worry about natural constraints on human economic activity; rare is the economic text that mentions the carrying capacity principle that is so fundamental to ecology. Advancing technology, economists believe, can push back any limits. Their view prevails in the worlds of industry and finance, and in national governments and international development agencies.[4]

In contrast, ecologists study the relationship of living things with each other and their environments. They see growth in terms of S-shaped curves, a concept commonly illustrated in high school biology classes by introducing a few algae into a petri dish. Carefully cultured at optimum temperature and with unlimited supplies of food, the algae multiply slowly at first, and then more rapidly, until growth eventually slows and then stops, usually because of waste accumulation. Charting this process over time yields the familiar S-shaped curve to which all biological growth processes in a finite environment conform.

Ecologists think in terms of closed cycles—the hydrological cycle, the carbon cycle, and the nitrogen cycle, to name a few. For them, all growth processes are limited, confined within the natural parameters of the earth's ecosystem. They see more clearly than others the damage to natural systems and resources from expanding economic activity.

Although the intellectual foundations of this view originate in biology, other scientific fields such as meteorology, geology, and hydrology also contribute. The ecological perspective prevails in most national academies of science, in international scientific bodies, and in environmental organizations. Indeed, it is environmentalists who are actively voicing this view, urging the use of principles of ecology to restructure national economies and to shape the emerging world order.

These divergent views of the world are producing a certain global schizophrenia, a loss of contact with reality. The events of 1990 typify this unhealthy condition. The celebration of Earth Day 1990 symbolized the growing concern for the environmental health of the planet. Estimates indicate that at least 100 million people in 141 countries participated in events on Sunday, April 22. Soon after, at the Group of Seven economic summit in Houston, national leaders from Europe, reflecting the mounting concern with global warming, urged the United States to adopt a climate-sensitive energy policy.[5]

A few weeks later, Iraq invaded Kuwait, unsettling oil markets. Almost overnight, concerns about energy shifted from the long-term climatic consequences of burning oil and other fossil fuels to a short-term preoccupation with prices at the local gasoline pump. More traditional views of energy security resurfaced, eclipsing, at least temporarily, the concern with fossil fuel use and rising global temperatures.

The ecological view holds that continuing the single-minded pursuit of growth will eventually lead to economic collapse.

This schizophrenic perspective is translating into intense political conflict in economic policymaking. To the extent that constraints on economic expansion are discussed on the business pages, it is usually in terms of inadequate demand growth rather than supply-side constraints imposed by the earth's natural systems and resources. In contrast, the ecological view, represented by the environmental public interest community, holds that continuing the single-minded pursuit of growth will eventually lead to economic collapse. Ecologists see the need to restructure economic systems so that progress can be sustained.

Both visions are competing for the attention of policymakers and, as more environmentally minded candidates run for office, for the support of voters. The different views are strikingly evident in the indicators used to measure progress and assess future prospects. The basic evidence cited by economists shows a remarkable performance over the last decade. (See Table 1–1.) The value of all goods produced and services rendered grew steadily during the eighties, expanding some 3 percent a year and adding more than $4.5 trillion to the gross world product by 1990, an amount that exceeded the entire world product in 1950. In other words, growth in global economic output during the eighties was greater than that during the several thousand years from the beginning of civilization until 1950.[6]

International trade, another widely used measure of global economic progress, grew even more rapidly, expanding by nearly half during the eighties. This record was dominated by the expanding commerce in industrial products, while growth in the trade of agricultural commodities and minerals lagged. Although the exports of some countries, such as those in East Asia, increased much more than others, all but a relatively small number of nations contributed to the rising tide of commerce.[7]

On the employment front, the International Labour Organization reports that the economically active population increased from 1.96 billion to 2.36 billion during the decade. Although impressive gains in employment were made in some regions, the growth in new jobs in the Third World did not keep pace with the number of new entrants, making this one of the least satisfying of the leading economic indicators.[8]

Using stock prices as a gauge, the eighties was a remarkable decade. Investors on the New York Stock Exchange saw the value of their portfolios growing by leaps and bounds, a pattern only occasionally interrupted, as in October 1987. The Standard and Poor Index of 500 widely held stocks showed stock values nearly tripling during the decade. Pension funds, mutual funds, and individual investors all benefited. (See Figure 1–1.) The value of stocks traded on the Tokyo Exchange climbed even more rapidly.[9]

The contrast between these basic

Table 1-1. Selected Global Economic and Environmental Indicators

Indicator	Observation
The Economy	
Gross World Product	Global output of goods and services totalled roughly $20 trillion in 1990, up from $15.5 trillion in 1980 (1990 dollars).
International Trade	World exports of all goods—agricultural commodities, industrial products, and minerals—expanded 4 percent a year during the eighties, reaching more than $3 trillion in 1990.
Employment	In a typical year, growth of the global economy creates millions of new jobs, but unfortunately job creation lags far behind the number of new entrants into the labor force.
Stock Prices	A key indicator of investor confidence, prices on the Tokyo and New York stock exchanges climbed to all-time highs in late 1989 and early 1990, respectively.
The Environment	
Forests	Each year the earth's tree cover diminishes by some 17 million hectares, an area the size of Austria. Forests are cleared for farming, harvests of lumber and firewood exceed sustainable yields, and air pollution and acid rain take a growing toll on every continent.
Land	Annual losses of topsoil from cropland are estimated at 24 billion tons, roughly the amount on Australia's wheatland. Degradation of grazing land is widespread throughout the Third World, North America, and Australia.
Climate System	The amount of carbon dioxide, the principal greenhouse gas in the atmosphere, is now rising 0.4 percent per year from fossil fuel burning and deforestation. Record hot summers of the eighties may well be exceeded during the nineties.
Air Quality	Air pollution reached health-threatening levels in hundreds of cities and crop-damaging levels in scores of countries.
Plant and Animal Life	As the number of humans inhabiting the planet rises, the number of plant and animal species drops. Habitat destruction and pollution are reducing the earth's biological diversity. Rising temperatures and ozone layer depletion could add to losses.

SOURCE: Worldwatch Institute, based on sources documented in endnote 6.

1941-43 = 10

Source: U.S. Dept. of Commerce

Figure 1-1. Index of Stock Prices, 500 Common Stocks, 1950–90

global economic indicators and those measuring the earth's environmental health could not be greater. While these particular leading economic measurements are overwhelmingly positive, all the principal environmental indicators are consistently negative. As the need for cropland led to the clearing of forests, for example, and as the demand for firewood, lumber, and paper soared, deforestation gained momentum. By the end of the decade, the world's forests were shrinking by an estimated 17 million hectares each year. Some countries, such as Mauritania and Ethiopia, have lost nearly all their tree cover.[10]

Closely paralleling this is the loss of topsoil from wind and water erosion, and the associated degradation of land. Deforestation and overgrazing, both widespread throughout the Third World, have also led to wholesale land degradation. Each year, some 6 million hectares of land are so severely degraded that they lose their productive capacity, becoming wasteland.[11]

During the eighties, the amount of carbon pumped into the atmosphere from the burning of fossil fuels climbed to a new high, reaching nearly 6 billion tons in 1990. In a decade in which stock prices climbed to record highs, so too

did the mean temperature, making the eighties the warmest decade since recordkeeping began more than a century ago. The temperature rise was most pronounced in western North America and western Siberia. Preliminary climate data for 1990 indicate it will be the hottest year on record, with snow cover in the northern hemisphere the lightest since the satellite record began in 1970.[12]

Air and water pollution also worsened in most of the world during the last 10 years. By 1990, the air in hundreds of cities contained health-threatening levels of pollutants. In large areas of North America, Europe, and Asia, crops were being damaged as well. And despite widespread reduction in water pollution in the United States, the Environmental Protection Agency reported in 1988 that groundwater in 39 states contained pesticides. In Poland, at least half the river water was too polluted even for industrial use.[13]

These changes in the earth's physical condition are having a devastating effect on the biological diversity of the planet. Although no one knows how many plant and animal species were lost during the eighties, leading biologists estimate that one fifth of the species on earth may well disappear during this century's last two decades. What they cannot estimate is how long such a rate of extinction can continue without leading to the wholesale collapse of ecosystems.[14]

How can one set of widely used indicators be so consistently positive and another so consistently negative? One reason the economic measures are so encouraging is that national accounting systems—which produce figures on gross national product—miss entirely the environmental debts the world is incurring. The result is a disguised form of deficit financing. In sector after sector, we are consuming our natural capital at an alarming rate—the opposite of an environmentally sustainable economy, one that satisfies current needs without jeopardizing the prospects of future generations. As economist Herman Daly so aptly puts it, "there is something fundamentally wrong in treating the earth as if it were a business in liquidation."[15]

To extend this analogy, it is as though a vast industrial corporation quietly sold off a few of its factories each year, using an incomplete accounting system that did not reflect these sales. As a result, its cash flow would be strong and profits would rise. Stockholders would be pleased with the annual reports, not realizing that the profits were coming at the expense of the corporation's assets. But once all the factories were sold off, corporate officers would have to inform stockholders that their shares were worthless.

In effect, this is what we are doing with the earth. Relying on a similarly incomplete accounting system, we are depleting our productive assets, satisfying our needs today at the expense of our children.

NEW MEASURES OF PROGRESS

Fortunately, there is a growing recognition of the need for new ways of measuring progress. Ever since national accounting systems were adopted a half-century ago, per capita income has been the most widely used measure of economic progress. In the early stages of economic development, expanded output translated rather directly into rising living standards. Thus it became customary and not illogical to equate progress with economic growth.

Over time, however, average income has become less satisfactory as a measure of well-being: it does not reflect either environmental degradation or how additional wealth is distributed. Mounting dissatisfaction has led to the development of alternative yardsticks. Two interesting recent efforts are the Human Development Index (HDI) devised by the United Nations and the Index of Sustainable Economic Welfare (ISEW) developed by Herman Daly and theologian John Cobb. A third indicator, grain consumption per person, is a particularly sensitive measure of changes in well-being in low-income countries.[16]

Average income does not reflect either environmental degradation or how additional wealth is distributed.

The Human Development Index, measured on a scale of 0 to 1, is an aggregate of three indicators: longevity, knowledge, and the command over resources needed for a decent life. For longevity, the U.N. team used life expectancy at birth. For knowledge, they used literacy rates, since reading is the key to acquiring information and understanding. And for the command over resources, they used gross domestic product (GDP) per person after adjusting it for purchasing power. Because these indicators are national averages, they do not deal directly with distribution inequality, but by including longevity and literacy they do reflect indirectly the distribution of resources. A high average life expectancy, for example, indicates broad access to health care and to adequate supplies of food.[17]

A comparison of countries ranked by both adjusted per capita gross domestic product and HDI reveals some wide disparities: some with low average incomes have relatively high HDIs, and vice versa. In Sri Lanka, for instance, per capita GDP is only $2,053, while the HDI is 0.79. But in Brazil, where GDP is twice as high at $4,307 per person, the HDI is 0.78, slightly lower. This is because wealth is rather evenly distributed in Sri Lanka, along with access to food and social services, whereas in Brazil it is largely concentrated among the wealthiest one fifth of the population. The United States, which leads the world in adjusted income per capita at $17,615, is 19th in the HDI column, below such countries as Australia, Canada, and Spain.[18]

Per capita grain consumption looks at the satisfaction of a basic human need and is far less vulnerable to distortion by inequities of purchasing power.

While the HDI represents a distinct improvement over income figures as a measure of changes in human well-being, it says nothing about environmental degradation. As a result, the HDI can rise through gains in literacy, life expectancy, or purchasing power that are financed by the depletion of natural support systems, setting the stage for a longer term deterioration in living conditions.

The Daly-Cobb Index of Sustainable Economic Welfare is the most comprehensive indicator of well-being available, taking into account not only average consumption but also distribution and environmental degradation. After adjusting the consumption component of the index for distributional inequality, the authors factor in several environmental costs associated with economic mismanagement, such as depletion of nonrenewable resources, loss of farmland from soil erosion and urbanization,

loss of wetlands, and the cost of air and water pollution. They also incorporate what they call "long-term environmental damage," a figure that attempts to take into account such large-scale changes as the effects of global warming and of damage to the ozone layer.[19]

Applying this comprehensive measure to the United States shows a rise in welfare per person of some 42 percent between 1950 and 1976. (See Figure 1–2.) But after that the ISEW began to decline, falling by just over 12 percent by 1988, the last year for which it was calculated. Simply put, about 15 years ago the net benefits associated with economic growth in the United States fell below the growth of population, leading to a decline in individual welfare.[20]

The principal weakness of the ISEW, which has been calculated only for the United States, is its dependence on information that is available in only a handful of nations. For example, few developing countries have comprehensive data on the extent of air and water pollution, not to mention information on year-to-year changes. The same drawback applies to the HDI, since life expectancy data depend heavily on infant mortality information that is collected at

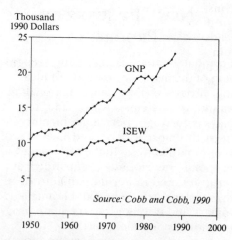

Figure 1-2. GNP and Index of Sustainable Economic Welfare (ISEW) Per Capita, United States, 1950–88

best once a decade in most of the Third World.

A measure in many ways more relevant to well-being in low-income countries is per capita grain consumption. It looks at the satisfaction of a basic human need and is far less vulnerable to distortion by inequities of purchasing power. The distribution of wealth between the richest one fifth of a country and the poorest one fifth can be as great as 20 to 1, as indeed it is in Algeria, Brazil, or Mexico, but the per capita consumption of grain by these same groups cannot vary by more than 4 to 1. Among more affluent countries, this figure peaks at about 800 kilograms a year, with the limit set by the quantity of grain-fed livestock products that can be consumed. At the lower end, people cannot survive if annual grain consumption drops much below 180 kilograms (about 1 pound a day) for an extended period. Thus, a gain in average grain consumption in a country typically means a gain in welfare.[21]

At the top end of this scale, the figure can be used to measure threats to health. Beyond a certain point—a point well below the level of consumption in the more affluent countries—rising grain consumption per person, most of it in the form of fat-rich livestock products, leads to increases in heart disease, certain types of cancer, and an overall reduction in life expectancy.

Grain production is also a more sensitive barometer of environmental degradation than income is, since it is affected more immediately by environmentally destructive activities outside agriculture, such as air pollution, the hotter summers that accompany global warming, and increased flooding as a result of deforestation.

In summary, the Index of Sustainable Economic Welfare is by far the most sophisticated indicator of progress now available, although its use is constrained by lack of data. In low-income countries where the relevant data to calculate the ISEW are not available, changes in grain consumption per person can tell more than income figures about improvements—or deterioration—in well-being.

WHAT FOOD INDICATORS SAY

Of all the sectors in the world economy, it is agriculture where the contrast between the economic and environmental indicators is most obvious. It is in the relentless push to produce more food that several decades of borrowing from the future are beginning to take a toll. In many countries, growth in the farm sector is pressing against the limits of land and water supplies. And in some, the backlog of technology available for farmers to raise food output is shrinking.

By traditional measures, world agriculture appears to be doing well. Western Europe worries about surpluses, particularly of dairy products, and the United States still idles cropland to control production. Grain-exporting countries use subsidies to compete for markets that never seem large enough. For an economist, there may be distribution problems in the world food economy, but not a production problem.

To an ecologist who sees a substantial fraction of current world food output being produced on highly erodible land that will soon be abandoned or by overpumping groundwater, which cannot continue indefinitely, the prospect is far less promising. As world agriculture presses against natural limits imposed by the area of productive land, by the amount of fresh water produced by the hydrological cycle, and by the geophysical processes that produce soil, growth in output is beginning to slow. Modest new additions to the cropland base are offset by the conversion of land to non-farm uses and by the abandonment of severely degraded land.[22]

The scarcity of fresh water is imposing limits on crop production in many agricultural regions. Competition among countries for the water from internationally shared rivers, such as the Tigris-Euphrates, Jordan, and Nile in the Middle East, is a source of growing political tension. In Soviet central Asia, the Amu Darya, the source of most of the region's irrigation water, now runs dry long before it reaches the Aral Sea. Falling water tables are now commonplace in heavily populated countries such as India and China, which are overpumping aquifers in their effort to satisfy the growing need for irrigation water. Under parts of the North China Plain, water tables are dropping up to a meter per year. And the vast Ogallala aquifer, which supplies irrigation water to U.S. farmers and ranchers from central Nebraska to the Texas panhandle, is gradually being depleted. Cities such as Denver and Phoenix are outbidding farmers in the intensifying competition for water.[23]

In addition to the degradation of land by farming practices, outside forces are also beginning to take a little-acknowledged toll on agriculture. Air pollution is reducing U.S. crop production by an officially estimated 5–10 percent, and is probably having a similar effect in the coal-burning economies of Eastern Europe and China. As deforestation progresses in the mountainous areas of the world, the term "flood-damaged harvests" appears with increasing frequency in world crop reports.[24]

Even as these environmental and resource constraints slow world food output growth, the backlog of unused agricultural technology is diminishing. In Asia, for example, the highest yielding

rice varieties available to farmers were released in 1966, a quarter-century ago. The International Rice Research Institute, the world's premier research facility in this field, observed in a strategy paper released for 1990 that "during the past five years, growth in rice yields has virtually ceased."[25]

One way of assessing the technological prospect for boosting food output during the nineties is to look at trends in fertilizer use, since the phenomenal growth in world food output from 1950 to 1984 was due largely to the ninefold growth in fertilizer use. In large measure, other major advances in agriculture, such as the near-tripling of irrigated area and the adoption of ever higher yielding varieties, greatly enhanced the potential to use more fertilizer profitably. But as the nineties begin many countries have reached the point where using additional fertilizer does little to boost food output.[26]

Nowhere was this potential for expanding the use of fertilizer more evident than in the United States, where fertilizer use multiplied five times between 1950 and 1981. (See Figure 1–3.) After three decades of extraordinary increase, the growth in fertilizer use abruptly stopped during the eighties, contributing to a levelling off of grain

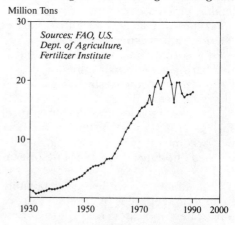

Figure 1-3. U.S. Fertilizer Consumption, 1930–90

output. A similar trend is unfolding in Western Europe. And in the Soviet Union, where fertilizer use has been heavily subsidized, the economic reforms leading to adoption of world market prices reduced its use nearly 10 percent between 1987 and 1990 as wasteful practices were minimized. In China, where the use of this agricultural input climbed even more rapidly than in the United States, growth is also slowing.[27]

There are still some countries, such as India—now a distant fourth among the big four grain producers—where there is a large potential for profitably boosting fertilizer use. But the worldwide opportunities for doing so are diminishing. Just as the enormous growth in fertilizer use goes a long way toward explaining the unprecedented growth in grain output from 1950 to 1984, so the slower growth in its use since then helps explain the slower growth in grain output. The Paris-based International Fertilizer Industry Association projects that the annual growth in world fertilizer use, which dropped from nearly 6 percent during the seventies to 2.6 percent in the eighties, will fall to 1.5 percent in the early nineties.[28]

Beyond the growing scarcity of productive cropland and fresh water, the yield-reducing effects of environmental degradation, and the shrinking backlog of new agricultural technologies, farmers are now in a period of consolidation. As noted, some of the growth in world food output during the late seventies and early eighties came from plowing highly erodible land and overpumping aquifers. By the mid-eighties, farmers were beginning to retrench, pulling back from the unsustainable margins. As they did so, they contributed to the slower growth in world grain output, dropping the increase in production per person to scarcely 6 percent between 1984 and 1990, or roughly 1 percent per year.[29]

The global downturn in per capita grain output reflects downturns in each geographic region, though the exact timing and the principal reasons vary. (See Table 1–2.) The worldwide rise that started following World War II was reversed first in Africa, where grain output per person peaked at 169 kilograms in 1967. By 1990, a combination of record population growth, land degradation, and economic mismanagement had dropped it to 121 kilograms, a fall of 28 percent.

The next region to peak was Eastern Europe and the Soviet Union, where production is dominated by the the latter. The regional high in 1978 coincided with the end of the rapid expansion in

Table 1-2. Regional and World Grain Production Per Person, Peak Year and 1990

Region	Peak Production		1990 Production	Change Since Peak Year
	(year)	(kilograms)	(kilograms)	(percent)
Africa	1967	169	121	−28
E. Europe and Soviet Union	1978	826	763	− 8
Latin America	1981	250	210	−16
North America	1981	1,509	1,324	−12
Western Europe	1984	538	496	− 8
Asia	1984	227	217	− 4
World	1984	343	329	− 4

SOURCE: Based on U.S. Department of Agriculture, Economic Research Service, *World Grain Database* (unpublished printouts) (Washington, D.C.: 1990), with updates for 1990 harvest.

Soviet grain area that followed the massive crop shortfall of 1972. Since then, that nation's grain harvested area has shrunk by 10 percent as land in alternate-year fallow has been increased to restore moisture and stabilize yields and as eroded land has been abandoned. For the region, grain production per person has fallen 8 percent since 1978.[30]

Per capita grain production in both Latin and North America peaked in 1981. In Latin America, the debt crisis that emerged in force in 1982 weakened consumer purchasing power and reduced the availability of foreign exchange to import needed inputs such as fertilizer. These economic stresses, combined with rapid population growth and land degradation, have dropped grain output per person 16 percent since 1981.[31]

By 1990, word carryover stocks of grain had dropped to 290 million tons, enough for just 62 days.

In North America, there were no restrictions on planting in 1981, and large amounts of highly erodible land came under the plow. After that year, land was again taken out under government set-aside programs to reduce "surpluses." Beginning in 1986, farmers began to retire highly erodible land under the new Conservation Reserve Program, returning nearly 14 million hectares to grass or trees by 1990. Even though the area in the more traditional "set-aside" program was sharply reduced in 1990 to meet expanding demand, the harvest per person was 12 percent below the peak of 1981.[32]

In the two remaining regions, Western Europe and Asia, production per person peaked in 1984. In Western Europe, where high price supports and advancing technology have led to a long sustained rise in yields, farmers are now experiencing difficulty in maintaining the rapid rise. If the Uruguay Round of General Agreement on Tariffs and Trade negotiations finally ends with an agreement to lower Europe's farm price supports, then the recent decline could continue for a few years. Fortunately for the region, which produces an exportable surplus of grain, food consumption levels are high and population growth is approaching zero.[33]

For Asia, which has over half the world's people and produces over 90 percent of its rice, grain yield per hectare is continuing to rise, but more slowly than a decade ago. Within East Asia, dominated by China, Japan, and Indonesia, population growth has slowed to 1.4 percent per year. It is in West Asia, where most of the 1.1 billion people in the Indian subcontinent live at subsistence levels, that the imbalance between food and people is greatest and likely to get worse.[34]

For the world as a whole, the annual growth in grain production from 1984 to 1990 was 1 percent, while that of population was nearly 2. The diminishing crop response to the additional use of fertilizer, the negative effect of environmental degradation on harvests, and the lack of any new technology to replace fertilizer as the engine of agricultural growth are each contributing to a potentially hungry future for much of humanity. In both 1984 and 1990, per hectare yields of the three grains that dominate the world diet—wheat, rice, and corn—set new records, indicating unusually favorable growing conditions in all the major grain-growing regions. If these two years are broadly comparable weather-wise, as they appear to be, then this slower growth in world grain output may indeed be a new trend.[35]

The slowdown in world food output since 1984 would have had even more severe consequences if it had not been for the record grain stores accumulated in the mid-eighties. World carryover stocks, perhaps the best short-term measure of food security, totaled a record 461 million tons of grain in 1987, enough to feed the world for 102 days. (See Figure 1–4.) But in each of the next three years, world grain consumption exceeded production, leading to a 173-million-ton drop in stocks to compensate for the downturn in per capita grain production. By 1990, carryover stocks had dropped to 290 million tons, enough for just 62 days. With the bumper grain harvest of 1990, carryover stocks in 1991 are projected to increase, but only to 66 days of consumption.[36]

When stocks drop below 60 days of consumption, roughly the amount of grain needed to maintain an uninterrupted flow from the farmer to the consumer, prices become highly volatile, rising and falling on the strength of weekly weather forecasts. The last time this happened, when only 55 days' worth of consumption were available in 1973, grain prices doubled in a matter of months. In 1990, stocks fell precariously close to this trigger point.[37]

The prospective shrinkage of cropland and fresh water per person during the nineties, along with the prospect of a likely reduction in per capita fertilizer use, raises basic questions of future food security. Buttressing this concern is the failure in 1990, a year of record harvests, to appreciably rebuild grain stocks. If stocks cannot be replenished in such an exceptionally good year, when can they be? What happens to stocks and world grain prices if we have an unusually poor harvest? Both these questions are likely to be answered within the next few years.[38]

In our modern, post-industrial information economy, where few of us remain on the land, we are largely isolated from the economy's agricultural foundations. We tend to take the land's capacity to satisfy our needs for granted. But the superficial economic indicators we rely on so heavily do mask serious underlying problems. As Harvard ecological anthropologist Timothy Weiskel quite rightly notes, "We live in a highly industrialized, urban culture, but it is important to remember that there is no such thing as a 'post-agricultural' society." As the agricultural foundations of the global economy weaken, so will the global economy itself. In effect, agriculture is likely to be the sector that first illustrates how profoundly environmental degradation will eventually shape global economic trends.[39]

Days of Consumption

Threshold of Price Instability

Source: U.S. Dept. of Agriculture

Figure 1-4. World Carryover Grain Stocks, 1963–91

POPULATION: THE NEGLECTED ISSUE

Nowhere is the conceptual contrast between economists and ecologists more evident than in the way they view population growth. In assessing its effect, economists typically have not seen it as a particularly serious threat. In their view, if a nation's economy is growing at

5 percent per year and its population at 3 percent, this leads to a steady 2-percent gain in living standards. Relying on economic variables alone, this situation seemed to be tenable, one that could be extrapolated indefinitely into the future.

Ecologists looking at biological indicators in the same situation see rising human demand, driven by population growth and rising affluence, surpassing the carrying capacity of local forests, grasslands, and soils in country after country. They see sustainable yield thresholds of the economy's natural support systems being breached throughout the Third World. And as a result, they see the natural resource base diminishing even as population growth is expanding.

The world is projected to add at least 960 million people during this decade.

Against this backdrop, biologists find recent population trends profoundly disturbing. Accelerating sharply during the recovery period after World War II, the annual growth of world population peaked at about 1.9 percent in 1970. It then slowed gradually, declining to 1.7 percent in the early eighties. But during the late eighties it again began to accelerate, reaching 1.8 percent, largely because of a modest rise of the birth rate in China and a decrease in the death rate in India. With fertility turning upward in the late eighties instead of declining, as some had expected and many had hoped, the world is projected to add at least 960 million people during this decade, up from 840 million in the eighties and 750 million in the seventies.[40]

Concern with the effects of population growth is not new. Nearly two centuries have passed since Malthus published his famous treatise in which he argued that population tends to grow exponentially while food production grows arithmetically. He argued that unless profligate childbearing was checked, preferably through abstinence, famine and hunger would be inevitable. Malthus was wrong in the sense that he did not anticipate the enormous potential of advancing technology to raise land productivity. He was writing before Mendel formulated the basic principles of genetics and before Von Leibeg demonstrated that all the nutrients taken from the soil by plants could be returned in mineral form.[41]

Malthus was correct, however, in anticipating the difficulty of expanding food output as fast as population growth. Today, hundreds of millions of the earth's inhabitants are hungry, partly because of inequitable distribution, but increasingly because of falling per capita food production. And as the nineties begin, the ranks of the hungry are swelling.

Malthus was concerned with the relationship between population growth and the earth's food-producing capacity. We now know that increasing numbers and economic activity affect many other natural capacities, such as the earth's ability to absorb waste. At any given level of per capita pollution, more people means more pollution. As the discharge of various industrial and agricultural wastes overwhelms the waste-absorptive capacity of natural systems, the cumulative effects of toxic materials in the environment begins to affect human health.

Another consequence of continuing population growth in much of the Third World is a shortage of firewood, the primary fuel. As the local demand for firewood for cooking exceeds the sustainable yield of local woodlands, the forests recede from the villages. Women, who gather most of the firewood, often find themselves trekking long distances to find enough to prepare meals. In some situations, families are reduced to only one hot meal a day. Malthus worried about whether there would be enough food, but he never reckoned that finding the fuel to prepare it would become part of the daily struggle for survival.[42]

The record population growth projected for the nineties means the per capita availability of key resources such as land, water, and wood will also shrink at an unprecedented rate. (See Table 1–3.) Since the total cropland area is not expected to change during the decade, the land available per person to produce our basic staples will shrink by 1.7 percent a year. This means that grainland per person, averaging 0.13 hectares in 1990, will be reduced by one sixth during the nineties. And with a projected growth in overall irrigated land of less than 1 percent per year, the irrigated area per person will decline by nearly a tenth.

Forested area per person, reduced both by the overall loss in forests and by population growth, is likely to decline by one fifth or more during this decade. The 0.61 hectares per person of grazing land, which produces much of our milk, meat, and cheese, is also projected to drop by one fifth by the year 2000 as population grows and desertification spreads. Maintaining an improvement in living conditions with this reduction in per capita natural resources will not be easy.[43]

One reason the world is now facing such dramatic per capita resource declines is the policy of benign neglect that seems to have affected family planning programs both at the national level and within the international development community. After two decades of strong U.S. leadership in international family planning efforts, the Reagan administration withdrew all U.S. funding from the United Nations Population Fund and the International Planned Parenthood Federation, the two principal sources of international family planning assistance. Yielding to pressures from the political far right, which used opposition to abortion to cut off this financing, the administration effectively forfeited leadership. Ironically, as a result more and more Third World women are denied access to family planning services and forced to resort to abortion. (See Chapter 7.)[44]

Within the international development community, leadership on population policy continues to be weak. The World Bank officially recognizes the need to slow population growth, but contributes little to doing so. The Secretary-General of the United Nations rarely mentions population, much less provides leadership on the issue. Deep-seated religious resistance in the Catholic church and in many Moslem societies has fostered this climate of neglect.

Table 1-3. Availability of Basic Natural Resources Per Person in 1990 and 2000

Resource	1990	2000
	(hectares)	
Grain land	0.13	0.11
Irrigated land	0.045	0.04
Forest land	0.79	0.64
Grazing land	0.61	0.50

SOURCE: Based on U.S. Department of Agriculture, Economic Research Service, *World Grain Database* (unpublished printouts) (Washington, D.C.: 1990); U.N. Food and Agriculture Organization, *Production Yearbook* (Rome: various years); and U.N. Department of International Economic and Social Affairs, *World Population Prospects 1988* (New York: 1989).

One of the rare family planning success stories during the eighties among the more populous countries was Brazil, where the average number of children per woman dropped from 4.4 in 1980 to 3.3 in 1990. Prominent among the causes was an expansion of government family planning services and growing access to modern contraceptives in commercial markets.[45]

Overall, however, the eighties was not a happy decade for efforts to achieve a sustainable balance between people and their natural support systems. Continuing rapid population growth and spreading environmental degradation trapped hundreds of millions in a downward spiral of falling incomes and growing hunger. With the number of people caught in this life-threatening cycle increasing each year, the world may soon be forced to reckon with the consequence of years of population policy neglect.

A NEW AGENDA, A NEW ORDER

With the end of the ideological conflict that dominated a generation of international affairs, a new world order, shaped by a new agenda, will emerge. If the physical degradation of the planet becomes the principal preoccupation of the global community, then environmental sustainability will become the organizing principle of this new order. (For a discussion of the rough outline of an environmentally sustainable global economy, see Chapter 10 in *State of the World 1990*.) The world's agenda will be more ecological than ideological, dominated less by relationships among nations and more by the relationship between nations and nature. For the first time since the emergence of the nation-state, all countries can unite around a common theme. All societies have an interest in satisfying the needs of the current generation without compromising the ability of future generations to meet their needs. It is in the interest of everyone to protect the earth's life-support systems, for we all have a stake in the future habitability of the planet.

This is not to suggest, by any means, that all international initiatives will be conflict-free. Issues of who assumes how much responsibility for achieving a given goal, such as climate stabilization, will plague international negotiations long after agreement is reached on the goal itself. Do those in wealthy countries have an obligation to reduce carbon emissions to the same level as those living in poor countries? If preservation of the earth's biological diversity is a goal, should the cost be borne by those who live in the tropical countries that contain the vast majority of the earth's plant and animal species, or is this the responsibility of the international community?

In the new age, diplomacy will be more concerned with environmental security than with military security. To be effective, diplomats will need a solid grounding in ecology as well as economics and politics. Toxic waste disposal, endangered species protection, carbon efficiencies, water-sharing agreements, substitutes for chlorofluorocarbons (CFCs), achievement of replacement-fertility levels, and the latest solar energy technologies are but a few of the matters that will command diplomatic attention in the battle to save the planet.

Although it is premature to describe the shape of the post–cold war world order, its determining characteristics can now be identified. A commitment to the long-term improvement in the human condition is contingent on substituting environmental sustainability for growth as the overriding goal of national economic policymaking and international development. Political influence will derive more from environmental and economic leadership than from military strength. And in the new order, the political stresses between East and West are likely to be replaced by the economic stresses between North and South, including such issues as the need to reduce Third World debt, access to markets in the industrial North, and how the costs of environmental protection initiatives are allocated between rich and poor.

In the emerging order, the United Nations seems certain to figure much more prominently in world affairs, particularly in peacekeeping, where its role is likely to be closer to that envisaged by its founders. Evidence of this new capacity emerged in 1990 as the United Nations took a leading and decisive role in the international response to Iraq's invasion of Kuwait. It was also evident in the U.N.-negotiated Kampuchean peace settlement of mid-1990. If the United Nations can effectively play the envisaged peacekeeping role, it will speed demilitarization and the shift of resources to environmental security.

Another indication of the expanding U.N. role was the June 1990 international agreement on a rapid phaseout of CFCs, to minimize further losses from the stratospheric ozone layer. Some 93 countries agreed to halt CFC production by the end of the nineties, going far beyond the 1987 Montreal Accord that called for a 50-percent cut by 1998. This essential advance hinged on the establishment of an international fund that will provide $240 million of technical assistance over the next three years to help the Third World obtain CFC substitutes. The funding mechanism was essential to broadening support for the phaseout among developing countries, importantly India and China, the world's two most populous countries.[46]

Reaching international agreement on a plan to stabilize climate, which in effect requires a restructuring of the world energy economy, will be far more difficult. (See Chapter 2.) The current schedule, designed to produce a draft agreement for the U.N. Conference on Environment and Development in June 1992, will be the first major test of the new world order.

Environmental alliances to deal with specific transnational threats are likely to become commonplace and far more numerous than the military alliances that have featured so prominently since World War II. To cite a few examples, European countries could work together to save the region's deteriorating forests, nations bordering the Baltic Sea could join together to reverse its degradation, and countries in the Indian subcontinent could combine forces to reforest the Himalayas and reduce the frequency of crop-damaging floods. New North-South alliances to save migratory birds, whether songbirds within the western hemisphere or waterfowl that migrate from Europe to Africa, are increasingly probable.

Political influence will derive more from environmental and economic leadership than from military strength.

As noted earlier, leadership in the new order is likely to derive less from military power and more from success in building environmentally sustainable economies. The United States and the Soviet Union, the traditional military superpowers, are lagging badly in this effort and are thus likely to lose ground to those governments that can provide leadership in such a shift. For example, the path-breaking June 1990 decision by the West German cabinet to reduce carbon emissions 25 percent by 2005, along with other ambitious environmental initiatives in material reuse and recycling (see Chapter 3), may cast the newly unified Germany in a leadership role.[47]

With time running out in the effort to reverse the environmental destruction of the earth, there is an obvious need for initiatives that will quickly convert our environmentally unsustainable global economy into one that is sustainable. The many means of achieving this transformation range from voluntary lifestyle changes, such as limiting family size or reducing waste, to regulated changes such as laws boosting the fuel efficiencies of automobiles and household appliances. But the most effective instrument of all promises to be tax policy—specifically, the partial replacement of income taxes with those that discourage environmentally destructive activities. Prominent among the activities to tax are carbon emissions, the use of virgin materials, and the generation of toxic waste. (See Chapter 10.)

We can see what environmentally unsustainable growth does to the earth. And we know what the outlines of an environmentally sustainable economy look like. If the move toward the latter is not speeded up, we risk being overwhelmed by the economic and social consequences of planetary degradation. This in turn depends on more of us becoming environmental activists, working on behalf of the future of the planet and our children. Unless we can reverse quickly some of the environmental trends that are undermining our economy, our dream of a better life for our children and grandchildren will remain just that.

2

Designing a Sustainable Energy System

Christopher Flavin and Nicholas Lenssen

The world is now lurching from one energy crisis to another, threatening at every turn to derail the global economy or disrupt its environmental support systems. The nineties are likely to be plagued by more frequent and more severe energy crises than ever before.

While the failure of societies to redirect their energy futures is in one sense a failure of policy, it is also a failure of vision. Political leaders have little concept of an energy system not based on fossil fuels. Nor do they seem to see that an alternative approach is possible. Society is entering a period of inevitable and rapid change in its energy systems, with little idea of where we are headed or how our course can be shaped.

The World Energy Conference, a triennial gathering of energy officials and experts, concluded in late 1989 that by 2020 the world would be using 75 percent more energy, and that most of it

would be supplied by coal, oil, and nuclear power. Yet this business-as-usual scenario would not lead to a more pleasant version of the status quo—the apparent goal of many planners.[1]

Such an approach would eventually entail relying on the Persian Gulf for more than two thirds of the world's oil, compared with 26 percent today. It would involve building three times as many nuclear plants in the next 30 years as in the past 30, accompanied by more frequent nuclear accidents and growing stockpiles of nuclear waste and plutonium. It would accelerate global warming as carbon dioxide emissions soared above today's levels. And the increasing centralization and growing scale of energy systems would require tight police supervision and restrictions on public participation. This picture of the future is neither attractive nor ultimately plausible.[2]

Three major considerations are now forcing the world's energy systems in a different direction. The first is the availability of fossil fuels, particularly the most

An expanded version of this chapter appeared as Worldwatch Paper 100, *Beyond the Petroleum Age: Designing a Solar Enonomy.*

economical and versatile one—petroleum. The constraint is not the global resource base but the geographical and political limits of having nearly two thirds of the world's current oil reserves in the Persian Gulf region.[3]

The second limit is environmental—the capacity of the world to cope with the overwhelming burden of pollution that is emitted by a $20-trillion world economy run on fossil fuels. The most intractable load is the nearly 6 billion tons of carbon added to the atmosphere each year. As no technical fix appears likely for this problem, slowing global warming will mean placing limits on fossil fuel combustion.[4]

Not only is the world addicted to cheap oil, but the largest liquor store is in a very dangerous neighborhood.

The third constraint is social and political. In recent years, citizens around the globe have rebelled against the energy "solutions" their governments pursue. The people of West Germany, for example, effectively ruled out nuclear expansion during the eighties, and those in the Soviet Republics are in the process of doing the same. Less controversial technologies have also been stopped. Coal-fired power plants are rarely constructed now in the northeastern United States, and the Indian government's efforts to build new hydro dams have met with massive public protest. Political leaders around the world are beginning to realize that people's passionate concerns cannot be swept aside by a tide of technocratic policymaking.[5]

Powerful economic, environmental, and social forces are now pushing the world toward a very different energy system in the decades ahead. But what might it look like? Ultimately, a sustainable economy must operate with much lower levels of fossil fuels, and probably without nuclear power. It would likely derive its power from solar resources replenished daily by incoming sunlight and by geothermal energy—resources available in far greater abundance than fossil fuels. It would also need to be much more energy-efficient, since renewable energy is unlikely ever to be as cheap as oil has been.

A solar economy will involve the creation of whole new industries and the restructuring of the job market. Ultimately, new transportation systems will likely evolve, and both cities and agriculture will be changed. The challenge ahead is in part one of continuing to develop new technologies that use energy efficiently and harness renewable resources economically. But the most important challenge is political: societies need to overcome narrow economic interests and revamp energy policies in order to develop energy systems that future generations can count on.

THE END OF THE PETROLEUM ERA

Just four decades ago, world oil consumption was one sixth the current level, with half of it being used in North America alone. As recently as 20 years ago, the petroleum economy had touched the lives of only a tiny fraction of humanity. While oil dependence may seem to our generation to be inevitable and permanent, it could turn out to be even more fleeting than the 200-year age of coal that preceded it.[6]

In the immediate future, a chaotic world oil market may do the most to knock world energy trends off their current course. When Iraq's tanks rumbled into Kuwait in August 1990, the world faced the third oil shock in the space of just 17 years. (See Figure 2–1.) This invasion, which immediately raised Iraq's share of world oil reserves from 10 to nearly 20 percent, caused a 170-percent increase in oil prices in three months and led to near panic in world financial markets.[7]

The forerunners to this crisis were the failed energy policies that allowed oil-consuming nations—both industrial and developing—to increase greatly their dependence on Middle Eastern oil in the late eighties. The world's addiction to cheap oil is as destructive and hard to break as an alcoholic's need for a drink. Since 1986, when oil prices fell back below $20 per barrel, the move toward more efficient homes, cars, and factories that began in the mid-seventies slowed to a crawl. As a result, world oil demand shot up by almost 5 million barrels per day, or nearly 10 percent.[8]

Virtually all the extra oil now being consumed is supplied by a handful of countries in the Middle East, a region that faces the stresses of rapidly growing populations, autocratic political systems, rampant poverty, and a deadly arms race. Not only is the world addicted to cheap oil, but the largest liquor store is in a very dangerous neighborhood.

The uneven distribution of world petroleum resources is growing more lopsided all the time. While the Persian Gulf region had 55 percent of proven global reserves as recently as 1980, by 1989 that figure reached 65 percent. Most of the nations in that area have at least 100 years of proven reserves left at current extraction rates, compared with less than 20 years' worth in Europe, North America, and the Soviet Union. (See Table 2–1.)[9]

Outside the Middle East, much of the cheap oil has already been consumed. In the Soviet Union and the United States—still the world's leading producers—output is now declining. The U.S. fall is hardly surprising since the country's heavily exploited oil fields have only 4 percent of global reserves while still accounting for 12 percent of pro-

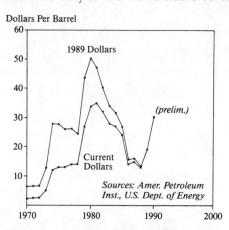

Dollars Per Barrel

Figure 2-1. World Price of Oil at End of Calendar Year, 1970–90

Table 2-1. World Oil Reserves by Region, 1980 and 1989

Region	Oil Reserves 1980	Oil Reserves 1989	Reserves Remaining at 1989 Production Rates
	(billion barrels)		(number of years)
Middle East	362	660	110
Latin America	70	125	51
Soviet Union & East. Eur.	66	60	13
Africa	55	59	28
Asia, Australia, & New Zeal.	40	47	20
North America	39	42	10
West. Europe	23	18	13
World	655	1,011	44

SOURCE: British Petroleum, *BP Statistical Review of World Energy* (London: various years).

duction. Whereas the average oil well in Saudi Arabia produces 9,000 barrels per day, the average well in the United States produces 15. The Soviet Union also appears poised for a steep decline as it cuts its disproportionate investments in the petroleum sector. Infusions of western oil technology could slow the decline but are unlikely to stop it entirely.[10]

If the past is any guide—and there is every reason to think it is—the nations of the Persian Gulf are in no position to provide a steady long-term supply of oil. To rely increasingly on them would set the world up for an unending series of price run-ups, economic crises, and oil wars. Developing countries with large debt burdens are particularly vulnerable to a continuation of the oil-price roller coaster. India, for example, was forced to cut its oil consumption by a remarkable 25 percent as prices skyrocketed in late 1990.[11]

Oil-consuming nations therefore face the imperative of reducing their petroleum dependence. But by how much? Current oil use per person averages 4.5 barrels a year, but it ranges from 24 barrels in the United States to 12 in Western Europe and less than 1 in sub-Saharan Africa. To stretch out oil supplies and reduce the environmental impacts of its use, the world is unlikely to be able to burn more than about 30 million barrels a day by the year 2030—one half the current level. Given population increases, this would allow for an average of just 1.2 barrels per person worldwide by then, implying extensive changes in the global energy economy.[12]

The capacity of the global biosphere to absorb the emissions of a fossil-fuel-based energy system may in the end prove even more constraining than the limits posed by oil. Nearly 6 billion tons of carbon are spewed into the air each year in the form of carbon dioxide, a greenhouse gas that is building steadily in the atmosphere and gradually heating

the planet. Although these concentrations rise slowly, future climate disruptions are likely to be abrupt and catastrophic.[13]

Despite the vast public attention paid to the problem of global warming over the past three years, the amount of carbon being released annually has risen by 400 million tons since 1986—exactly the opposite of what many scientists believe is necessary. (See Figure 2–2.)[14]

A major scientific study released in 1990 by the United Nations-commissioned Intergovernmental Panel on Climate Change confirmed that a rapid and highly disruptive increase in global temperatures would occur unless emissions are cut. Upon releasing the report, Dr. John Houghton, head of the British Meteorological Service, noted that it represented "remarkable consensus," with fewer than 10 of 200 scientists dissenting. Although major cuts in carbon dioxide emissions will take decades to accomplish, the targets will be far more difficult to achieve if emissions continue to rise.[15]

Somewhat balancing this bleak global trend, 15 nations produced plans over the past two years to limit their production of carbon dioxide—and, by implication, their use of fossil fuels. The leader

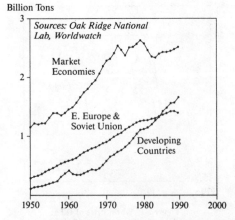

Figure 2-2. **Carbon Emissions from Fossil Fuels, 1950–89**

is Germany, which aims to cut emissions within the former West Germany by 25 percent over the next 15 years. Yet in order to stabilize the atmospheric concentration of carbon dioxide, scientists believe global emissions must eventually be cut by at least 60-80 percent—to about 2 billion tons annually.[16]

A world that produces only that much carbon a year will be far different from one that produces 6 billion. (See Table 2–2.) Per capita carbon emissions some 40 years from now would need to be one fourth the level in Western Europe today, given the inevitable growth in world population over the next few decades. These are stringent targets, especially when one considers that fossil fuels now account for 75 percent of world energy supplies.[17]

An annual carbon budget of 2 billion tons can only be met if use of coal, the most carbon-intensive fossil fuel, is cut by roughly 90 percent. Small amounts of coal would still be burned in countries like China and India, which have large populations and only limited reserves of other fossil fuels. Oil shale and other synthetic fuels can be ruled out entirely due to their high carbon content.[18]

For most nations, however, natural gas will likely be the predominant fossil fuel still used—as it produces roughly twice as much energy per kilogram of carbon released as coal does. Natural gas resources are also better disbursed than those of oil; the largest known reserves are, however, in the Middle East and the Soviet Union. Forty years from now, natural gas could still be producing as much energy as it does today.[19]

In a world with an energy system that is truly sustainable—economically and socially—nuclear power will probably not be a major source of energy. During the past 10 years, the pace of nuclear expansion has slowed almost to a halt in countries around the world. All existing reactors are scheduled to be retired within the next 40 years, and it seems likely that most will not be replaced.[20]

Although there is much that can be debated about the new energy technologies to be deployed and the ways in

Table 2-2. World Energy Use and Carbon Emissions, 1989, with Goals for 2030

Energy Source	1989		2030	
	Energy	Carbon	Energy	Carbon
	(mtoe[1])	(million tons)	(mtoe[1])	(million tons)
Oil	3,098	2,393	1,500	1,160
Coal	2,231	2,396	240	430
Natural Gas	1,707	975	1,750	1,000
Renewables[2]	1,813	—	7,000	—
Nuclear[3]	451	—	0	0
Total	9,300	5,764	10,490	2,590

[1]Million tons of oil equivalent. [2]Renewable biomass energy results in net carbon emissions only if not replaced as a result of new growth. [3]Nuclear energy produces carbon dioxide as a result of the fuel processing that precedes power generation.
SOURCE: Worldwatch Institute, based on British Petroleum, *BP Statistical Review of World Energy* (London: 1990); J.M.O. Scurlock and D.O. Hall, "The Contribution of Biomass to Global Energy Use," *Biomass*, No. 21, 1990; Gregg Marland et al., *Estimates of CO₂ Emissions from Fossil Fuel Burning and Cement Manufacturing, Based on the United Nations Energy Statistics and the U.S. Bureau of Mines Cement Manufacturing Data* (Oak Ridge, Tenn.: Oak Ridge National Laboratory, 1989).

which cities and economies will be restructured, one point is clear: a sustainable energy system is possible only if energy efficiency is vastly improved. Overall, the world will have to be producing goods and services with a third to half as much energy as today. The member countries of the Organisation for Economic Co-operation and Development have lowered their energy use per unit of gross national product 24 percent since 1973, but plenty of opportunities for further improvement remain. The Soviet Union, Eastern Europe, and developing countries have an even larger, untapped potential.[21]

Technologies are already available that will quadruple the efficiency of most lighting systems and double the efficiency of new cars. Electrical efficiency improvements could reduce the need for power by 40–75 percent at an average cost of less than 2¢ a kilowatt-hour. Heating and cooling needs of buildings can be cut to an even smaller fraction of current levels through improved furnaces and air conditioners, as well as better insulation and windows.[22]

Over the next 30 years, industrial countries could reduce their energy use per capita by at least half without having a detrimental effect on their economies. In developing countries, improved efficiency could allow energy consumption per capita to remain constant while economies grow. Developing nations are unlikely to be able to afford to continue pursuing expensive, centralized technologies at the neglect of simpler and cheaper means to improve energy efficiency.[23]

Quadrupling the output of renewable energy is also essential to achieving a sustainable energy system in the foreseeable future. This will entail expanding the use of biomass and hydropower, but more importantly will require that solar and geothermal energy become a major part of the world energy mix, as discussed in the next section.

The technologies are at hand to initiate this historic energy transition, but it will not occur without major changes in energy policy. The first step is to redirect a host of government policies so that they are aimed at achieving the central goals of improving energy efficiency and reducing fossil fuel use. The purchase of efficient cars could be rewarded, for example, and gas guzzlers discouraged through government levies. In areas such as requiring tighter building standards or encouraging local transportation alternatives to the automobile, state and local governments can play a leading role.

A second key is the gradual restructuring of energy industries, particularly the publicly owned or regulated electric utility companies. Ideally, they would be taken out of the power plant construction business and charged with improving end-use efficiency, which would be financed with utility revenues.

Last, but not least, governments will need to raise taxes on fossil fuels so that prices reflect the full security and environmental costs involved. (See Chapter 10.) This would provide a great boost to the development of energy-efficient and renewable energy technologies.

POWER FROM THE SUN

Renewable energy resources are available in immense quantity. The U.S. Department of Energy estimates that the country's annual influx of accessible resources is more than 200 times its use of energy, and more than 10 times the total reserves estimated for fossil and nuclear fuels. According to a new study by several government scientific laboratories, renewables could supply the equivalent of 50–70 percent of current U.S. energy use by the year 2030.[24]

Contrary to popular belief, renewables—primarily biomass and hydropower—already supply about 20 percent of the world's energy. Biomass alone meets 35 percent of developing countries' total energy needs, though often not in a manner that is renewable or sustainable in the long term. And in certain industrial countries, renewables play a central role: Norway, for example, relies on them, mainly in the form of hydropower, for more than 50 percent of its energy.[25]

Steady advances have been made since the mid-seventies in a broad array of renewable energy technologies. Many of the devices, machinery, and processes that could provide energy in a solar economy are now economically competitive with fossil fuels. Further reductions in costs are expected in the next decade as technologies continue to improve. (See Table 2–3.) But the pace of advance will be determined by energy prices and government policies. After a period of neglect in the eighties, many governments are now supporting new energy technologies more effectively.[26]

Direct conversion of solar energy is likely to be the cornerstone of a sustainable world energy system. Not only is sunshine available in great quantity, it is more widely distributed than any other source. Solar energy is especially well suited to supplying heat at or below the boiling point of water, which accounts for 30–50 percent of energy use in industrial countries and even more in the developing world. A few decades from now, societies may use the sun to heat most of their water, and new buildings may take advantage of natural heating and cooling to cut energy use by more than 80 percent.[27]

Solar rays are a free resource that can be harnessed with modest modifications in building construction, design, or orientation. In Cyprus, Israel, and Jordan, solar panels already heat between 25 and 65 percent of the water in homes. More than 1 million active solar systems and 250,000 passive solar homes have been built in the United States. Advanced solar collectors can produce water so hot—200 degrees Celsius—that it can meet process steam needs for many industries. Indeed, using electricity or directly burning fossil fuels to heat water

Table 2-3. Costs of Selected Renewable Electricity Sources, 1980–2030[1]

Technology	1980	1988	2000	2030
		(1988 cents per kilowatt-hour)		
Wind	32[2]	8	5	3
Geothermal	4	4	4	3
Photovoltaic	339	30	10	4
Solar Thermal				
trough with gas assistance	24[3]	8[4]	6[5]	—
parabolic/central receiver	85[6]	16	8	5
Biomass[7]	5	5	—	—

[1]All costs are levelized over the expected life of the technology and are rounded; projected costs assume return to high government R&D levels. [2]1981. [3]1984. [4]1989. [5]1994. [6]1982. [7]Future changes in biomass costs are dependent on feedstock cost.

SOURCE: Worldwatch Institute, based on Idaho National Engineering Laboratory et al., *The Potential of Renewable Energy: An Interlaboratory White Paper,* prepared for the Office of Policy, Planning and Analysis, U.S. Department of Energy, in support of the National Energy Strategy (Golden, Colo.: Solar Energy Research Institute, 1990), and other sources.

and buildings may become rare during the next few decades.[28]

Solar collectors, along with other renewable technologies, can also turn the sun's rays into electricity. In one system, large troughs reflect the sun's rays onto an oil-filled tube that produces steam for a turbine. One southern Californian company generates 354 megawatts of energy with these collectors and has contracts to install 320 megawatts' worth more. The newest systems turn 22 percent of the incoming sunlight into electricity. Spread over 750 hectares, the collectors produce enough power for around 170,000 homes at a cost as low as 8¢ per kilowatt-hour—competitive with some conventional power sources.[29]

Solar cells are the least expensive source of electricity for much of the rural Third World.

Future solar thermal technologies are expected to produce electricity even more cheaply. Parabolic dishes follow the sun and focus sunlight onto a single point where a small heat engine can be mounted or the energy can be transferred to a central turbine. The standardized units mean that generating capacity can be added incrementally as needed. By the middle of the next century, vast areas of arid and semiarid countryside could be used to produce electricity for export to power-short regions.[30]

Photovoltaic cells, which convert sunlight into electricity directly, will almost certainly be ubiquitous by 2030. These small, modular units can power anything from a pocket calculator to a large city. Within a generation, solar cells will likely be installed on building rooftops, along transportation rights-of-way, and at central generating facilities. One Japanese company, Sanyo Electric, has incorporated them into roofing shingles.[31]

Over the past two decades, the cost of photovoltaic electricity has fallen from $30 a kilowatt-hour to just 30¢. The force behind the decline is steady improvement in cell efficiency and manufacturing as well as a demand that has more than doubled every five years. These cost reductions mean that pumping water with photovoltaics is cheaper than using diesel generators in remote areas of Africa. Solar cells are also the least expensive source of electricity for much of the rural Third World; more than 6,000 villages in India now rely on them, and Indonesia and Sri Lanka have also initiated ambitious programs.[32]

If projected cost reductions for the two technologies are realized, photovoltaics might eventually take over the central generating role of solar thermal power. Solar cells have another advantage: because they can be more decentralized, they require less investment in transportation and distribution systems. By the end of this decade, when solar cell electricity is expected to cost 10¢ a kilowatt-hour, some countries may be turning to photovoltaics to provide power for well-established grids. Two decades later, photovoltaics could provide a large share of electricity, and for as little as 4¢ a kilowatt-hour.[33]

Another form of solar energy, wind power, captures the energy from the sun's differential heating of the earth's atmosphere. Electricity is generated by propeller-driven mechanical turbines perched on strategically located towers. The cost of this source of electricity has fallen from more than 30¢ a kilowatt-hour in the early eighties to a current average of just 8¢. By the end of the nineties, the cost is expected to be around 5¢. Most of the reductions have come from experience gained in California, which accounts for nearly 80 percent of the world's wind-produced electricity.

Denmark, the world's second-largest wind energy producer, got about 2 percent of the country's power from wind turbines in 1990.[34]

Wind power has a huge potential. It could provide many countries with 20 percent or more of their electricity. Some of the most promising areas have been found in northern Europe, northern Africa, southern South America, the U.S. western plains, and the trade wind belt around the tropics. A single ridge in Minnesota, 160 kilometers long and 1.6 kilometers wide, could be used to generate three times as much wind power as California gets today. Even more productive sites have been mapped out in Montana and Idaho.[35]

Living green plants provide another means of capturing solar energy. Through photosynthesis, they convert sunlight into biomass that, burned in the form of wood, charcoal, agricultural wastes, or animal dung, is the primary source of energy for nearly half the world—about 2.5 billion people in developing countries. Sub-Saharan Africa derives some 75 percent of its energy from biomass, most of it using primitive technologies and at considerable cost to the environment.[36]

Some uses of bioenergy will undoubtedly increase in the decades ahead, though not as much as some enthusiasts assume. Developing nations will need to find more sophisticated and efficient means of using biomass if their rapidly increasing fuel needs are to be met.

With many forests and croplands already overstressed, for example, and with food needs pressing against agricultural resources, it is unrealistic to think that ethanol distilled from corn can supply more than a tiny fraction of the world's liquid fuels. And shortages of irrigating water may complicate matters, especially in a world undergoing a rapid warming.[37]

In the future, ethanol will probably be produced from agricultural and wood wastes rather than precious grain. By employing an enzymatic process, scientists have reduced the cost of wood ethanol from $4 a gallon to $1.35 over the past 10 years, and expect it to be about 60¢ a gallon by the end of the nineties. Within a few decades, however, liquid fuel will be at a premium; it will probably be saved for specialized uses.[38]

Improving the conversion of agricultural and forestry wastes to energy could boost biomass energy's role in the future, particularly in developing countries already so reliant on this source. Wood stoves that double or treble efficiency exist today, and better designs are being worked on. Conversion can also be improved by using more efficient combustion technologies. For electricity production, highly efficient advanced gas turbines fueled by biomass can be built as small as 5 megawatts. Some 50,000 megawatts of generating capacity, 75 percent of Africa's current total, could come from using residues in today's sugarcane industry alone. In the future, integrated farming systems known as agroforestry could produce much fuel, food, and building materials.[39]

Hydropower now supplies nearly a fifth of the world's electricity. Although there is still ample growth potential, particularly in developing countries, environmental constraints will greatly limit such development. Small-scale projects are generally more promising than the massive ones favored by governments and international lending agencies. Smaller dams and reservoirs cause less social and ecological disruption. In deciding which hydropower resources to develop, issues such as land flooding, siltation, and human displacement will play an important role. These considerations will likely keep most nations from exploiting all of their potential.[40]

Another important element of a renewable-based energy system is geothermal energy—the latent heat of the earth's core. This is not strictly a renewable resource, however, and it needs to be carefully tapped so as not to deplete the local heat source. Since geothermal plants can produce power more than 90 percent of the time, they can provide electricity when there is no sun or wind.

Geothermal resources are localized, though found in many regions. Worldwide, more than 5,600 megawatts' worth of geothermal power plants have been built. El Salvador gets 40 percent of its electricity from the earth's natural heat, Nicaragua 28 percent, and Kenya 11 percent. Most Pacific Rim countries, as well as those along East Africa's Great Rift and around the Mediterranean, could tap geothermal energy. Iceland, Indonesia, and Japan are among the nations with the greatest potential.[41]

Renewable energy can protect developing countries from the devastating fluctuations in the world oil market.

While fossil fuels have been in storage for millions of years, renewable energy is in constant flux—replenished as the sun shines. The intermittent nature of sunshine and wind mean that the use of renewables will eventually need to be backed up with a way to store the energy for later use. Indeed, biomass energy and hydropower are the only forms that in themselves can be easily stored. Developing new and improved storage systems is therefore one of the key challenges in building a sustainable energy economy.

Low-temperature heat can be stored in simple systems that rely on water, bedrock, or materials such as oil or salt. Thermal storage systems pump heat available on sunny summer days through these substances to ensure that buildings remain warm—even through long winters. Such systems can recover as much as 85 percent of the heat originally captured and stored. Already, some 30 large installations have been built in Europe, including 10 district heating systems for schools, office buildings, and apartments in Sweden.[42]

A greater challenge comes in storing electricity. Pumped hydroelectric storage systems—which elevate water to a reservoir, then drop it through a turbine to produce electricity—are now used in some regions. As with other hydroelectric plants, pumped storage systems will be limited by their environmental drawbacks, though their use is likely to grow. Another, less disruptive large-scale alternative is a storage system that uses available electricity to compress air into an underground reservoir. When electricity is needed, the air is withdrawn, heated up, and forced through a turbine. As with pumped-hydro, compressed-air storage systems can achieve about 70 percent efficiency. A 290-megawatt system is already operating in Germany.[43]

Battery storage is a more flexible alternative. Batteries are modular, chemical devices that can be used on a small or large scale. Home photovoltaic panels can be hooked up to batteries, as can utility-scale wind or solar plants. Batteries could also play a role in transportation without substantially increasing electricity demand. If one quarter of U.S. passenger vehicle miles were traveled in electric cars, total electricity consumption would rise only 7 percent.[44]

During the early nineties, electric vehicles are scheduled to be introduced by several major auto companies. More advanced batteries have the potential to bring costs down in the following years. New batteries also have less of the toxic heavy metals used in lead-acid batteries, though no batteries avoid the need for careful reuse and recycling. (See Chapter 3.) One type, the sodium sulfur battery, is more efficient, more compact, longer lasting, and lighter than current models. It requires further improvements before commercial use, however, including less expensive means to maintain the batteries at the high temperature necessary for proper functioning.[45]

Hydrogen is the strongest candidate for large-scale storage. It can be burned in place of petroleum, coal, or natural gas. The chemical industry currently produces hydrogen from fossil fuels, but it can also be produced by running an electric current through water, splitting the molecules into oxygen and hydrogen. German and Saudi engineers are working on this process using electricity from photovoltaic cells.[46]

Proponents of solar hydrogen envision huge desert photovoltaic farms connected by pipelines to cities. Hydrogen can be stored in metal hydrides, pressurized tanks, or underground reservoirs, thus providing a readily accessible form of energy.[47]

Hydrogen is the cleanest-burning fuel—producing only water vapor and small amounts of nitrogen oxides (formed by the combination of atmospheric nitrogen and oxygen). These emissions can be reduced through lower combustion temperatures and nearly eliminated by using a catalytic converter designed to remove them. Today's catalytic converters have the more difficult task of reducing multiple pollutants at the same time.[48]

Electricity can also be generated chemically by combining hydrogen with oxygen in a fuel cell, yielding no emissions of nitrogen oxides. Fuel cells can be used in hydrogen-powered electric cars in place of inefficient internal combustion engines. Cells fueled with natural gas now convert 40 percent of the energy to electricity, while those using hydrogen operate at an efficiency of nearly 70 percent. Internal combustion engines rarely convert even 25 percent of gasoline to usable energy, while standard power plants generally operate at 33 percent efficiency. Furthermore, waste heat could be captured from stationary fuel cells for use in a cogeneration system.[49]

The shape of a renewable energy system is beginning to emerge. One thing that seems certain is that a solar age will tend to be more decentralized and diverse; the mix of energy sources would reflect the climate and natural resources of each region. Northern Europe, for example, is likely to rely on a mixture of wind, biomass, solar, and hydropower, while northern Africa and the Middle East will depend more on direct sunlight. Wood, agricultural wastes, sunshine, and geothermal energy will probably provide energy throughout Southeast Asia.

No completely new technologies are needed, only modest, achievable advances in those already in use or under development. Renewable energy is well ahead of fusion energy technologies, for example, which have received billions of dollars of government funds over several decades without yet producing even a detailed design for a workable power plant.[50]

One significant aspect of a renewable energy system is that all countries will have to start virtually from scratch in building it. Although the rich nations will have an obvious advantage in terms of investment capital, developing countries in many cases have extensive renewable energy resources, and will not face such broad conversion costs. And renewable energy can protect developing countries from the devastating fluctuations in the world oil market that have so complicated their development plans in recent years.

Vastly improved energy efficiency—along with being intrinsically important in any effort to move away from fossil fuels—is the key to making a renewable energy system work. If a home's electricity needs are cut by two thirds, for example, the investment cost for a rooftop photovoltaic power plant could be halved. Similarly, a highly efficient electric car would go further and would need smaller batteries, reducing its cost and weight. The development of more energy-efficient technologies is thus as crucial to the viability of an economy based on renewable energy as the solar technologies themselves.

EMPLOYMENT IMPLICATIONS

Successful economies are dynamic, changing constantly as technologies develop and as societies' needs shift. This evolution naturally leads to changes in the jobs people hold. With the advent of the automobile, for example, blacksmiths and wainwrights were replaced by service station attendants and mechanics. Although this process is painful for those whose jobs disappear, it opens new opportunities for them and for other workers.

Industry lobbyists often argue that reduced energy consumption will lead to a massive loss of jobs in energy-producing industries. To the contrary, a sustainable energy economy would likely have more jobs than one based on fossil fuels—primarily because improving the efficiency of energy use creates more jobs than supplying energy. In the future, the number of jobs in energy will probably grow, and the skills in demand will shift dramatically.

Today, few countries have much of their work force involved in energy production. In Poland, Canada, and India, for example, 4.4, 2.5, and 1 percent of jobs respectively are in energy and min-

ing. Some 1.5 million Americans—1.4 percent of the labor force—worked in energy production and conversion in 1988. This includes jobs in coal mining, the oil and gas industry, and electric and gas utilities.[51]

The trend in industrial countries is toward fewer such jobs. Coal mining jobs in the United States fell nearly 40 percent between 1980 and 1988, from 246,000 to 151,000, despite a 14-percent increase in total coal production. Those in the nation's oil and gas industry shrank from 715,000 to 528,000 over the same period. One minor exception is the electric utility sector, in which the number of employees, primarily service workers, rose 10 percent to 648,000 workers. However, most of this increase has likely been offset by the loss of construction jobs following a 40-percent decline in utility construction expenditures in the eighties.[52]

Harnessing energy entails relatively few jobs because these are among the most capital-intensive industries. The oil and gas industry in Alberta, Canada, for instance, generates 1.4 jobs for $1 million worth of capital investment, while other sectors of the economy average over 10 jobs. Manufacturing, by comparison, yields 9.2 jobs per $1 million; agriculture, 13; and services, more than 32.[53]

The electric power industry is also highly capital-intensive. One quarter of the foreign debts in Costa Rica and Brazil are due to borrowing by their power sectors. Centrally planned economies went the furthest in this direction: In the Soviet Union, energy accounted for nearly one fifth of all capital expenditures in the late eighties. Poland poured nearly 40 percent of total industrial investment into energy in 1986, with 21 percent in coal alone.[54]

Reduced employment in coal mining is among the trends likely to continue in the decades ahead. Governments will need to compensate workers, ensure that they learn new skills, and cooperate with businesses to form new industries in the affected areas. Countries such as the United Kingdom and Germany have experience with this problem, since the number of coal miners is already falling as automation increases—despite the opposition of unions. Hundreds of thousands of Polish, Czech, and east German coal miners are poised to lose their positions as energy prices are deregulated. Even in China, with more than 4 million coal miners, increased automation and worker productivity ensures a leveling off of jobs in this sector.[55]

There is a way, however, to meet energy needs in the future while creating jobs. Theoretical studies and post-project evaluations have found the same thing: for each dollar invested, efficiency improvements generate more jobs than producing energy does. A 1979 Council on Economic Priorities report found that investments in energy efficiency, conservation, and solar technologies provided more than twice as much employment as those in new energy resources, whether oil, natural gas, or new power plants. At the local level, where the savings from efficiency improvements would be recirculated in the economy, a dollar spent on energy efficiency produced four times as many jobs as one invested in a new power plant.[56]

Similar conclusions were reached by a 1985 study of Denmark, France, the United Kingdom, and West Germany done by the Commission of the European Communities. Investments in district heating, building insulation, and biogas plants, for example, were found to save money and produce more jobs than traditional energy investments. A study in Alaska found that home weatherization created more jobs and personal income per dollar than any other investment studied, including the construction of hospitals, highways, or hy-droelectric projects. Post-project evaluations of energy-saving programs in Connecticut and Iowa have found that they were less expensive and created more work than energy supply alternatives such as electric power stations.[57]

For each dollar invested, efficiency improvements generate more jobs than producing energy does.

As communities invest more in improving energy efficiency and tap local renewable energy resources, rather than purchase imported energy, economic benefits ripple through the economy. A city plan drawn up by San Jose, California, for example, would create 170 jobs over 10 years with an initial investment of just $645,000. The program includes education campaigns to show consumers how to save energy, and technical assistance, such as energy audits and the development of a home energy rating system. Prominent in the San Jose plan are initiatives to reduce energy use in government buildings and transportation, in effect providing an example for the community. The city investment, which would spur nearly $20 million in private spending, is expected to pay for itself in two-and-a-half years, and result in reduced carbon dioxide emissions.[58]

Even among electricity-generating technologies, there is a wide gap in employment levels. For the amount of energy produced, traditional fossil fuel and nuclear power plants employ fewer people than today's solar power systems do, even when coal mining is included. (See Table 2–4.) As the technologies are further refined, and as companies strive to cut costs, however, the difference between renewable and conventional technologies may be narrowed. Photovoltaic companies, for example, are now cutting costs by opening fully automated manufacturing lines, as Maryland-based Solarex did in 1990.[59]

Biomass energy, particularly from sustainably harvested wood, also generates more jobs than fossil fuel alternatives. A recent Canadian study found that increasing wood use in New Brunswick over the next 20 years would create more income, more jobs, and more tax revenue for the province than would the same amount invested in oil or coal development. Researchers in the Northeast and Great Lakes regions of the United States have come to similar conclusions.[60]

In the move to a solar economy, the fastest growing jobs would be traditional skilled and semiskilled positions such as insulation installers, carpenters, and sheet metal workers. Wind prospectors, photovoltaic engineers, and solar architects are among the new professions that would expand rapidly. Numbering

Table 2-4. United States: Direct Employment Generated by Electricity-Producing Technologies

Technology	Jobs
	(per terawatt-hour a year)
Nuclear	100
Geothermal	112
Coal[1]	116
Solar Thermal	248
Wind	542

[1]Includes coal mining.
SOURCE: Worldwatch Institute, based on Department of Energy (DOE), Energy Information Administration (EIA), *Electric Plant Cost and Power Production Expenses 1988* (Washington, D.C.: 1990); DOE, EIA, *Coal Production Statistics 1988* (Washington, D.C.: 1989); Mark Sisinyak, Vice President, California Energy Company, Coso Junction, Calif., private communication, June 19, 1990; Kathleen Flanagan, Director of Government Relations and Public Affairs, Luz International Limited, Los Angeles, Calif., private communication, June 18, 1990; Paul Gipe, Gipe & Assoc., Tehachapi, Calif., private communication, April 12, 1990.

in the thousands today, jobs in these fields may total in the millions within a few decades. Some of the skills now used in a fossil-fuel-based energy system would still be valued. Petroleum geologists and oil-well crews, for example, could focus their energies on drilling for geothermal resources.

The Iraqi invasion of Kuwait did not affect the cost of sugarcane ethanol in Brazil or of wind turbines in Denmark.

A highly efficient, renewable-energy-based economy would create not only more jobs, but cleaner and safer ones. Some of the jobs added by moving toward nuclear power, by comparison, would require people to clean up radioactive spills or decommission hot plants. Adding pollution equipment to coal plants also creates employment, but some of the new jobs involve disposing of toxic ash. Passive solar builders and energy service managers are spared such occupational hazards.

A few nations currently rely on energy production as the cornerstone of their economies. The Persian Gulf nations would experience vast changes if fossil fuel use declined precipitously, since petroleum exports generate virtually all their foreign exchange. The oil reserves of most countries, however, will be largely depleted over the next 50 years, leading to a gradual phasedown anyway as reserves are used up. Ironically, the Middle East may end up with another energy export in the future—solar energy, via hydrogen-bearing pipelines.

Oil-importing developing countries, particularly those burdened with high foreign debt, have a further incentive to follow a labor-intensive, improved-efficiency energy strategy. Most Latin

American and African nations have far more labor to spare than capital; indeed, underemployment and unemployment are creating major social problems in many developing countries. By following a solar strategy, developing countries would provide more jobs while reducing expenditures on imported oil and other fossil fuels.

As energy supplies become more diverse and less dependent on high-value fuels, local economies will be free from the boom-and-bust cycles that plague today's energy markets. The Iraqi invasion of Kuwait, it should be noted, did not significantly affect the cost of solar hot-water equipment in Jordan, of sugarcane ethanol in Brazil, or of wind turbines in Denmark. Indeed, the unquantifiable benefits of the greater self-reliance that flows from local jobs and investments based on local energy resources could offer stability in an otherwise volatile world.

Toward a Solar Economy

In 1976, *Foreign Affairs* published an article that challenged the comfortable assumptions of energy planners. In "Energy Strategy: The Road Not Taken?" physicist Amory Lovins proposed a heretical vision of the future in which the world relied on improved energy efficiency and renewable technologies instead of fossil fuels and nuclear power.[61]

The experience of the past 15 years is beginning to prove Lovins right. In the mid-seventies, conventional energy planners predicted that the United States would be using around 135 quadrillion Btus (quads) of energy in 1990, while Lovins projected just under 100 quads. The actual figure for 1990 was just 83 quads, only 10 percent higher than in 1973. Once portrayed as a wild-eyed advocate of "soft energy," Lovins actually underestimated the rapidity of efficiency's gains.[62]

It would seem, then, that the world has taken the first step down Lovins' road, though most policymakers remain oblivious to it. The big question is when we will take the next step—the building of a decentralized renewable energy system. The answer may be soon.

In contrast to the efficiency success story, Lovins' 1990 quota for solar energy has only been half met. This can be explained in large measure by government neglect and even hostility during the eighties. Still, renewable energy technologies are far more mature now than they were in the mid-seventies. Production costs have plummeted and reliability has substantially improved. A commercial takeoff can be predicted with confidence for several of these technologies during the next five years. This surge will be driven not only by technological progress but by the obvious unsustainability of world oil and climate trends.[63]

The shape of this new energy system is beginning to emerge and, as Lovins predicted, decentralization is its hallmark. In contrast to the huge coal and nuclear plants of today, power from renewable technologies—whether photovoltaic cells, wood-fired plants, or wind generators—can be developed cost-effectively in various sizes. Solar, wind, and cogeneration facilities can be built economically on a scale that is less than one one-thousandth the typical size of a large nuclear or coal-fired plant. Some renewable energy systems can be built, literally, for households.[64]

Wind turbine manufacturing currently focuses on 100-kilowatt machines that cost roughly $100,000 to install. The manufacturing processes and investments are more akin to today's automobile assembly lines than to central power plants. Costs will fall dramatically as the market grows. A wind power developer could install 10, 100, or 1,000 machines, depending on how much power is needed. The same machine could also be used by itself to supply an entire village in a developing country.

Given the diversity and decentralization of renewable resources, transmission and distribution losses can be minimized. Assisting this would be the development of a hydrogen system that can move energy long distances with virtually no energy losses compared with today's electricity transmission grids. Hydrogen can also be used to power cars, buses, and other modes of transportation.[65]

Areas where renewable sources are abundant and the need for energy great will likely see the arrival of a range of new technologies. Solar thermal power systems will be deployed extensively in deserts, while wind turbines will proliferate in windy regions. Photovoltaics can be used virtually everywhere. No matter the energy technology, however, environmental and land use considerations need careful attention. Although many areas will remain off-limits for energy production due to environmental concerns, this will not substantially hinder renewable energy development.

Solar electric technologies do require land, but they are no more land-intensive than some of today's power sources. (See Table 2–5.) In fact, if the land devoted to mining coal is included, many renewable systems actually require less space than coal does. In coal-rich areas of Eastern Europe, the United States, and India, for example, vast strip mines now cover huge areas. These enormous gashes in the earth's surface will in many cases be permanent—rendering large areas useless for generations to come.[66]

Nor do solar technologies need to be deployed uniformly over a wide swath of land. Photovoltaics can be placed on rooftops and in areas of "wasted" space. On wind farms, only 10 percent of the land is actually occupied by turbine towers and service roads; the remainder can be used for grazing animals or cultivating crops. Around a nuclear power plant, by contrast, large areas are fenced off to provide security zones. And researchers have not yet calculated the amount of land needed for nuclear waste disposal and uranium tailings—land that may be off-limits for millennia.[67]

Land availability would not be a constraint to the harnessing of solar energy, even from large, central generating facilities. Researchers at the Electric

Table 2-5. United States: Land Use of Selected Electricity-Producing Technologies

Technology	Land Occupied
	(square meters per gigawatt-hour, over 30 years)
Coal[1]	3,642
Solar Thermal	3,561
Photovoltaics	3,237
Wind[2]	1,335
Geothermal	404

[1]Includes coal mining. [2]Land actually occupied by turbines and service roads.
SOURCE: Worldwatch Institute, based on Meridian Corporation, "Energy System Emissions and Materiel Requirements," prepared for U.S. Department of Energy, Alexandria, Va., February 1989; Paul Gipe, "Wind Energy Comes of Age," Gipe & Assoc., Tehachapi, Calif., May 13, 1990; Paul Savoldelli, Luz International Limited, Los Angeles, Calif., private communication and printout, July 11, 1989; Paula Blaydes, California Energy Company, San Francisco, Calif., private communication, June 19, 1990.

Power Research Institute in California have determined that all current U.S. electricity needs could be met by solar cells deployed over an area of 59,000 square kilometers—just twice the size of the U.S. Air Force's bombing ranges. Pacific Northwest Laboratories estimates that 25 percent of current U.S. generating capacity could be met by installing wind machines on the windiest 1.5 percent of the contiguous United States. Most of this is barren, privately owned grazing land in the western states that would hardly be changed by wind farm development. In Europe, the largest wind farms will likely be placed in the North and Baltic Seas.[68]

Still, no one envisions that wind or photovoltaics alone would provide all the world's power. Rather, a variety of renewable technologies, deployed at different scales, seems more likely. Within a few decades, a geographically diverse country like the United States might get 30 percent of its electricity from sunshine, 20 percent from hydropower, 20 percent from wind power, 10 percent from biomass, 10 percent from geothermal energy, and 10 percent from natural-gas-fired cogeneration. A north African country may get half its electricity from solar power, while northern Europe is likely to rely more on wind, and the Philippines on geothermal energy.

Contrary to the assumptions of some, it is unlikely that vast stretches of cropland will be turned into energy farms. Less than 3 percent of the sun's rays are converted to biomass in photosynthesis. Photovoltaics, by contrast, already convert 10 percent of sunlight to electricity, and solar thermal units reach 22 percent. Thus if land is to be dedicated to energy production, more energy can be squeezed from direct solar technologies than from biomass. For example, it takes nearly one hectare of corn to run a U.S. automobile for a year on ethanol, yet the same amount of land devoted to today's solar thermal troughs could power more than 80 electric vehicles. Moreover, solar technologies can be placed on less valuable land. A hectare of Wyoming scrubland is worth around $100, while a plot of Iowa farmland the same size costs more than $3,000.[69]

The pattern of human settlements, now shaped by cheap oil and the automobile, could be redrawn during the next several decades.

Other environmental issues to consider include the loss of biodiversity, a concern if natural ecosystems are converted to energy farms that exacerbate pesticide contamination and soil erosion. And geothermal development in Hawaii and the Philippines has run into conflicts with tropical forest protection, while California's wind turbines have been associated with bird kills. But solutions can be found. In the Netherlands, wind developers agreed with ornithological society representatives not to build in locations where birds might be affected.[70]

The pattern of human settlements, now shaped by cheap oil and the automobile, could be redrawn during the next several decades. Over half of total energy use in industrial countries is now related in some way to spatial structure—that is, to the relative location of homes, jobs, and shopping sites—according to Susan Owens, geography professor at Cambridge University. It is this placement of work and living space over the landscape that partially drives the wasteful use of energy.[71]

Although major changes in land use will obviously take time, the early stages of that transition may begin almost immediately. One thing that is almost certain to be supplanted are the sprawling suburbs found in some countries today. Not only are large detached homes prone to high levels of energy consumption, the current suburban structure itself forces people to rely on automobiles and to use enormous amounts of energy performing the ordinary tasks of daily life.

Energy constraints are therefore likely to push societies toward more compact communities, where work and shopping are often within easy walking or cycling distance. (See also Chapter 4.) European cities already provide a model of this; they typically have a density about three times that of modern American cities. In many climates, new buildings might be constructed so as to capture as much sunlight as possible—both for household heating and for electricity—perhaps supplemented by a hydrogen-powered cogenerator in the basement.[72]

There is sufficient flexibility for solar design not to conflict with the need to make societies relatively compact. Passive solar residences can be built at 35 or even 50 dwellings to the hectare, a concentration that is typically considered by planners in the United States to be a high-density development. A normal U.S. residential suburb, in contrast, is zoned for no more than 10 homes to the hectare.[73]

District heating and cooling can offer efficient energy for more compact cities and towns. This concept, already widely used in the Soviet Union, employs a central heating plant that delivers steam or hot water to neighboring buildings. In Denmark, 40 percent of the heating is provided by such plants, some of it using straw as fuel. District plants often produce electricity as well as heat (cogener-ation), allowing for more efficient use of fuels.[74]

More compact urban designs also reduce transportation energy needs, and diminish traffic and pollution. Mixing homes and businesses can be more energy-efficient than concentrating work and shopping away from residential neighborhoods. It allows people to rely more on walking and cycling. And lower energy use would be one result of better public transportation. Some 40 years from now, rail travel and telecommunications could replace many of the shorter trips now covered by planes.[75]

The transition to a sustainable energy system is one that the world as a whole must achieve. By the year 2030, today's developing countries will have upward of 80 percent of the world's population. It is their transition that ultimately is the most important. These nations have little hope of achieving their basic development goals if they follow the energy path taken 100 years ago by the West. But they also have an opportunity to in effect "leapfrog" industrial countries and follow an energy strategy that is sustainable from the start. Only then would the Third World be able to meet the basic needs of its people while sustaining its environment.[76]

The world has in a sense already embarked on the next great energy transition—under the pressures of economic, environmental, and social limits that have made the old system unsustainable and obsolete. The main danger is that new energy systems will evolve too slowly, overtaken not only by environmental problems but by the social and economic upheavals that could accompany them. Societies have only a short time to chart a sustainable energy course—and then to muster the political will to follow it.

3

Reducing Waste, Saving Materials

John E. Young

In his 1977 book *Soft Energy Paths*, Amory Lovins offered a startlingly simple critique of the notion that the well-being of a society is inexorably tied to its level of energy use. Energy is a means, he argued, not an end: "People do not want electricity or oil . . . but rather comfortable rooms, light, vehicular motion, food, tables, and other real things."[1]

By the same token, people do not need materials but the services they provide. The amount of wood, stone, or steel used to make a house or office building, for example, is irrelevant to its occupants if the building is sturdy and stays at a comfortable temperature. Rice bought straight from a bin at the local store and carried home in an old jar is no less tasty or nutritious than that bought in a throwaway box.

Today's industrial economies were founded on the use of vast quantities of materials and energy, and the economic

health of nations has often been equated with the amount of raw materials consumed. But prosperity need not be so closely linked to consumption. (See also Chapter 9.) A kilogram of steel may be used in a building that lasts hundreds of years or in several cans that end up in a dump after one use. A few hundred grams of glass may be fashioned into a bottle reused 50 times or one immediately discarded.

The amount of material that originally enters an economy tells us nothing about the material's eventual fate or its contribution to human well-being. It does tell us a good deal, however, about the damage inflicted on the environment at both ends of the production cycle.

Extraction and processing of raw materials are among the most destructive of human activities. Logging usually ruins forest ecosystems, and transforming trees into paper and other wood products involves several highly polluting processes. Mining regularly obliterates whatever ecosystems or human settlements sit atop ore deposits. Making met-

An expanded version of this chapter appeared as Worldwatch Paper 101, *Discarding the Throwaway Society*.

als from ores takes great quantities of energy and produces large amounts of pollution and waste. Unfortunately, much of the damage from producing raw materials occurs in remote areas, so most people know little of it.

The other end of the cycle is more familiar. Industrial economies eventually excrete as waste most of the raw materials they devour. This refuse presents a massive disposal problem. As the dirty and expensive legacies of careless dumping have come to light, the most visible symptom of profligate materials consumption—the "garbage crisis"—has generated political heat in communities around the world.

The primary danger of high levels of resource consumption lies in the continuing damage that extraction and processing impose on the environment.

Though the symptom gets attention, politicians rarely diagnose the disease: a global economy built on the inefficient use of raw materials and energy. As a result, the usual prescription—increasingly more sophisticated technology for destroying waste—allows the illness to progress unchecked. Garbage output continues to grow (often faster than population), along with the environmental damage from waste disposal and materials production.

Fortunately, societies need not limit themselves to purely technological approaches. They can attack the problem at its source. From the attempts of people around the world to find alternative solutions to waste problems, a "soft materials path" can be mapped out. Its operating principle is efficiency: meeting people's needs with as little as possible

of the most appropriate materials available.

MATERIALS AND THE ENVIRONMENT

Human use of raw materials—with the notable exception of timber—was almost insignificant by today's terms until the rise of modern industrial economies in the nineteenth century. From then on it grew at an explosive rate, particularly the use of minerals. Per capita production and consumption of raw materials by industrial nations continued rising until the last two decades. In the United States, for example, per capita consumption of steel, cement, paper, and inorganic chemicals expanded from the twenties through the sixties as the economy grew.[2]

Since the seventies, however, per capita consumption of raw materials in Western Europe and the United States appears to have leveled off or declined slightly. Some observers now believe that basic changes in western industrial economies have made continued growth in raw materials consumption unnecessary and unlikely.[3]

Rapidly growing new industries—producing computers, pharmaceuticals, and high-technology goods, among other things—are accounting for an increasing share of economic output. These industries use materials and energy far less intensively than do traditional extractive and manufacturing ones, which have grown little or have even shrunk in recent years. Raw materials are needed mostly for replacement rather than new construction of infrastructure in highly industrialized economies, and as a result are now mainly used to satisfy immediate consumer demands.[4]

Although these trends appear to be common to most industrial market nations, absolute levels of consumption vary significantly. In 1987, for example, each West German used three fourths more steel than someone in France or the United Kingdom did, and nearly two thirds more zinc than each American. The Japanese require more than twice as much copper per person as the British do.[5]

Differences between industrial and developing countries are even more dramatic. The average Japanese consumes nine times as much steel as the average Chinese, and Americans use more than four times as much steel and 23 times as much aluminum as their neighbors in Mexico. U.S. paper consumption per person is over a dozen times the average for Latin America, and Americans use about 25 times as much nickel apiece as someone who lives in India.[6]

The now fairly stable levels of materials consumption in various western industrial nations are nevertheless quite high in comparison with historical levels. Over the last century, U.S. per capita consumption of steel has grown fourfold, copper fivefold, paper sevenfold, and concrete sixteenfold. According to one estimate, the United States alone consumed more minerals from 1940 to 1976 than did all of humanity up to 1940.[7]

The danger of such high levels of consumption lies less in running out of resources, as was commonly argued in the seventies, than in the continuing damage that their extraction and processing impose on the environment. Oil provides an instructive example: though resource exhaustion is easier to envision with petroleum than with other materials, rising levels of carbon dioxide in the atmosphere make it unlikely the world will run out of oil before the environmental cost of its use—in the form of global warming—becomes prohibitive.

Each year, the production of virgin materials damages millions of hectares of land, destroys millions of trees, produces billions of tons of solid waste, and pollutes air and water to a degree only exceeded by the production and use of energy—much of which is generated in order to extract and process materials.

Millions of hectares of forest are logged each year to satisfy the world's voracious appetite for wood. Manufacturing of non-fuel wood products, including paper, lumber, and plywood, currently requires 1.7 billion cubic meters of wood per year. Wherever it occurs, logging inflicts damage on the environment. Increased soil erosion, damage to fisheries, more severe floods, and destruction of wildlife habitat are but a few of the common effects. (See Chapter 5.)[8]

Mining, which supplies most of the raw materials for industrial societies, is one of the most damaging human activities, and unfortunately one of the most poorly documented. Private companies, governments, and international organizations collect and publish exhaustive statistics on mineral production, but information on its environmental costs is usually fragmented and out of date.

Although no precise global statistics are kept, it is clear that past and present mines cover a vast area of land. In the United States alone, current and abandoned metal and coal mines cover an estimated 9 million hectares—a figure that does not include the sizable but unmeasured area used for extracting sand, gravel, and stone for construction materials. By comparison, U.S. roads, parking lots, and other paved areas take up roughly 16 million hectares.[9]

The 1980 *Global 2000 Report to the President* of the U.S. Council on Environmental Quality estimated that 571,000 hectares were mined worldwide during 1976. Non-fuel minerals extraction accounted for two thirds of this area, and coal mining the remainder. The study projected that an area about half the size of Spain would be mined in the last quarter of this century. This estimate may be high, as production has not increased as much as the report anticipated, but the inevitable movement to lower-grade ores as better resources are exhausted tends to increase the area mined each year.[10]

Mining involves the movement of enormous quantities of soil and rock. According to geologist John Wolfe, the materials and energy used in the construction of a typical building require the excavation of a hole equal to the size of that building. Since about half, on average, of what comes out of the hole is not useful material, mining and processing minerals produces large quantities of waste. In the United States, non-fuel mining produces an estimated 1.0–1.3 billion tons of waste material each year—six to seven times the amount of municipal solid waste produced.[11]

Most waste is generated early in the production process. Unless a mineral deposit lies at the surface, soil and rock (called overburden) must be removed to reach the ore. Surface mining—which accounts for most current mineral production—produces far more such waste than underground mining, in which ore is brought to the surface through shafts and tunnels. After either type of mining, the process of concentrating the ore leaves more residues, which are called tailings. Finally, in metal production, smelting and refining remove remaining impurities, in the form of slag.[12]

Not all these wastes are hazardous. Overburden is often relatively inert material, though even chemically benign waste may cause problems if eroded by wind or water. But both ore-bearing and waste material can contain acid-forming chemicals, heavy metals, and other environmental contaminants, which water and wind can carry far beyond the mine.

For example, acidic or toxic drainage from mines and mining wastes has damaged an estimated 16,000 kilometers of streams in the western United States.[13]

Pollution from mineral extraction is not limited to water. Smelting and refining release large amounts of air pollutants, the composition of which depends on the metal or metals being produced. Sulfur oxides, arsenic, lead, and other heavy metals are all among the pollutants commonly produced by smelters.

Added together, these effects can spell environmental disaster for communities and ecosystems in mining areas. One hundred years of mining and smelting in Montana created the largest hazardous-waste cleanup site in the United States, which stretches for nearly 200 kilometers along the Clark Fork River and its tributaries. Children who grew up in the shadow of a now-closed smelter in neighboring Idaho's Silver Valley—also the site of over a century of mining—were found to have enough lead in their blood to require emergency medical treatment.[14]

Although the most visible and immediate impacts of mining, logging, and other such activities are local, their global effects may be even more profound. Industries that produce bulk materials are about 10 times as energy-intensive as other manufacturers. This high level of energy use, combined with the lack of reforestation in many logged areas, makes the production of basic materials a large contributor to rising carbon dioxide levels and, therefore, global warming.[15]

THE MESS WE ARE IN

"Historians," wrote social critic Vance Packard in his 1960 classic, *The Waste Makers*, "may allude to this as the

Throwaway Age." Three decades later, his description of the second half of the twentieth century is still apt for residents of industrial nations. Many now accept this historical aberration as the norm.[16]

Most of the raw materials that enter industrial economies eventually emerge from the other end as waste. Although municipal solid waste, or garbage, is neither the largest nor the most dangerous category of waste materials in industrial nations, it is certainly an indicator of overall profligacy. And producing the items that end up as trash accounts for much of the other waste generated by industrial societies. Ironically, as intensity of materials use appears to be falling in industrial production, continuing growth in solid waste generation indicates it is probably increasing in the consumer products sector. Societies that wish to improve their overall materials efficiency would thus do well to direct attention to reducing their output of garbage.[17]

The rapid increases in materials use in the United States, Western Europe, and Japan after World War II were accompanied by correspondingly sharp growth in garbage output. In the United States, for instance, the amount of solid waste generated per person has been rising since at least 1960.[18]

Mounting piles of garbage are a feature of virtually all industrial market nations. In the Organisation for Economic Co-operation and Development (OECD), 14 of the 16 members for which data are available showed increases in solid waste generation per person between 1980 and 1985. (See Table 3–1.) Only Japan and West Germany produced less trash, and in recent years output appeared to be rebounding in both. Before West Germany merged with East, its garbage output was rising 1–2 percent a year.[19]

The limited information available hints at a similar situation elsewhere. Ac-

Table 3-1. Change in Municipal Solid Waste Generation, Selected Countries, 1980–85

Country	Total	Per Person
	(percent)	
Ireland[1]	+72	+65
Spain[2]	+32	+28
Canada	+27	+21
Norway	+16	+14
United Kingdom[3]	+12	+11
Switzerland	+12	+ 9
Denmark	+ 6	+ 6
Sweden	+ 6	+ 5
France	+ 7	+ 5
Italy	+ 7	+ 4
Portugal	+13	+ 4
United States	+ 8	+ 3
Austria[4]	+ 3	+ 3
Luxembourg	+ 2	+ 2
Japan	0	− 3
West Germany[1]	− 10	− 9

[1]Data for 1980–84. [2]Data for 1978–85. [3]Data for 1980–87; includes England and Wales only. [4]Data for 1979–83.
SOURCES: Organisation for Economic Co-operation and Development, *OECD Environmental Data Compendium 1989* (Paris: 1989); U.S. Environmental Protection Agency, Office of Solid Waste and Emergency Response, *Characterization of Municipal Solid Waste in the United States: 1990 Update* (Washington, D.C.: 1990).

cording to a recent report based on articles in the Soviet press, people are throwing away 2–5 percent more garbage each year. Little documentation is available for Eastern Europe, but waste generation there and in the Soviet Union is likely to rise as formerly insular economies are opened to the consumer goods of the West. East German solid waste output reportedly skyrocketed after German economic unification.[20]

Industrialization and economic growth have brought not only increases in garbage but changes in its characteristics. While paper and paperboard usually remain the largest component (15–40 percent by weight) of municipal solid waste in industrial democracies, other types of waste are growing much more rapidly. Aluminum, plastics, and other relatively new substances are increasingly displacing traditional materials such as glass, steel, and plant fibers. The most startling change has been in plastics, the tonnage of which in U.S. solid waste rose 14 percent a year, on average, between 1960 and 1988; plastics now constitute 9 percent of U.S. waste by weight and 20 percent by volume. Many modern consumer products also contain toxic substances that can pose disposal problems: batteries contain heavy metals such as lead, mercury, and cadmium; household cleaners, solvents, paints, and pesticides often include hazardous chemicals.[21]

The amounts of garbage produced vary widely around the world. OECD data for the mid-eighties show Americans and Canadians generating roughly twice as much garbage per person as West Europeans or Japanese do. Though other estimates indicate that the gap between North Americans and the rest of the world might not be quite so wide, even U.S. government documents cite the nation as the world's top producer of garbage—660 kilograms per person in 1988.[22]

The greatest divide in waste generation, as in materials use, lies between the industrial and developing worlds. Though garbage is not unique to rich countries, it is generated there on a different scale. Residents of New York City, for example, throw away three or more times as much as people in Calcutta and Manila. In developing countries, waste is a luxury only available to a wealthy minority. Reuse and recycling are a way of life, and many survive by scouring the garbage of the rich for valuable scraps.[23]

Over the last two decades, virtually all the industrial market nations have come to realize that the new scale and character of waste are incompatible with con-

tinued reliance on landfills, the traditional method of disposal. All landfills eventually leak, releasing into groundwater an often toxic soup of rainwater and decomposing waste called "leachate." This can contain a wide variety of hazardous substances, including heavy metals and organic chemicals. The severity of the problem is illustrated by the fact that more than one fifth of the hazardous-waste sites on the U.S. Superfund cleanup list are municipal landfills. Decay of garbage in oxygen-starved dumps also produces methane gas, which is both a major contributor to global warming and a fire hazard.[24]

Higher population densities in Japan and a number of countries in Western Europe forced them to face the environmental faults of landfills long before the United States had to. Those nations experienced shortages of dumping space and rising landfill costs much sooner. Their lower waste generation rates, higher levels of recycling, and greater reliance on incineration reflect this earlier awakening to landfill problems.

Japan, for instance, burns 43–53 percent of its garbage and recycles another 26–39 percent. West Germany, when it was a separate nation, incinerated 27 percent of its solid waste, and planned to increase that number to 50 percent by 1995. Its citizens recycled about a third of their paper, aluminum, and glass. Several West European nations, including Denmark, France, Sweden, and Switzerland, throw half or less of their waste into landfills.[25]

In contrast, the United States landfilled over 80 percent of its waste until the late eighties. Nearly three fourths of American garbage still ends up in landfills, with half the remainder burned and half recycled. The United Kingdom is similarly dependent on landfills, with an even lower rate of recycling.[26]

Many industrial nations share a common official approach to garbage—the waste management hierarchy. This spells out a list of management options in order of priority: source reduction (avoiding garbage generation in the first place), direct reuse of products, recycling, incineration (with recovery of energy), and—as the last resort—landfilling. The U.N. Environment Programme endorses this hierarchy, as do citizen groups, many industry leaders, and government officials from Europe, North America, and Japan. And it has been enshrined in U.S. law since the passage of the Resource Conservation and Recovery Act in 1976.[27]

Unfortunately, practice has run directly counter to principle. Most governments continue to focus on managing rather than reducing waste. When faced with disposal crises, they tend to fund waste management options in inverse proportion to their position on the hierarchy, usually moving one notch up the ladder, from landfilling to incineration. Ubiquitous incinerators throughout Europe and Japan are the product of such decisions.

In the United States, the states—which have almost total responsibility for waste management—have focused heavily on building incinerators rather than on other options. A 1987 *Newsday* survey found that state governments had spent 39 times as much money on incineration as on recycling programs. Since 1970, Massachusetts has arranged for over a half-billion dollars in tax-exempt financing for incinerators, yet it did not fund a state recycling plan until 1987. Similarly, New York's 1972 Environmental Quality Bond Act budgeted $215 million for incinerators and only $1 million for recycling; additional legislation during the eighties provided only $31 million more for recycling. Although state governments are increasingly planning and budgeting for recycling, according to a recent survey, 18 in the Northeast and Midwest still expect to spend 8–10 times more on incineration than on recycling over the next five years.[28]

Major misconceptions persist about the nature of incineration. It is commonly referred to as a form of recycling and an alternative to landfilling. Strictly speaking, it is neither. It can reduce the amount of materials requiring final disposal and recover some energy in the process, but it does not recover materials or eliminate the need for landfills.

Americans and Canadians generate roughly twice as much garbage per person as West Europeans or Japanese do.

Mass-burn incinerators are technically capable of cutting the weight of garbage fed into them by 65–75 percent, and the volume by 80–90 percent. Due to maintenance shutdowns and the substantial share of waste that is too bulky or inert to be burned, however, actual reductions in the amount of solid waste that must be landfilled are usually considerably lower—closer to 50 percent by weight and 60 percent by volume.[29]

Incineration has several major drawbacks in comparison with the options higher in the waste management hierarchy. Most important in the long run, it is a destructive process that wastes both materials and energy. Though many incinerators produce energy, the amount recovered is considerably less than that needed to produce the items they burn. For example, recycling paper can save up to five times as much energy as can be recovered through incineration, though the amount saved varies substantially with the type of paper. For high-density polyethylene—the plastic from which milk jugs and laundry detergent bottles are commonly made—recycling saves almost twice as much energy as incineration. Repeated reuse of a durable container can save even more.[30]

Waste reduction, reuse, and recycling can reduce landfill needs by at least as much as incineration would.

Burning garbage is not a clean process. It produces air and water pollution and tons of toxic ash. High-temperature combustion breaks chemical bonds that render the toxic metals in many products inert, freeing them to leach from landfilled incinerator ash into groundwater. Incinerators pump into the air nitrogen and sulfur oxides (both precursors of acid rain), carbon monoxide, acid gases, dioxins and furans (extremely toxic substances suspected of causing cancer and genetic defects), and heavy metals like lead, cadmium, and mercury. Smokestack devices can trap some of these substances, but at a price: air pollution controls create additional toxic ash. Another form of pollution is created by using water to quench hot ash; the water inevitably becomes contaminated with chemicals, and poses a disposal problem if not saved and reused.[31]

Incinerators are also extremely expensive. They usually receive a variety of explicit government subsidies plus hidden ones such as higher-than-normal rates for the energy they produce. Although day-to-day operating costs of incinerators may be lower than those of recycling and composting programs, such savings are far outweighed by the extremely high capital cost of incineration. The Institute for Local Self-Reliance (ILSR) in Washington, D.C., estimates the capacity to incinerate one ton per day costs $100,000–150,000, whereas the same amount of materials

recovery capacity is pegged at $10,000–15,000, and composting at $15,000–20,000. Rough calculations using conservative figures for capital costs reveal that an $8-billion investment in additional incinerators could allow the United States to burn a fourth of its projected solid waste output in the year 2000, whereas the same sum spent on recycling and composting facilities could provide enough additional capacity to handle three fourths of the nation's garbage that year.[32]

Finally, as biologist Barry Commoner of Queens College puts it, "the only insurmountable hindrance to recycling is building an incinerator." Although their operators argue that incineration and recycling are compatible—because removal of some recyclables from waste makes the facilities burn more efficiently—they actually have an incentive to remove only noncombustible materials like glass and aluminum. Recycling, reuse, and source reduction programs compete directly with incinerators for approximately 80 percent of the waste stream.[33]

Since many incinerators depend on revenue from energy sales, they must run near capacity to stay profitable. Effective recycling and waste reduction programs can cut the amount of waste flowing to such facilities enough to put them in the red. In 1989, for example, waste disposal officials in Warren County, New Jersey, attributed a large part of a local incinerator's weekly $59,000 losses to implementation of a state law requiring a 25-percent recycling rate. The community was forced to reimburse the incinerator's builder and operator for its losses.[34]

Luckily, communities have more attractive alternatives than incinerators. Waste reduction, reuse, and recycling—the three options above incineration in the waste management hierarchy—can, taken together, reduce landfill needs by at least as much as incineration would. In addition, these soft-path solutions can lower not only the environmental impacts of waste disposal, but also the much greater environmental damage caused by extraction and processing of raw materials.

CHANGING PRODUCTS—AND PEOPLE

Source reduction—cutting waste by using less material in the first place—is the top choice on virtually everyone's list of waste management strategies, and for obvious reasons: it is the only option that eliminates the need for disposal, the extraction and processing of virgin materials, and even the reduced energy and pollution of recycling. Yet it is often dismissed as unrealistic.

Many maintain that reducing waste is impractical in today's industrial societies, that people want and need the things they buy, use, and discard. In an age in which the terms "consumer" and "person" are used interchangeably, disposing of bagfuls of garbage each day has become a routine, seemingly inescapable fact of life. Younger people forget that life was not always this way. Until recently, thrift was a way of life for those in industrial and developing countries alike, and people chose products that would last.

Several historic developments helped create the huge amounts of waste and voracious demand for raw materials that characterize today's consumer societies. After World War II, the United States and U.S. companies created and exported a new life-style: consumerism. (See also Chapter 9.) Total sales of all the commodities produced by a nation became a widely accepted indicator of economic health. Emphasis on sales created a peculiar set of industrial design standards. As one critic quoted in Vance Packard's *The Waste Makers* put it: "Maximum sales volume demands the cheapest construction for the briefest interval the buying public will tolerate." Packard termed this an "iron law" of American marketing.[35]

Convenience eclipsed durability as a top marketing point, and the ensuing decline of durable, reusable products disrupted many established services. Repairs became relatively more expensive and, in general, more difficult to arrange. Consumers had to return to the manufacturer many items, such as radios and small appliances, that had commonly been fixed by owners or in local shops—if the maker even still offered repair service. This greater inconvenience and expense led many people to throw away the old and just buy new items, as did annual style changes that outmoded many products soon after their purchase.[36]

The rise of synthetic materials also had a dramatic effect. A few decades ago, most products were composed of a relatively limited number of materials, many of them biological in origin. Today's products contain a bewildering mix of synthetic and natural, new and old, recyclable and nonrecyclable. Some traditional recycling systems, such as the collection of old woolen clothing to be turned into blankets and other products, have nearly vanished as a result.

Simultaneous initiatives on two broad fronts could help arrest or reverse some of these trends, reducing both waste and raw materials production. Manufacturers need to be convinced, cajoled, or forced to improve their products, so that people have the opportunity to choose items that are less harmful to the environment. And consumers need information about what, or whether, to purchase, along with incentives to make the right choices, so that the conscience need not do battle with the pocketbook.

On the first front, perverse incentives now lead manufacturers to produce wasteful and overpackaged goods. Industry representatives regularly point out that the costs of raw materials already give businesses adequate incentives to reduce waste. But their argument has three major flaws.

Selective purchasing by informed buyers might be the strongest incentive for manufacturers to produce low-waste, safer items.

First, companies pay artificially low prices for virgin materials. This is in part because the environmental costs of making them are rarely included in their price, but also because virgin production is often subsidized by governments (a problem discussed at the end of this chapter). Second, the public, not the maker, usually ends up footing the bill for disposal of consumer products and packaging, giving the manufacturer no reason to consider their eventual fate. Third, maximum profits—the primary concern of any business—are not always obtained by minimizing costs. The extra expense of elaborate, more wasteful packaging, for instance, may be offset by the additional purchasers it attracts.

If they want to cut waste, however, manufacturers have a variety of options. Industrial designers could undoubtedly uncover many opportunities for source reduction if they focused on development of durable, repairable products, for example, rather than the single-use items now rapidly proliferating.

Packaging is an obvious first target. In industrial countries, a large share of it is thrown away after a single use, so packaging (including containers) in the West

accounts for a large portion of solid waste. In 1988, for instance, packaging constituted 32 percent of U.S. garbage and 21 percent of domestic waste in the Netherlands, and it was responsible for one third of household and commercial waste in West Germany in recent years.[37]

Appropriate goals for packaging reduction programs include eliminating unnecessary wrappings and reusing as much as possible of what remains indispensable (while recycling the leftovers). Reuse is a particularly appropriate option for rigid containers that hold liquid or powdered products. The best example is refillable beverage bottles, which only a few decades ago were typical around the world. They are still dominant in many countries, including Finland, Germany, and a good deal of the Third World, but have lost much of their market share in the United States, the United Kingdom, and a number of other nations.[38]

In addition to obvious savings of materials, using refillables saves energy. Repeated studies have shown that it takes far less energy to wash out an old bottle than to melt it and make a new one, or to make a new bottle from virgin material. According to a 1981 study, a 12-ounce refillable glass bottle reused 10 times requires 24 percent as much energy per use as a recycled aluminum or glass container, and only 9–16 percent as much as a throwaway made of those materials. (See Figure 3–1.) Even a 1989 study commissioned by a plastics trade group found that a 16-ounce glass refillable bottle used eight times was the lowest energy user of nine containers considered. The key to savings is the number of times a bottle is used, which can be 50 or more in areas where refillables dominate the market. Deposits are nearly always placed on refillables to ensure their return.[39]

In the former West Germany, where

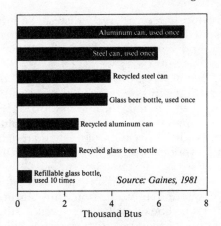

Aluminum can, used once

Steel can, used once

Recycled steel can

Glass beer bottle, used once

Recycled aluminum can

Recycled glass beer bottle

Refillable glass bottle, used 10 times

Source: Gaines, 1981

0   2   4   6   8
Thousand Btus

Figure 3-1. Energy Consumption Per Use for 12-Ounce Beverage Containers

disposable containers recently made inroads into a market dominated by refillables, environment minister Klaus Töpfer vowed in mid-1990 to dramatically cut packaging's 30-percent share in household waste. He proposed putting deposits on virtually all containers for liquid products, requiring retailers, distributors, and manufacturers to collect used packaging from consumers, and excluding packaging waste from government disposal systems. Also being considered (in the newly unified Germany) is a ban on the large-scale incineration of cardboard, plastic, and laminated packaging, a move that could promote reuse and recycling. Industry responded by volunteering to set up a packaging return system that would not require collection by individual retailers. Töpfer has expressed interest in establishing centers—already common in eastern Germany—where consumers could redeem used packaging for deposits.[40]

Several other European nations, including Denmark, the Netherlands, Sweden, and Switzerland, are also trying various measures to reduce waste. Denmark, for instance, banned throwaway containers for soft drinks in 1977 and for beer in 1981, and has vigorously defended its beverage packaging regula-

tions against charges of protectionism from other European Community members.[41]

Beyond the issue of reducing wastage in packaging is the issue of safety. A number of jurisdictions have laws or regulations aimed at reducing the toxicity of products and packaging, or ensuring that wastes containing hazardous materials receive special treatment. In the United States, eight states have passed legislation—based on a model developed by the Coalition of Northeastern Governors—that targets toxic metals in packaging for reduction. In Japan and several European nations, a number of products, including batteries and certain plastics, have been banned or are collected separately from other waste to avoid release of toxic substances during incineration.[42]

In the long run, selective purchasing by informed buyers might be the strongest incentive for manufacturers to produce low-waste, safer items. The degree to which widespread environmental concern has changed buying habits is as yet unclear. Brisk sales of "green" products and of numerous guidebooks to them are reason for hope on this front, but people also still seem willing to pay more for "convenience" products that are among the most wasteful. The most important choice of all—the choice to skip a purchase altogether—is the hardest to measure.

It will do no good if manufacturers produce durable products and consumers choose not to buy them, or if people continue to opt for discard over repair. Over their lifetime, durable products can often be cheaper than throwaways, despite a higher price tag. Supermarkets now commonly provide unit price information so buyers can compare the costs of products in different size packages; similar details are needed on the long-term costs of different products. This type of information, coupled with greater understanding of environmental issues, could help consumers substantially cut the amount of waste they produce.

PUSHING THE LIMITS OF RECYCLING

Recycling has suddenly become fashionable in the West. As many communities turn to recycling programs, marketers are eagerly promoting "recyclable" products, and a few have even set up small demonstration programs. But recycling as currently constituted in most countries is far from the last word in resource conservation. And while they express their support for the concept, many firms are still unwilling to make their products from secondary materials. Some recycling programs seem to exist largely to soothe the conscience of consumers while most waste continues to be incinerated or landfilled.[43]

Though it may be the latest sign of being a good environmentalist, recycling cannot take care of all waste—and it is not the best possible waste management option. Source reduction and reuse are both superior in terms of overall environmental impact. But combined with strong efforts to promote these two approaches, recycling and composting offer a cheaper, more effective alternative to incineration, one that can cut landfill needs to a bare minimum. And community recycling programs, especially those involving household separation of waste, can help make people more aware of the amount and types of garbage they generate.

Not all recycling is created equal. Unfortunately, the term has become a catchall used to describe any scheme involving collection and use of materials previously considered wastes. Simply defined, however, recycling is the recovery and conversion of waste materials into new products.

The relative worth of different types of recycling can be ranked: the most valuable is the manufacture of new products from similar, used items; the least valuable is the conversion of waste materials into products with inferior physical characteristics. The key criterion is whether the recovered material is substituted for a virgin one in production, thus closing the loop. The overall aim is to reduce the amount of materials that enter and exit the economy, thus avoiding the environmental costs of extracting and processing virgin materials and of waste disposal.

Glass, steel, and aluminum recycling—all of which commonly save virgin material from being used—unquestionably rank very high by this standard. All three save considerable amounts of energy and pollution over virgin materials production. Thanks to the inflexible laws of thermodynamics, the reduction of ores to pure metal is a particularly energy-intensive process. Avoiding this step makes metal recycling a major energy-saver.[44]

Some forms of plastic recycling, such as the manufacture of new bottles from old ones, could also rank high. Other forms, however, such as the production of "lumber" from mixed plastics, are less valuable. Furthermore, despite major efforts by manufacturers to publicize it, plastics recycling has not yet reached rates close to those now achieved for metals, glass, and paper.

Paper recycling tends to fall somewhere in between. Each time paper is recycled, the fibers it contains become somewhat shorter, making the new paper weaker. Luckily, plant fibers are a renewable resource, and more efficient paper-making methods and technology could be applied. Combined with minimizing demand, maximizing recycling, and exploring nonwood sources of fiber, new techniques might allow paper needs to be met without disastrous effects on the world's forests. (See also Chapter 5.)

Community recycling programs have generally fallen into two broad categories, according to researchers at the Center for the Biology of Natural Systems (CBNS) at Queens College in New York. "Partial recycling" is usually aimed at a limited number of materials—newsprint, glass bottles, aluminum cans—and participation is generally voluntary. Such programs are usually designed as an adjunct to waste management systems that rely primarily on landfills or incinerators. They rarely achieve overall recycling rates higher than 10–15 percent.[45]

The second type of program is termed "intensive recycling." It includes comprehensive separation of materials, recovery of all reusable or recyclable items, and composting of organic waste. Intensive recycling is viewed as a substitute rather than a complement to incineration, and, if properly designed and operated, can bring the tonnage of waste requiring disposal down to levels comparable to incinerators.[46]

The CBNS researchers estimate that a theoretical upper limit of 85–90 percent of today's U.S. solid waste stream could be recovered through intensive recycling. A pilot project with 100 volunteer families in East Hampton, New York, achieved a recycling rate of 84 percent—far higher than any existing program. At the time, only a dozen communities in the nation were recycling 25 percent or more of their waste.[47]

In the United States, the potential of intensive recycling has led many communities to cancel or delay plans to build incinerators while they strive to achieve recycling rates previously considered unreachable. Perhaps the best-known—and most successful—program is in Seattle. Facing the imminent closure of

its only landfill, the City Council originally proposed building a large incinerator. But in 1988, up against strong citizen opposition to that plan, the city instead adopted an extremely ambitious waste reduction, recycling, and composting scheme. The primary goal is to reduce by 60 percent the amount of waste requiring disposal by 1998, with an interim target of 40 percent by 1991. With a 1989 recycling rate of 37 percent—the highest of any city its size in the nation—Seattle is well on its way.[48]

The overall aim is to reduce the amount of materials that enter and exit the economy.

Although Seattle is in a class by itself among large U.S. cities, at least 10 smaller communities have equal or higher recycling rates, according to a 1990 study from the Institute for Local Self-Reliance: Berlin Township, New Jersey, with a population of about 6,000, recycled 57 percent of its waste in 1989; Wellesley, Massachusetts, had a rate of 41 percent that same year.[49]

Heidelberg, in Germany, has also achieved a 37-percent recycling rate. This city of 134,000 people requires households to separate food and yard waste—together, one fourth of total trash—and encourages people to return glass and paper to neighborhood drop-off centers. The separated waste is composted in a central facility. Other German cities are also turning to source separation to boost rates, partly because citizens are increasingly opposed to incineration.[50]

Successful intensive recycling programs are built from many pieces. Curbside and apartment-house pickup programs, publicly and privately operated neighborhood drop-off centers, privately run buy-back centers for particularly valuable materials, and public and private commercial-waste hauling all have roles to play.

Composting plays a particularly critical part. Households can easily compost food and yard wastes, which account for one fourth of U.S. garbage. Seattle, for example, promotes backyard composting through a network of volunteer "master composters." For those who lack the will to do the job themselves, communities can collect materials for composting at central plants. In 1989, the top 10 U.S. recycling communities listed in the 1990 ILSR study composted 20 percent of their waste on average. Composting is an effective option for yard clippings and food leftovers, but not for all waste. Plastics and other synthetic waste materials are fundamentally unsuitable because they do not degrade in the same manner as biological material. Even worse, if they do degrade, they can release toxic substances, rendering compost unsuitable—and unmarketable—for many agricultural uses.[51]

Prices that accounted for the real costs of using materials would be the single most effective incentive for source reduction, reuse, and recycling.

The success of programs that have received adequate funding and attention makes it difficult to argue that recycling is impractical. Those who still maintain that it is too much trouble for most people have short memories. As *Washington Post* columnist Jonathan Yardley writes, "By contrast with what my generation's parents went through in World War II, when almost everything was saved for reuse, the inconvenience of recycling is . . . scarcely noteworthy."[52]

There is now little question that high recycling rates are possible. It is important to remember, however, that these efforts are a means, not an end. Recycling is but one piece of a strategy—which must also include strong efforts to reduce waste at the source and directly reuse products—to build a society that consumes and discards a bare minimum of materials.

DISCARDING THE THROWAWAY SOCIETY

Essayist Wendell Berry argues that misplaced values are at the root of our waste problem: "Our economy is such that we 'cannot afford' to take care of things: Labor is expensive, time is expensive, money is expensive, but materials—the stuff of creation—are so cheap that we cannot afford to take care of them."[53]

Increasing the value of raw materials is an essential first step toward improving the efficiency of materials use and reducing waste. Virgin materials are now artificially cheap, in relation both to secondary materials and to other factors of production. Prices that accounted for the real costs of using materials would be the single most effective incentive for source reduction, reuse, and recycling.

Governments' first task is to eliminate the wide variety of subsidies for virgin production. In mining, depletion allowances are the most explicit subsidies: the United States grants massive tax exemptions to the mining industry, theoretically to compensate for the depletion of mineral reserves. The allowances, usually between 7 and 22 percent, are not available to those who produce the same materials from recycled goods. Many governments also give large subsidies to logging, artificially reducing the price of virgin paper and other wood products. (See Chapter 5.)[54]

Archaic laws that make public mineral or timber resources available at low or no cost to multinational corporations also underwrite virgin materials extraction and environmental destruction. A particularly egregious example is the U.S. General Mining Act of 1872, which allows anyone who finds metallic minerals in public territory to buy the land for $12 per hectare or less, and does not require the miner to pay the government anything for the minerals extracted. The U.S. Treasury received nothing for the $4 billion worth of hard-rock minerals (such as gold, silver, lead, iron, and copper) taken from former federal lands in 1988.[55]

Weak or nonexistent regulation of the environmental effects of mining and logging allows industries to reap profits while nature and future generations pick up the tab. Mining rules are notably lax in most nations, and logging firms are also rarely forced to repair or mitigate the environmental damage they cause.

Taxes on virgin materials would also bring their prices closer to real costs. The U.S. Congress considered such taxes in 1990 in proposed revisions to the Resource Conservation and Recovery Act. The state of Florida has already put a 10¢ per ton tax on virgin newsprint, and other states may follow suit. The higher energy taxes often discussed as central to averting climate change would also serve to boost the prices of virgin materials.[56]

If the prices of virgin materials do rise substantially, demand is likely to fall, and regional and national economies that subsist on their production would probably suffer. Zambia, for example, gets 90 percent of its export earnings from copper, and Guinea relies on mineral ores and concentrates for 91 percent of its exports. Policymakers should explore ways to help such areas develop economies based on sustainable industries, and phase in new taxes over a period of years to soften the immediate impact.[57]

Beyond getting prices right, governments can try a variety of strategies to promote source reduction, reuse, and recycling. Minimum warranty requirements might encourage production of more durable products. Deposits can ensure that manufacturers retain some responsibility for products and packaging. Where deposits are not successful in promoting reuse over recycling—as has been noted with beverage containers in most U.S. jurisdictions with deposit legislation—additional regulations may be in order.

Waste reduction measures aimed at industry will generally be more effective if implemented nationally rather than locally, because single markets may be too small to provide leverage on large manufacturers. In large nations, states or provinces may find it effective to band together. Similarly, groups of nations unified for trade purposes, such as the European Community, will probably find market-wide measures most effective, as long as they resist pressures to adopt the lowest common denominator as the standard. (See Chapter 10.)

Governments or civic-minded businesses might find it fairly easy to revive some once-common reuse practices. For instance, the return of the refillable bottle—usually considered a thing of the past in the United States—is still possible. Eleven out of twelve breweries owned by Anheuser-Busch, the largest U.S. beer producer, still turn out some refillable containers, and they have enough capacity to provide the entire country with nondisposable bottles. In Seattle, Washington, and Portland, Oregon, sister breweries Rainier and Blitz-Weinhard switched from disposable bottles back to refillables in the spring of 1990.[58]

A convenient network of facilities for collection and exchange of used but still serviceable goods could cut waste and provide employment. Though many people stigmatize used goods, "it's not waste until it is wasted," according to Dan Knapp, who runs Urban Ore, a small firm that recovers and sells useful items from garbage collected at the municipal transfer station in Berkeley, California. For instance, many of the 280 million tires thrown away each year in the United States could be retreaded to serve another useful life. Examples abound of other serviceable products commonly discarded before their time.[59]

The trick to getting consumers to reduce waste is to build a framework of incentives that encourage them.

Consistently available markets for secondary materials are essential to the success of recycling programs. The public and private sectors can support recycling by purchasing materials recovered from waste. Legislation requiring the U.S. government to do so has been on the books since 1976, but the law has yet to be fully implemented. In choosing recycled products—paper in particular—buyers should ensure that their purchase contains waste collected from consumers, not just industrial scraps that are already commonly recycled, thus supporting public recycling programs. Government scrutiny of eco-marketing claims could also help consumers pick products with genuine environmental merit.[60]

As with businesses, the trick to getting consumers to reduce waste is to build a framework of incentives that encourage them. On the theory that the quickest way to consumers' brains is through

their pocketbooks, many communities are charging for garbage disposal by the can or bag. Even more effective, some cities are charging a higher price for a second container of trash.

Such programs have been notably successful in reducing garbage and spurring recycling. In Seattle, where households subscribe for garbage removal by the can, the average number of cans per customer has fallen from 3.5 to 1 since the program was introduced in 1981. Limits on weight per container keep people from simply compacting their garbage. Per-can rates also helped the city reach one of the highest recycling rates in the United States—24 percent—before the city-sponsored recycling program had begun.[61]

Education programs conducted by governments and public interest groups can also help promote source reduction, reuse, and recycling. Many communities insert informational flyers or booklets with solid waste collection bills. King County, Washington, for example, gives its citizens a 40-page "Home Waste Guide," which includes a quiz and an extensive list of recycling and waste reduction information sources. Creatively designed public advertising campaigns, perhaps after the fashion of the successful U.S. anti-smoking television spots of the sixties, could help get the message to people through the din of product advertising.[62]

Eco-labeling programs can put basic environmental information into the hands of shoppers at the time of purchase. Canada, France, Japan, the Netherlands, Norway, Sweden, West Germany, and other nations have implemented or are now exploring national labeling schemes, and the European Community is considering a label for use throughout the Common Market. In the United States, at least two organizations plan to award labels:

Green Cross, the first to do so, was sponsored by four West Coast supermarket chains, while Green Seal is being set up by a coalition of environmental and consumer groups.[63]

Programs that take a "cradle-to-grave" approach—measuring the impacts of products from production to disposal—will probably be more effective in promoting waste reduction, reuse, and recycling than those that award labels based on single characteristics, such as whether a container is made of recycled paper. The best-known eco-label, the German Blue Angel, uses limited criteria, while the relatively new Canadian and Japanese government programs and the nascent Green Seal program in the United States look at the bigger picture.[64]

A few rules of thumb can guide people who want to be part of the solution. The most important is that the least wasteful choice is usually not to buy at all. Another is to avoid heavily packaged goods. Buying staples such as cereal or rice in bulk can dramatically reduce waste. When buying durable goods, shoppers should compare the lifetime costs of different options: longer-lasting products may have higher purchase prices, but they can turn out to cost less in the end.

Environmentalists can support firms that make superior products by buying their goods and letting them know why. If better product options are not available at the local store, consumers can ask for them—or take their business elsewhere. Finally, the best option for carrying purchases home is a sturdy reusable bag, not disposable paper or plastic.

In the long run, more efficient use of materials could virtually eliminate incineration of garbage and dramatically reduce dependence on landfills. It could also substantially lower energy needs, which would help slow global warming, the most ominous of all environmental threats. Taken together, source reduction, reuse, and recycling—the elements of a soft materials path—can not only cut waste but also foster more flexible, resilient, diverse, self-reliant, and sustainable economies. Decentralized collection and processing of secondary materials can create new industries and jobs.

Finally, the soft materials path offers societies the chance to solve garbage problems without creating new ecological risks. It moves us toward the ultimate goal of providing, in the words of E.F. Schumacher, "the maximum of well-being with the minimum of consumption."[65]

4

Rethinking Urban Transport

Marcia D. Lowe

The automobile once promised a dazzling world of speed, freedom, and convenience, magically conveying people wherever the road would take them. Given these alluring qualities, it is not surprising that people around the world enthusiastically embraced the dream of car ownership. But societies that have built their transport systems around the automobile are now waking up to a much harsher reality. The problems created by overreliance on the car are outweighing its benefits.

These problems are numerous and widespread. Traffic congestion and air pollution plague all major cities, and oil dependence makes economies vulnerable. Cities with streets designed for cars instead of people are increasingly unlivable. In developing countries, automobiles serve only a small elite and leave the vast majority with inadequate transport. In Eastern Europe and the Soviet

An expanded version of this chapter appeared as Worldwatch Paper 98, *Alternatives to the Automobile: Transport for Livable Cities*. Research for the chapter was supported by the Surdna Foundation.

Union, recent reforms could add the problems of automobile dependence to overwhelming economic and environmental crises.

A new, more rational approach to transportation is needed, one that puts the automobile in its rightful place in a city as one among many options for travel. Buses and trains are more appropriate than private cars as the centerpieces of transportation systems, particularly in the world's most congested urban areas. At reasonable occupancy rates, public transport uses space and energy many times more efficiently than cars do, and creates much less pollution.

In this new transport environment, walking and bicycling would also play important roles, complementing public transport with the convenience of individual mobility. These nonmotorized forms of travel have the potential to provide a considerable share of transportation—as long as cities cater to the needs of pedestrians and cyclists.

Getting away from automobile dominance also requires gradually restructuring cities and suburbs to lessen the need for driving. Development can be planned to create compact cities in which jobs, homes, and services are consolidated and near public transport. In both industrial and developing countries, careful urban planning can help meet future transportation needs by minimizing the demand for travel.

FROM SERVANT TO MASTER

Perhaps more than any other invention, the automobile embodies author Jacques Ellul's observation about all technologies: it makes a good servant but a bad master. Yet obeying the demands of the private car has become a passive routine for many of the world's cities. Automobile access has dictated the very character of urban life, most obviously in the design of the modern city. Vast roads and parking lots distort cityscapes into proportions that dwarf and intimidate humans. Once all available surface space has been surrendered to private cars, engineers turn to space overhead and underground. In a final gesture of submission, entrepreneurs in Yokohama, Japan, recently opened a floating parking lot in the local bay.[1]

Growth in the world's 400-million-strong auto fleet makes it clear that if societies fail to regain mastery over this servant, car-related problems will become global crises. The average annual rate of growth in car ownership has slowed from 5 percent in the seventies to 3 percent in the eighties because of saturation in the industrial countries, which account for about 80 percent of the global fleet. But while the world fleet is no longer growing as quickly as it did before 1970 (now taking two decades to double instead of one), the absolute number of cars added is huge; currently,

a net total of 19 million cars is added to the world fleet each year.[2]

Along with the increase in the automobile's numbers come ubiquitous problems. Traffic congestion, now a fact of life in major cities, has stretched daily rush hours to 12 hours or longer in Seoul and to 14 in Rio de Janeiro. In 1989, London traffic broke a record with a 53-kilometer backup of cars at a near standstill. Roaring engines and blaring horns cause distress and hypertension, as in downtown Cairo, where noise levels are 10 times the limit set by health and safety standards. Half of U.S. business leaders surveyed in 13 major cities said that traffic conditions affected their employees' morale, productivity, punctuality, and emotions.[3]

Careful urban planning can help meet future transportation needs by minimizing the demand for travel.

Motor vehicles are the single largest source of air pollution, creating a haze of smog over the world's cities. The main component of car-induced smog is ozone, a gas formed as nitrogen oxides and hydrocarbons react with sunlight. Ozone and other pollutants—including carbon monoxide, nitrogen oxides, and hydrocarbons—aggravate bronchial and lung disorders and are often deadly to asthmatics, children, and the elderly. Automobiles also emit carbon dioxide, the greenhouse gas responsible for over half the global warming problem. Passenger cars account for more than 13 percent of the total carbon dioxide emitted from fossil fuels worldwide, or more than 700 million tons of carbon annually.[4]

The economic and political vulnerability of a car-dependent society becomes painfully clear whenever there is an oil crisis. The United States, which devotes 43 percent of its petroleum use to run cars and light trucks and imports half its oil, was sharply jolted in August 1990 when Iraqi troops invaded Kuwait, claiming control over nearly 20 percent of the world's proven oil reserves. Even when the current crisis subsides, the Middle East may never again be counted on for a stable supply of oil. (See Chapter 2.)[5]

The enormity of these auto-related problems defies mere technical fixes. Without alternatives to cars, progress in fuel economy and emissions reduction can be offset by increased driving. In the United States, for example, dramatic reductions in hydrocarbon and carbon monoxide emissions made possible by catalytic converters have been partly offset by greater use of cars, which are now logging an additional 120 billion kilometers each year. In 1989, 96 metropolitan areas—home to more than half the people in the country—failed to meet the U.S. Environmental Protection Agency's ozone safety standard, and 41 areas violated the carbon monoxide standard.[6]

While some technical changes hold great promise, they do not address all the problems of automobile use. Improving new-car fuel economy could ease dependence on oil, and together with stricter emissions standards and improved exhaust controls could also reduce air pollution considerably. But these changes do nothing to ease traffic congestion. Even electric cars, which could greatly reduce fossil fuel consumption and pollution, would still get stuck in traffic jams.

Moreover, no automobile technology can fully address the negative societal consequences of a car-dominated society. Traffic deaths are an example. In the United States, some 49,000 people died in motor vehicle accidents in 1988—more than from all other accidents combined. Worldwide, despite safety improvements, more than a quarter of a million people were killed in road accidents in 1988, and several million more were injured or permanently disabled. The greatest danger of road accidents is in the Third World's dense, chaotic mix of motorized and nonmotorized traffic, where road fatality rates are 20 times those in the industrial world. A study of 15 developing countries found that road accidents were second only to intestinal diseases as the leading cause of death.[7]

Finally, no new car technology will serve the majority of humanity who will never own an automobile. A Fiat minicar in China sells for roughly $6,400—a moderate sum in wealthy countries, but equal to about 16 years' wages for an ordinary worker there. In much of the developing world, higher sales figures just mean that a small elite is improving its travel options, while the vast majority's mobility and accessibility remain impaired. Even in the cities of car-oriented industrial countries, those who either cannot afford a car or are unable to operate one often have no way to get to jobs, schools, health centers, and other important destinations.[8]

Creating sustainable urban transport systems that meet people's needs equitably and that foster a healthy environment requires putting the automobile back into its useful place as a servant. With a shift in priorities, cars can be part of a broad, balanced system in which public transport, cycling, and walking are all viable options.

GETTING ON TRACK

Public transport plays a central role in any efficient urban transport system. In developing countries, where at least 16 cities are expected to have more than 12 million people each by the end of this decade, failing to give priority to public transport would be disastrous. But neither the exploding Cairos and Delhis nor the relatively stabilized New Yorks and Londons can sustain future growth in automobile use. As the nineties begin, a new oil crisis, mounting pollution and congestion, and global warming all call for a greater commitment to public transport.[9]

The term "public transport" covers many different types of vehicles, but most commonly it refers to buses and trains. Buses take many forms, from minibuses to double-length vehicles with pivoting centers. Rail services fall into four major categories: rapid rail (also called the underground, tube, metro, or subway), which operates on exclusive rights-of-way in tunnels or on elevated tracks; streetcars (or trams), which move with other traffic on regular streets; light rail (or trolleys), quieter, more modern versions of streetcars that can run either on exclusive rights-of-way or with other traffic; and suburban or regional trains, which connect a city with surrounding areas.

The concept of public transport also includes organized car pools and van pools. For U.S. commuters in areas with inadequate bus and train service, this is the only "public" transport option. But even where other systems are comprehensive, there is vast potential for car pooling; recent research shows that in cities the world over, private cars during commuting hours on average carry just 1.2–1.3 persons per vehicle.[10]

Public transport modes vary in fuel use and emissions and in the space they require—but if carrying reasonable numbers of passengers, they all outperform one-occupant private cars on each of these counts. Although energy requirements vary according to the size and design of the vehicle and how many people are on board, buses and trains require far less fuel per passenger for each kilometer of travel. In the United States, for example, a light-rail vehicle carrying 55 passengers needs an estimated 640 Btus of energy per passenger per kilometer; a city bus with 45 passengers would use some 690 Btus per passenger-kilometer; and a car pool with four occupants, 1,140 Btus. A single-occupant automobile, by contrast, burns nearly 4,580 Btus per passenger-kilometer.[11]

The emissions savings from public transport are even more dramatic. (See Table 4–1.) Since both rapid and light rail have electric engines, pollution is

Table 4-1. United States: Pollution Emitted During Typical Work Commutes[1]

Transport Mode	Hydrocarbons	Carbon Monoxide	Nitrogen Oxides
	(grams per 100 passenger-kilometers)		
Rapid rail	0.2	1	30
Light rail	0.2	2	43
Transit bus	12	189	95
Van pool	22	150	24
Car pool	43	311	43
Auto[2]	130	934	128

[1]Based on national average vehicle occupancy rates. [2]Based on one occupant per vehicle.
SOURCE: American Public Transit Association, "Mass Transit: The Clean Air Alternative," pamphlet, Washington, D.C., 1989.

measured not from the tailpipe, but from the power plant, which is usually located outside the city, where air quality problems are less acute. For typical U.S. commutes, rapid rail emits 30 grams of nitrogen oxides for every 100 passenger-kilometers (that is, for every 100 kilometers each rail passenger travels), compared with 43 grams for light rail, 95 grams for transit buses, and 128 grams for single-occupant automobiles. Public transport's potential for reducing hydrocarbon and carbon monoxide emissions is even greater.

Although diesel buses—especially in developing countries—can be heavy polluters, existing technologies can control their exhaust. In Athens, some buses are fitted with traps to prevent particulates from being emitted into the air. Buses can also run on less polluting fuels such as propane (used in parts of Europe) and natural gas (used in Brazil and China). Test buses in the Netherlands that run on natural gas are estimated to emit 90 percent less nitrogen oxides and 25 percent less carbon monoxide than diesel engines do.[12]

In addition to reducing fuel consumption and pollution, public transport saves valuable city space. Buses and trains carry more people in each vehicle and, if they operate on their own rights-of-way, can safely run at much higher speeds. In other words, they not only take up less space but also occupy it for a shorter time. Thus, comparing ideal conditions for each mode, an underground metro can carry 70,000 passengers past a certain point in a single lane in one hour, surface rapid rail can carry up to 50,000 people, and a trolley or a bus on a separate lane, more than 30,000. By contrast, a lane of private cars—even with four occupants each—can move only about 8,000 people an hour.[13]

The cost of providing public transport is, understandably, the overriding factor for many governments faced with these dramatic differences in mobility and efficiency. But many public officials fail to make a full accounting. A fair comparison must consider the full costs of all systems, including the environmental impacts and social consequences, and which approach can move the most people. With public transport's lower impacts, higher capacities, and greater affordability for the general public, governments could get more for their money.

Similarly, drivers would find public transport more attractive if they kept the full costs in mind. Few U.S. drivers realize that, when the costs are factored in—including fuel, maintenance, insurance, depreciation, and finance charges (but excluding the portion of their taxes that goes toward driving subsidies)—they pay $21 per 100 kilometers of driving, or about $1,700 annually just to commute to work. By contrast, the average public transport fare is under $9 per 100 kilometers. In highly car-dependent cities, a viable public transport option for commuting could save some families from having to buy a second or third car.[14]

The availability and use of public transport vary widely in cities around the globe, from infrequent, near-empty buses that lumber across sprawled U.S. urban areas to Tokyo's crowded, minute-to-minute subways, where hired "pushers" pack passengers into the train so the doors can close. Since variations in distances and city densities affect the total kilometers of travel, the annual number of trips each person takes by public transport provides a better standard for comparing its importance in various cities. The frequency of public transport use ranges from more than 700 trips annually per person in Moscow to 22 trips a year per person in the auto-oriented city of Dallas, Texas. (See Table 4–2.)[15]

Cities in the Soviet Union and Eastern

Table 4-2. Dependence on Public Transport, Selected Cities, 1983

City	Population	Mode[1]	Trips Per Person Per Year
	(million)		
Moscow	8.0	bus, tram, metro	713
Tokyo	11.6	bus, tram, metro, rail	650
East Berlin	1.2	bus, tram, metro, rail	540
Seoul	8.7	bus, metro	457
West Berlin[2]	1.9	bus, metro	389
Buenos Aires[3]	9.0	bus, metro	248
Kuala Lumpur[4]	1.0	bus, minibus	224
Toronto	2.8	bus, tram, metro	200
Nairobi	1.2	bus, minibus	151
Abidjan	1.8	bus, boat	132
Beijing	8.7	bus, metro	107
Chicago[3]	6.8	bus, metro, rail	101
Melbourne[5]	2.7	bus, tram, rail	95
Dallas[3]	1.4	bus	22

[1]In this table, "rail" refers to suburban rail. [2]1982. [3]Metropolitan area. [4]Excludes cycle rickshaws and private minibuses. [5]1980.
SOURCES: Worldwatch Institute estimates, based on Chris Bushell and Peter Stonham, ed., *Jane's Urban Transport Systems: Fourth Edition* (London: Jane's Publishing, 1985); Peter Newman and Jeffrey Kenworthy, *Cities and Automobile Dependence: An International Sourcebook* (Aldershot, U.K.: Gower, 1989).

Europe provide extensive and comprehensive public transport options, including buses, tramways, metros, and suburban trains. Although quality varies along with public spending constraints—from showpiece metros in the largest cities to undependable, overcrowded systems elsewhere—the various transport modes offer widespread service to the many people who do not own cars. Of the roughly 300 streetcar and trolley systems in the world, about 110 are in the Soviet Union and another 70 in Eastern Europe.[16]

Urban public transport has long been a government priority in Western Europe. Although all major European cities contend with automobile traffic, well-developed bus and rail systems are available for those who choose public transport. While high car ownership makes for stiff competition, public transport in large cities in Western Europe typically accounts for between 20 and 30 percent of passenger-kilometers. In recent years, several large West European cities have stepped up their commitment to public transportation, combining further investments with complementary policies to restrict auto use.[17]

High-income Asian countries also make extensive use of public transport. Japanese cities are particularly rail-oriented; authorities since the sixties have primarily used commuter railroads to link expanding suburbs with urban centers. In Tokyo, 95 percent of all passenger-kilometers by public transport are on trains. Metro lines in Tokyo, Seoul, and other Asian cities not only move millions of passengers within the city but also lend their tracks to through-trains from surrounding suburbs. In Hong Kong, public transport accounts for about 9 million out of the 10 million daily passenger trips.[18]

Public transport also plays an important role in urban areas of the Third World. In many cities in Asia, Latin America, and Africa, buses—in their various forms—make 50–80 percent of all motorized trips. Buses are sometimes hopelessly overcrowded; it is not uncommon to see several riders clinging to the outside. Yet most Third World cities have lower public transport use per person than those in Western Europe, reflecting the inability of meager bus fleets to keep up with population growth.[19]

Cities in car-infatuated California are leading the trend toward reviving rail transport.

Private bus operators often take up where publicly owned systems leave off, and in many cases provide the bulk of all service. In Calcutta, for example, private companies hold roughly two thirds of the market; three quarters of public transport trips in Buenos Aires are made by some 13,000 private buses, or *colectivos*. Flexible, informal forms of public transport—including minibuses, jeepneys (converted jeeps), vans, pickups, shared taxis, and cycle rickshaws—give crucial service, especially in the parts of cities that are hard to get to.[20]

Over the past two decades, some 21 large cities, including Mexico City, Shanghai, and Cairo, have built metro systems. These projects have greatly improved transportation in dense city centers but at great financial cost, raising widespread doubts about their economic viability in developing countries. Still, in several cities of such extreme density that even greatly expanded bus service cannot cope with demand, new metros are being planned despite the cost.[21]

Among the world's major cities, those in Australia and the United States make the least use of alternatives to the private car. Although less than 5 percent of U.S. work trips are by public transport, ridership is heavy in New York City, Chicago, and other places that provide extensive service. Indeed, nearly one quarter of the entire country's public transport trips are in New York City. But several large and medium-sized American cities, having reached the limits of automobile dependence, are either building or considering light-rail systems, and others are adding light rail to their existing lines.[22]

Cities in the car-infatuated state of California are leading this trend toward reviving rail transport, with projects such as an expansion of San Diego's highly successful trolley and a light-rail line in San Jose. Even Los Angeles has an extensive new rail system under way, expected to include 240 kilometers of light and rapid rail when completed.[23]

The recent trend in many cities is toward light rail over "heavy" rapid-rail systems. Whereas metros require exclusive rights-of-way, which often means building costly and time-consuming elevated or underground lines and stations, light rail can be built on regular city streets at lower cost. The capital costs of recently constructed light-rail lines range from $5 million per kilometer for San Diego's surface trolley to $39 million per kilometer for a tunnel light-rail line in Hannover, Germany. By contrast, the underground metro in Santiago, Chile, cost $40 million per kilometer; a metro extension in Osaka, Japan, needed $64 million; and the new underground line in Caracas, Venezuela, rang up a bill of $117 million per kilometer.[24]

One increasingly popular transport alternative is to upgrade old suburban rail systems, improving their speed and convenience for much less than the cost of a new metro. For example, Hong Kong completely modernized and rebuilt its suburban rail system and added new vehicles for $13.2 million per kilometer, a little more than 10 percent of the cost of the city's underground Island Line. Rail upgrading projects are now under way in at least 50 major cities, including London, Jakarta, Melbourne, and São Paulo.[25]

CITIES FOR PEOPLE

Walking and cycling are the most common forms of individual transport. Because they are economical and clean, save space, and require no fuel other than a person's most recent meal, they are also the most appropriate way to make short trips. Yet nonmotorized transport is often ignored as part of transport systems. Few cities, if any, adequately address the needs of pedestrians and cyclists.

In both rich and poor countries, serving the needs of people who do not have cars is crucial for creating a sustainable transport system. There are several ways to make cities for people, not just for cars. Among them are providing various facilities to improve the access of bikers and walkers to points throughout the city, giving them priority in city centers, and integrating cycling and walking with public transport.

The most effective way to make cities safer and more convenient for nonmotorized transport is to keep motor traffic from commandeering urban space. Because of their mass and speed, cars automatically take over streets, intimidating and endangering people on foot or on bicycles. For cycling and walking to be viable means of transport, people must be able to move safely throughout the city under their own steam. This calls for separate lanes and paths in some situations (where motor traffic is heavy and traveling quickly), but more often it requires making motor vehicles share regular streets with other travellers.

It takes active restrictions on cars to make some streets safe for slower traffic. Many European cities use these restrictions, known as "traffic calming," to turn streets into places for people who live, work, and shop there, instead of for drivers just passing through. Traffic calming's chief contribution is to safely accommodate pedestrians and cyclists on city streets without shunting them to often-inferior lanes or paths.

For more than two decades the Dutch have calmed traffic by changing the layout of the residential street, transforming it into a *woonerf*, or "living yard." In the *woonerf*, cars are forced to navigate slowly around carefully placed trees and other landscaping. Since motor traffic cannot monopolize the entire breadth of the street, much of the space becomes more open to walking, cycling, and children's play. Automobiles are free to enter the *woonerf*, but only as "guests," while nonmotorized traffic has priority. Experience with traffic calming has shown that it is most effective if widely implemented, so that motor traffic problems are not simply diverted to nearby streets.[26]

West Germany's similar *Verkehrsberuhigung* schemes multiplied into the thousands throughout that former country since they were started in the seventies. Originally intended for residential areas, the technique is now spreading over whole cities. Traffic calming greatly improves the quality of life in neighborhoods where it is implemented, and so is gathering popularity in many countries, including Italy, Japan, Sweden, and Switzerland. Such restraints are so well-received in Denmark that local residents themselves are often willing to pay for the measures.[27]

Another way to give street space to nondrivers is to restrict cars in city centers. Several West European cities have successfully restrained traffic in the core by dividing it into cells. In Göteborg, Sweden, for example, the city center is divided into five pie-shaped zones, all accessible by a large ring road on the periphery. Automobiles are not allowed to cross the zone boundaries, but public transport, emergency vehicles, bicycles, and mopeds may. Since this system was instituted in 1970—along with reserved lanes for buses and trams, and some streets closed to all but pedestrians—the city has had fewer accidents and improved public transport service. Traffic cells are also found in Bremen, Germany (where they originated); Besançon, France; the Dutch city of Groningen; and Tunis, the capital of Tunisia.[28]

Making bicycling practical depends largely on creating continuous routes throughout a city, which may require some separate cycle lanes and paths. But simply providing these facilities is not enough; traffic planners need to analyze data on movement patterns and accident potential when designing such paths. It is important for bicycle paths to be sufficiently wide and smooth—otherwise they create safety hazards.

The most dangerous situations arise at intersections where bicycles and motor vehicles cross paths. Some cities provide separate overpasses and underpasses for nonmotorized traffic at such junctions. But what many cities call "safety improvements" often mean overhead skywalks, isolated bike paths, and other physical schemes that merely clear children, cyclists, and pedestrians from space meant to be the sole domain of cars. Although these separate facilities are sometimes necessary, it is usually preferable to restrain the motor traffic so

that people can cross safely. This can be done with special traffic lights, for example, or by designating space for cyclists to stop ahead of cars at an intersection, together with a light that allows them to proceed first.[29]

Where separate lanes or paths for nonmotorized traffic are provided, the trick is to avoid using them as justification for restricting pedestrians and cyclists from regular streets. In the Netherlands, where some 30 percent of work trips and 60 percent of school trips are made by bicycle, some cities have combined traffic measures on regular roads with separate paths where necessary—thus seeking to create direct, uninterrupted bicycle routes, rather than to just keep cyclists out of the way of drivers. Chinese cities often provide pedestrian/cyclist lanes and bridges for the country's 300 million cyclists, along with restrictions on turns by motor vehicles at dangerous junctions.[30]

Another effective way to make streets more amenable to pedestrians and cyclists is to restrict car parking downtown. Such limits not only free space for nonmotorized traffic but also encourage people to choose transport options other than driving. Paris Mayor Jacques Chirac, apparently impressed by the reduced traffic resulting from temporary parking restrictions for France's 1989 bicentennial, announced plans to remove permanently more than 100,000 street parking spaces in central Paris. Geneva prohibits car parking at workplaces in the central city, motivating commuters to use the city's excellent public transport system.[31]

Belying conventional wisdom, research in 10 major German cities has shown that parking spaces do not always attract more shoppers to commercial areas. In fact, too much parking can even hurt business by creating an atmosphere unfriendly to pedestrians. Bicycle parking is much less expensive to provide and brings in quieter, safer, nonpolluting traffic.[32]

Copenhagen's city council has reduced car traffic in the city center by banning all on-street parking in the core, replacing parking spaces in public squares with landscaping, and increasing the amount of bicycle parking at commuter train stations. Public policy in Harare, Zimbabwe, requires merchants to provide bike parking downtown. Although bicycle parking is relatively simple to supply, it must be designed carefully to be secure. High theft rates naturally deter potential cyclists. Perhaps the most effective security measure is guarded bicycle parking, common in many Asian countries, including China and Vietnam, and at rail stations in industrial countries, including Denmark, Japan, the Netherlands, and Germany.[33]

City centers benefit greatly from the creation of auto-free pedestrian zones. Nearly all major European cities devote part of their centers to people on foot. Munich's impressive 85,000-square-meter pedestrian zone owes much of its success to easy access via public transport. Third World cities with heavy concentrations of foot traffic and street vendors could enhance safety and improve traffic conditions with such schemes. After pedestrian streets were established in Lima, Peru, attracting both street traders and shoppers on foot, traffic flow through the center improved dramatically.[34]

Although cycling and walking are often used for short journeys, they can serve for longer trips if integrated well with trains and buses. This requires safe access to transit stops and stations for cyclists and pedestrians. Station entrances can also be made more accessible to passengers who do not arrive by car through the placement of bicycle parking, bus lanes, and car parking. For example, a Dutch national railway program seeks to give the highest priority at station entrances to pedestrians, followed in descending order by bicyclists, bus riders, taxi passengers, people dropped off by car, and, finally, those who park a car at the station.[35]

"Bike-and-ride" facilities, which encourage commuters to cycle to rail stations instead of drive, are increasingly popular in Japan and Western Europe. For years, Japanese commuters have preferred bicycles over slow feeder buses for getting to suburban rail stations. Japan's 1980 census showed that 7.2 million commuters, or about 15 percent of the total, rode bicycles to work or to commuter rail stations. In Europe, the portion of rail passengers in suburbs and smaller towns who bicycle to the station varies from 10 to 55 percent. Stations often have spaces for hundreds of bicycles, and many public transport systems allow cyclists to bring their bikes on the bus or train.[36]

In the Netherlands, some 30 percent of work trips and 60 percent of school trips are made by bicycle.

For many people in developing countries, nonmotorized travel is essential because auto ownership is out of the question. Motorcycles and mopeds are increasingly popular in much of the developing world, but in addition to being heavily polluting, they are often too costly for those with low incomes and require expensive, scarce fossil fuels. Even buses are out of reach for many; it is estimated that people in one fourth of the households in Third World cities cannot afford public transport.[37]

Governments that are overwhelmed by the costs of expanding public transport can greatly improve people's travel options for less investment by subsidizing bicycle purchases. In countries such as Tanzania, where a bike can cost seven or eight times the average monthly wage, cycling can be a luxury. Some city governments in China have bought some time to expand bus service by paying commuters a monthly allowance for cycling to work. Credit schemes to help people acquire bicycles, rickshaws, and other nonmotorized vehicles are in place in India, Ghana, and other countries; city employees in Harare receive low-cost loans for buying bicycles.[38]

Cities can thus address many of their transportation problems by facilitating cycling and walking. They can take steps to displace car travel for short trips, make public transport more convenient, and provide high-quality mobility and accessibility to people for a fraction of the cost of motorized transport. At the same time, the quality of life will improve in cities that are oriented to people, not just motor vehicles.

THE ROAD NOT TAKEN

A city's potential to expand public transport and to facilitate cycling and walking depends on much more than providing buses, trains, and safe streets. The layout of a city helps determine whether or not these transport options are appropriate or even feasible. Many urban areas are designed around the automobile, with planners using road building to combat the inevitable traffic congestion. The result is a treadmill effect in which new roads fill to capacity as soon as they are completed; cities begin to look like Los Angeles, where two thirds of urban space is paved over for cars.[39]

Instead of further catering to autos, cities can step off the road-building treadmill by changing land use patterns to reduce the need for driving. For the long haul, reducing automobile depen-

dence calls for a fundamental rethinking of the very shape of cities.

Although all major urban areas struggle with traffic congestion to some degree, those with the least sprawl are most able to promote alternatives to driving. In a study of 32 of the world's major cities, Australian researchers Peter Newman and Jeffrey Kenworthy found that low urban densities (fewer than 40 people and jobs per hectare of land) and dependence on the automobile go hand-in-hand. Sprawling cities in the United States and Australia are highly car-oriented; medium-density cities in Western Europe and Canada have greater use of public transport; and highly concentrated metropolises in Asia have more commuters who walk and cycle. (See Table 4–3.)

Newman, Kenworthy, and other researchers have concluded that strong land use policies to increase urban densities are crucial in fostering viable alternatives to automobile dependence. Very high densities are not necessary; even having 60–100 people and jobs per hectare, as is typical in many European capitals, can greatly enhance travel options. The difference that land use controls make is striking when development patterns in Japan or Western Europe, which have strict regulations encouraging compact development, are compared with those in the United States or Australia, where loose planning has promoted sprawled suburban growth. In most European cities a greater share of people in cities live in the center instead of the periphery. Even Europe's suburbs are more concentrated than those in the United States and Australia, and they are nearly always provided with public transport.[40]

While many cities have evolved compactly because of clear constraints on space, others with plenty of available land have purposely contained sprawl in the interest of efficiency. Sweden's cit-

Table 4-3. Urban Densities and Commuting Choices, Selected Cities, 1980

City	Land Use Intensity	Private Car	Public Transport	Walking and Cycling
	(people and jobs/hectare)	(percent of workers using)		
Phoenix	13	93	3	3
Perth	15	84	12	4
Washington	21	81	14	5
Sydney	25	65	30	5
Toronto	59	63	31	6
Hamburg	66	44	41	15
Amsterdam	74	58	14	28
Stockholm	85	34	46	20
Munich	91	38	42	20
Vienna	111	40	45	15
Tokyo	171	16	59	25
Hong Kong	403	3	62	35

SOURCE: Peter Newman and Jeffrey Kenworthy, *Cities and Automobile Dependence: An International Sourcebook* (Aldershot, U.K.: Gower, 1989).

ies—compact centers surrounded by vast stretches of rural, largely forested land—demonstrate the success of the country's strong urban land use policies. The Soviet Union also makes efficient use of urban space despite its great size.[41]

European governments have long recognized the need to let societal gain, not individual profit, determine how urban space will be used. Columbia University professor Kenneth Jackson cites the example of a large German city: "When truck farmers tend their crops within 2,000 yards of the skyscrapers of Düsseldorf, the richest city on the continent, [it is] not because alternative land uses would not yield a higher return, but because the government rejects the very possibility of development." In much of Europe, development of private land is guided by zoning, tax incentives, bans on low-density projects, and other measures. Urban planners try to position new developments within cycling or walking distance of public transport stops.[42]

Although the term "high density" evokes images of towering apartment buildings and little open space, dense developments can be pleasant and livable if planned well. A more compact urban form, far from precluding green spaces and structures on a human scale, can actually facilitate them. According to a study done for the U.S. Environmental Protection Agency, a compact development can mix two- to six-story apartments and town houses with clustered single-family homes, and still leave 30 percent of the area for open space and parks. In a typical low-density sprawl community, according to the study, only 9 percent of the land is devoted to open space.[43]

Land use controls should do more than simply increase density; ideally, they should mix different land uses. Zoning can be used to foster a mix of homes and commercial uses instead of separating them and thus creating long commutes. University of California researcher Robert Cervero points out that in much of the industrial world there is no longer a strong case for separating homes from jobs, because today's workplaces are not the smokestack factories and slaughterhouses of the industrial era. The original purpose of separating the two was to prevent nuisances springing from proximity. But today, according to Cervero, "the 'nuisance' facing most suburban areas seems . . . more one of traffic congestion."[44]

The issue is not whether to reject or accept growth, but how to use it to reduce dependence on cars and make communities more livable.

Stockholm is a good example of a decades-old scheme to mix land uses and integrate development with transport. The capital is ringed with satellite communities of 25,000–50,000 people each, linked closely with a rail network and expressway. Shops, apartments, and offices are clustered around train stations that give people access to jobs on the periphery and in the center. The plan has also allowed city officials to restrict driving and parking downtown, and to make the center more amenable to walking and cycling. Paris has followed similar development policies.[45]

Zoning changes could help offset the common problem of imbalance between jobs and housing, a major contributor to automobile dependence. Since developers often prefer more profitable office and retail projects over housing, and since cities and suburbs want to expand their tax base by attracting corporate investments, housing gets shunted elsewhere, creating long commutes, or gets neglected entirely. Without development controls, affordable housing is not likely to be interspersed with job centers because it is less profitable to developers.[46]

Such controls include strong pro-residential policies in the city center, for example, tying office space development to a required minimum amount of space for homes. An alternative is to levy fees on developers whose projects will worsen the imbalance, and use the revenues to create employment in job-poor areas and homes in housing-poor areas. The Southern California Association of Governments' Regional Mobility Plan, a 20-year undertaking launched in 1990 to address the region's transport problems, is considering using this strategy to improve its balance of jobs and housing.[47]

It is not too late for well-established cities to change their auto-oriented land use patterns, as some Canadian cities have shown. Toronto, for example, has combined public transport expansion with zoning and incentives for developers to create higher densities and shorter travel distances. Half of all apartments built since 1954 are within walking distance of rapid-rail transport, and 90 percent of all new offices are adjacent to stations downtown and at three other locations. Toronto's overall density is now comparable to several major West European cities, and, despite increasing auto ownership, public transport ridership has increased 80 percent in a little more than 20 years. Toronto has grown so quickly (the population doubled during the period of subway construction) that in the eighties local residents began to protest further growth. The city's recent land use plans limit development in the center and use newer rail lines to help divert development out to subcenters.[48]

The rapid-rail system seems to have shaped metropolitan Toronto: viewed from an airplane, the rail stations are clearly marked by the dense clusters of development around them. But more precisely, the successes of both the transport system and the related land developments have been mutually reinforcing. Rail can be an important force in urban development, but in the absence of specific land use policies, a new rail line by itself will not induce high density. In Paris, Stockholm, Hamburg, and many other cities, rail systems and deliberate land use controls have created compact, efficient developments.[49]

Even cities in Australia and the United States are beginning to rethink their inefficient use of land. Portland, Oregon, took some federal funds it received for road building and constructed a light-rail system instead, while working out plans to intensify development along the rail corridor. The city intends to use revenues from joint development projects (such as leasing air rights over stations to private developers) to make the light-rail line self-sufficient. Portland is encouraging multifamily housing in low-density areas, and emphasizing housing in the city center. City officials also are restricting downtown parking and giving traffic priority to both the light rail and some bus routes.[50]

The time may be ripe for more careful development in other parts of the United States. In a public opinion poll of New Jersey residents, 25 percent of the respondents said development controls should be "very strict" and 50 percent said "extremely strict." However, many popular no-growth initiatives actually undermine the goals of mixing land use and concentrating higher densities near public transport by trying to stop growth altogether. This just diverts inevitable development to areas where the controls are looser, leading to further sprawl. The issue is not whether to reject or accept growth, but rather how best to use it to reduce dependence on cars and make communities more livable.[51]

Housing and taxation policies can either support or undermine land use controls and transportation improvements. For example, suburbanization in the United States has been fueled largely by the subsidy of single-family homes through property tax and mortgage interest deductions from federal taxes. Canadians and Western Europeans, who generally do not receive such benefits, tend to live in denser multifamily housing. Tax codes that favor new construction over improvements to existing buildings also encourage sprawl.[52]

Land use controls have had relatively little success in developing countries because of rapid growth, lax enforcement, and inability to meet regulations, among other obstacles. Particularly in Asian cities, high densities already overwhelm the public transport systems. Yet since so few people have cars, it is important for urban distances to be on a walking or cycling scale. Hong Kong, Seoul, and Singapore have helped manage travel demand by drawing development into designated subcenters outside their cores. Singapore's plan used an extensive low-income housing program to place jobs and homes close to each other, partially relieving downtown congestion without expanding the transport system.[53]

In Pakistan, Karachi's "Metroville" program for urban development operates on a similar principle. The plan enables people to build their own homes within walking distance of jobs, and eliminates some commutes by promoting home-based workshops for producing textiles, furniture, and other goods. In Africa and Latin America, similar schemes that plan urban development to bring together jobs, services, and affordable housing hold great potential for solving city-wide transport problems and giving people access to vital amenities.[54]

A POLICY OVERHAUL

Automobile dependence plagues the world's major cities with problems that further tinkering with car technology will never solve. To fully confront congestion, pollution, oil dependence, and increasingly unlivable cities, governments will need to end the reign of the car. The surest way to lessen overdependence on cars is through a wholesale reordering of transportation priorities.

The first step is to bring to light the hidden costs of driving, such as air pollution, municipal services, and road construction and repair. Perhaps least-recognized of these expenses are items such as police, fire, and ambulance services. According to an analysis of the salaries and personnel time of the Pasadena Police Department in California, 40 percent of department costs are auto-related—primarily accidents, thefts, and traffic control. Extending this finding to the entire United States suggests that driving costs local governments alone at least $60 billion each year. Only when such hidden costs are acknowledged will governments recognize that transportation alternatives are economical.[55]

Employer-provided parking represents an even more direct subsidy of driving. In the United States, where fewer than 10 percent of employees pay for parking, employers can deduct the expense of providing parking from their taxes. But deductions for public transport fare reimbursements are strictly limited. Employees receive parking as a tax-free fringe benefit, worth an estimated $12-50 billion a year nationwide.[56]

Tax benefits for company cars are another common subsidy. Light taxation of company cars in the United Kingdom, for example, diverts some $5 billion annually from the public treasury, and encourages more driving and purchase of larger, less fuel-efficient cars. Company cars on average log nearly twice as many miles per week as household cars, mostly for private purposes. In response to growing public ire over this subsidy, taxes on U.K. company cars have been hiked each year since 1988—provoking vehement protests from the auto industry. The subsidy is still sizable, however, and needs further reduction.[57]

So long as automobile owners are showered with these inducements, they will stay in their cars and leave trains, buses, and bike paths empty. This creates a vicious cycle, since transport planners are unlikely to invest in improved alternative transport when existing systems are underused. Given the gross imbalance in many cities' transport systems, it makes sense to levy auto-related fees and taxes, and spend some of the revenues to develop pedestrian and cycling facilities and public transportation.

Removing parking subsidies, for example, discourages the one-person-per-auto commute. In April 1975, when Canada began charging federal employees 70 percent of the commercial rate for parking, the number driving alone to work dropped 21 percent and commuting by public transport increased 16 percent. In a study of workers commuting to Los Angeles' Civic Center, employees who paid for their parking were 44 percent less likely to commute alone and 175 percent more likely to use public transport than their colleagues who parked for free.[58]

A reasonably high gasoline tax, such as the $1–2 per gallon now common in Europe, would discourage driving, encourage people to use public transport where it is available, and raise revenues to expand transit service. It would also serve as a steadying influence on widely varying petroleum prices. Particularly in the United States and Canada, where the price of gas is comparatively low, steady increases in these taxes are needed during the next decade.[59]

It makes sense to levy a sizable tax on new cars as well and to raise annual registration fees. Such charges encourage people to consider the full costs of driving when they purchase a car, and serve as a disincentive for households to buy a second or third auto. One approach is the new German policy of tying these fees to a car's emissions of pollutants. Another is to base the tax on the car's fuel economy.[60]

The Philippines has achieved remarkable results since 1975 with a transport program that raised fuel prices nearly 100 percent, introduced car sales and registration fees based on engine size, and put a light-rail line in Manila. Between 1976 and 1985, the country's total gasoline consumption dropped by 43 percent, despite expanding population and rising per capita income. In the vicinity of the rail system, travel time on roads has decreased by about a third.[61]

Creating a sustainable transportation system hinges largely on making the alternatives attractive. Surveys show that even Americans choose to drive not out of blind love for cars but rather from consideration of the time and money required for a trip. Because people base their transportation choices on the cost, convenience, time, and dependability of their options, making the alternatives convenient helps cities achieve a better transport balance.[62]

Transit service should be reliable for off-peak as well as commuting trips. Drivers will only use public transport regularly if the standard of service is high and the systems are convenient; aiming to attract these riders creates a more effective system than one that only serves carless citizens. Paris, Hamburg, Copenhagen, Tokyo, Toronto, and other cities have shown that such a strategy can boost ridership markedly.[63]

Municipalities can share the cost of expanding transport services by striking deals with private land developers who benefit from enhanced access to their projects. Joint development schemes can be planned at new metro stations, helping to defray costs. The Metropolitan Area Transit Authority of Washington, D.C., has estimated that the long-term benefits of joint development projects at just two metro stations will exceed public costs by more than $200 million.[64]

Eastern Europe and the Soviet Union are uniquely positioned to avoid the excesses of auto dependence.

A mix of public and private participation in bus and train services can increase efficiency and take financial pressure off city governments—so long as the public sector remains a principal provider, and also plays a strong regulatory role. Throughout Asia, Latin America, and Africa, privately run minibuses and minivans help fill the public transport gap where government services alone cannot meet demand. But such arrangements require careful regulation to ensure that both profitable and unprofitable routes are covered, fares are reasonable, and safety standards enforced.

Eastern Europe and the Soviet Union are uniquely positioned, with extensive public transport systems, to avoid the excesses of auto dependence—even though the near future will bring a flood of opportunities to repeat industrial countries' mistakes. There is ample argument for these governments to focus future transport investments on improving the often-inadequate quality of transit service, and to structure auto costs to reflect accurately their environmental and social impacts.

In developing countries, the deterioration of public transport systems and the neglect of nonmotorized transport are largely the result of lending biases among international development banks, which favor road building. Although the rationale for emphasizing motorization has been to transport goods and thus boost economic development, this strategy has created unbalanced systems that leave those who cannot afford cars with severely inadequate transportation.

With the right incentives, employers may prove the best promoters of public transport.

The extent of developing countries' unmet transport needs and their overwhelming financial debt make it clear that an auto-dominated future is not viable for the Third World. This argues strongly for an international effort to help developing countries finance public transport projects—particularly rail expansion, where appropriate—through increased taxes on fuel, car manufacture, or related items. Such a move would only partially compensate for the industrial countries' disproportionate share of world oil consumption, as well as their responsibility for global warming and other environmental problems.[65]

In cities that are building public transport systems from scratch, dedicated lanes for buses would speed service, helping to attract more passengers where demand is low and greatly improving efficiency where demand is high. Another intermediate step toward public transport is to encourage car pools and van pools by reserving some lanes solely for vehicles with three or more occupants.

Charging drivers for the right to use congested roads is a further incentive for ride sharing. Since 1975, Singapore has successfully used an Area Licensing Scheme, levying a fee on vehicles entering the city center—except for buses, commercial trucks, and cars carrying four or more people. The scheme is part of a package of traffic measures, including expanded bus service, heavy parking charges, and high car taxes, that have reduced congestion and traffic accidents, and have helped avoid further road building.[66]

With the right incentives, employers may prove the best promoters of public transport. Local governments can require large employers to provide bus and train route information and offer financial bonuses to employees to promote ride sharing, use of public transport, and cycling and walking. In Southern California, for example, the South Coast Air Quality Management Plan requires businesses employing more than 100 people to submit plans for reducing one-person-per-car commuting; stiff fines face those who do not.[67]

Effective land use planning is another key to a viable new transportation system. Several studies suggest that there is a threshold level of urban density—30-40 people per hectare—below which reliance on the automobile soars. This is about the density level found in Copenhagen, Toronto, and Hamburg. Comparing Copenhagen (30 people per hectare) with Denver (12 people per hectare), it appears that a 60-percent decrease in density corresponds with a 285-percent increase in gasoline use per person. This dramatizes the difference that relatively moderate land use changes can make, and provides a practical minimum density that planners can use as a guide.[68]

It is important for local land use policies to fit into more comprehensive regional plans. Otherwise, communities may solve their own transport problems—particularly congestion—at the expense of neighboring areas. The experience of fragmented local planning boards in the United States has also shown that without broader coordination, private developers can play one body off another and so escape controls.[69]

Particularly in the developing world, allotting street space logically and efficiently would mean setting aside exclusive space for buses and giving pedestrians and cyclists priority over cars. In all cities, local authorities can improve people's transport options with ordinances that require buildings to provide secure bicycle parking and convenient access to main entrances for people who arrive on foot, by bicycle, or by public transport.

Peter Newman and Jeffrey Kenworthy have noted that parking is almost a "litmus test" of a city's car orientation. Their 32-city study found that generally there were 150-200 parking spaces per 1,000 jobs in the central business district. But in the most auto-dependent cities there were more than 500 parking spaces per 1,000 jobs. They suggested that these cities should limit their central business districts to no more than 200 parking spaces per 1,000 jobs.[70]

What would the future look like if cities were not dominated by cars? The very heart of a city would be reserved for people on foot and passengers arriving by metro or trolley. Proceeding outward from the center, streets would become the shared domain of pedestrians, cyclists, trolleys, and buses. Slow automobile traffic would be allowed beyond the city's densest core, but convenient bus and rail services—running between stops placed within walking or cycling distance of most points—would offer a faster way to get around. Express public transport routes would link outlying areas to each other and to the downtown. Car parking would be progressively less restricted as you moved away from the city center.

People would make most short trips by foot or on a bicycle, and longer ones by walking or biking to transport stops, then continuing by bus, metro, or trolley. Many long drives between cities would be replaced by train trips. Cars would be used mainly for trips for which these other modes are inconvenient, such as the transport of loads of things or groups of people, travel at odd hours when public transport is running infrequently, and some recreational outings.

The challenge of creating an alternative transport future is ultimately a political one. As elected officials in most societies are well aware, many people continue to support the policies that have nurtured overreliance on cars—from driving subsidies, to tax benefits, to expansion of parking lots and roads. Even more resistance to change lies in the colossal power of the automobile and road lobby.

But as the enormous problems caused by excessive dependence on the automobile continue to plague cities, a political transformation may occur. Indeed, people around the world are beginning to see that the costs of depending on cars are already outweighing the benefits. If cities are to achieve the dream of clean, efficient, reliable transportation once promised by the automobile, they will have to steer toward sustainable alternatives.

5

Reforming Forestry

Sandra Postel and John C. Ryan

From the fate of the northern spotted owl in the U.S. Pacific Northwest to the survival of the Penan people struggling to save their Malaysian homeland from the bulldozer and saw, conflicts over timber are raising difficult questions about economic progress and environmental protection. Long considered a limitless resource, forests are fast becoming too scarce and degraded to provide all the products people need and want, and all the ecological services a healthy planet requires.

Over the last 10,000 years, the earth's mantle of forests and woodlands has shrunk by a third as trees were cleared to make way for crops, pasture, and cities. Even as this transformation continues, with some 17 million hectares of tropical forest being lost per year, demand for forests' main commodity—wood—is at an all-time high and growing. Meanwhile, greater appreciation for the role of forests in maintaining climate, stabilizing soil and water resources, and safeguarding biological diversity has made clear the need for their protection.[1]

Though few nations have taken inventories of the biological values of their forests, the best estimate is that just 1.5 billion hectares of undisturbed, primary forest remain out of the 6.2 billion that existed before settled agriculture began. (See Table 5–1.) Half the original area of tropical forests has disappeared at the hands of peasants, loggers, ranchers, and land speculators, and half of what is left has already been logged for timber or degraded in some way that compromises its ecological integrity.[2]

Virtually all of Europe's original forests are gone, replaced largely by intensively managed tree stands composed of just a handful of species. In the United States, excluding Alaska, less than 5 percent of primary forest is intact. Vast uncut areas remain in the northern reaches of Canada and the Soviet Union, where most woodlands have been too remote and unproductive for large-scale economic exploitation or human settlement.[3]

No secondary forest or plantation can compete with the biological richness or ecological importance of primary forests. From their large, centuries-old trees and huge volumes of wood per hectare, the timber industry has enjoyed a one-time bonanza of harvesting. One 500-year-old Douglas-fir from the Pacific Northwest can provide enough timber to build the average U.S. home.[4]

But this rapid forest mining exacts a

Table 5-1. Estimated Remaining Area of Primary Forest, Selected Countries, Regions, and Total, Late Eighties

Country/Region	Original Forest Cover	Current Forest Cover	Current Primary Forest	Current Primary as Share of Original Forest
	(million hectares)			(percent)
Soviet Union	n.a.	944	444[1]	n.a.
Canada	530	453	274[2]	52
Brazil[3]	286	220	180	63
Zaire[3]	125	100	70	56
United States	438	296	65[4]	15
Indonesia[3]	122	86	53	43
Peru[3]	70	52	42	60
Venezuela[3]	42	35	30	71
Colombia[3]	70	28	18	26
Papua New Guinea[3]	43	36	18	42
Australia	244	151	13[5]	5
China	476	117	6[6]	1
New Zealand	22	7	5	24
Europe	n.a.	157	< 1[7]	0
Other	n.a.	1,563	295	n.a.
World[8]	6,200	4,244	1,514	24

[1]Figure based on surveys for roadless areas greater than 400,000 hectares, where development is unlikely to have occurred; may include non-primary forest areas and exclude smaller areas.   [2]Consists mostly of "unproductive" forest (189 million hectares). Based on age-class survey, 85 million hectares of "productive" primary forest, with more than 50 cubic meters of wood per hectare, remain.   [3]Figures for tropical nations refer to tropical moist forest only.   [4]Consists mostly of Alaskan forests (52 million hectares); figure for lower 48 states (13 million hectares) is midpoint of estimated range of 2–5 percent of original forest area.   [5]Consists mostly of woodland (with low-growing trees); 1.7 million hectares of tall primary forest are estimated to remain.   [6]Figure, based on age-class survey, represents "over-mature" non-plantation forest area.   [7]The only extensive primary forests left in Europe (excluding the Soviet Union) are 450,000 hectares in northern Sweden.   [8]Columns may not add to total due to rounding.
SOURCE: Worldwatch Institute, based on sources documented in endnote 2.

severe economic and ecological toll. The World Bank expects overcutting will drop the number of net tropical wood-exporting countries from 33 to as few as 10 over the next decade. In the Pacific Northwest and other regions dependent on temperate old-growth forests, the timber industry will shrink once remaining stands are logged. Meanwhile, the societal costs—in extinguished species, soil erosion, and other ecological damage—go largely uncounted.[5]

TIMBER TRENDS

More than 3.4 billion cubic meters of wood are extracted from the world's forests and woodlands each year, roughly half for fuel and half for lumber, plywood, paper, and other industrial products. Firewood scarcity has reached crisis proportions in many parts of the Third World and is an important cause of woodland loss and degradation in regions such as sub-Saharan Africa and India. Yet seldom does the gathering of wood for fuel result in the destruction of rich primary forests.[6]

Industrial timber cutting, on the other hand, is a major cause of primary forest destruction in both temperate and tropical nations, and is the focus of this chapter. Logging in the tropics, for example, degrades some 4.5 million hectares of rain forest annually and leads to deforestation by making woodlands more susceptible to fire and more open to clearing by peasants and ranchers, the leading direct causes of forest loss.[7]

Having expanded by more than 50 percent since 1965, the world's commercial timber harvest now amounts to nearly 1.7 billion cubic meters per year, and supports an international forest products trade worth $85 billion annually. Three timber giants—the United States, the Soviet Union, and Canada—supply more than half of the world's industrial wood. (See Table 5–2.)

As with many commodities, demand for timber is driven by population growth, economic conditions, and the extent to which substitutes are found. Though total industrial wood consumption has been increasing, the worldwide rate of growth has slowed since the postwar boom years. Compared with average annual growth rates of about 3.5 percent during the fifties, growth during the seventies and eighties hovered between 1 and 2 percent a year. Two relatively recent forecasts project demand levels for 2030 of 2.0–2.6 billion cubic meters, or 18–53 percent higher than today.[8]

Though no meteoric rise in consumption is anticipated globally, trends in

Table 5-2. World Production of Industrial Roundwood, Top 15 Nations and World, 1988[1]

Country	Volume	Share of Total
	(million cubic meters)	(percent)
United States	417	25
Soviet Union	305	18
Canada	173	10
China	98	6
Brazil	67	4
Sweden	48	3
Finland	46	3
Indonesia	40	2
Malaysia	36	2
France	32	2
West Germany	31	2
Japan	28	2
India	24	2
Poland	20	1
Australia	18	1
Others	281	17
World	1,664	100

[1]Includes all wood products except fuelwood and charcoal.
SOURCE: U.N. Food and Agriculture Organization, *Forest Products Yearbook 1988* (Rome: 1990).

some key countries are unsettling, to say the least. Demand skyrocketed in China following the economic reforms of the late seventies. Annual wood harvests jumped from 196 million cubic meters in 1976 to 344 million cubic meters in 1988, of which industrial uses accounted for about 60 percent. Officials estimate that annual cutting in China now exceeds regrowth by 100 million cubic meters. The area of timber production forests has shrunk by nearly 3 million hectares since 1980; at current harvest rates, all the remaining production forests of harvestable age will be gone within a decade. Officials in China now speak openly of a timber supply crisis, one that imports—totaling 25 million cubic meters in 1989 and an estimated 15 million in 1990—will only partially resolve.[9]

India's situation is equally dire. Its forests have been shrinking by 1.5 million hectares per year; because of their low productivity, these woodlands can support an annual harvest of no more than 39 million cubic meters. That amounts to only 0.046 cubic meters per person for both fuelwood and industrial wood, compared with U.S. industrial wood consumption of 1.86 cubic meters per person—40 times higher. Government projections show India's demand for wood climbing to 289 million cubic meters by 2000, more than seven times the estimated annual growth, virtually assuring continued wood deficits.[10]

On the brighter side of the supply-demand picture, harvests from large areas of plantations coming on-line in a number of countries—including Argentina, Australia, Brazil, Chile, New Zealand, Portugal, South Africa, Spain, and Venezuela—will help satisfy increased demands. These tree farms can yield 20–35 cubic meters per hectare per year, up to 10 times the average annual yield from natural stands, and so can help ease logging pressures on forests. Because the plantations are so fast-growing, they can be harvested on much shorter rotations. As monocultures, however, they face increased risks from pests and disease, as described in the next section, and offer few of the ecological values natural forests do.[11]

In Latin America, industrial plantations account for less than 1 percent of forestland but one third of the region's industrial wood output. Chile now has 1.3 million hectares of plantations, of which about 85 percent contain just Monterey pine. Unfortunately, in the push to make plantations the cornerstone of the country's forest products industry, much natural forest was converted to pine monocultures. Forestry exports have more than doubled in value since 1983, and with plantings of about 77,000 hectares per year between 1978 and 1986, marked increases in Chile's timber supply are expected by early next century.[12]

Industrial timber cutting is a major cause of primary forest destruction in both temperate and tropical nations.

Brazil, too, has greatly expanded its plantation area in recent years, though exports are likely to be constrained by a shortage of capital and greater domestic wood needs. An excellent climate for fast-growing eucalyptus trees, relatively low land costs, and new pulping technologies that allow eucalyptus (a hardwood) to substitute for softwoods in the manufacture of many paper products give Brazil a strong competitive advantage. It can produce hardwood pulp for one fourth the cost of softwood pulp in Sweden and half that in the southeastern United States.[13]

The Soviet Union, with a fifth of the world's forest area and nearly a quarter of its growing stock, would seem to hold a large untapped supply potential. In recent years, Soviet foresters have replanted about 1 million hectares annually and aided natural regeneration on a slightly larger area, helping ensure that total forest area and standing timber volume were increasing. Much forest in the European North, Siberia, and the Far East, however, suffers from unfavorable climates and poorly drained soils, keeping productivity low. Overall, Soviet timber harvest levels are not likely to increase considerably, though forest product output may expand through more efficient use of the wood harvested.[14]

With some regional gaps but no looming global crisis in supply and demand for industrial wood, the real tragedy of forestry today becomes all the more striking. A great deal of timber production is both economically and environmentally wasteful, and is needlessly degrading and fragmenting unique forest ecosystems.

In the tropics, overcutting has turned one nation after another into a major timber supplier as the forests of the previous leading exporter have been depleted and raw log exports curtailed. Southeast Asia's exports to Japan (by far the world's biggest importer of tropical wood) were dominated first by the Philippines during the sixties, followed by Indonesia during much of the seventies, and then by Malaysia during the eighties.[15]

While debate rages over how much ancient forest to protect, the last stands are disappearing.

The east Malaysian states of Sabah and Sarawak now supply the bulk of the world's tropical logs, but with harvest levels more than twice the so-called sustained yield—the amount of wood that can be cut without diminishing future timber supplies—their forests are rapidly disappearing. Malaysia's timber exports brought in a record $3.1 billion in 1989, but the nation could find itself a net importer of wood in less than a decade.[16]

A similar story has unfolded in West Africa, which sends most of its tropical logs to Europe. Nigeria, once a major tropical log exporter, saw its timber shipments fall off dramatically after

many years of overcutting forests and the rapid expansion of slash-and-burn cultivation. In 1988, the country earned only $6 million from these exports while spending $100 million on forest product imports.[17]

Sadly, Côte d'Ivoire and Ghana are following in Nigeria's footsteps. More than 80 percent of the tropical moist forest in these countries has already disappeared, and both are likely to become net importers of wood by the end of the decade. The value of timber exports in Côte d'Ivoire plummeted from $490 million in 1980 to $81 million in 1987.[18]

Destructive logging is by no means confined to the tropics. In Canada's British Columbia, logging of old-growth forest proceeds at a rate of 270,000 hectares per year, and timber companies hold licenses to harvest almost all of what remains. The 85 million cubic meters of wood logged from British Columbia's forests in 1989 exceeded sustained yield by 30 percent.[19]

The United States gets nearly a third of its softwood lumber and plywood from a band of forests stretching from the state of Washington down to northern California, bounded by the Pacific Ocean to the west and the Cascade Mountains to the east. This area contains virtually all the country's remaining old-growth forest outside Alaska. During the first half of the eighties, harvests from industry-owned lands in the region surpassed the sustained yield by more than a fourth, and those from the 12 national forests—which harbor most of the remaining ancient stands—by 61 percent.[20]

As stocks dwindle and production costs rise, the U.S. timber industry has shifted its center of gravity to an expanding area of plantations and secondary forests in the Southeast. By 1986, the southern states accounted for 47 percent of the nation's timber harvest, compared with 25 percent from the Pacific coast states. And the latter's share is expected to decline further.[21]

Market forces will continue to shift timber production away from old-growth forests gradually. But how much of the world's biological heritage will be left when that shift is complete? Without major changes in government policies, only the most inaccessible and least productive primary forests will remain by the time industry has turned exclusively to secondary forests and plantations. While debate rages on in Canada, the United States, and elsewhere over how much ancient forest to protect, the last stands are disappearing. Even worse, in many countries the debate has not even begun.

THE LEGACY OF LOGGING

Forestry methods vary nearly as much as the ecosystems they are applied to. But almost everywhere, logging tends to deplete, fragment, and homogenize forests. The worst, most widespread type of degradation is timber mining—a cycle of overcutting and moving on to richer territory. Wherever the cut exceeds sustained yield, future harvests will suffer and loggers will seek out new areas to exploit. Having depleted forests in their own regions, for example, timber companies in both the western Soviet Union and the U.S. Pacific Northwest are setting their sights on the largely untouched forests of the Soviet Far East. And Thai loggers, having been banned from their own nation's forests after catastrophic floods in November 1988 left whole villages buried in mud and logs from cutover hillsides, are now depleting the world's last great teak forests in neighboring Myanmar (formerly Burma).[22]

The alternative to this frontier approach of always finding virgin land to exploit is sustained-yield forestry. Yet a 1989 study for the International Tropical Timber Organization (ITTO) concluded that less than 0.1 percent of tropical logging was being done on a sustained-yield basis. Outside the tropics, the goal of modern forestry has been to strip forests of their natural complexity in order to maximize wood yields. In all regions, sustainable forestry—a broader concept than sustained yield that includes maintenance of the biological diversity and environmental services of forests as well as their stocks of wood—has been equally elusive.[23]

Timber harvesting typically begins with a dense network of roads, which themselves deforest large areas. In Southeast Asia, as much as 14 percent of logging areas are cleared to build roads. And in U.S. national forests, more than 570,000 kilometers of logging roads—a network eight times the size of the interstate highway system—cover roughly 1.4 million hectares.[24]

Roads expose forests to exotic pests, diseases, and wildlife and, especially in steeper regions, can severely increase soil erosion and sediment buildup in streams and rivers. Logging roads have accelerated the spread of a number of destructive pests in the U.S. Northwest, including a fatal root rot that is moving rapidly into the remaining upland groves of the Port Orford cedar, the region's most highly prized timber tree. In Idaho, forest roads have caused erosion more than 200 times greater than on undisturbed sites. Logging roads near Bacuit Bay in Palawan, the Philippines, cover only 3 percent of the watershed but are responsible for 84 percent of the erosion caused by logging.[25]

Great as these impacts are, the most serious effect roads have on forests is the chain of devastation they begin. They open once-impenetrable forests to miners, hunters, ranchers, and poor farmers. Because deforestation is a sequence of events, it is impossible to state exactly how much is caused by the timber trade, but it is clearly a major contributor to the alarming pace of deforestation in Africa and Southeast Asia. At current rates of destruction, according to British environmental consultant Norman Myers, "by early next century there will be little left of tropical forests except for a few large blocks in New Guinea, the Zaire basin, western Amazonia in Brazil and the Guyana highlands."[26]

When diverse populations of trees are replaced with genetically uniform stands, future timber harvests are put at risk.

As roads, logging, and forest clearance spread, large areas of habitat become islands in a sea of degraded lands. Biological diversity depends on large areas of contiguous habitat, and edges of forest "islands" can deteriorate rapidly from exposure to damaging winds, exotic species, and dramatic changes in temperature, humidity, and light levels. Long before forests actually disappear, their biological integrity will be lost. In the Pacific Northwest, for example, for each 10-hectare clear-cut, an additional 14 hectares of old-growth forest are degraded by these edge effects; 37 percent of remaining old-growth occurs in islands smaller than 160 hectares in size.[27]

Reforestation after logging can reduce some of the soil erosion, nutrient loss, and water runoff that results from loss of tree cover. On many sites, however, the severe disturbances that typically follow large-scale logging make reforestation difficult or impossible. Heavy machinery used to skid logs across the ground com-

pacts soils and, in the Soviet Union, for example, destroys up to 80 percent of young growth. Removing large amounts of vegetation from tropical rain forests, where nutrients are found mostly in the plant life itself and not in the soil, leaves behind a nutritionally impoverished system that may take hundreds of years to recover. Reforestation failures are also common in northern forests and in high-elevation stands in western North America.[28]

Even highly selective logging in the tropics is typically quite destructive because of the tremendous diversity of tree species: loggers "cream" the forest—taking only a handful of desired species but degrading much wider areas than they would if other, lesser-known species were harvested. One study in the eastern Amazon found that while 3 percent of the trees were removed, 54 percent were uprooted, crushed, or damaged during road building and logging. As experience in the Amazon and Indonesia has shown, selective logging can also disrupt local climates, turning rain forests that were practically fire-proof into dried-out, easily burned stands.[29]

The role of tropical deforestation in global warming is well known, accounting for on the order of 20–30 percent of annual carbon emissions worldwide. Less well known is that ancient rain forests of northwest North America store up to three times as much carbon per hectare as their tropical counterparts. The conversion of those stands to plantations over the past 100 years has resulted in a net release of 1.8 billion tons of carbon to the atmosphere, according to Mark Harmon of Oregon State University and his colleagues. They note that the loss of these unparalleled carbon storehouses, covering only 0.017 percent of the earth's land surface, has been responsible for 2 percent of the carbon emissions released through deforestation and other land use changes over the past century.[30]

The establishment of industrial plantations, almost always consisting of one species of tree or one genetic variety within a species, has also eliminated much of the plant and animal diversity of the world's temperate latitudes. Woodpeckers and the array of species that depend on old and dead trees are endangered throughout Europe because most of its forests have been converted to monocultures. Ninety-seven percent of western Germany's woodlands, for example, are covered by just three species of tree. The Pacific yew, the bark of which contains an anti-cancer drug, faces possible extinction as Douglas-fir tree farms proliferate across the northwestern United States.[31]

These environmental losses also have tangible economic costs. In the Peruvian Amazon, where the wealth of fruits and rubber yield greater long-term revenues per hectare than timber, botanist Charles M. Peters and his colleagues found that if as few as one in six fruit trees were damaged by logging, the net financial gains of timber harvesting would be zero. The annual catch of the $700-million salmon fishing industry in British Columbia, where steep-slope clear-cutting has filled streams and bays with silt and where pulp mills have polluted rivers and coastal waterways, is now half the previous levels.[32]

The costs of timber extraction usually fall on those who depend on intact woodlands, such as forest dwellers, downstream communities, and tourism-based economies. But loggers can also cut themselves out of business. A number of commercially important tropical timbers—including *Virola surinamensis*, the most valuable timber tree in the eastern Amazon, and Masson pine, once a major timber species throughout southern and central China—are on the brink of extinction in the wild due to overharvesting.[33]

When diverse populations of trees are replaced with genetically uniform stands, future timber harvests are put at risk. Because natural systems of checks and balances have been stripped in order to maximize tree growth, monocultures are prone to unravel. Widespread disease and pest outbreaks—common throughout the conifer plantations of the United States, central Europe, and China, and a chronic problem in tropical plantations—can decimate entire landscapes, rather than just localized groups of trees.[34]

As Jerry Franklin, forest ecologist at the University of Washington, and his colleagues note, "creating uniform stands with a narrowed genetic base increases the vulnerability of forests to changes in climate, pollutants, and pests and pathogens." In Germany, scientists have speculated that the long-term degradation caused by intensive forestry may have helped speed *Waldsterben*, the widespread "forest death" linked to air pollution and acid rain. Since there is virtually no natural forest left for comparison, it is impossible to prove their hypothesis.[35]

Beyond the impacts on specific parts of forest ecosystems, logging destroys wild places. In Canada's British Columbia, where only 6 of 89 large watersheds on Vancouver Island remain unlogged—and only one is protected—rain forests are an endangered ecosystem. Ninety percent of Clayoquot Sound, a remnant area of wilderness on the island's west coast, is slated to be logged, even though it contains three of the last six intact watersheds. When a cathedral grove of millennia-old *alerce* trees in Chile—containing some of the world's oldest living organisms—is cut, no statistics can capture the world's loss.[36]

NEW DIRECTIONS FOR FORESTRY

How can the timber industry get wood without destroying forests? Answers to this question will vary regionally, from massive tree planting efforts in denuded lands to improved management of forests where they remain. But a common thread in all strategies is a fundamental philosophical shift for foresters. Instead of treating biological diversity as an impediment to timber production, forestry will need to maintain and restore the complexity of life that gives rise to both forests and wood.

Around the world, government and corporate interest in "sustainable forestry" has soared in the past year in response to growing public concern. Where this new-found environmental awareness is sincere, it is surely welcome. But because old-growth forests are a form of natural capital that has taken centuries or millennia to accumulate, "sustainable logging" of these nonrenewable resources is, strictly speaking, an oxymoron.

Beyond their inherent value as the world's greatest storehouses of life, and the economic value of their nontimber products, undisturbed forests are vital to the long-term success of the forest industry. Intact stands of native trees are valuable as sources of insect predators and as physical barriers to stop the spread of pest outbreaks on adjacent plantations. According to Oregon State University entomologist Timothy Schowalter and others, old-growth forests can support more than 100 times as many predators as plantations, and their pest outbreaks tend to be limited.[37]

When these forests disappear, the timber industry also loses its reservoirs of genetic variety and its scientific laboratories for elucidating the many hidden relationships that make timber growth possible. While most foresters still focus narrowly on wood production, a few researchers and land managers, primarily in the U.S. Pacific Northwest, have begun paying attention to other, overlooked components. Their ecosystem-oriented work, known as New Forestry, makes it clear that diversity—at the genetic, species, and ecosystem levels—is crucial to forests' long-term productivity.[38]

One element ignored until recently is the underground organisms that help keep soils fertile. Among the most important are mycorrhizal fungi attached to the roots of 90 percent of the world's plant species; when eaten and dispersed by small mammals, the fungi enable trees to absorb nutrients and water from the soil and to fix nitrogen. Conventional logging removes host plants and disturbs soils, often causing fungus species to disappear. Similarly, foresters are now starting to recognize dead trees and logs as integral to healthy forests. They provide important wildlife habitat, return organic matter and nutrients to the soil, and help control erosion. Removing too much dead wood or other organic matter from an ecosystem can cause the entire system to break down.[39]

These and other linkages discovered within forest communities demonstrate the importance of maintaining as many prelogging conditions as possible throughout the timber cutting cycle. These findings were first applied in an integrated fashion on portions of the Willamette National Forest in Oregon in 1988, and use of the new, constantly evolving approach is now spreading throughout the Northwest. Managers have begun leaving both live and dead trees, streamside corridors, and small and large woody debris. They have also begun to lump timber cutting areas together in order to reduce fragmentation and road building.[40]

Unfortunately, New Forestry is often

pushed as a substitute for ancient forest protection. At least one project in southwest Oregon's Siskiyou National Forest appears to be taking a more enlightened approach, however. Now in its final planning stages, the stated goal is to maintain the biological health of the Shasta Costa Valley, including protection of its old-growth forests. Logging will be concentrated near existing roads and in younger stands, and will be designed to leave trees, nitrogen-fixing shrubs, and other legacies of the natural landscape behind to ensure the forest's recovery.[41]

A handful of promising forestry operations in the tropics share this diversity-centered approach. Since 1985 the Yanesha Forestry Cooperative, the first such Indian group in Amazonia, has been operating in Peru's Palcazu Valley, with local people owning and processing the forest products and with timber cutting specifically designed to protect diversity. By clear-cutting in narrow strips, leaving large areas of forest intact, the Palcazu project seeks to mimic small-scale natural disturbances. Creating gaps in the forest canopy allows shade-intolerant seedlings of hundreds of different species from the uncut areas to colonize the strips; leaving bark and branches as nutrient sources, instead of burning them off, is expected to maintain long-term soil fertility. Unfortunately, unstable social conditions in impoverished, war-torn Peru threaten to make sound management of the area impossible.[42]

Whether tropical rain forests are physically capable of sustained timber production without losing their nontimber values is still under debate. Researchers may some day understand enough about how disturbances, such as fires, windstorms, and indigenous agricultural systems, foster natural diversity to create diversity-sustaining logging systems. But the social context of most tropical forest nations—poverty, debt, landlessness, and excessive political influence of the timber industry—makes anything approaching sustainable logging of primary forest a remote possibility.[43]

Since 1985 the Yanesha Forestry Cooperative has been operating in Peru's Palcazu Valley, with timber cutting specifically designed to protect diversity.

Second-growth forests—areas that have grown back after being logged or cleared for farming—are an often underutilized resource in both tropical and temperate latitudes. Accounting for perhaps two thirds of the world's forest cover, these areas serve important environmental functions. But because they are often close to access roads and scattered in small fragments, timber can be cut from them with a minimum of ecological damage. In addition, forest management, including the extraction of wood, can be used to restore the biological health of these areas.

Frank Wadsworth of the Institute of Tropical Forestry in Puerto Rico has estimated that the present area of logged-over forest in the tropics could provide more than enough wood to meet the area's anticipated requirements at the end of this decade. Although many of the trees in these stands are not now deemed valuable by the international timber trade, they are viable sources of wood products nonetheless.[44]

A greatly stepped-up effort to plant trees on lands already cleared is urgently needed to slow the atmospheric buildup of carbon dioxide, stabilize degraded watersheds, and provide fuelwood. But it can also, in the long run, become a major source of industrial wood. While tree planting can be costly compared with management of existing forests, plantation trees grow much faster than native forests, and wood needs can be met from a smaller area. In China, for example, it is estimated that an additional 10 million hectares of plantations (4 percent of the area now available to timber harvest) could double the nation's timber production.[45]

Especially in wood-poor nations, much tree planting will have to be designed and managed to provide timber as quickly as possible. A number of factors, however, argue for a more diverse approach to plantations than simply repeating the intensive monoculture systems dominant today. As noted earlier, stands of just one or two species are especially vulnerable to disease and pollutants.

In the tropics, tree planting efforts will only succeed if they revolve around local people's ideas and interests.

In addition, because most plantations have fast-growing trees that are harvested relatively young, the quality of plantation wood tends to be low. Besides their smaller diameter, young trees contain a higher percentage of "juvenile" wood, which is not as strong, as useful for pulp production, or as pleasing to the eye as older wood. Without more attention to wood quality, plantations can only complement, not substitute for, natural forest timber. Of those in the tropics, just 12 percent grow high-quality hardwoods that can be used instead of wood extracted from tropical forests. Northern regions, which cannot grow wood as fast as plantations in warmer climates, may find their market niche in growing higher quality wood than their competitors.[46]

Although there is often a short-term trade-off between diversity and wood production, evidence is building that intensive plantation practices often harm long-term timber productivity. Managers may begin to see the wisdom of restoring some of the natural resilience and variety they have always sought to eliminate. Biological diversity is no luxury: reducing the risk of future pest outbreaks and ensuring that soil is not robbed of its nutrients makes sense wherever wood is harvested.[47]

In contrast to monocultures, plantations with a mixture of species and ages can offer a variety of wood and nonwood products and, with multilayer canopies, can provide wildlife habitat as well. Even in clonal plantations (where every tree is genetically identical), some diversity can be restored. In clonal plantations of *Gmelina* in the Subri Forest Reserve in Ghana, ground vegetation and some small trees are left undisturbed after harvest to protect the soils and mycorrhizal organisms, and galleries of natural forest are left in the valley bottoms to reduce pest outbreaks. As elsewhere, tree growth is faster where site damage from logging is minimized.[48]

Even if measures to promote biological diversity and long-term productivity reduce short-term yields, tree planting on degraded lands has considerable scope to increase wood supplies once new trees reach maturity. To get some idea of the potential, a conservative assumption can be made that diversified tropical plantations with a mix of fast- and slow-growing species and managed to provide both fast-growing fiber and high-quality timber would yield 10 cubic meters per hectare per year. Establishing such plantations on just 5 percent of the 600 million hectares of tropical rain forest already cleared could provide almost twice as much industrial wood as is currently harvested from all tropical forests.

In the tropics, where rural people depend directly on the array of products available from natural forest, tree planting efforts will only succeed if they revolve around local people's ideas and interests. Forestry projects that have not done so have been plagued by illicit felling. Ideally, most tree planting will take place in small-scale efforts oriented toward community needs and the stabilization of farmland soils through agroforestry (the combined cultivation of crops and trees). But industrial timber-oriented plantations can also incorporate a range of tree types to provide nontimber products such as fruits and fodder and thereby gain the support and protection of local people.[49]

REDUCING INDUSTRIAL DEMANDS FOR WOOD

Because sustainable forestry will often yield less wood per hectare in the short term than timber mining, and because greater recognition of forests' nonwood values will mean less area is available for logging, reducing demands for timber is essential to balancing the need for both wood and healthy forests. Fortunately, a quick review of the world's industrial wood economy reveals numerous opportunities to eliminate wasteful and frivolous uses of timber.

Approximately half of the world's industrial wood is sawn into lumber, one quarter turned into pulp for paper and other products, and more than one eighth cut or chipped into panels such as plywood and chipboard. Although no global breakdown on the precise end-uses of wood is available, clearly the building industry makes the single largest claim on the world's timber. In North America and Europe, regions for which

figures are available, new housing is by far the single largest end-use for lumber and panels.[50]

Waste in the construction sector is rife. Almost one third of Japan's plywood in 1987 went to make *kon-pane* forms, panels used to mold concrete that are typically discarded after two or three uses. Even worse, nearly all of them are made from high-quality Southeast Asian tropical hardwoods. In Finland, about 10 percent of the wood used in construction is lost. And during the building of an average home in Toronto, Canada, 845 kilograms of wood are wasted— roughly the equivalent of a year's worth of paper use by the family that will live there.[51]

In addition to these obvious losses, much hidden waste occurs. Walls in most U.S. houses, for example, are built with beams at 40-centimeter intervals; placing them 60 centimeters apart could reduce lumber requirements with no noticeable effect on wall strength or quality. The U.S. Forest Service estimates that a handful of similar techniques to reduce "overbuilding" could save 10 percent of the lumber used in conventional homes.[52]

Inefficient manufacturing processes also cause much high-quality wood to go to waste. Strictly speaking, little wood is actually wasted in sawmilling: most sawdust and other manufacturing residues become raw material for pulp mills or are burned for energy. But a good deal of valuable solid wood is lost in manufacturing as it is turned into chips and sawdust. Heavily subsidized plywood mills in Southeast Asia convert as little as 40 percent of raw wood into final products. Mills in Japan generally achieve the world's highest efficiencies, 65–70 percent, well above the 50 percent typical elsewhere. In addition to using more efficient machinery, they put greater effort into getting the most out of each piece of wood by substituting abundant human labor for scarce raw materials, a practice that makes sense in many regions.[53]

A variety of technologies are available to reduce manufacturing waste. Thinner saw blades can reduce kerf—the wood chewed up by the blade—from the 7 millimeters common in U.S. mills to less than 3 millimeters. Improved lathes, used in plywood mills to peel thin layers of wood from a log, can capture all but a 5-centimeter core at the log's center, instead of the 10- to 20-centimeter cores now typically left behind. Computerized log scanning can detect interior defects and determine a cutting approach to maximize the yield of high-quality wood. The U.S. Forest Service estimates that market forces alone will spur enough use of such techniques to reduce the amount of wood needed to make a plank of plywood or lumber by one third by 2040. A concerted effort to foster efficiency could achieve these gains much sooner.[54]

In the Soviet Union, a good deal of wood is lost during logging operations. Biologist Alexei V. Yablokov, Deputy Chairman of the Ecological Committee of the Supreme Soviet, reports that most rivers in the northern and far eastern Soviet Union are laden with logs lost during transport. More than 3 million cubic meters of timber may disappear this way every year.[55]

With some notable exceptions, such as the *kon-panes* and the 20 billion disposable chopsticks used annually in Japan, solid wood products are manufactured for durable, essential uses. Paper, however, is often used wastefully and frivolously, and so offers perhaps the most immediate potential for reducing industrial demands on the world's forests.[56]

Paper and paperboard use has risen dramatically in industrial nations over the past several decades, driven in large part by offices, packaging needs, and advertising. (See Figure 5–1.) Continued

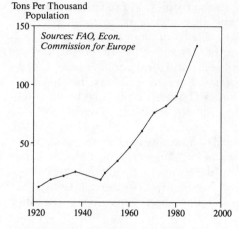

Tons Per Thousand Population

Sources: FAO, Econ. Commission for Europe

Figure 5-1. Per Capita Paper and Paperboard Consumption in Europe, 1922-88

rapid growth is projected for both industrial and developing countries.[57]

Much of the pulp used in papermaking comes from plantations and sawmill residues, so there is not always a direct link between consuming less paper and saving forests. But many natural areas of global ecological importance are being logged for pulp, including Alaska's Tongass National Forest and Southeast Asia's last great expanse of coastal mangroves in Bintuni Bay, Indonesia. More than half the newspaper used in the United States and almost one third of the world's newsprint originates in Canada, where logging for pulpwood damages large areas of natural forest.[58]

In addition, much of the low-quality pulpwood and wood waste that is now turned into paper could be processed to substitute for wood taken from primary forests. The use of particle board, for example, made of small wood pieces glued together, has grown faster than any other wood product in recent decades and is now a major raw material for European furniture. In addition, new technologies can convert knotty, warp-prone wood from pulpwood plantations into structural-grade lumber.[59]

People in industrial nations use staggering amounts of paper, much of it designed to be discarded after one use. West Germans, for example, got through 76 kilograms of paper packaging per person a year, 40 percent of their overall paper consumption. And a full 50 percent of U.S. paper production goes into packaging. Worldwide, 15 million tons of wood—1 percent of total pulp production—are thrown away every year in the form of disposable diapers.[60]

Paper consumption per person is high virtually everywhere in industrial nations compared with the Third World, but great disparities still exist among the wealthy countries. (See Table 5–3.) Each Swede, for example, uses more than twice as many paper products as a neighboring Norwegian. Such differences, along with those in paper recycling rates—20 percent in Canada versus 50 percent in Japan—suggest a vast potential for reducing consumption of paper without diminishing the quality of life. The Ontario Ministry of Government Services is already saving 29 tons of paper a year simply by using double-sided photocopying.[61]

In the United States, the world's largest wood consumer, an effort to reduce wasteful wood use would yield surprisingly large benefits. (See Table 5–4.) Improved efficiency in forest product manufacturing, to levels approached in Japan, would alone save enough wood to leave standing one out of four trees now cut nationwide. Together, available methods of reducing waste and increasing recycling and efficiency could more than halve U.S. wood consumption.[62]

Poor or nonexistent data preclude a similar analysis of potential timber savings globally. But overall consumption patterns in wealthy nations make it clear that far larger areas of forest are being degraded than is necessary. Any serious effort to protect forests will include reducing wood waste, increasing manufac-

Table 5-3. Per Capita Paper and Paperboard Use, Selected Countries and Regions, Late Eighties

Country or Region	Consumption[1]	Share Recycled[2]
	(kilograms/year)	(percent)
United States	317	29
Sweden	311	40
Canada	247	20
Japan	204	50
Norway	151	27
Soviet Union	35	19
Latin America	25	32
China	12	21
Africa	5	17
India	2	26

[1]1988. [2]Amount of waste paper recycled compared with total paper consumption; 1987 figures. SOURCE: Greenpeace, *The Greenpeace Guide to Paper* (Vancouver: 1990).

turing efficiency, and stepping up paper recycling.

TOWARD SUSTAINABLE FORESTRY

Unless actions are taken soon to put an end to today's cut-and-run style of forestry, little of the earth's natural forest heritage will remain for the next generation. The basic challenge is to halt the rapid mining of irreplaceable old-growth stands, hasten the transition to sustainably managed secondary forests and tree plantations, and reduce wood demands.

Reorienting forestry's goals and practices will not be easy. In many countries, entrenched timber interests profit from large government subsidies and scant regulation of their practices. Public agencies often operate more like timber

Table 5-4. United States: Potential Wood Savings Through Demand Management

Activity	Savings
	(million cubic meters, roundwood equivalent)
Increased Manufacturing Efficiency[1]	
Sawmills	114.3
Plywood mills	10.6
Elimination of Construction Waste[2]	26.1
Disposables Reduction and Paper Conservation[3]	68.5
Doubled Paper Recycling[4]	12.5
Total Savings	232.0
Total U.S. Consumption	460.4
	(percent)
Savings as Share of Consumption	50.4

[1]Assumes efficiency increases as predicted by USDA Forest Service (USFS) for 2040, based on spread of best currently available technologies, from 42–66 percent for sawmills, and from 50–73 percent for plywood mills; calculated at current consumption levels.   [2]Based on USFS estimates of lumber wasted through outdated building practices and on rates of wood waste reported for Finland; savings reduced to account for increased manufacturing efficiency.   [3]Assumes various measures (such as reduction of packaging, diapers, and other disposable products, conservation of office paper, and reduction in advertising) could reduce per-capita paper consumption to Norwegian levels, about 48 percent of U.S. levels.   [4]From current rate of 29 percent to 60 percent; savings reduced to account for lower consumption levels.
SOURCE: Worldwatch Institute, based on sources documented in endnote 62.

suppliers than forest managers. Saving forests, especially in tropical nations, will require fundamental reforms outside the forestry sector as well as within.

Unfortunately, the countries best situated to lead the way are failing to do so. In the United States, legislators have put forth several proposals for protecting old-growth forests in the Pacific Northwest, including the establishment of an "ancient forest reserve system" that would designate areas of old growth and adjacent younger forests off-limits to logging, road building, and other damaging activities. Included in the reserves would be all habitat deemed suitable for the threatened northern spotted owl; by 1995, this would reduce timber harvests from federal lands by 10 million cubic meters, just over 2 percent of current nationwide production. Legislation passed in October 1990 will protect an additional 400,000 hectares of the Tongass National Forest, about 6 percent of its total area, from timber cutting but will not necessarily curtail subsidized logging of the forest. With timber interests and the Bush administration opposed to major reductions in logging in national forests, it remains unclear how much of the remaining old growth will be protected.[63]

No legislation that sweeping has been introduced in Canada yet. Environmental groups in British Columbia are calling for an end to old-growth liquidation and, most urgently, a moratorium on logging several pristine areas of western Vancouver Island. They lost one round in April 1990, when provincial premier William Vander Zalm decided to allow logging in half of the Carmanah Valley, home of the world's tallest spruce. But among the hopeful signs is a move within the provincial forest ministry to develop an old-growth strategy that in the short term could include bans on logging and in the longer term would establish a reserve system similar to that proposed in the United States.[64]

Given the pressures of population growth, poverty, and debt, saving the most ecologically important and biologically rich tropical forests is far more complex. Success hinges on respect for and cooperation with the 200 million or so people living in or on their outskirts. The boldest move to date has been taken by the government of Colombia, which returned legal rights to some 18 million hectares—nearly half the Colombian Amazon—to some 70,000 Indians belonging to more than 50 different ethnic groups. Although there is no guarantee that the Indians will not exploit the forest for quick profit (nor that oil and minerals will not be extracted, since the government retains subsurface rights), chances for sustainable use are good under their management, since they have lived there for centuries.[65]

Broader use of "debt-for-nature swaps," which to date have proved the most effective instrument for local conservation financing in the Third World, can also help protect forests. These arrangements involve a third party, usually an environmental organization or industrial-country government, purchasing a portion of a developing country's debt at a heavy discount and converting it into local currency for use in various conservation projects. As of August 1990, 15 swaps had been arranged—in Bolivia, Costa Rica, Dominican Republic, Ecuador, Madagascar, the Philippines, Poland, and Zambia. These transactions have barely made a dent in the debt or deforestation crises (the face value of the debt traded totals less than $100 million), but the potential to expand them

clearly exists since so much tropical forest is found in deeply indebted countries.[66]

As with any conservation scheme, debt swaps need the support and cooperation of local people if they are to be effective and equitable. A swap in Bolivia, for example, has run into complications because of competing claims to the land by local Indians. When it was arranged in 1987, the Bolivian government did not recognize indigenous land claims, and had already awarded logging concessions in several areas that became part of the buffer zone of the Beni Biosphere Reserve. In late August 1990, hundreds of Bolivian Indians began a 650-kilometer march to the capital to petition for land rights and draw attention to their concerns. The government responded in September by granting several territories to local tribes and curtailing logging in parts of the contested forest area. It remains to be seen whether all parties will be satisfied. Certainly, earlier recognition of the native people's land claims would have eased an effective compromise.[67]

An international moratorium on the logging of primary forest now seems necessary before most of what is worth saving is gone.

Beyond the limited aid provided by the new mechanism of debt swaps, more drastic measures are clearly needed. An international moratorium on the logging of primary forest—both temperate and tropical—now seems necessary to end the timber industry's devastation before most of what is worth saving is gone. An international ban would not necessarily last forever, but it could brake the destruction long enough to put more precious areas under protection and to introduce more sustainable forest management. To be effective, it would take international support, including funds to compensate tropical countries that lose foreign exchange when a good portion of the $7-billion tropical timber trade grinds to a halt.

Such a ban would certainly cause short-term economic disruption in regions dependent on timber mining and would be opposed by those who justify unsustainable logging as a means of creating employment in rural areas. But shifts in employment are inevitable whether remaining forests are liquidated or protected: jobs and profits based on a rapidly diminishing resource simply will not last.

In Oregon, where the ancient forest controversy has been misleadingly popularized as a conflict between "jobs and owls," even record levels of timber cutting could not prevent employment in the industry from falling 15 percent between 1979 and 1989, due to increased mechanization and raw log exports. Continued cutting of the last ancient forests will do little to sustain timber industry jobs. Moreover, it will foreclose the option of diversifying from narrow wood-based economies to broader forest-based economies that capitalize on such nontimber values as tourism.[68]

In the tropics, the relatively small number of jobs in mechanized commercial logging are usually held by full-time workers in the industry who travel with the machines from place to place. Rarely do jobs go to local forest dwellers, whose poverty, ironically, is often cited as a reason to exploit forests for timber. Rather than benefiting local people, logging tends to impoverish them by disrupting their community-oriented forest management systems and depriving them of their sources of food, medicines, and other materials. Wherever logging operations are subsidized by the government, whole societies in effect pay to en-

rich a handful of loggers and wealthy timber concessionaires.[69]

As a prelude to a complete ban on primary forest logging, importing countries might levy a hefty surcharge on high-quality woods from primary forests. This would discourage inappropriate and wasteful uses, such as Japan's conversion of valuable tropical hardwoods into throwaway concrete moldings or the use of Canadian old-growth for pulp. Revenues from the levy could be used for a fund to compensate countries that lose vital export earnings, with the monies going to support conservation efforts, the creation of extractive reserves (areas managed sustainably for their nontimber products), or other needed investments.

Beyond safeguarding more primary forest from logging, eliminating government subsidies for timber harvesting is critical. In the United States, minimum bids for logging rights are set so low that timber sale revenues in 1989 failed to cover the government's costs in 102 out of the 120 national forests. The U.S. Forest Service spent more than $40 million each year during the eighties selling timber in the Tongass National Forest, but recouped barely 2 percent of that from Tongass timber revenues. Requiring timber sales from national forests to at least break even would help eliminate overcutting, would allow a larger area to be managed for recreation, biodiversity protection, and other forest functions, and, by valuing timber closer to its real cost, would promote more efficient use of wood.[70]

Reforms are equally needed to curb logging's destruction in tropical forests. Detailed studies by World Resources Institute (WRI) economist Robert Repetto and his colleagues have shown that logging concessions generally encourage practices irreparably damaging to forests. Most governments, for example, base logging fees on the volume of wood harvested rather than on the volume of merchantable timber in a given stand. This encourages the "high-grading" that destroys so many unwanted trees for every one cut. Contract terms often allow loggers to re-enter forests for a second cut before sufficient time for re-generation and recovery has passed. In Indonesia, for example, concession agreements typically allow a second harvest after just 20 years.[71]

Governments could also slow logging's destruction by capturing more of their fair share of the timber harvests' value. To entice foreign contractors, many nations have set appallingly low timber royalties. Between 1979 and 1982, for instance, the Philippines and Indonesia took in, respectively, only 17 percent and 38 percent of logging rents, the rest going to private, typically foreign concessionaires. The resulting high rates-of-return on logging investments have fueled rapacious overcutting. In recent years, a number of governments—including Ghana, Indonesia, and the Philippines—have taken steps to raise timber royalties and fees; in many cases, though, the reforms are too little, too late.[72]

Unfortunately, most major international initiatives launched to slow tropical deforestation have fallen far short of their missions, and urgently need redirection. Recent assessments of the Tropical Forestry Action Plan (TFAP) launched in 1985 by the World Bank, the U.N Development Programme, the U.N. Food and Agriculture Organization, and WRI strongly suggest it is more likely to accelerate deforestation than arrest it. The plan for Cameroon, for example, calls for a doubling of log production and the construction of a 600-kilometer road to open new areas of southern forest; astonishingly, it fails to even mention the 50,000 Pygmies who live in these areas. Peru's Forestry Action Plan calls for a four- to sevenfold increase in logging in Amazonia, while proposing no controls on the wave of colonization that will result from further opening up the forest.[73]

If the Tropical Forestry Action Plan is not fundamentally overhauled soon, it is best abandoned.

A sadly misused opportunity, the TFAP has so far done little more than coordinate donor efforts at business-as-usual forestry. In a recent review of the program, Robert Winterbottom of WRI states that "the TFAP should not encourage logging of remaining natural forests until a management system is in place and demonstrated to be both feasible and responsive to the needs and concerns of local communities." That this must even be said shows how far from sustainable development the TFAP has deviated. If it is not fundamentally overhauled soon, it is best abandoned.[74]

Efforts of the International Tropical Timber Organization, formed in 1985 and composed of 48 producing and consuming nations, have also generally been disappointing. The initial agreement called for national policies that encourage "sustainable utilization and conservation of tropical forests and their genetic resources," a unique mandate for a commodity organization. Based in Yokohama, Japan, the ITTO unfortunately has made little progress toward these goals. A positive step was taken, however, at the May 1990 meeting in Indonesia, when participants set the year 2000 as a target for the entire tropical timber trade to be based on sustainable production, though that remains undefined. While many countries cannot wait nine years for this to happen, the goal correctly focuses the ITTO on the sustainability of the timber trade rather than simply its promotion.[75]

In virtually all countries, wood-rich or wood-poor, increased investments in secondary forest management and tree plantations are essential to putting commercial forestry on a sustainable track. Rather than subsidizing uneconomic and destructive logging of national forests, the U.S. government, for instance, could give private nonindustrial landowners—who supply half the nation's timber—incentives to plant and manage more trees. In 1988, three federal assistance programs resulted in contracts with small farmers and woodland owners to seed and plant trees on 329,000 hectares, nearly a fourth of the total seeding and planting done that year. Government payments for these reforestation efforts totaled $37 million, less than it spent to open up roadless areas in the Tongass National Forest to below-cost timber sales.[76]

Chinese officials, faced with worsening wood shortages, have established a tree planting goal of 30 million hectares by the year 2000. And a new agency in India, the Technology Mission for Wasteland Development, has set a target of reforesting 17 million hectares by 1995, of which 6 million would be for industrial use. Achieving such high planting rates—and assuring the seedlings' survival—is no easy task, as shortfalls of past efforts have shown.[77]

Improving the efficiency of wood use and curbing the waste of forest products can greatly reduce harvest levels, easing pressures on forests. Yet rarely do governments or development agencies promote these measures. In many cases, the World Bank would do far more good for a country's economy and environment by investing in more-efficient plywood mills and paper recycling facilities than in opening up more forest to logging.

Few if any of the deepest reforms needed to make forestry sustainable will happen without international cooperation. The vested interests in logging the last tree are too strong, and governments too beholden to those interests—or too impoverished—to go it alone. At the Group of Seven Summit in Texas in July 1990, President George Bush proposed that negotiations begin on a global convention on forests, to be ready for signing by 1992. To pay more than lip service to this concept, the U.S. administration should actively support a ban on logging in the ancient forests of the Pacific Northwest, end subsidized timber sales in national forests, require federal offices to use recycled paper, and extend financial aid to poorer countries wishing to take similar measures.[78]

Putting forestry on a sustainable footing worldwide is as complex an undertaking as it is vital to the planet's health. The interests of indebted governments, indigenous forest dwellers, loggers, and local communities all come into play, as do concerns of people everywhere about the accelerating loss of species, global warming, and the destruction of irreplaceable ecosystems. Glimpses of a new kind of forestry, one that respects forests' diversity of life and multitude of benefits, inspire hope. But unless change comes soon, the next generation is guaranteed a vastly diminished biological inheritance.

6

Restoring the East European and Soviet Environments

Hilary F. French

When a relatively unknown Hungarian biologist named János Vargha began to campaign against a proposed hydroelectric dam on the Danube River in the early eighties, he could never have anticipated the flood he would unleash. Before the decade was over, mass protest against the dam was instrumental in the development of an effective political opposition in Hungary, which eventually undermined the Communist Party's exclusive hold on power.[1]

Elsewhere in the region, the environment in the pre-revolution days also served as a rallying point from which broader demands for political change emerged. Protests against pollution quickly turned into protests against Communist rule. Initially perceived by governments as relatively benign, envi-

An expanded version of this chapter appeared as Worldwatch Paper 99, *Green Revolutions: Environmental Reconstruction in Eastern Europe and the Soviet Union*.

ronmental movements in the region soon acquired unstoppable momentum.[2]

The political changes that swept both Eastern Europe and the Soviet Union over the past few years offer the hope of myriad positive changes, environmental reconstruction among them. But although the political climate has been transformed, the environmental problems remain. Under the assault of air pollution and acid deposition, medieval cities are blackened and crumbling, whole hillsides are deforested, and crop yields are diminishing. Rivers serve as open sewers, and clean drinking water is in scarce supply. Perhaps most alarming of all, people are dying from pollution: in the worst parts of the region, life expectancies are years lower and rates of cancer, reproductive problems, and a host of other ailments far higher than in cleaner areas.

Though bound together by the post–

World War II legacy of Communist rule and in some cases by a common Slavic heritage, Eastern Europe and the Soviet Union are distinct culturally, historically, and geographically. Many people in Eastern Europe underscore this point by referring to the region as Central Europe. But their shared experience with central planning and authoritarian regimes as well as their common current experience with momentous political change yield some similar environmental traits worth considering as a whole.

Throughout the region, cleaning up the environment is by no means a luxury.

Focusing on environmental issues will not be easy for Eastern Europe and the Soviet Union as they struggle with economic and political reform. The voices calling for the environment to be short-changed for budgetary and other reasons threaten to drown out those pushing for its restoration. And the short-term costs of environmental cleanup, such as investments in pollution control and jobs lost due to plant shutdowns, may be more readily apparent than the economic and quality-of-life benefits.

Throughout the region, however, cleaning up the environment is by no means a luxury. Though precise figures are hard to come by, economists estimate that environmental degradation is costing Poland 10–20 percent of its gross national product (GNP) every year and Czechoslovakia, 5–7 percent. The health costs alone of pollution in the Soviet Union were reported to be 190 billion rubles ($330 billion, at the October 1990 official rate) in 1987, or 11 percent of that nation's estimated GNP. Investments in environmental protection are

thus virtually guaranteed to provide economic benefits.[3]

The fate of the environment in the region is of concern not only to its residents but to the entire world. The Soviet Union pumps out 19 percent of world emissions of carbon dioxide (CO_2), the gas chiefly responsible for global warming. And a significant share of Eastern Europe's air and water pollution winds up in Western Europe. Indeed, investing in pollution control in East European countries is a cost-effective way for West European nations to clean up at home.[4]

Given the important role that environmental protest played in the recent upheavals in Eastern Europe and the Soviet Union, environmentalists can fairly claim a mandate for strong environmental controls. Respecting that call will require a sustained commitment from both national governments and the international community. Without it, damages will only mount.

INDUSTRIAL WASTELANDS

Until recently, billowing smokestacks were regarded as a symbol of national prowess in Eastern Europe and the Soviet Union. But the intense emphasis on rapid industrialization, widely celebrated in Communist propaganda posters, has exacted a heavy toll. Air and water pollution are at levels reminiscent of the fifties and sixties in the West. Pollutants not spewed into the air or water have been dumped on land. Hazardous waste disposal has apparently been largely unregulated.

Air pollution is staggering in the region. In Eastern Europe, the primary cause is the burning of indigenous supplies of lignite, also known as brown or soft coal. Lignite is low in energy content, and the variety burned there is high in sulfur. Prior to German unification, East Germany and Czechoslovakia burned nearly one third of the world's lignite. Many coal-burning plants in the region have no pollution control technology whatsoever; in those that do, the controls are significantly less effective at removing pollutants than western varieties.[5]

Extremely inefficient use of energy also contributes to degraded air quality. Government subsidies that keep energy costs very low and the lack of a meaningful pricing structure give industries and individuals little incentive to conserve. Thus, the region missed out on the large efficiency gains made elsewhere following the oil price increases of 1973 and 1979. Open-hearth steel manufacturing and other outdated, inefficient technologies are still widely used by East European and Soviet industries. On average, these countries use 50–100 percent more energy than the United States to produce a dollar of gross domestic product (GDP), and 100–300 percent more than Japan. (See Figure 6–1.)[6]

The combination of coal dependence, few pollution controls, and energy inefficiency has given Eastern Europe some of the highest sulfur dioxide (SO_2) levels in the world. Ranked by emissions per dollar of GNP, these countries are the most heavily polluting. (See Table 6–1.) A single lignite-burning power plant in the former East German town of Boxberg emits 460,000 tons of sulfur dioxide annually, more than Denmark and Norway combined.[7]

Emissions of nitrogen oxides (NO_x), which contribute to both acid deposition and ground-level ozone (formed when NO_x reacts in sunlight with hydrocarbons, and harmful to humans, crops, and trees), are also high. These emissions are caused by automobiles, factories, and power plants. Per unit of GNP, Czechoslovakia has the worst record, with Poland close behind.[8]

Auto emissions contribute a significant share of the total air pollution in spite of far lower car ownership rates than in the West because pollution per automobile is high. The Trabant and the Wartburg, from the former East Germany, are particularly dirty because of their two-stroke engines. These vehicles burn a combination of gasoline and oil, emitting far more hydrocarbons, particulates, and aldehydes (a class of organic chemicals), though fewer nitrogen oxides, than four-stroke engines do. Indeed, the smoking Trabants became a potent symbol of the area's environmental crisis when they started pouring across the border after the Berlin Wall came down. Other autos produced in the region have four-stroke engines, but are nonetheless more polluting than West European cars.[9]

Industrial emissions of a variety of toxic chemicals are also a major source of air pollution. Throughout Eastern Europe and the Soviet Union, highly polluting heavy industries were established in the postwar industrialization drive. In Hungary, for example, the chemical industry's share of gross production rose from 3.5 percent in 1950 to 19.1 percent in 1986. The economic base remains largely heavy-industry ori-

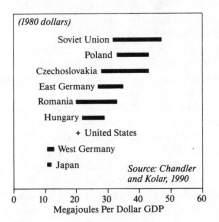

Figure 6-1. Estimated Energy Intensity, Selected Countries, 1985

Table 6-1. Emissions of Air Pollutants, Selected Countries, 1988[1]

Country	Nitrogen Oxides		Sulfur Dioxide	
	Emissions	Emissions Per Unit GNP	Emissions	Emissions Per Unit GNP
	(thousand tons)	(grams)	(thousand tons)	(grams)
East Germany	708	4	5,258	31
Czechoslovakia	950	8	2,800	24
Bulgaria	150	3	1,030	21
Poland	1,550	7	4,180	20
Romania[2]	390	4	1,800	19
Hungary	259	4	1,218	17
Soviet Union[3]	4,510	2	18,584	10
United Kingdom	2,480	3	3,664	5
United States[4]	19,800	4	20,700	4
Sweden	390	2	214	1
France	1,615	2	1,226	1
West Germany	2,860	3	1,300	1

[1]Preliminary data. [2]SO_2 estimate from 1980, NO_x estimate from 1985. [3]Stationary sources only; 1987 data. [4]Sulfur data are for sulfur oxides.
SOURCE: Worldwatch Institute, based on U.N. Economic Commission for Europe, *The State of Transboundary Air Pollution: 1989 Update* (Geneva: 1990); Christer Ågren, "Tracking Air Pollutants," *Acid News,* January 1, 1990. Emissions for United States from U.S. Environmental Protection Agency, *National Air Quality and Emissions Trends Report for 1988* (Washington, D.C.: 1990); Soviet data from unofficial translation of Statistical Supplement to USSR State Committee for the Protection of Nature, *Report on the State of the Environment in the USSR* (Moscow: 1989). Population data from Population Reference Bureau, *1988 World Population Data Sheet* (Washington, D.C.: 1988). GNP extrapolated from adjusted purchasing power parity 1980 levels in Paul Marer, *Dollar GNP's of the USSR and Eastern Europe* (Baltimore: Johns Hopkins University Press, 1985), using growth rates from U.S. Central Intelligence Agency, *Handbook of Economic Statistics* (Washington, D.C.: 1989).

ented, in contrast to the service-driven economy that has developed in the West. In each country of the region, industry accounts for more than half the economic base, and services, less than a quarter. In Sweden, in contrast, industry makes up only 32 percent of the total and services, 65 percent—a pattern found in other western countries.[10]

The area's heavy industries tend to be clumped in isolated geographic areas, where they pump large quantities of toxic fumes into the air. These industrial zones have some of the highest concentrations of pollution ever recorded. For example, the town of Yana in Bulgaria, midway between the Kremikovtsi metal works and a uranium mine, has been dubbed a "doomed village" by the local press owing to the high levels of toxic chemicals in the air. After medical evidence showed that only one out of every nine children in the village could be considered healthy, authorities decided to investigate the possibility of resettling all 1,550 residents.[11]

Complicating the picture is air pollution's transboundary nature. Sulfur dioxide emissions are continually traded back and forth between countries. East European countries export 68–97 percent of their SO_2 emissions, but then import 40–91 percent of the SO_2 deposited within their borders. Nor do toxic emissions respect borders. The town of Ruse, Bulgaria, has been poisoned over the years by chlorine emissions from a noxious Romanian plant just across the Danube. Protests against this factory in early 1987 constituted the first stirrings of environmentalism and antigovernment sentiment in Bulgaria. The plant's continuing emissions are becoming a major irritant in Bulgarian-Romanian relations.[12]

Industrial by-products not pumped into the air tend to be dumped into bodies of water at levels almost unimaginable in the West. The Buna chemical plant in the former East German district of Halle, for instance, discharges 20 kilograms of mercury every day—10 times as much as a chemical plant in the former West German district of Ludwigshafen does in an entire year. Industrial discharges, combined with untreated sewage and agricultural runoff, have contaminated most rivers, lakes, and seashores in Eastern Europe and the Soviet Union.[13]

In Czechoslovakia, only 40 percent of wastewater is adequately treated. In Hungary, some 1.3 billion cubic meters of untreated sewage are discharged into the country's surface waters every year. Half of Poland's cities, including Warsaw, and 35 percent of its industries do not treat their wastes at all. In 1988, the Soviet Union could adequately treat only 30 percent of its sewage. Half was improperly purified, and the remaining 20 percent was dumped into the environment raw. Many large Soviet cities, such as Kaunas in Lithuania and Riga, the capital of Latvia, still do not have any sewage treatment facilities.[14]

Clean drinking water is scarce throughout the region. Of Hungary's 3,000 towns and cities, around 700—home to some 300,000 people—now rely on bottled water or water piped in from neighboring communities because their own wells are contaminated with pesticides and nitrates from fertilizer runoff. Half of Czechoslovakia's drinking water does not meet the national health standards. Because of nitrate contamination, pregnant women and infants in Czechoslovakia are advised not to drink tap water in many regions. Sixty-five percent of Poland's river water is so corrosive that it is unfit for industrial use, let alone for drinking. And in the Soviet Union, 18 percent of water samples taken nationwide in 1988 failed to meet health standards.[15]

Industrial pollution and agricultural runoff in the Soviet Union are also threatening Lake Baikal, the largest body of fresh water in the world. The lake contains an astounding 80 percent of the country's supply of fresh water and supports 2,400 species of plants and animals, more than two thirds of which are found nowhere else on earth. A comprehensive plan was put in place in 1987 to clean up the offending enterprises; unfortunately, progress has been slow. By January 1989, only 26 of 41 environmental projects (such as improving sewage treatment and enforcing discharge limits from paper mills) had been completed as planned. Nearly two thirds of the projects that were scheduled to commence in 1988 never even started.[16]

Because many of the rivers of the region cross borders, water pollution is another source of international conflict. Romania's pollution of the Tisza River's headwaters has long been a point of contention with neighboring Hungary. In 1988, the Polish government asked Czechoslovakia to pay damages for the contamination of the Polish stretch of the Odra River caused by a heavy fuel-oil leak in November 1986. And the Danube travels through western Germany, Austria, Czechoslovakia, Yugoslavia, Bulgaria, Romania, and the Soviet Union, picking up industrial and biological waste along the way; few of the cities and towns on its East European route treat their sewage.[17]

The polluted rivers of the region ultimately find their way to the seas. Each year, for example, the Elbe carries 10 tons of mercury, 24 tons of cadmium, and 142 tons of lead through what was West Germany and then into the North Sea. The Caspian Sea receives 40 percent of the Soviet Union's 28.6 cubic kilometers of polluted wastewater annually, most of it from the Volga. The Black Sea receives 4,300 tons of nitrogen compounds, 900 tons of petroleum products, 600 tons of lead, and 200 tons of detergents from industrial wastes, much of it from the Danube and Dnieper rivers. The Baltic receives more than 46 percent of its nitrogen load and more than 53 percent of its organic waste from Poland, eastern Germany, and the Soviet Union, though they occupy only a third of its coastline. Poland's Vistula river is a prime culprit.[18]

The catastrophic state of these seas has economic repercussions. At one time, the Caspian held 90 percent of the Soviet Union's caviar-producing sturgeon fishery. But populations of sturgeon and other valuable fish have declined by between 66 and 96 percent over the past 20 years. On the Black Sea, fish populations are dropping precipitously as a hydrogen sulfide cloud rises toward the surface. Beaches along these two seas and the Baltic have had to close periodically over the last few years because of pollution. Resorts such as Yalta on the Black Sea and Yurmala on the Baltic are imperiled as a result.[19]

Though data are scarce, hazardous wastes appear to have been indiscriminately dumped throughout the region. Some 15,000 dump sites are awaiting evaluation in former East German territory. Prague's city planners cannot account for 80 percent of the estimated 40,000 tons of hazardous waste produced in the city annually. Little wonder, then, that illegal dumps are being uncovered throughout Czechoslovakia. For instance, the national radio station reported that a dump with 3,500 tons of toxic waste containing nerve poison was discovered near Karlovy Vary, a spa famous for its mineral hot springs.[20]

In the Soviet Union, over half of nearly 6,000 official landfills do not meet sanitary regulations. In the republics of Uzbekistan, Georgia, Moldavia, Latvia, and Turkmenistan, over three quarters of the landfills do not comply with regulations. Again, of greatest concern is illegal dumping. One of the more notorious cases occurred in Sillamae in northeast Estonia. When 300 children attending two kindergartens began to lose their hair, residents were horrified but baffled. Eventually, after months of speculation, the former director of a local factory revealed that his company had dumped radioactive wastes where the schools were later built.[21]

THE HEALTH TOLL

Of all the data from Eastern Europe and the Soviet Union released in the last year, perhaps none are as shocking as the health statistics. Shortened life expectancies, soaring cancer rates, and a score of other maladies have been recorded in highly polluted regions. Residents of the hardest hit areas do not need statistical confirmation of the toll taken on their health: in the northern Bohemia region of Czechoslovakia, home to much of the country's heavy industry and power plants, residents term the financial compensation they receive for living there "burial money."[22]

Because environmental factors are superimposed on a more general health care crisis, sorting out precise causes and consequences is impossible. Poor diets and high rates of smoking and alcohol use are thought to contribute heavily to adverse health trends. Inadequate health care systems are also to blame. Interactions between the various factors combine to create a situation where the whole is undoubtedly worse than the sum of its parts. Though it is difficult to pinpoint the role played by environmental factors in the region's health crisis, a mounting body of evidence suggests it is a substantial one.[23]

The Soviet Ministry of Public Health has studied the health of populations where industrial pollution is unusually high. According to the national environmental report, air pollution levels are clearly linked to the incidences of a variety of ailments. The higher the overall level of pollution, the higher the rates of malignant tumors, respiratory disease, and skin disease. The Ministry also found a correlation between the types of sickness observed and the kind of industry in the region. Fertilizer production appeared to be related to an increase in cancer rates and in blood and cardiovascular diseases. Nonferrous metal works were associated with increased cancer rates among children and with skin disease. Young children in regions where pesticide use is high have overall sickness rates five times those of children living in relatively clean areas.[24]

Recent disclosures of the scope of the Chernobyl disaster have shocked the public in the Soviet Union. As a result of newly released information about the extent of the fallout, 200,000 evacuations are expected by 1992 from contaminated areas in the Ukraine, Byelorussia, and the Russian republics. Concern is rising that the health impact of the disaster may be far greater than originally supposed. Soviet authorities now admit that the thyroid glands of more than 150,000 people were "seriously affected" by radioactive iodine, that rates of thyroid cancer among people living in the affected area are 5 to 10 times higher than would normally be expected, and that leukemia rates among children are

two to four times normal levels. Though debate rages over whether these increases can be attributed to the accident, numerous reports of grossly deformed farm animals being born in the contaminated zone do not lend comfort to the many people convinced their health is endangered.[25]

Concern is rising that the health impact of the Chernobyl disaster may be far greater than originally supposed.

Long-rumored stories of reduced life expectancy in the most polluted regions of Eastern Europe are also beginning to be confirmed. In the dirtiest areas of Czechoslovakia, life expectancy is as much as five years less than in relatively clean parts of the country. In heavily industrialized Silesia, Poland, people die three to four years younger than the average for the rest of the country. In Halle, Germany, a center of the chemical industry, people can expect to live five years less than their neighbors in what was East Germany. People born and raised in environmental disaster areas are only now entering middle age, and many of them may become ill in the years ahead.[26]

Research conducted by Dr. Kiriaki Basmadjieva of the Bulgarian Health Ministry reveals that asthma and ulcer rates among people living near heavy industrial complexes in Bulgaria are nine times those of people living in relatively pristine areas; rates of skin disease are some seven times higher, of rickets and liver diseases four times higher, and of hypertension and nervous system diseases three times as high. Children in the industrial town of Kuklen, Bulgaria, have so much lead in their blood that they would be rushed to a hospital for detoxification if they lived in the United States, according to Dr. Ellen Silbergeld, a toxicologist with the Environmental Defense Fund.[27]

Researchers at the Institute of Hygiene and Epidemiology in Prague have also found a correlation in areas of Czechoslovakia between high air pollution levels and elevated rates of a number of health problems, including acute respiratory illnesses. Children in these regions exhibit retarded bone development, diminished immunity, and a higher incidence of enlarged lymph nodes and cranial infections. In areas with high lead and arsenic pollution, hair samples indicate heightened levels of these heavy metals in childrens' hair. Over the last decade, the number of people suffering from pollen allergies increased by six times in adults and tenfold in children, with about 30 percent of all children suffering from some kind of allergy.[28]

The state of health in Hungary, as elsewhere in the region, is clearly on the decline. Heart disease and cancer rates are increasing, leading to shorter life expectancies. Rising mortality rates coincide with a period of growing pollution, but showing a causal relationship is problematic. Yet studies in the industrial cities of Dorog, Ajka, and Pápa demonstrated that children living in highly polluted air develop twice as many diseases of the upper respiratory system as do those living in areas with clean air. Asthmatic diseases are also on the rise in polluted areas. Another report established a correlation between the incidence of congenital birth defects and environmental pollution. According to the National Institute of Public Health, 1 out of every 24 disablements and 1 out of every 17 deaths in Hungary is caused by air pollution.[29]

In Poland, several illnesses—including tuberculosis, pneumonia, bronchitis, and leukemia—are more common in heavily polluted areas. A collaborative report prepared by the Institute for Environmental Engineering in Zabrze, Upper Silesia, and the Environment Center of Berlin indicates that residents of Upper Silesia have 155 percent more circulatory illnesses, 30 percent more cancer, and 47 percent more respiratory illness than the national average. Researchers believe these trends help explain why life expectancy for Polish men aged 40–60 has fallen back to 1952 levels.[30]

Though the links between them are obvious, public health and environmental quality are viewed all too often as separate domains. In Eastern Europe and the Soviet Union, the connection is indisputable. Unless environmental quality is restored, improving the population's poor state of health will be an uphill battle.

DIMINISHED BIOLOGICAL PRODUCTIVITY

Just as the health of humans is threatened in Eastern Europe and the Soviet Union, so is that of plants and animals. Agricultural productivity is declining in response to land degradation and pollution, forests are ravaged by both air pollution and acid rain, and biodiversity is threatened. In essence, the natural resource base that underlies the economy is dangerously depleted.

Land degradation is a major barrier to raising agricultural productivity in the Soviet Union. At least 1.5 billion tons of topsoil erode away annually. Roughly two thirds of arable land, some 152 million hectares, has lost fertility because of wind and water erosion. Production losses attributable to soil erosion cost the Soviet economy 18–20 billion rubles

($31–35 billion) annually. Twelve percent of irrigated farmland, amounting to 2.5 million hectares, is contaminated with salt or salt compounds due to poor drainage systems. Between 1975 and 1985, the area of salinized land nearly doubled.[31]

The Aral Sea disaster is an infamous example of the land degradation that can result from faulty irrigation practices. Until 1973, the Aral was the fourth largest inland body of water in the world. But water from the two rivers that feed it, the Amu Darya and the Syr Darya, has been diverted to irrigate cotton and other crops. As a result, since 1960 the Aral's volume has dropped 66 percent, its surface area has decreased 40 percent, and its level has fallen nearly 13 meters. The former seabed has become a saline desert from which vast dust storms sweep up salt and sand that is then deposited on the surrounding farmland at a rate of almost half a ton per hectare each year.[32]

Several East European countries also report growing problems with land degradation. In Bulgaria, 80 percent of cultivable land is affected by erosion. In Czechoslovakia, 54 percent of agricultural land is endangered by water- and wind-induced soil erosion; about 5 million tons of soil are lost annually. In both Hungary and Romania, water and wind erosion endanger more than 30 percent of arable land. Several countries also report salinization and waterlogging problems.[33]

Fertilizer and pesticide use in the countries of the region varies considerably. Although use per hectare in general is on a par with that in the West, the chemicals are often applied inappropriately. Prices for these agricultural inputs are heavily subsidized, leading farmers to dump more and more of them on the land whether they are raising yields commensurately or not. Application rates are often determined by a planner in a farwaway city who is unlikely to know the appropriate rates or whether a pest has developed resistance to a chemical, rendering it ineffective.

In the Soviet Union, an audit conducted by the State Planning Office (Gosplan) found that 11 percent of fertilizer production never reaches the field because of transport and storage problems. *Pravda*, perhaps only half in jest, suggested that Soviet farmers should sow their crops along the railroad tracks because so much fertilizer is lost on the way from the factory to the farm. Similar problems plague pesticide use. According to Alexei Yablokov, Deputy Chair of the Supreme Soviet's environmental committee and a leading environmentalist, nearly a third of all pesticides used in the country are lost on their way to the fields. The Soviet statistical agency (Goskomstat) reports that soils have been significantly contaminated by pesticides in Azerbaijan, Armenia, Kirghizia, Moldavia, Tajikistan, and Uzbekistan.[34]

In the Soviet Union, at least 1.5 billion tons of topsoil erode away annually.

Industrial pollution is lowering crop yields. Many different pollutants are thought to contribute to the problem, including acid deposition, low-level ozone, and heavy metals. By unhappy coincidence, the major pollution sources in the Soviet Union are located in agricultural areas. The worst culprits are the metallurgical centers: in 1988, for example, lead concentration in soils surrounding Glubokoe, a nonferrous metallurgical center, were found to be 22 times the permitted level, while cobalt and zinc concentrations exceeded allowed levels by 10 and 100 times, respectively. In Czechoslovakia, yields of alfalfa, cereals, and lettuce are thought to be affected by pollution; sulfur dioxide-induced crop damage is estimated to cost the economy 3 billion koruna ($192 million) annually.[35]

Forests are also at risk. Air pollution-related forest damage in Eastern Europe is among the worst in the world. Woodlands in the brown coal belt of southeastern Germany, southern Poland, and northern Czechoslovakia are dying or dead. Vast expanses of mountaintops are filled with skeleton-like trees. A count by the U.N. Economic Commission for Europe (ECE) in 1989 found 82 percent of Poland's forests showing some signs of damage, 78 percent of Bulgaria's, 73 percent of Czechoslovakia's, 57 percent of East Germany's, and 36 percent of Hungary's.[36]

According to the Soviet national environmental report, forest damage from industrial air emissions is becoming increasingly severe. Extensive regions near several industrial cities have been affected over the last 20 years. The report implicates sulfur dioxide, nitrogen oxides, hydrogen fluoride, and ammonia emissions in the damage. The forest damage problem previously had not been acknowledged, and detailed data have yet to be released. But a photo of the Noril'sk region provides some chilling evidence—vast tracts of dead stumps.[37]

Attesting to the extent of overall biological impoverishment is the region's diminishing diversity of life: In the Soviet Union, every tenth bird species, every fifth plant and mammal species, and every fourth amphibian and reptile species is endangered. Fifty-three animal species and 40 plant species have become extinct in Hungary over the last century. The Bulgarian Academy of Sciences has declared 150 animal and 763 plant species endangered or rare, a situation partly caused by encroachment of development on the region's plentiful nature reserves.[38]

GREEN MOVEMENTS

The magnitude of the environmental problems in Eastern Europe and the Soviet Union has produced a broad-based green movement. (See Table 6–2.) In the space of just a few years, environmental activism has come out from underground, forming an integral part of the new political landscape. The successes this young movement can claim are nothing short of remarkable given the obstacles placed in its way. Until recently, independent nongovernmental organizing was strictly illegal throughout the region, and environmental data and information were tightly guarded state secrets. Many challenges lie ahead, however, as the movement adapts to rapidly changing political circumstances.[39]

Though Soviet environmentalists only recently have been allowed to play an active and open political role, the roots of their movement run deep. As many ecologists there like to point out, the Soviet Union made some early contributions to environmental thought in the pre-Communist era. V.I. Vernadsky, for one, in the late nineteenth century developed a concept of the world being divided into the biosphere and the "noosphere"—that part of the natural world under the influence of human activity. Though conservationists were respected in the early years of Communist rule, they were attacked in the thirties by Stalinists who felt that the natural world was to be exploited.[40]

In the sixties, a student nature protection movement developed at Moscow State University that fought for nature preserves and the protection of bio-

Table 6-2. The Environmental Movement in Eastern Europe and the Soviet Union, Mid-1990

Country	Description
Bulgaria	Ecoglasnost, which played role in unseating Prime Minister Zhivkov, now active as both environmental group and political party. Recently posted highest approval rating of any political party. There is also another Green Party, and at least 18 other groups.
Czechoslovakia	Official environmental groups from old era, such as Brontosaurus and Czech and Slovak Unions of Nature Protectors, now independent and being joined by many small groups. The Green Circle is umbrella organization for three major groups and 30 smaller ones. There is a national Green Party and "Trend of the Third Millenium," a Slovakian Green party.
East Germany	The network ARK, which developed before the revolution under auspices of the Lutheran Church, merged with other groups in 1990 to form the Green League. Green Party established in late 1989. With political union, environmental movements and Green parties merging.
Hungary	In Budapest, environmental movement emerged out of battle against the Danube Dam. Environmental research institute called ISTER established, along with an Independent Ecological Center serving as a resource group for many local groups. Several small Green parties exist.
Poland	Polish Ecological Club grew out of Solidarity in early eighties. Some leading members now have environmental posts in new government. Several Green parties exist, as well as more than 40 groups, including the Green Federation, Zoology and Health, and the Franciscan Ecological Movement.
Romania	MER (Ecological Movement of Romania), which operates as both environmental group and Green Party, has taken on leading role. Several small Green parties outside of MER. By one estimate, 112 local groups with some 100,000 members.
Soviet Union	Four umbrella organizations—the Social Ecological Union, the Ecological Union, Ecology and Peace, and the Green Movement—attempting to link numerous local groups into national movement. Viable Green parties in Latvia, Lithuania, Estonia, Moldavia, Byelorussia, and the Ukraine.

SOURCES: Worldwatch Institute, based on sources documented in endnote 39.

diversity. The movement was tolerated so long as it stuck to nature protection; confronting industrial pollution was considered to be subversive. During the same period, a movement of writers, scientists, and other intellectuals launched a crusade to save Lake Baikal. A variation on this same group coalesced in the early eighties to stop a grandiose plan that would have reversed the direction of Siberian rivers in order to irrigate arid Soviet central Asia. In 1986, the group achieved a major victory when the new General Secretary, Mikhail Gorbachev, mothballed the river diversion scheme.[41]

The Polish Ecological Club was the first fully independent environmental group established in Eastern Europe.

These early efforts revolved around a small, elite group that was able to exert influence through back channels to those in power. In the words of Russian environmentalist Natalya Yourina: "In the sixties, only individuals protested. A movement didn't exist." This changed when the Chernobyl disaster in April 1986 combined with *glasnost* to give rise to a widespread movement encompassing diverse segments of society. Across the vast nation, people began to protest in a fashion never before witnessed in the Soviet Union. Haltingly at first, and with greater confidence as they stretched the limits of official tolerance, thousands and sometimes tens of thousands turned out for mass demonstrations to protest nuclear power plants, air and water pollution, beach closings, and all manner of environmental degradation.[42]

In the republics, most of which are struggling for some measure of sovereignty if not complete independence from Moscow, environmentalism tends to take on highly political overtones. Protests about pollution in the early days of *glasnost* in the Baltic republics quickly turned into independence movements. Now environmentalism is helping to fan the nationalist fire in the Ukraine and other republics. Currently, many of these "nationalist environmentalists" are preoccupied with independence politics. If and when the republics do become independent, they will have the opportunity to use their newfound autonomy to improve conditions.[43]

Though most environmental groups in the Soviet Union are focused around local issues, efforts are being made to coordinate their work at the national level. The Social Ecological Union is an umbrella group for more than 150 nongovernmental organizations (NGOs) in 260 cities and towns. Other coordinating bodies include the Association for the Support of Ecological Initiatives, the Ecological Union, Ecology and Peace, and the Green Movement. The groups vary in their levels of cooperation with the government, with some intentionally taking a confrontational stance while others try to work from within the system. For now, they are overwhelmingly amateur operations, working out of committed peoples' apartments on shoestring budgets.[44]

Independent environmentalism in Eastern Europe has just emerged in the last few years. Previously, official nature protection clubs existed that mainly focused on the politically "safe" issues of wildlife conservation and nature reserves. In addition to these, some dissident groups viewed environmental issues as part of their agenda. For example, the Czechoslovakian Charter 77 movement clandestinely published a report in 1983 produced by members of the ecological section of the Czechoslovakian Academy of Sciences detailing the scope of the country's environmental catastrophe and its impact on human health. The study was smuggled to western newspapers, and then made its way back into the country via radio broadcasts.[45]

In September 1980, during the liberalization that accompanied Solidarity's rise, the Polish Ecological Club was founded in Krakow, Poland. It was the first fully independent environmental group established in Eastern Europe. After the revolutions, officially sponsored nature protection groups became independent, underground dissident groups surfaced, and many new groups formed. Independent environmental movements now exist in every East European country, although the Romanian movement still reports some repression. These groups are struggling with organizational questions: What kind of relationship should they have with government environment ministries? What should their platform be? How should they fund themselves? Is there room for a variety of groups with different approaches?[46]

The Green movements in the region are also trying their hand at electoral politics. Each East European country now has a Green Party, as do the Soviet republics of Latvia, Lithuania, Estonia, Moldavia, Byelorussia, and the Ukraine. In Bulgaria, Ecoglasnost (the movement that helped unseat President Zhivkov) and the Green Party together hold 32 seats in Parliament. The Green Party holds seven seats in the Estonian Parliament, six seats each in the Latvian and Slovakian bodies, and nine in the Lithuanian. And in the Romanian legislature, the Green Party and the Green Movement hold 23 seats between them.[47]

Although the Green Parties did not do as well as initially expected in the spring 1990 elections, their loss is in some sense a measure of the movement's success: virtually all the competing political parties had strong environmental plat-

forms. For many parties, however, including a clause on environmental degradation in the platform was simply another way of criticizing the old regime. The fledgling environmental movement faces the task of pressuring the new governments to abide by their campaign promises.[48]

OFFICIAL RESPONSES

Though their environments do not show it, both the Soviet Union and East European countries have stringent environmental regulations on the books. Air and water quality standards actually tend to be stricter than those of western nations because they are based on a scientific determination of the level necessary to avoid health problems. Unlike in the West, the standards do not have to survive the vicissitudes of the political process.

Unfortunately, enforcement of these laws has been poor. Because most industry continues to be state-owned, the regulator and the regulated are one and the same, posing a formidable conflict of interest. Moreover, the ministries charged with industry, agriculture, and forestry have considerably more clout than the new agencies charged with environmental enforcement. The production ministries have often succeeded in getting themselves exempted from fines. The penalties that are levied have barely made a dent: the offending industry, being state-owned and monopolistic, simply passes the bill on to the central government. Thus the production target—the overriding goal for which a plant manager is rewarded or penalized—is unaffected.[49]

Efforts to reform environmental policymaking depend on the broader political transformations now under way. The strength of Soviet regulatory institutions, for example, will be influenced by President Gorbachev's plan to transfer power away from the Communist Party toward the executive branch and the legislature (the Congress of Peoples' Deputies and the Supreme Soviet).[50]

Goskompriroda, the Soviet environment agency, was created in early 1988. It was charged with coordinating work previously spread out among many ministries, and was given broad enforcement powers over other agencies. Unfortunately, Goskompriroda was beset by early problems, such as the resignation of its first head and an unwillingness on the part of other ministries to cede jurisdiction. Hopes for the agency were raised in late 1989 by the appointment of a new Minister, Nikolai Vorontsov, a highly regarded biologist and the first non–Communist Party member ever to hold a ministerial post.[51]

The Congress of Peoples' Deputies and the Supreme Soviet are playing an active role in the reform of environmental policies. According to one analysis, as many as 300 deputies (13 percent) could be classified as Greens. During the first meeting of the Soviet Congress, 80 percent of the speeches reportedly contained references to the environment. This created public momentum for aggressive governmental cleanup efforts. The Supreme Soviet now has an Ecology Committee with many prominent and highly respected scientists, writers, and environmental activists as members.[52]

Together, Goskompriroda and the Supreme Soviet are in the process of overhauling the country's environmental legislation. A major bill the agency sent to the Supreme Soviet in the fall of 1989 called for, in Vorontsov's words, "the primacy of ecology over economics, of the interests of citizens over the interests of departments." It also called for environmental impact assessments, public

participation in decision making, and the establishment of fees for the use of natural resources. The Supreme Soviet responded with a resolution of its own, which called for a variety of measures roughly in parallel with the Goskompriroda proposal.[53]

As discussion continues on these long-term measures, the public is increasingly demanding immediate results. The easiest response for the government has been to simply close plants. In 1989, 240 factories in the Soviet Union were shut down for environmental reasons. As a result, 1990 output will be reduced by 5.2 million tons of fertilizer, 951,000 tons of soda, 400,000 tons of cellulose, 387,000 tons of methanol, and over 250,000 tons of synthetic rubber, among other goods. Such losses could lead to a backlash: many plants producing essential medicines and scarce paper have been closed. When the heavily polluting Sloka pulp and paper mill in Jurmala, Latvia, was shut down, for instance, the republic's newspapers ceased to appear for lack of newsprint.[54]

Across the region, perhaps no issue has been as contentious as nuclear power. Though governments continue to voice commitment to their nuclear programs, the disclosures about Chernobyl and new information about brushes with serious accidents in Eastern Europe have undermined public faith. In the face of public concern, the future of the region's nuclear programs is seriously in doubt. Plans for 30 nuclear power plants in the Soviet Union have been abandoned or indefinitely suspended since Chernobyl. In Eastern Europe, four operating reactors have been shut down since December 1989 and construction was halted or plans were canceled for 14 reactors.[55]

The new governments in Eastern Europe are also beginning to formulate broader environmental strategies. Though many of the declarations of environment ministries and newly formed parliaments are impressive, it remains to be seen how they will fare against entrenched economic interests and the public's longing for rapid improvements in material well-being.

Eastern Germany is a special case, as it is now part of a unified Germany. Newly built factories, smokestacks, or engines must meet standards of the former West Germany; existing enterprises have until the end of the decade to either conform or close down. For the other countries of the region, however, there is no "rich uncle." Still, Poland and Czechoslovakia are both launching ambitious cleanup plans.[56]

In Poland, new Minister of the Environment Bronislaw Kaminski has already publicized a "hit list" of 80 major industrial polluters. The ministry and local authorities will develop a timetable for bringing these enterprises into compliance with environmental regulations or shutting them down. Additionally, loopholes for polluters will be closed, existing environmental legislation overhauled, and environmental auditing required. Kaminski has also outlined an extensive program of environmental protection investments, including 3,000 new wastewater treatment plants, to be completed by 1995.[57]

In Czechoslovakia, President Vaclav Havel made it clear from the beginning of his term that the environment would be a priority. In his address upon becoming Provisional President on New Year's Day 1990, Havel stated: "We have laid waste to our soil and the rivers and the forests that our forefathers bequeathed to us, and we have the worst environment in the whole of Europe today." He proceeded to appoint prominent environmentalists to head up environmental agencies at the Czech and Slovak republic and federal levels.[58]

Minister of the Environment Josef Vavroušek recently spelled out a policy designed to make environmental protection a central element in Czechoslovakia's shift to a market economy. Under his plan, financial incentives—such as emissions taxes or refundable deposits—would play a large role. Vavroušek says the environmental plan must succeed, even "at the cost of delaying the growth of material consumption." He is expected to soon send to Parliament draft laws calling for environmental impact assessment, tightened waste management, and air pollution regulations. Though his proposals are good, environmentalists fear that they will be opposed by other ministries and interests. Indeed, an economic plan presented in September 1990 did not incorporate Vavroušek's proposals.[59]

During the first meeting of the Soviet Congress, 80 percent of the speeches reportedly contained references to the environment.

Hungary, Bulgaria, and Romania are moving somewhat more slowly. Hungary still has a relatively ineffective environment ministry that until September 1990 was combined with a public-works-style water development agency. It is too soon to tell whether the separation of the agencies will enable the environment ministry to pursue its mandate more effectively. The Prime Minister of Bulgaria presented a $1.2-billion plan in March 1990 to combat industrial pollution, but skeptics question whether the government will be able to come up with this sum. In Romania, environmentalists did not waste much time taking advantage of the revolution: a new environment ministry was formed on December 28, 1989, just days after Ceausescu loyalists stopped shooting on the streets of Bucharest. Unfortunately, continuing political instability in Romania does not bode well for the environment receiving soon the attention it needs.[60]

A Policy Agenda

Given the degraded environment's toll on human health and biological productivity, decontaminating Eastern Europe and the Soviet Union is best seen as a precondition to economic development, not an obstacle. Many of the most polluting plants would be closed for purely economic reasons during a transformation from an industrial-based economy to a more service- and consumer goods-oriented one. As new investment occurs, it can be marshaled to help meet environmental needs.

The challenge is to design cleanup programs that offer maximum long-term gain for minimum short-term cost.

But cleaning up the region will cause large short-term economic and social dislocations. According to the German Institute of Ecological Economic Research, bringing eastern Germany's environment up to the new Germany's standards will take 10 years and cost $249–308 billion. Poland's environment minister estimates that improving the situation in that country will cost $20 billion over the next 10–20 years. Czechoslovakians believe they will need to spend at least $23.7 billion on pollution control in the next 15 years. According to one estimate, the Soviet Union must spend 100 billion rubles ($174 billion) initially and then 10 billion rubles annually just to cut air pollution to the ac-

cepted limits. In addition, many jobs are threatened: the closing of just one chemical works at the notoriously polluted Bitterfeld plant in eastern Germany put 10,000 people out of work. Thus the challenge is to design cleanup programs that offer maximum long-term gain for minimum short-term cost.[61]

Eastern Europe and the Soviet Union have a unique opportunity to cull from 20 years of western experience in addressing environmental problems. They could "leapfrog" the West in both policies and technologies. By implementing strategies that have proved most effective, this region could realize the greatest possible return on environmental investments.

One such strategy is to encourage energy efficiency. (See Chapter 2.) This is particularly important in light of pent-up demand for consumer goods that, as it is met, could lead to large increases in energy consumption. Energy efficiency offers the advantage of being both economically and environmentally beneficial. The less energy burned, the less pollution produced. And the savings from forgoing construction of new power plants can more than offset the costs of installing pollution control technologies such as scrubbers on existing plants.[62]

As these nations move toward a greater reliance on markets, energy efficiency will improve. Higher energy prices and the profit motive will spur conservation. Energy-hungry heavy industries are likely to prove uncompetitive under such a shift. Aggressive efforts to replace outmoded equipment with more efficient technologies would yield still greater returns. According to case studies coordinated by William Chandler of Pacific Northwest Laboratories, the Soviet Union could reduce projected energy consumption over the next 15 years by an amount equal to a quarter of current levels and Poland by an amount equal to 40 percent of current levels while still saving money: it would cost less to invest in efficient technologies than to build new power plants.[63]

Unfortunately, golden opportunities are being lost. For example, the U.S. Overseas Private Investment Corporation recently underwrote General Electric's $150-million project to refurbish 13 Hungarian incandescent light bulb factories. If this money had been spent instead on plants to manufacture compact fluorescent bulbs, it could have saved the Hungarian government $10 billion in the construction of new coal-fired, polluting power plants.[64]

Transportation policy also presents leapfrogging opportunities. Two decades of attempts to improve urban air quality in the West have made it clear that combatting automotive pollution by technological means, such as catalytic converters, is not sufficient. Increasingly

large car fleets have wiped out any gains. Recognizing this, many North Americans regret that they allowed their public transportation systems to atrophy.[65]

In Eastern Europe and the Soviet Union, in contrast, public transportation systems are extensive and widely used. Hungary, for example, relies on public transport for 58 percent of total passenger trips and automobiles for 11 percent, while in the United States only 3 percent of trips are made by public transportation and 82 percent by car. (See Table 6–3.) There is a danger that public transportation in Eastern Europe and the Soviet Union will go the way it did in the United States, as consumers fulfill long-standing dreams of auto ownership. Careful public policy decisions could prevent this by treating automobiles as one component, rather than the dominant player, in a diversified transportation scheme. (See Chapter 4.)

Without measures to encourage recy-

Table 6-3. Share of Urban Passenger Trips by Transportation Mode, Selected Countries[1]

Country	Auto	Pedestrians and Bicyclists	Public Transport
		(percent)	
Soviet Union[2]	12	—	88
Poland[2]	15	—	85
Hungary	11	31	58
Czechoslovakia	13	35	52
East Germany	24	48	27
United Kingdom	45	33	19
Sweden	36	49	11
France	47	35	11
West Germany	48	40	11
Netherlands[3]	45	48	5
United States	82	10	3

[1]Data range from 1978 to 1987, depending on the most recent year for which information is available, and reflect split of modes for all trip purposes; due to variations in measurement, sum of shares for any one country may not equal 100 percent.   [2]Data refer only to automobiles and public transport, and thus exclude pedestrian and bicycle trips.

SOURCE: John Pucher, "Capitalism, Socialism, and Urban Transportation: Policies and Travel Behavior in the East and West," *Journal of the American Planning Association*, Summer 1990.

cling and waste reduction, production of household garbage in the region is likely to skyrocket as western packaging practices take hold. The republic of Russia now produces about 186 kilograms of household and commercial waste per capita annually; the former West Germany, by comparison, produced 473 kilograms per person. In the industrial arena, western experience shows that reducing the amount of waste generated in the production process is cleaner and often cheaper than trying to trap emissions or effluents at the end of a pipe. (See Chapter 3.)[66]

It would be unfortunate if Eastern Europe and the Soviet Union followed the West down the path toward wanton materialism. Many of the region's intellectuals who led the recent revolutions are wary of consumerism. In his essay "The Power of the Powerless," Czech President Vaclav Havel writes of "the omnipresent dictatorship of consumption, production, advertising, commerce, and consumer culture" in the West. But most of the region's people, who often lack even basic goods such as soap, are understandably unenthused by the notion of restraining consumption. The challenge is to find the proper balance between sufficiency and excess. (See Chapter 9.)[67]

The move toward market-based pricing offers environmental bonuses. As energy, water, and other industrial and agricultural resources are priced closer to their market value, it will create an incentive to conserve. However, the market is by no means a panacea; it fails miserably at taking environmental costs into account. Eastern Europe and the Soviet Union might look seriously at measures now under study in the West to help correct this. For example, many governments are now considering expanding their use of eco-taxes, which penalize activities that pollute or degrade the environment. (See Chapter 10.)[68]

International cooperation will be critical to the region's restoration. At the nongovernmental level, environmentalists in both the Soviet Union and Eastern Europe are increasingly cultivating ties with western environmental groups and Green parties. The Green parties of countries bordering the Baltic Sea, for instance, have established the Balto-Scandian Information Center to press governments to respect previous commitments to reduce discharges into the sea. A "Common House of Europe" project among East and West European NGOs is pushing for converting former border areas into parks.[69]

At the governmental level, environmental aid programs for Eastern Europe have blossomed over the past year. The World Bank made an $18-million loan to Poland to help improve environmental management practices, and a loan for Hungary is in preparation. One arm of the Nordic Investment Bank, the Nordic Environmental Financing Corporation, is expected to approve its first investments in Eastern Europe soon—$45 million to help establish joint venture projects to reduce air and water pollution and improve energy efficiency. The new European Bank for Reconstruction and Development may be another important contributor. An international NGO campaign succeeded in placing an environmental mandate in the bank's charter; it remains to be seen if it will be honored when the bank begins lending in March 1991.[70]

The European Community has so far committed $131 million for environmental programs in Bulgaria, Czechoslovakia, the former East Germany, Hungary, and Poland. These countries will be included in the new European Environmental Agency, a primary function of which will be the collection of uniform, continent-wide environmental data. In another multilateral effort, a regional center in Budapest initiated by the United States and funded by it along with the European Community, Austria, Canada, Finland, Hungary, the Netherlands, and Norway opened its doors in September 1990. The center will mediate between advocacy groups and the governments of the region, according to Peter Hardi, the center's executive director.[71]

Bilateral programs are also flourishing. The United States has provided Hungary and Poland with $40 million in environmental aid, and will soon provide funds as well to Bulgaria, Czechoslovakia, and Romania. In addition to its commitment to clean up the eastern part of its new nation, Germany has launched a $120-million aid program for Poland, which also expects to receive $60 million from Sweden, $70 million from Denmark, and $35 million from Finland.[72]

The reluctance of the United States and, until recently, Western Europe to provide financial help to the Soviet Union means that little, if any, western governmental money has yet reached there for environmental assistance. However, the Soviets have been cooperating with western countries on a non-remunerative basis for decades. Some projects that involve financial transfers now appear to be in the works: the European Community and the Soviet Union are working on a joint nuclear safety project, and the Norwegian, Finnish, and Swedish governments plan to help install pollution controls on two Soviet nickel smelters that export acidic emissions to Scandinavia.[73]

The aid offered so far will help, but the funds set aside for the environment are very small compared with the total packages of economic assistance. Thus, it is important that environmental considerations form an integral component of all aid and trade deliberations. Lending for isolated environmental schemes at the same time as giving larger amounts of funding for damaging industrial, trans-

port, or energy projects is like taking a small step forward and then a giant step back.

The West has an obvious role in preventing "ecological colonialism"—the export of environmentally hazardous forms of resource extraction or industry to countries with lax regulations and a thirst for hard currency. For example, an enormous petrochemical complex being built in the Tyumen region of Siberia by Japanese, American, German, and Italian firms is raising the ire of Soviet environmentalists. At the very least, corporations can ensure that their new plants meet western environmental standards. The European Community is planning to establish an environmental code of conduct for investment in Eastern Europe. Occidental Petroleum has taken the promising step of announcing that all its new overseas facilities must meet U.S. or local environmental standards, whichever are stricter.[74]

It is important that environmental considerations form an integral component of all aid and trade deliberations.

Given the transboundary nature of environmental problems in Eastern Europe and the western republics of the Soviet Union, international agreements will be critical. Under the auspices of the Economic Commission for Europe, two air pollution reduction protocols have been signed and a third is being prepared. In addition, member states of the Commission on Security and Cooperation in Europe have requested the ECE to begin work on a transboundary water pollution treaty. It is important that treaties take account of the need for technology transfer. Several East European nations are thought unlikely to meet agreed-upon air pollution reduction targets in part because they lack the necessary technology.[75]

Finally, the West could consider creative means of reducing the debt burdens of East European countries. Poland is saddled with a $42-billion debt, 64 percent of its annual GNP. Hungary's debt of $18 billion is 65 percent of its GNP. Czechoslovakia and Bulgaria also have large outstanding bills, though official numbers are not yet available. Debt-for-nature swaps are one way out of the morass. Two swaps have been negotiated thus far with Poland—one by the German government that will generate $60 million in environmental cleanup funds, and one by the Washington-based World Wildlife Fund that will raise $50,000 for a project to help clean up the Vistula River.[76]

The political transformation of Eastern Europe and the Soviet Union offers both opportunities and pitfalls. Though the countries of the region have a unique chance to avoid some of the West's mistakes, powerful forces pull them toward repeating the errors. An international effort will be required to see that this does not happen. The revolutions of 1989 offer the hope of a brighter future. But the hope will only be realized if the countries of the region move quickly to restore their environments.

7

Coming to Grips with Abortion

Jodi L. Jacobson

Among the first actions taken by Romania's provisional government following the execution of dictator Nicolae Ceausescu in December 1989 was the repeal of a ban on abortion. The 14-year-old edict, created by Ceausescu in a fruitless attempt to raise the nation's birth rate, outlawed contraceptives and made abortion a criminal offense punishable in some instances by death. Despite the harsh law, data show that in the eighties the country outranked virtually all other European nations in rates of abortion and abortion-related maternal mortality.[1]

In legalizing abortion, Romania joined 35 other countries that have made similar changes since the late seventies. In fact, a 30-year tide of liberalization in laws governing access to family planning—contraceptives and abortion—reduced the relative number of unintended pregnancies and deaths due to illegal abortion in many countries,

leading to vast improvements in public health and lower fertility worldwide. Today, however, abortion is at the center of an intense public controversy over religious and moral beliefs about the status of the fetus and a woman's right to make choices about pregnancy and motherhood.[2]

From the standpoint of public policy, few would disagree that reducing the number of unintended pregnancies and terminations worldwide is a desirable goal. A growing body of evidence suggests that dealing with abortion as part of a comprehensive strategy of public health and family planning, rather than making it illegal, is the most direct route to this end.

But abortion politics has become deadlocked in a no-win dispute over the ideology and criminality of various procedures, yielding a tug-of-war over laws that do not even begin to address the complexity of this social phenomenon. This stalemate postpones the day when the energies spent fighting over reproductive freedom can be directed fully to-

An expanded version of this chapter appeared as Worldwatch Paper 97, *The Global Politics of Abortion*.

ward improving the health and welfare of women and children worldwide.

A dispassionate debate on abortion seems a remote possibility. But the current polemic reflects scant understanding of its real place in demographic and public health trends, or of the social forces that influence abortion rates. Important questions go unasked: How many abortions are there and how many are legal? Where are the rates climbing, where falling? Who has this procedure, and why? What role does abortion play in social change? What are the costs to society of illegal abortions? How can the number of abortions be reduced without forcing women to carry unwanted pregnancies to term?

Abortions are carried out in every country, no matter the law.

Irrefutable evidence remains unconsidered. Abortions are carried out in every country, no matter the law. History has shown that women determined to exercise control over the number of children they bear will do so, even if it means having dangerous illegal procedures. Worldwide, perhaps 50 million abortions are performed each year, nearly half of them illegal. Romania's experience is only one illustration that, irrespective of restrictive laws and religious doctrines and in spite of financial, logistical, and social obstacles, women everywhere continue to terminate unwanted pregnancies.[3]

It is the number of maternal deaths, not abortions, that is most affected by legal codes. Criminalizing abortion makes one of the safest of all surgical procedures highly dangerous by driving it into the hands of unskilled and often unscrupulous practitioners. High rates of maternal death and even higher rates

of permanent physical impairment, along with exorbitant fees, fear of discovery, ostracism, and loss of vital income due to illness, are only a few of the realities of life for women who seek to end unwanted pregnancies in societies with restricted access to abortion. Where the incidence of illegal procedures is high, a disproportionate share of scarce medical resources goes to treating complications. Moreover, because abortion—whether legal or illegal—plays a significant role in the move from high to low fertility, policies that restrict access actually delay the demographic transition.

Looking beyond the rhetoric to the reality of abortion—its incidence, its social and health costs when illegal, its place in the fertility transition, the way it fits in with the broader struggle for human equity and equality—makes crystal clear the urgency of moving the abortion debate from the realm of crime to common sense.

THE PACE OF LIBERALIZATION

Liberalization of abortion laws began full force in the fifties, as recognition of the need to reduce maternal mortality and increase reproductive choices became widespread. Social justice was also an issue. Bringing abortion into the public domain narrowed the difference between those who could afford adequate medical care and those forced to resort to unsafe practitioners.

The strategy worked. France, Poland, Tunisia, the United Kingdom, and the United States are a few examples of countries where the relative number of births due to unintended pregnancies and deaths due to illegal procedures fell following liberalization. Between 1970 and 1976, for instance, abortion-related mortality among women in the United States fell from 30 per 100,000 live births to 5. And in Poland, an analysis by the Commission on Health and Physical Culture concluded that legalization had, among other things, contributed to the elimination of infanticide and of suicides by pregnant women, and had initiated a fall in abortion-related deaths.[4]

The term "liberal" is generally applied to policies that recognize the rights of a pregnant woman to terminate an unwanted pregnancy under various conditions to be greater than those of a developing embryo or fetus . . . up to a point. In countries with the most liberal laws, that point is legally set at "viability," the gestational stage at which a fetus can first reasonably be expected to live outside the womb, albeit with intensive medical assistance.

The crucial stages in the development of brain, heart, and lungs—the organs central to life, and hence to the question of viability—begin around the 20th week of pregnancy and proceed rapidly through birth. In medical circles, viability is generally recognized to occur at between 24 and 28 weeks of pregnancy. For this reason, most countries that use the viability framework severely circumscribe abortion rights after the 24th week, the end of the second trimester. The United Kingdom passed a law in early 1990 reducing the legal limit on abortion from 28 to 24 weeks.[5]

Abortion laws are usually grouped according to "indications," the circumstances traditionally used to justify legal terminations. These categories are broad, representing a diverse set of statutes. (See Table 7–1 for examples of countries in each category.)

Countries with the narrowest laws either completely ban abortions or restrict them to cases where pregnancy poses a

Table 7-1. Conditions Under Which Abortions Are Allowed, Selected Countries, 1989

Life Endangerment[1]	Other Maternal Health Reasons[2]	Social and Socio-Medical Reasons[3]	No Mandated Conditions[4]
Bangladesh	Costa Rica	Argentina	Canada
Brazil	Egypt	India	China
Chile	Ghana	Peru	Czechoslovakia
Colombia	Israel	Poland	Italy
Indonesia	Kenya	United Kingdom	France
Ireland	Morocco	West Germany	Netherlands
Lebanon	Zimbabwe		Soviet Union
Mexico			Sweden
Nigeria			Tunisia
Pakistan			United States
Philippines			
Sudan			

[1]When a woman's life would be endangered by carrying the child to term; some countries in this category prohibit abortion without exception. [2]Such as a threat to the woman's overall health, and sometimes in the case of fetal abnormality, rape, or incest. [3]Social factors, such as insufficient income, poor housing, or marital status, may be considered in evaluating a "threat" to the women's health, or may be deemed sufficient conditions in and of themselves to warrant termination of a pregnancy. [4]Countries in this category have liberal abortion laws, commonly known as "on request," which indicates the lack of legal obstacles to abortion but not necessarily the lack of social or administrative ones.
SOURCE: Rebecca J. Cook, "Abortion Laws and Policies: Challenges and Opportunities," *International Journal of Gynecology and Obstetrics*, Supplement 3, 1989.

risk to the woman's life; some allow the operation in the case of rape and incest. Other laws consider risks to physical and mental health; still others, the case of a severely impaired fetus. Some societies allow the operation for what are known as "social" reasons, as in the case where an additional child will bring undue burdens to an existing family. The broadest category is that recognizing contraceptive failure as a sound basis for abortion, or allowing procedures on request (usually within the first trimester).[6]

Most governments leave specific interpretations to the discretion of the medical community. The definition of "health," for example, is flexible. In some countries, doctors follow the broad definition of the World Health Organization (WHO): "a state of complete physical, mental, and social well being and not merely the absence of disease or infirmity."[7]

According to Rebecca Cook, professor of law at the University of Toronto, several of the 35 countries that liberalized their laws since 1977 created new categories, such as adolescence, advanced maternal age, or infection with the AIDS virus, as a basis for legal abor-

tion. Cyprus, Italy, and Taiwan, for instance, all broadened their regulations to consider "family welfare," while Hong Kong included adolescence as a valid consideration.[8]

France and the Netherlands added clauses pertaining to pregnancy-related distress. In Hungary, one of the first East European countries to liberalize its laws (in 1956), abortion rights have been extended to women who are single or who have been separated from their husbands for up to six months, to women over 35 who have had at least three previous deliveries, and to women caught in economic hardship, such as the lack of appropriate housing.[9]

Most people in the world now live in countries that have moved from blanket prohibition of abortion to a more reasoned acceptance of its role as a backup to contraceptive failure and unwanted pregnancy. The Alan Guttmacher Institute (AGI) indicates that about 40 percent of the world's population in theory has access to induced abortion on request. (See Table 7–2.)

Again, laws in countries grouped in the same category vary widely. In Tunisia—one of the few Muslim countries

Table 7-2. Abortion Laws Worldwide, by Number of Countries and Share of World Population

Legal Conditions	Countries[1]	Share of World Population
	(number)	(percent)
Life Endangerment[2]	53	25
Other Maternal Health Reasons	42	12
Social and Socio-Medical Reasons	14	23
No Mandated Conditions[3]	23	40

[1]Countries with populations of at least 1 million. [2]Technically, in some countries in this category abortion is prohibited without exception. [3]Includes some of the world's most populous countries (China, the Soviet Union, and the United States).
SOURCE: Stanley K. Henshaw, "Induced Abortion: A World Review, 1990," *Family Planning Perspectives,* March/April 1990.

with liberalized laws—abortion is legally available on request until viability, while in France abortions on request are sanctioned only through the first trimester. Other countries with similar on-request status through varying stages of gestation are Canada, China, the Soviet Union, the United States, and virtually all of Eastern and Western Europe.[10]

Adding the share of the world covered by social or maternal health indications—including India, with its 835 million people—brings the total to 75 percent (nearly 4 billion people) who are governed by laws that permit abortion on medical or broader social and economic grounds. Included in this second group, it should be noted, however, are countries like Ethiopia and Costa Rica, where abortion is legal only in cases of risk to the woman's health.[11]

Another 20 percent of the world lives in 49 countries that have resisted liberalization and still totally prohibit abortion, except in some cases to save the woman's life, while the remaining 5 percent (in four other countries) is governed by laws that add rape and incest to this restrictive set of conditions. One in four women in the world, therefore, has little access to abortion—and she is likely to live in Africa, Latin America, or Muslim Asia, where she also has the least access to safe, affordable means of contraception to prevent unwanted pregnancy.[12]

ROADBLOCKS TO ACCESS

Access to abortion and other family planning services, like health care in general, is determined by four variables: laws, policies and the way they are interpreted, the commitment of public funds to provide services, and personal resources, particularly money. Control

over many of these factors—from the enforced shortage of available facilities to the personal views of physicians—is used by opponents of abortion rights to limit access to services.

Interpretations of laws are often as important as the statutes themselves in determining the availability of abortions. Stanley K. Henshaw, deputy director of research at AGI, finds that "in most Muslim countries, and in Latin America and Africa, few legal abortions are performed under the health exception, while in Israel, New Zealand and South Korea, the legal abortion rates [under the health indication] are comparable to those in countries that allow abortion on request."[13]

In many countries where women should be able to get an abortion on demand, they find it difficult to exercise their legal rights for a variety of reasons, including stricter-than-usual medical regulations, burdensome administrative requirements, lack of public funds for services, lack of information or referral networks, lack of trained providers, extreme centralization of services, and local opposition or reluctance to enforce national laws.

Access is determined in part by medical regulations governing how, where, and by whom services can be provided. In most countries with liberal laws, abortions must generally be performed by licensed providers (though not necessarily physicians), a regulation that safeguards public health. Some countries take this one step further, however, by requiring that the operations be carried out only in designated hospitals or centers, or by highly trained specialists.

These and other laws often work against the goal of ensuring that abortions are carried out at the earliest possible point. New laws in Bermuda, Qatar, and the Seychelles, while more liberal than the former ones, include hospital committee authorization requirements before an abortion can be performed. In most cases, these regulations, strongly supported by opponents of abortion rights, act only to delay abortion until later stages of pregnancy—when procedures are riskier and the fetus more developed. Unfortunately, several American states are considering such restrictions.[14]

The lack of a government or public commitment to provide or fund services can severely undermine legal rights.

These institutional and third-party authorization requirements have come under legal attack in many countries, and have been overturned in the courts or defeated in legislatures in several, including Canada and Czechoslovakia. In 1988, the Canadian Supreme Court struck down that nation's standing abortion law, which required that terminations be performed only in hospitals and that women receive the permission of a hospital authorization committee. Among other findings, the Court stated that the delays in procuring abortions resulting from these administrative requirements interfered with "a woman's right to physical and bodily integrity."[15]

The lack of a government or public commitment to provide or fund services can severely undermine legal rights. Abortion became legal on broad grounds in India in 1971. But because registered practitioners are clustered in urban areas, rural women have little access to services. Survey data from 1984 showed that only about 1,000 out of a total of 15,000 physicians trained to perform abortions were living in rural areas, although 78 percent of the country's population falls in this category.[16]

Not surprisingly, just 388,000 of the estimated 4 million to 6 million abortions in India were carried out legally in government-regulated facilities. Were the Indian government to commit funds to expanding the number of outlets for reproductive health care, literally millions of women could avoid the dangers of illegal terminations.[17]

In Turkey, abortion is in theory available on request through the 10th week of pregnancy. But Turkish law states that an abortion may be carried out only by or under the supervision of a gynecological specialist trained in such procedures, as opposed to, say, a general practitioner or a trained paramedic.[18]

The scarcity of trained specialists even in urban areas limits access. In rural Turkey, where medical services of any kind are generally hard to come by, such services are virtually nonexistent. Many potential outlets—health clinics staffed by medical personnel but without a trained specialist—are excluded from delivering services. Rural women without the information and financial resources to reach a doctor in a city are left with the choice of having an illegal abortion or carrying the pregnancy to term.

The many roadblocks to access are illustrated by the situation in Zambia, a country with one of the most liberal laws in Africa. Abortions are legal through the 12th week of pregnancy on broad grounds, but they may only be performed in a hospital setting. What is more, to get permission for a legal abortion a woman must obtain the signatures of three physicians (one of them a specialist) on a form that lists her previous births and abortions. The physicians must agree on one of three grounds for termination of the pregnancy—a medical condition of either the woman or the fetus or a nonmedical condition that justifies termination.[19]

Despite the relatively liberal law, illegal abortions far outnumber legal ones in Zambia. First, the administrative requirements are neither widely known nor understood, especially among rural women. In fact, several Zambian doctors interviewed by Renee Holt, a nurse and lawyer who studies abortion trends, believe that "many Zambian women are not [even] aware of their right to an abortion and visit backstreet abortionists rather than a hospital." Second, the requirements themselves are virtually impossible to fulfill: Only three specialists in the entire country—one of whom now lives in Kenya—are legally empowered to sign the forms. Only one hospital in Lusaka performs the operation; sanctioned facilities—and hence legal abortions—virtually do not exist elsewhere.[20]

Holt reports that "obstetricians and gynecologists at the University Teaching Hospital (UTH) did not have enough operating time to perform all abortions requested. They were turning away half of the requests each day, and these were returning to UTH as incomplete or septic [infected] abortions, which then demanded their time [to save the woman's life], setting up a vicious cycle." Small wonder, then, that even Zambian women aware of their legal rights resort to illegal practitioners.[21]

Conversely, in some countries where abortion is illegal in principle it is carried out quite freely in practice. Such "lapsed law" countries include Brazil, Egypt, Indonesia, Mexico, Nigeria, and Thailand. In Colombia, abortions are technically legal only in cases where the woman's life is in danger. Observers note, however, that safe, dependable, and affordable services are available in most urban areas, and are freely advertised in local newspapers and on billboards. In Bogotá, private clinics provide comprehensive reproductive health services, including prenatal care, contraceptive counseling, and abortion. In fact, in at least one area local policewomen are on hand to escort neighborhood clients to a clinic.[22]

Access to abortion in Colombia is enhanced by the tacit or active willingness of a government to overlook restrictive legislation, which serves to placate opponents of legal abortion. It is essential to note, however, that in Colombia—as in several other countries where a blind eye is similarly turned—extreme inequalities persist in who can get safe services, and the incidence of illegal abortion remains high. Low-income rural women are particularly disadvantaged in not having the resources—the connections, education, money—to gain access to or information on safe abortions.[23]

Money is among the most critical factors in securing safe abortions, especially where laws are prohibitive. In Mexico, for example, access to safe procedures is restricted even when legally indicated under the country's narrow but ambiguous law. Safe services can be obtained in urban areas—for a price. The cost for medical abortions ranges from $215 to $644. Even the lower estimate is more than twice the monthly minimum wage of $103. According to one report, "many experts believe that safe medical abortion is now beyond the reach of the middle class."[24]

The resolution of a number of issues now under debate throughout the world could have a negative effect on abortion rights by restricting access. Those being considered are when and to what extent government health care programs should cover the costs of legal procedures, whether a husband's consent or notification should be required before a married woman can obtain an abortion, and whether laws should require parental notification or consent in the case of adolescents. Placing limits on access is only one part of a broader attack on legalized abortion. A glance beneath the surface waters of liberalization reveals a strong undertow tugging at recently codified reproductive rights.

Opponents of abortion rights, dismayed at the extent of legalization, have devised a three-pronged strategy. First, they seek to reinstate restrictive policies in countries where they have been liberalized—Canada, France, Italy, Poland, Spain, the United States, and Germany, to name a few. Second, they aim to maintain or reinstate restrictions in the Third World by supporting the growth of parallel movements there. Third, they are using legal and economic stoppers to plug every hole in the dam restricting access to services. This movement has scored some significant successes since 1977, most notably in countries where laws have been made considerably more restrictive.

Finland and Israel, for example, made their liberal laws more restrictive, while Iran and Ireland have forbidden abortions altogether. A Honduran law permitting abortions in cases where they would protect the life and health of the mother and in cases of rape and fetal deformity was rejected because it was perceived to conflict with constitutional provisions stating that the "right to life is inviolable." Changes in the constitutions of Ecuador (1978) and the Philippines (1986) incorporated provisions giving the right to life "from the moment of conception."[25]

Abortion has played an integral though varied role in the transition from high to low fertility in virtually every country that has achieved replacement-level fertility.

In July 1989, the United States—a country with one of the world's most liberal policies—took a step backward on reproductive rights. The U.S. Supreme Court's ruling in *Webster v. Reproductive Services* in effect gave the green light to those states seeking to regulate abortion procedures strictly. In *Webster*, the court threw out the trimester framework of viability established in the landmark 1973 *Roe v. Wade* decision, which permitted states to regulate abortions only after the first trimester and to ban them only in the last.[26]

The case upheld the State of Missouri's law that physicians must carry out extensive tests for viability before performing abortions after 20 weeks. Furthermore, *Webster* severely curtailed access to services in that state by upholding Missouri's ban on the use of public facilities for the operation. Since then, restrictive laws of various shades have been introduced in a number of state legislatures, although only a few have been passed.

Global trends in abortion politics are both reflected in and fueled by events in the United States. The U.S. decision in *Webster*, a major success of the so-called pro-life movement, sent shock waves through ranks of activists in Western Europe. The abortion debate there has been far less emotional than in the United States but is becoming more polarized. Europeans from both camps have described the decision as a "wind from the west."[27]

The struggle over abortion rights is now an international affair, with money and anti-abortion protestors crossing the Atlantic from the United States. Moreover, a broader global effort to repeal or restrict abortion rights is being coordinated by the U.S.-based umbrella group Human Life International, which has set up branch offices in 31 countries. Its agenda in developing countries focuses on restricting abortion rather than providing couples with the means to prevent unintended pregnancies. Yet studies show that millions of Third World couples still lack access to contraceptives. Not surprisingly, poor women in these countries already suffer the highest rates of death due to complications of pregnancy and illegal abortion.

A SENSE OF SCALE

Broadly speaking, abortion rates are governed by the cultural and economic pressures about family size in a given society and the mix of laws and policies that determine access to family planning. The numbers of illegal versus legal procedures in a given country, the degree to which pregnancy termination is used to regulate fertility, and the demographic makeup of the groups relying most heavily on this method are all shaped by social and economic pressures to limit or delay childbearing, by the availability and reliability of contraceptives, and by the legal, cultural, and political climate that surrounds abortion services.[28]

Abortion rates tend to be low where desired family size is large and fertility rates are limited only by traditional practices such as heavy reliance on breastfeeding and postpartum abstinence. In rapidly modernizing societies, however, changes in the status of women, in levels of education and income, and in the composition of the work force, among other things, lead to equally rapid changes in desired family size.

As the number of children that they prefer falls, couples look for ways to avoid or terminate unwanted pregnancies. Abortion rates then tend to rise rapidly (irrespective of the legal status), especially if there is no strong tradition of contraceptive use or if contraceptives are not widely available. It is at this point in the transition that abortion's effect on birth rates is highest.

Although rates of contraceptive use and abortion may rise together for a while, eventually the latter peak and begin to decline. In South Korea, for instance, both rates rose rapidly from the late sixties throughout the seventies, reflecting an increasing desire for smaller families. But between 1979 and 1985, the rate of adoption of contraceptives continued to climb, while the abortion rate fell back to the level of 1973. Induced abortion clearly played a major role in South Korea's fertility transition: without it birth rates would have been some 22 percent higher in that period.[29]

In this way, abortion has played an integral though varied role in the transition from high to low fertility in virtually every country that has to date achieved replacement-level fertility (approximately two children per family). The transition to lower abortion rates and birth rates is slowed wherever access to family planning information and supplies is limited.

True to the pattern, the incidence of abortion has declined most rapidly in those countries where legalized abortion has been included as part of truly comprehensive voluntary family planning services—among the few to note are Denmark, France, Iceland, Italy, and the Netherlands. But in contrast, in societies on the cusp or in the process of this transition throughout Africa, Asia, and Latin America, illegal abortion is now widely relied upon to limit family size, though at a tremendous price in women's lives and health.[30]

Based on available data about legal procedures, abortion appears to rank fourth in terms of birth control methods used, behind female sterilization, intrauterine devices, and oral contraceptives. Use of these other methods, however, is heavily concentrated in China, India, and the industrial nations, whereas abortion is relied on everywhere.[31]

Estimates of the number of illegal abortions and maternal deaths for individual developing countries are generally drawn from hospital- or community-based studies that offer but a fragmented picture of the real situation. In both Bangladesh and Brazil, for example, demographic studies indicate that 20–35 percent of all pregnancies are aborted. Yet because of legal restrictions, bureaucratic indifference, and social disapproval, abortion in these countries is largely undocumented and clandestine.[32]

In fact, so few countries keep accurate statistics on abortion that the omission itself has political implications of tremendous import. If society remains ignorant of the number of legal versus illegal procedures, if the number of women who die or are physically impaired due to illegal abortions remains unknown, if the costs in terms of health and productivity (not to mention individual freedom) remain untallied, then there is no empirical basis on which to challenge opponents of abortion rights. In effect, the pathetically poor quality of data narrows the debate on which set of societal and individual priorities should prevail.

Despite the lack of hard numbers, several researchers have made estimates based on available evidence, from which a number of conclusions about trends at the global and regional level can be drawn. Demographers calculate that from a third to half of all women of reproductive age undergo at least one induced abortion in their lifetimes. According to calculations by Stanley Henshaw of the Alan Guttmacher Institute, some 36–51 million abortions were performed worldwide in 1987. He estimates the annual number of illegal procedures at 10–20 million, leaving from 26–31 million legal ones. Other estimates put the total number at between 40 million and 60 million. Using either set of figures implies close to one induced abortion for every two to three births worldwide.[33]

Comparisons of trends within and between countries are made using abortion rates, the number of procedures per 1,000 women of reproductive age. Again, lack of data for many countries makes true comparisons difficult. But by using figures from countries with reliable statistics as well as figures adjusted for illegal abortions in those without data, a sketch can be drawn of regional and national trends.

In many countries, abortion has become the primary method of family planning as a direct result of government policies (or lack of them) that result in limited access to contraception. The connection is made plain by the situation in Eastern Europe and the Soviet Union, where a "contraceptive iron curtain" has hung for decades.[34]

With the exceptions of Albania (which retains restrictive policies) and of the former East Germany and Yugoslavia (which liberalized their laws in the seventies), abortion laws were changed in most of Eastern Europe in the fifties, making legal a practice that was already widespread. Few of these governments, however, concurrently made the availability of contraceptive information or supplies a priority; consequently, couples continued to rely on less effective methods, such as withdrawal, using abortion as a backup.[35]

This pattern held as social ills, economic hardship—evident in housing shortages and long lines for basic rations—and environmental deterioration reinforced the strong desire of East Europeans to limit the size of their families. With virtually only one way to achieve this goal, throughout the sixties and seventies rates of induced abortion in the region were the highest recorded in the world. Even today, abortion rates in most of Eastern Europe are high for women throughout their reproductive years. (See Table 7–3.)[36]

The lack of effective contraceptives in

the Soviet Union has led to heavy reliance on abortion there. The nation has some 70 million women of childbearing age yet not a single factory producing modern contraceptives, except the poor-quality condoms widely disparaged as "galoshes." Writing in the Soviet magazine *Ogonyok*, medical researcher Andrei Popov states that "the way out [of unwanted pregnancies] is well-known—abortions . . . child abandonment [and] infanticide."[37]

Abortions are available throughout the Soviet Union on demand and at low cost. And the average Soviet woman, who terminates between five and seven pregnancies during her reproductive years, will likely take advantage of the system at some time. Still, administrative and technological barriers combined with public disapproval drive the majority of women to obtain what are essentially illegal procedures that they must pay for out of pocket. Many are reluctant to request state-funded abortions because, by law, the procedure must be recorded in work and health documents.[38]

It is clear the Soviet Union's share of total abortions worldwide is large; what is less clear is just what that share is. Official statistics put the number of terminations in 1987 at nearly 7 million, well in excess of the 6 million recorded live births; official rates were 100 per 1,000 women of reproductive age in 1985. Estimates made by independent researchers imply the true numbers are far higher. Henshaw calculates that possibly 11 million abortions are performed annually. Demographer Tomas Frejka, citing estimates of 13 million unauthorized procedures, claims the number could approach 20 million, a figure close to one put forward by Murray Feshbach, a researcher on Soviet health at Georgetown University.[39]

The Soviet Union has some 70 million women of childbearing age yet not a single factory producing modern contraceptives.

Three East European countries—Czechoslovakia, the former East Germany, and Hungary—apparently kept their abortion rates relatively low by encouraging widespread contraceptive practice. Hungary, for example, relied on a campaign that included dissemination and education on the use of modern contraceptives. Between 1966 and the late seventies, the share of Hungarian women using modern contraceptives increased dramatically, leading to a substantial decline in terminations. In the words of Henry David, Director of the U.S.-based Transnational Family Research Institute, Hungary went from being "an abortion culture" to one relying on education and modern contraception.[40]

In Latin America, abortion rates have been consistently high for over two decades, despite quite restrictive laws and the firm opposition of the Catholic church to any kind of modern family planning. Indeed, there is evidence of a

Table 7-3. Legal Abortion Rates, Selected East European Countries, 1987

Country	Abortions
	(per thousand women aged 15–44)
Bulgaria	65
Czechoslovakia	47
East Germany[1]	27
Hungary	38
Romania[2]	91
Yugoslavia[1]	71

[1]1984 data. [2]Includes official estimates of illegal abortion.
SOURCE: Stanley K. Henshaw, "Induced Abortion: A World Review, 1990," *Family Planning Perspectives*, March/April 1990.

long tradition of induced abortion in the region. In 1551, the King of Spain was notified that the indigenous population in his Venezuelan colony practiced induced abortion, through the use of medicinal herbs, to prevent their children from being born into slavery.[41]

During the seventies, the International Planned Parenthood Federation estimated that abortion rates in Latin America and the Caribbean were higher than in any other developing region: an estimated one fourth of all pregnancies in Latin America were intentionally aborted in that period, compared with estimates of less than 10 percent in Africa and 15–20 percent in South and Southeast Asia.[42]

Fertility rates have fallen since the sixties, but the desire for even smaller families is strong throughout the region. Data from the World Fertility Survey in the seventies showed that while the average family contained at least four children, over half the women interviewed wanted to have only two to four. And over half the women with three children in all Latin American countries except Paraguay wanted no more.[43]

Induced abortion continues to account for about one fourth of total fertility control in Latin America.

Because political and religious opposition has kept contraceptive outlets to a minimum, the number of illegal abortions is high and shows no signs of falling in the near future. Experts put the total in excess of 5 million, but some claim the number in Brazil alone may surpass 4 million.[44]

Tracking illegal abortions in Latin America is difficult at best. Tomas Frejka reports that "a large proportion of the induced abortions are performed in violation of existing laws and [providers] have a vested interest not to report them. Even after the fact, women tend to deny having had an abortion, and health personnel who treat abortion complications will under-report cases . . . to avoid involvement with the law." A hospital study in Campinas, Brazil, for instance, found maternal deaths due to abortion were underreported by 40 percent.[45]

Today, induced abortion continues to account for about one fourth of total fertility control in Latin America. Although use of contraceptives has been increasing steadily since the sixties, it is still relatively low and supplies remain unevenly distributed throughout the region. Access to services is unequal: those most at risk of unwanted pregnancy—teens, the unmarried, and low-income women—are those for whom contraceptives and safe abortion services are most out of reach. Rates of contraceptive failure are still high, too. Frejka claims that "the incidence of induced abortion in Latin America will remain high, at least through the 1990s, even if its legislation continues to be restrictive. [This] situation implies serious reproductive health, and economic as well as social, problems for a large number of women and their families."[46]

A similar picture is developing in Africa, where the number of induced abortions and the related health and social costs of illegal or clandestine procedures are likely to continue rising for at least the next decade. The predominantly young population is characterized by high fertility and low rates of contraceptive use. Access to both contraceptives and safe abortion services is limited geographically and by income. Although fertility rates in Africa are among the highest in the world, the desire to limit family size is growing.

Yet laws circumscribing reproductive rights in Africa, inherited from colonial governments, remain largely intact.

Among the former British colonies, for instance, only Zambia has liberalized its law. Francophone Africa lags even further behind in this regard. In addition to criminalizing abortion, the French law of 1920 outlawed the sale, distribution, and advertisement of all contraceptives. Only Burundi, Togo, and the Seychelles among the Francophone countries have liberalized their laws enough to allow abortions for social indications.[47]

Social and cultural limitations on women in Africa are an equally important factor, and may be much harder to change than laws. Nolwandle Nozipo Mashalaba, a private family practitioner in Botswana, sees the lack of communication between African couples on matters of sexuality and the desire to maintain male dominance within the household as the primary roadblocks to preventing pregnancies that women themselves may not want. She notes that where "men migrate . . . for work, they keep the wife in a continuous state of pregnancy and lactation as a way to keep her (possible) infidelity to a minimum."[48]

Studies show that these and other constraints can hamper contraceptive use even where knowledge of modern methods is high. A 1984 survey in Botswana found that more than 70 percent of women in both rural and urban areas knew at least one modern method of family planning; a more recent survey in Zimbabwe indicated that 9 out of 10 knew at least one method and the majority were familiar with five or more. But a number of factors—including the inaccessibility of clinics, fear and anxiety over side effects, ineffective counseling, and the lack of programs for men—keep rates of contraceptive use well under 15 percent throughout most of Africa. Illegal abortion, in Mashalaba's words, is "the only solution."[49]

In Asia, abortion rates are high regardless of the law. Indonesia provides a classic example of the inevitable clash between rapidly changing social values and restrictive legal codes. According to Indonesian researchers Ninuk Widyantoro and Sarsanto W. Sarwono, rates of both abortion and contraceptive use in the country are climbing rapidly, indicating that "couples desire much smaller families than traditionally prevailed." They estimate that between 750,000 and 1 million abortions are performed annually.[50]

The legal status of the procedure has long been cloudy in Indonesia. A profusion of laws and morals concerning abortion and other family planning methods reflects the country's diverse national heritage, drawn from the traditions of indigenous ethnic groups melded together with the mores and practices of Buddhism, Christianity, Hinduism, Islam, and former Dutch colonizers. In the seventies, high rates of maternal illness and death from unsafe procedures prompted the members of the medical community to seek clarification of the welter of statutes from the Indonesian High Court.[51]

Although abortion was not then technically liberalized, nor has its status changed since, the court's decision that "procedures could not be regarded as illegal if they were carried out within the framework of normal medical practice by specialists and doctors" paved the way for an increase in trained providers. Since then, access to safe services has improved. Many doctors, although mainly in urban areas, have been trained in the use of and provided with vacuum aspiration equipment. Moreover, the Indonesian government has made a major commitment to increasing access to contraceptive information and supplies. Still, Widyantoro and Sarwono estimate that due to unequal access, social ambivalence about abortion, and lack of information on services, perhaps as many as 800,000 illegal abortions are carried out each year, "with many more unsuccessful attempted terminations going unnoticed." As a result, complication and fatality rates remain high.[52]

Looking at the pattern of induced abortions in various nations according to age, marital status, educational level, and current family size provides an indication of which demographic groups have the greatest numbers of unwanted pregnancies, and even suggests who has least access to effective, affordable, and acceptable contraceptives. In most industrial countries, for example, as in Canada and the United States, abortion rates tend to be highest among teenagers and women aged 20–24, groups that seek to delay childbearing either because of their marital status (single) or for other reasons, such as the desire to complete their education. (See Table 7–4.)

Making sex education and contraceptives more available to these groups lowers their abortion rates. The Transnational Family Research Institute compared approaches to family planning in Denmark and the United States to see how different strategies can result in different rates of unintended pregnancy and abortion among particular demographic groups.[53]

The Institute found that inability to pay limits access to contraceptives more often in the United States than in Denmark, especially among those groups most at risk of unwanted pregnancy. In the absence of national health insurance, women rely largely on private physicians to obtain contraceptives, and many are disadvantaged by cost constraints, their ineligibility for public assistance, or their place of residence.[54]

Data show that 17 percent of American women with low incomes lack health insurance of any kind; this group includes one fourth of women under 25, one fourth of unmarried women, and one third of women whose incomes fell below 150 percent of the federal poverty level—all groups with the highest rates of unwanted pregnancy and abortion. Many of these women cannot afford to purchase contraceptives. In Denmark, by contrast, national health insurance provides contraceptives, counseling, and pre- and postpregnancy health care for everyone, regardless of income.[55]

Federally funded family planning clinics do exist in the United States, but a lack of political commitment has kept their budgets spare, leading to limited hours, long waits for appointments, and a narrower menu of services offered. Moreover, services have been declining in the wake of recent budget cuts: less

Table 7-4. Legal Abortion Rates by Age of Woman, Selected Countries, Most Recent Year

Country	19 or Younger	20–24	25–29	30–34	35–39	40 or Older
	(legal abortions per thousand women in age group)					
Canada	15	19	12	8	5	2
East Germany	17	26	31	31	24	11
England/Wales	21	24	16	11	7	3
Hungary	26	45	47	46	41	22
Tunisia	1	13	27	36	31	16
United States	46	52	31	18	10	3

SOURCE: Stanley K. Henshaw, "Induced Abortion: A World Review, 1990," *Family Planning Perspectives,* March/April 1990.

than half as much funding was made available to these clinics in fiscal year 1989 than in 1981.[56]

Danish family planning programs focus on preventing unwanted pregnancies to the greatest extent possible by making contraceptive services universally available, even to teenagers. The results are clear. Today, pregnancy rates among Danish teens are less than half those in the United States. Abortion rates among women age 15–19 fell by nearly half between 1977 and 1985. (See Table 7–5.)

The situation regarding teen access to contraceptives in the United States is vastly different. Proposals for starting U.S. programs similar to those in Denmark are hotly contested. As a result, rates of teenage pregnancy and of abortion in the United States well exceed those of other industrial countries, even though the ages at which teens first experience sex are comparable.[57]

The growing disparity between low rates of contraceptive use and increasing desires to limit family size—the unmet need for family planning that is evident throughout the Third World—is a sure prescription for even higher rates of illegal abortion. Regional surveys suggest that 50–60 percent of couples in Latin America, 60–80 percent in low-income Asian countries (except China), 75 percent in the Middle East and North Africa, and 90 percent of sub-Saharan Africa do not use any form of modern contraception. On the other hand, the same studies show that a majority of couples in Latin America and Asia—and a growing percentage throughout the Middle East and Africa—wish to space the timing or limit the number of their children.[58]

In most developing countries, abortion rates are highest among married women with several children who have little means of preventing additional, unwanted pregnancies. In Latin America, abortion rates among women over 35 are twice those for women age 20–34; the rate among women with five or more children is more than twice that for women with only one. A clinic-based study from Allahabad, India, found that a large majority of women seeking abortions were married, between 20 and 29, and that most had several children already. Studies in Indonesia documented almost identical results—the majority of clients were married, had two to three children, and were over 25.[59]

It is commonly believed that abortion in Africa is used primarily by women in their teens and early twenties who want to delay childbearing. This fits with the social and demographic makeup of urban areas, for example, where higher levels of education and broader opportunities for women encourage a desire to delay marriage and childbearing. Data from Nairobi bear this out: 79 percent of the induced abortion patients in one hospital study were young, single women.[60]

But additional data point to the growing reliance on abortion here as well of older women with several children, es-

Table 7-5. Teen Abortion Rates, United States and Denmark, 1977–85

Year	United States	Denmark
	(abortions per thousand women aged 15–19)	
1977	37	25
1978	40	24
1979	42	22
1980	43	23
1981	43	20
1982	43	18
1983	43	18
1984	43	17
1985	44	16

SOURCE: Henry P. David et al., "United States and Denmark: Different Approaches to Health Care and Family Planning," *Studies in Family Planning,* January/February 1990.

pecially in rural areas. In Tunisia, for instance, rates are highest among women age 25–39. A sample in Nigeria showed that 30 percent of complications from abortion in one hospital were reported in women over 25; of all the women, 52 percent had two or more children.[61]

What consigns so many women to death or physical impairment is not a deficiency in technology, but a deficiency in the value placed on women's lives.

Likewise, a Kenyan study found that 46 percent of abortion patients had one to three children, 22 percent had four to six, and 7 percent had seven or more. Under increasing social and economic stress, more married women are turning to abortion as their primary means of birth control. The striking implication of this finding is that the unmet need for family planning in Africa may be far higher than is currently assumed. If this is true, then the need to improve access to contraceptives, the safety of abortion services, and general reproductive health care throughout Africa—especially to stave off a precipitous rise in illegal operations not to mention to reduce fertility—is far more urgent than the spending and policy priorities of most African governments indicate.[62]

Abortion trends throughout the developing world could be predicted from what is known about the downward pressure on birth rates created by economic growth and rising incomes. But evidence is mounting that quite a different process is at work. A growing share of the world's population lives in poverty, and inequalities in income, housing, and access to social services are increasing. These trends have been exacerbated by

consistently high levels of international debt, widespread environmental degradation, and a pattern of development that has relentlessly ignored the needs and priorities of women.

THE INVISIBLE PLAGUE

Each year, according to WHO, at least a half-million women worldwide die from pregnancy-related causes. Of these, roughly 200,000 lose their lives as a result of an illegal abortion, most of which are performed by unskilled attendants under unsanitary conditions or are self-inflicted with hangers, knitting needles, toxic herbal teas, and the like. In terms of sheer numbers, more than half the abortion-related deaths worldwide occur in South and Southeast Asia, followed by sub-Saharan Africa, and then Latin America and the Caribbean. And for every woman who dies, 30–40 more suffer serious, often lifelong health problems—among them hemorrhaging, infection, abdominal or intestinal perforations, kidney failure, and permanent infertility—that affect their ability to provide for themselves and for any children they already have.[63]

Here again, simple public recognition of problems related to women's health is stymied by lack of accurate data to assess and publicize the true extent of the problem. Reliable statistics on the incidence of induced abortion and related maternal mortality rates are available from only a handful of countries—the United States and most European countries are among those keeping accurate statistics. Even data from WHO are incomplete.

Perhaps the most distressing fact about abortion-related deaths and illnesses is that the vast majority of complications that lead to these outcomes are totally preventable. What consigns so many women around the world to death or physical impairment is not a deficiency in technology, but a deficiency in the value placed on women's lives. Technologically simple, inexpensive, easy-to-use tools for safe early abortion are well known, and widely used in some countries. But social intransigence, religious intolerance, economic self-interest, and political apathy all narrow the options for millions of women. Society's message to these women is, in effect, "carry this unwanted pregnancy or risk your life to end it."

Because of the social stigma of abortion, the dispersion of medical technologies for safe procedures is held back even while progress is made on other forms of health care. According to Julie DeClerque of the International Projects Assistance Services (IPAS), "data on infant mortality and hospital admissions for abortion complications in Santiago, Chile over a 20-year period show that while infant mortality dropped by over half, hospitalization from abortion complications increased by over 60 percent."[64]

Equally disturbing is the resounding silence on the part of international bodies concerned with health and development—the World Bank and the U.S. Agency for International Development, to name two—about the human and economic costs of illegal abortion. Abortion-related deaths and illness are to them an invisible plague.

The number of abortion deaths is a direct reflection of access to safe services. WHO studies in various settings indicate that the share of maternal deaths caused by induced abortion ranges from 7 percent to more than 50. On average, between 20 and 25 percent of maternal mortality is attributable to illegal or clandestine abortion. In Latin America, complications of illegal abortion are thought to be the main cause of death in women between the ages of 15 and 39.[65]

Abortion-related deaths are estimated to reach 1,000 per 100,000 illegal abortions in some parts of Africa, as opposed to less than 1 death per 100,000 legal procedures in the United States. Hospital admissions in African cities, virtually the only available indicator of abortion trends, are rising in tandem with reliance on abortion as a method of birth control. Khama Rogo, a medical doctor and faculty member at the University of Nairobi, indicates that admissions of women suffering from complications of illegal abortions have risen 600–800 percent at Nairobi's Kenyatta National Hospital over the past decade. He estimates that in 1990 more than 74,000 African women may have died following an illegal termination.[66]

Rogo notes that in East and Central Africa at least 20 percent of all maternal deaths are due to complications of induced abortion, and that the share has reached 54 percent in Ethiopia. He suspects that "gross underreporting" of abortion cases may be responsible for the fact that studies in several West African hospitals imply overall maternal death rates from abortion of only 10 percent.[67]

Hospitals in many developing countries are literally inundated with women seeking treatment for complications of illegal abortion. Over 30 percent of the beds in the gynecological and obstetric wards of most urban hospitals in Latin America are filled with women suffering abortion complications. At Mama Yemo hospital in Kinshasa, Zaire, and at the Kenyatta National Hospital in Nairobi, Kenya, some 60 percent of all gynecological cases fall in this same category. And at a hospital in Accra, Ghana, between 60 and 80 percent of all minor surgery performed relates to the aftereffects of illegal abortions; in 1977, half that hospital's blood supply was allocated to related transfusions.[68]

From a fifth to half of all maternal deaths worldwide could be prevented by providing access to safe abortion services. No international effort to accomplish this is on the horizon, but in a few countries individual groups are working to furnish the technical means and training to deal more efficiently, at least, with complications. IPAS, for one, has been working in sub-Saharan Africa to train clinicians in safe use of the manual vacuum aspiration technique. Use of this in the treatment of incomplete abortions has reduced the time needed to treat women suffering from poorly executed operations, and lowered their risk of hemorrhage and infection. Pilot projects at hospitals in both Kenya and Nigeria have yielded "a great savings in health resources," according to Ann Leonard of IPAS.[69]

Each roadblock to safe abortion raises the social costs of illegal procedures severalfold. Illegal abortions drain health resources. Complications from them require treatments that are in short supply. A study of 617 women suffering abortion complications who were admitted to 10 hospitals in Zaire found that 95 percent required antibiotics, 62 percent anesthetics, and 17 percent transfusions. Oftentimes, hospital supplies in Africa are so scarce that women must go to the local pharmacy and provide their own antibiotics—or not receive treatment. The increased competition for health resources posed by the growing numbers of illegal abortions in Africa will make coping with another health crisis there—AIDS—that much more difficult.[70]

A recent accounting by the Alan Guttmacher Institute of U.S. national and state expenditures on contraceptive counseling and supplies hints at the broad social costs of unwanted births. AGI estimated that every dollar spent to provide contraceptive services to women

who might otherwise find it difficult or impossible to obtain them without help saved $4.40. In 1987, a total of $412 million was spent by federal and state governments for family planning. The study's authors calculated that without this funding about 1.2 million more unintended pregnancies would have occurred nationwide, leading to 509,000 mistimed or unwanted births and 516,000 abortions. Averting these unwanted pregnancies saved $1.8 billion that would otherwise have been spent on medical and nutritional services and on welfare payments.[71]

FROM CRIME TO COMMON SENSE

The impact of unwanted pregnancy embraces but extends beyond the individual to encompass broader objectives, including the struggle for women to become equal partners in society and efforts to improve health among women and children. Less well recognized but equally important is the role that abortion plays in the transition from high to low fertility.

An international consensus among a diverse body of policymakers already exists on the adverse effects of rapid population growth on economic performance, the environment, family welfare, health, and political stability. For reasons of politics, many of these same leaders shy away from or ignore the role played by abortion in slowing birth rates. Yet as public health researchers Stephen Mumford and Elton Kessel note, "no nation wanting to reduce its growth to less than 1 percent can expect to do so without the widespread use of abortion." Policymakers who call for slower population growth while remaining silent on the issue of access to safe abortion are willing to achieve this goal at a high price in women's lives.[72]

The tremendous social gains to be reaped from eliminating illegal abortions cannot be ignored. First among them is a reduction in abortion-related maternal mortality of at least 25 percent and in related illnesses of far more. Reductions in illegal abortions and unwanted pregnancies would save billions in social and health care costs, freeing these resources for other uses.

Only by increasing access to family planning information and supplies, offering couples a wider and safer array of contraceptives, and improving the delivery of comprehensive reproductive health care services can the number of abortions be reduced. Some countries have already chosen this commonsense approach. Italy, for instance, now requires local and regional health authorities to promote contraceptive services and other measures to reduce the demand for abortion, while Czech law aims to prevent terminations through sex education in schools and health facilities and through the provision of free contraceptives and associated care. Some countries now require postabortion contraceptive counseling and education; some mandate programs for men as well.[73]

Many of these efforts register success quickly. On the Swedish Island of Gotland, for example, abortions were nearly halved in an intensive three-year program to provide information and improved family planning services. Similar results have been seen in France and elsewhere.[74]

The steps needed to make these gains universal are plain. Decriminalization and clarification of laws governing abortion would secure the rights of couples around the world to plan the size and spacing of their families safely. Policies that put abortion into the context of public health and family planning would immediately reduce the incidence of illegal operations. Removal of the administrative, financial, and geographic roadblocks to access both to safe abortions and to family planning services in general would reduce overall abortion rates and further improve public health.

Reductions in illegal abortions and unwanted pregnancies would save billions in social and health care costs, freeing these resources for other uses.

While the way is evident, the will is lacking. The missing ingredient is political commitment. Natural allies—representatives of groups concerned with women's rights, environmental degradation, family planning, health, and population growth—have failed to mount a concerted effort to dispel abortion myths. And despite the overwhelming evidence of the high human and social costs incurred by restrictive laws, abortion politics remains dominated by narrowly drawn priorities that reflect only one set of beliefs and attitudes. Respect for both ethical diversity and factual accuracy is a precondition for a truly "public" policy on the question of abortion.

Reforming restrictive laws may stir opposition. Failing to do so exacts an emotional and economic toll on society—and sentences countless women around the world to an early grave.

8

Assessing the Military's War on the Environment

Michael Renner

More than three decades ago, President Dwight D. Eisenhower warned that "the problem in defense is how far you can go without destroying from within what you are trying to defend from without." Meant as a warning against creating an all-powerful military-industrial complex, Eisenhower's statement is equally applicable to a problem the world is just beginning to grapple with: the military's war on the environment.[1]

The end of East-West confrontation and rising environmental awareness have combined to bring into sharper focus some problems long considered subsidiary to geopolitics. Sam Nunn, chairman of the U.S. Senate Armed Services Committee, recently made an explicit linkage between the military and the environment, proposing that the technological resources of the Defense Department be marshaled to address ecological problems. Far from being the savior of the biosphere, however, the world's armed forces are quite likely the single largest polluter on earth.[2]

Modern warfare entails large-scale en-

vironmental devastation, as conflicts in Vietnam, Afghanistan, Central America, and the Persian Gulf amply demonstrate. In some cases, environmental modification has consciously been employed as a weapon. And it is generally agreed that nuclear war is the ultimate threat to the global environment.[3]

But even in "peacetime"—preparing for war—the military contributes to resource depletion and environmental degradation, in some instances heavily. The production, testing, and maintenance of conventional, chemical, biological, and nuclear arms generates enormous quantities of toxic and radioactive substances, and contaminates the earth's soil, air, and water. Keeping troops in a state of readiness imposes a heavy toll on large tracts of often-fragile land.

The military's troubling relationship with the environment is moving up on the world's agenda for a number of reasons. Military wastes are literally surfacing: the effects of decades of pervasive disregard for the environment in the nuclear weapons production complex, for example, simply cannot be hidden from public view. Suddenly vanished, the cold war no longer provides a convenient smokescreen to deflect public concerns. As some of the superpowers' troops and bases are withdrawn from foreign lands, unpleasant discoveries are being made. And with the dramatic improvement in East-West relations, people are beginning to ask why massive maneuvers and low-level flights of military jets are necessary. Rising environmental awareness has sensitized ordinary citizens to issues neglected earlier, while a stream of shocking revelations of past environmental destruction by the military is forcing governments to acknowledge and begin to address the problems.

Data that would permit a truly comprehensive picture of the military's resource use and its health and environmental effects are by and large unavailable. Shielded by the mantle of "national security," the armed forces and military contractors have either been exempt from environmental regulations or ignored them.

The bulk of the data concerns the United States, which publishes by far the most information. Other governments wrap themselves in silence and denial, or release insufficient and contradictory data. While the frequent reference to U.S. examples in this chapter may seem lopsided, it must be remembered that the United States and the Soviet Union (for which only anecdotal evidence is available) account for the preponderance of global military activities.

Information about the Third World is particularly sparse. As developing nations' share of global military spending rose from 6 percent in 1965 to around 20 percent in the mid-eighties, their energy and materials consumption must have gone up in both absolute and relative terms. And while few of them produce major weapons, their imports of modern weaponry suggest they face

some of the same problems, at least with regard to hazardous wastes, as the United States does.[4]

LAND AND AIR: THE BATTLEFIELDS AT HOME

Modern armed forces require large expanses of land and airspace. Not only have the arsenals of many nations grown to simply phenomenal proportions, but the amount of space needed to maneuver agile jet fighters, fast tanks, huge aircraft carriers, and giant submarines has risen an astonishing amount. (See Table 8–1.) A 1982 U.N. study noted that "military requirements for land have risen steadily over the course of this century owing to the increase in the size of standing armed forces and, more particularly, the rapid pace of technological advances in weaponry." The report predicted continued growth in the military demand for land.[5]

During World War II, a U.S. mechanized infantry battalion with about 600 soldiers needed fewer than 16 square kilometers to maneuver; a similar unit today has to have more than 20 times as much space. A World War II fighter plane required a maneuvering radius of about 9 kilometers, compared with 75 kilometers today and a projected 150–185 kilometers for the next generation of jets. Beyond the seeming dictates of technological developments, however, military bureaucracies have shown a propensity to enlarge their command over society's resources.[6]

Global estimates of direct military land use outside of wartime are sketchy at best. In 1981 it was estimated at 1 percent of total territory for 13 industrial nations, but is believed to be in the range of 0.5–1.0 percent worldwide (ap-

Table 8-1. Historical Growth in Space Requirements of Armed Forces

Event	Required Front Area
	(square kilometers per 100,000 soldiers)
Ancient times	1
Napoleonic wars (late 18th-early 19th century)	20
World War I (1914–18)	248
World War II (1939–45)	3,000
Yom Kippur war (1973)	4,000
NATO maneuver in West Germany (1978)	55,500

SOURCE: Paul J.M. Vertegaal, "Environmental Impact of Dutch Military Activities," *Environmental Conservation,* Spring 1989.

proximately 750,000 to 1.5 million square kilometers). This may sound small, but it represents an area roughly the size of Turkey or Indonesia, respectively. To arrive at a truly comprehensive measure, however, the space occupied by arms-producing enterprises would need to be added to the land controlled by the armed forces themselves. Unfortunately, it appears that no data permit even a rough calculation of this bigger picture.[7]

In a world dramatically short of productive land, any unproductive and destructive use of territory seems a misplaced priority. The military appetite for land increasingly collides with other needs, such as agriculture, wilderness protection, recreation, and housing. It is ironic that in the name of defending a nation's territorial integrity against foreign threats, larger and larger areas are given over to the armed forces, effectively withdrawing them from public access.

Beyond the land formally under the military's domain lie far larger areas that are used to varying degrees by the armed forces. While these may not be off-limits to civilians, they are often damaged or rendered dangerous or unusable even by occasional military use. Maneuvers spread devastation far beyond the confines of military bases. Tanks rumbling across fertile fields decimate harvests, and low-flying jets target residential areas in simulated attacks. War games leave a swath of death and destruction in their wake: NATO maneuvers that were conducted in West Germany, for example, caused at least $100 million in assessed, quantifiable damages to crops, forests, and private property in a typical year.[8]

The best information on military land use exists for the United States. The Department of Defense directly holds 100,-000 square kilometers. This is roughly equivalent to the state of Virginia. Fierce citizen opposition forced the Pentagon in September 1990 to suspend indefinitely a plan to acquire an additional 18,-000 square kilometers—an area bigger than Connecticut and Rhode Island combined.[9]

The military also has access to other land. The armed services lease a total of about 80,000 square kilometers from other federal agencies, and an unknown amount of land owned by the states is devoted to military purposes. The nuclear weapons complex of the U.S. Department of Energy (DOE), meanwhile, spreads over 10,000 square kilometers. Altogether, at least 200,000 square kilometers—2 percent of total U.S. territory—is devoted to military purposes. In addition, the Pentagon controls about 8,100 square kilometers of land outside the United States. An expanse of 700 square kilometers in the Philippines, much of it left idle, makes the U.S. military the single largest holder of agricultural land in that country.[10]

The immense size of the Soviet military apparatus suggests that nation also commits vast expanses of land to its armed forces. Some 200,000 square kilometers of land just in Kazakhstan (the second largest republic) are devoted to that purpose—more than is used to grow wheat. The Semipalatinsk nuclear test ground in eastern Kazakhstan, for example, occupies roughly 2,000 square kilometers.[11]

Direct military land use in Western Europe is estimated at 1–3 percent of the total land mass. Yet indirect or nonexclusive use tends to be much higher. In the Netherlands, for instance, direct use stands at 1.15 percent of the country's territory, but indirect uses of both land and water surface areas (and the airspace above) are believed to add another 10.5 percent. At least one third of the ecologically unique but fragile Waddensea and half the Dutch sector of the North Sea are used militarily.[12]

In West Germany, when it was still a separate nation, the armed forces (including those of other NATO countries) had exclusive access to an estimated 6,000 square kilometers. At 2 percent of that country's total territory, this came to almost three times the combined area of all nature preserves. "Protective areas" surrounding military facilities brought the military's direct and indirect land use to 14,000 square kilometers, about 5.6 percent. Some 5,000 maneuvers each year were held on as much as a quarter of the country's territory. In what used to be East Germany, the Soviet military alone reportedly controlled

4 percent of all land, while installations of the East German army covered 0.5 percent. The limits adopted for a unified German army and the withdrawal of many foreign troops will decrease land use to a certain degree.[13]

Preparing for war resembles a scorched-earth policy against an imaginary foe.

With its choreographed violence, the military destroys large tracts of the land it is supposed to protect. Land used for war games is prone to suffer severe degradation. Maneuvers demolish the natural vegetation, disturb wildlife habitat, erode and compact soil, silt up streams, and cause flooding. Bombing ranges transform the land into a moon-like wasteland, pockmarked with craters. Shooting ranges for tanks and artillery contaminate soil and ground water with lead and other toxic residues. Some anti-tank shells, for example, contain uranium rods. Preparing for war resembles a scorched-earth policy against an imaginary foe.[14]

In fragile desert environments, the recovery of natural systems may take thousands of years. The southern California desert still bears the scars of tank maneuvers conducted by General George S. Patton in the early forties. And the damage is far heavier in Libya, where British and German armies fought major battles during World War II.[15]

One of the most enduring and perilous legacies of war preparation are large tracts of land strewn with unexploded bombs. In November 1989, the Pentagon had to close off some 275 square kilometers of public land in Nevada after discovering 1,389 live bombs, 123,375 pounds of shrapnel, and 28,136 rounds of ammunition accidentally dropped outside an Air Force bombing range. Robert Stone, Deputy Assistant Defense Secretary and the Pentagon's top land manager, acknowledged that land used for bombing practice has to be closed to human use permanently because even an intensive effort will fail to locate all unexploded bombs.[16]

The armed forces have far broader access to airspace than they have to land. This has been particularly the case in the former West Germany, perhaps the country most intensively used by the military. Virtually the country's entire airspace was open to military jets, and two thirds of it to low-level flights. Each year, anywhere from 700,000 to 1 million military sorties took place, accounting for approximately 15 percent of all air traffic in the skies over that nation. The extent to which this will be changed in the wake of unification remains to be seen.[17]

Much of the military flying in the United States is done in the relatively open spaces of the West. Some 90,000 training sorties a year, a fifth of them at very low levels, are flown in a 47,000-square-kilometer expanse above California's Mojave desert, for example. According to Citizen Alert, a Nevada grassroots group, 180,000 square kilometers of airspace, about 70 percent of the state's total, is either designated "special use" or is used for training purposes. For the United States as a whole, at least 30 percent and perhaps as much as 50 percent of airspace is used militarily in one way or another.[18]

Canada may have the world's most extensive military-purpose airspace. The zone assigned to Goose Bay Air Base at the northeastern coast of Labrador extends over 100,000 square kilometers, an area larger than the entire neighboring New Brunswick province. The total number of sorties flown in the zone by Canadian and other NATO planes increased fivefold to almost 10,000 between 1976 and 1987, and is projected to top 30,000 by 1996. Cold Lake Air Weapons Range in Alberta and Saskatchewan covers some 10,000 square kilometers, but the total flying area available there stretches over 450,000 square kilometers.[19]

Low-level and supersonic flights are the most dangerous and health-detrimental aspect of military aviation. They impose a growing, underdocumented health and psychological toll, impairing the habitability of certain areas. A plane flying at an altitude of 75 meters generates noise levels up to 140 decibels, at which acute hearing damage may occur. An F-18 jet flying at supersonic speed for 10 minutes, for example, can "boom" an area of more than 5,000 square kilometers. Startled by a sudden sonic boom, the human body releases adrenalin, causing high blood pressure, an increased heart rate, and disturbances of the intestinal tract and other organs. What the U.S. Air Force refers to as "the sound of freedom" is frightening to those forced to endure it, particularly children.[20]

In response to growing political opposition to low-level flights, West Germany's air force had to relocate its aerial maneuvers to Canada and Turkey. Canada continues to ignore protests not only by the peace and environmental movements but also by the Innu, the native people of Ntesinan (Labrador), about the illegal use of their land. Their livelihoods are imperiled because the exercises disturb the migration and feeding behavior of caribou herds. Such unwelcome intrusions also occur in the United States, where flight training is conducted on the territories of 14 Native American nations. Thus in the name of defending one society's freedom and life-style, another's is compromised.[21]

A Drain on Energy and Materials

Whether it is jets roaring through the skies, tanks rumbling across the land, or warships navigating the high seas, the armed forces clearly use large amounts of energy. (See Table 8–2.) An F-16 jet taking off for a regular training mission is likely to consume as much as 3,400 liters of fuel before returning to its base. In less than an hour, the plane thus uses almost twice as much gas as the average U.S. motorist during one year. After-burners will triple a jet's speed to supersonic levels, but also increase consumption twentyfold. And a modern battle tank's fuel consumption is so voracious that it is better measured in gallons per mile than in miles per gallon.[22]

Unfortunately, however, few aggregate statistics are available. Petroleum products account for roughly three quarters of all energy use by the armed forces worldwide, but by far the most important is jet fuel. Worldwide, nearly one quarter of all jet fuel—some 42 million tons per year—is used for military purposes. The share rises to 27 percent in the United States, to 34 percent in the Soviet Union, and to 50 percent in West Germany. (See Table 8–3.)[23]

Again, data are most readily available for the United States. The Department of Defense consumes about 37 million tons of oil equivalent a year. This works out to 2–3 percent of total U.S. energy demand and 3–4 percent of oil demand, but would be somewhat higher if military-related activities of the Department of Energy and the National Aeronautics and Space Administration were included. The Pentagon is the single largest consumer domestically, and very likely worldwide. Put differently, it uses enough energy in 12 months to run the entire U.S. urban mass transit system for almost 14 years. During wartime, the military's share of U.S. energy consumption could reach 15–20 percent. During World War II, the Pentagon's share of national energy use leapt from 1 percent in 1940 to 29 percent in 1945.[24]

Data for other countries are more difficult to come by and often less reliable. Official figures for West Germany when it was a separate nation indicated

Table 8-2. United States: Energy Consumption of Selected Military Equipment

Equipment	Operating Distance or Times	Consumption
		(liters of fuel)
M-1 Abrams tank, average use	1 kilometer	47
F-15 jet, at peak thrust	1 minute	908
M-1 Abrams tank, peak rate	1 hour	1,113
F-4 Phantom fighter/bomber	1 hour	6,359
Battleship	1 hour	10,810
B-52 bomber	1 hour	13,671
Non-nuclear aircraft carrier	1 hour	21,300
Carrier battle group	1 day	1,589,700
Armored division, of 348 tanks	1 day	2,271,000

SOURCES: "Defending the Environment? The Record of the U.S. Military," *The Defense Monitor*, Vol. 18, No. 6, 1989; Tom Cutler, "Myths of Military Oil Supply Vulnerability," *Armed Forces Journal International*, July 1989; Greg Williams, "The Army's M-1 Tank: Has It Lived up to Expectations?" Project on Government Procurement, Washington, D.C., June 12, 1990; Center for Disarmament, *Economic and Social Consequences of the Arms Race and Military Expenditures*, Disarmament Study Series No. 11 (New York: United Nations, 1983).

Table 8-3. The Military's Use of Petroleum Products, United States and the Soviet Union, 1987

Petroleum Product	United States		Soviet Union	
	Military Use	Share of Total Use	Military Use	Share of Total Use
	(million tons)	(percent)	(million tons)	(percent)
Jet Fuel	18.6	26.9	11.8	33.9
Diesel Distillate	4.4	3.0	3.8	4.9
Residual Fuel Oil	0.5	0.9	n.a.	n.a.
Gasoline	0.3	0.1	1.4	1.7
Other[1]	0.7	0.4	0.3	0.4
Total, Military	28.1[2]	3.4	17.4[3]	3.9

[1]Includes lubricants, greases, refined products, and refinery fuel. [2]Includes 3.6 million tons purchased for stockpiling. At least one third of the total is used on U.S. bases abroad. [3]Total does not add up due to rounding.
SOURCE: Worldwatch Institute, based on Tom Cutler, "Myths of Military Oil Supply Vulnerability," *Armed Forces Journal International,* July 1989.

that the *Bundeswehr* (the armed forces) accounted for just under 1 percent of the country's total energy demand, while a calculation by a private study group put that portion at 1.44 percent during 1981–88. (Neither figure seems to include the energy consumption of NATO troops stationed in West Germany.) Military-related energy consumption in the Netherlands is estimated at 2–5 percent of national demand. The British military purchased 4.8 percent of that country's output of petroleum products in 1985, 1.6 percent of its electricity, and 0.9 percent of U.K. coal and coke.[25]

These figures may not seem exceptional when compared with the military's share of gross national products, but would be considerably higher if energy used in manufacturing weapons were included. Up-to-date data in this regard, however, are virtually unavailable. In 1971, producing arms in the United States used about 47 million tons of oil equivalent. Leaving the issue of energy intensity aside, an estimate for 1989 based on 1971 and 1989 expenditures for U.S. arms procurement and revenues

from arms exports yields a usage figure of about 68 million tons of oil equivalent, almost twice the armed forces' direct use of energy.[26]

Worldwide, energy use for weapons production is probably relatively lower because most countries do not have a significant arms industry. Still, the military sector's share of total oil and energy use may well be double the armed forces' direct share of 3–4 percent. If these assumptions are correct, the world uses about as many petroleum products for military purposes as Japan, the world's second largest economy, does for everything.[27]

With more complete statistics on military energy use, it might be possible to draw a picture of the military's contribution to air pollution. In addition, however, information is needed on jet and tank engine characteristics in order to consider the generation of pollutants. Because military equipment obviously is designed for superior combat performance, not for energy efficiency, it seems reasonable to assume that the military's share of pollution surpasses its share of energy consumed. Any assessment would also need to look at the pollution created in arms manufacturing, an effort hampered by the fact that industrial emission statistics do not distinguish between civilian and military sources.

According to a 1983 estimate by Gunar Seitz, a German environmental writer, emissions from the operations of the armed forces alone account for at least 6–10 percent of global air pollution. The Research Institute for Peace Policy in Starnberg, Germany, estimated that 10–30 percent of all global environment degradation is due to military-related activities. Others have calculated the contribution of the West German armed forces to air pollution as having been 6.5 percent of carbon monoxide, 5.4 percent of nitrogen oxides, 3.9 percent of hydrocarbons, and 1.3 percent of sulfur dioxide emissions. Since warplanes consume the bulk of the military's petroleum use, tallying their emissions of air pollutants tells a large part of the story. (See Table 8–4.) Again, in West Germany, military jets emitted 58 percent of air pollutants generated by all air traffic over that country's territory.[28]

Little work has been done to date on the military's contribution to ozone depletion and global warming. In 1988, the Pentagon's activities resulted in carbon emissions of about 46 million tons, or roughly 3.5 percent of the U.S. total. If approximations of energy use in arms production are correct, the total military-related carbon release could be as high as 10 percent.[29]

Estimating a global figure for carbon emissions from the military is fraught with uncertainty. The release from military jet fuel consumption alone comes to about 37 million tons. If the U.S. share of global military spending—just under a third—is any indication, then the U.S. armed forces' carbon emissions would have to be tripled to arrive at a rough global estimate. The result of such a back-of-the-envelope calculation is about 150 million tons: almost 3 percent of the global total, or nearly equal to the annual carbon emissions of the United Kingdom. Again, if the energy consumption of arms-producing industries were included, these numbers could well double.[30]

A similar dearth of information per-

Table 8-4. Fuel Consumption and Estimated Air Pollutant Emissions of Military Aircraft, Selected Countries and World, Late Eighties

Area	Fuel Consumption		Emissions[1]			
	Total	Share	CO	Hydrocarbons	NO$_x$	SO$_2$
	(million tons)	(percent)	(thousand tons)			
United States	18.6	44.1	381	78	157	17.9
Soviet Union	11.8	28.1	244	50	100	11.4
West Germany[2]	1.5	3.5	31	6	13	1.4
World	42.2	100.0	865	178	357	40.6

[1]Global, U.S., and Soviet emissions data calculated on basis of West German data, assuming, that is, similar aircraft engine characteristics and flight patterns. Emissions are given for carbon monoxide, nitrogen oxides and sulfur dioxide. [2]Jets of the German Air Force and those of NATO contingents stationed in former West Germany, including U.S. planes whose fuel consumption is included in the U.S. total. SOURCE: Worldwatch Institute, based on Olaf Achilles, "Militär, Rüstung und Klima," MÖP Studie VII, Arbeits-und Forschungsstelle Militär, Ökologie und Planung, Bonn, West Germany, June 1990, and on Tom Cutler, "Myths of Military Oil Supply Vulnerability," *Armed Forces Journal International*, July 1989.

vades the military use of ozone-depleting substances. The U.S. Defense Department is a major user of Halon-1211 and CFC-113, accounting for 76 percent and just under 50 percent of total U.S. use of these two compounds, respectively. Together, these two chemicals are responsible for 13 percent of overall ozone depletion. The military accounts for a much smaller share of other substances implicated in this global problem.[31]

On the other hand, the armed forces are using ozone-destroying substances that have no civilian counterpart. For example, the B-2 Stealth bomber relies on a fuel additive that reduces emission particles and thus the plane's visibility on radar screens. It is unclear how much of the additive is in use and just how potent an ozone depleter it is. Further, the combustion of solid rocket fuel, used in strategic and tactical missiles and on the U.S. Space Shuttle (some of the missions of which are military), releases hydrogen chloride gas that damages the ozone layer. According to Lenny Siegel, director of the Pacific Studies Center in California, each shuttle launch deposits 56 tons of chlorine into the upper atmosphere.[32]

It appears that the worldwide use of aluminum, copper, nickel, and platinum for military purposes surpasses the entire Third World's demand for these materials.

Without better data, it remains difficult to sketch a realistic picture of military-related energy use and pollution. While the military sector's contribution may not seem large in comparison with other human activities, it is nonetheless substantial, given that military operations do not contribute anything directly to people's social and economic well-being.

The military has a larger impact on certain non-fuel minerals and other materials. Iron and steel are the traditional backbones of any military machine. Currently, some 9 percent of global iron consumption, or roughly 60 million tons, goes to military purposes. The construction and deployment of a single land-based mobile intercontinental missile requires 4,450 tons of steel, 1,200 tons of cement, 50 tons of aluminum, 12.5 tons of chromium, 750 kilograms of titanium, and 120 kilograms of beryllium. (The two superpowers controlled almost 2,400 land-based and another 1,600 sea-based missiles in 1987.)[33]

As the emphasis of the arms race has shifted to qualitative advances, the relative importance of iron and steel has declined, while that of more "exotic" materials has increased. Many of these are essential ingredients for high-temperature alloys desired for their strength and extreme resistance to heat, wear, and corrosion.

Titanium, for example, accounts for some 20–30 percent of the weight of a sophisticated combat aircraft today, compared with 8–10 percent in the fifties. Titanium is also an important component of submarine hulls. Manufacturing a single F-16 jet engine requires almost 5,000 kilograms of materials, including 2,044 kilograms of titanium, 1,715 of nickel, 573 of chromium, 330 of cobalt, and 267 of aluminum. An M-1 battle tank engine, by comparison, requires only about 150 kilograms of materials.[34]

Global figures, in the absence of reliable data, are once again of necessity rough estimates. (See Table 8–5.) Moreover, the lack of interest in this issue during the eighties means that most available information is fairly old. It appears, though, that the estimated worldwide use of aluminum, copper, nickel, and

Table 8-5. Estimated Military Consumption of Selected Non-Fuel Minerals as a Share of Total Global Consumption, Early Eighties

Mineral	Share
	(percent)
Copper	11.1
Lead	8.1
Aluminum	6.3
Nickel	6.3
Silver	6.0
Zinc	6.0
Fluorspar	6.0
Platinum Group	5.7
Tin	5.1
Iron Ore	5.1
Mercury	4.5
Chromium	3.9
Tungsten	3.6
Manganese	2.1

SOURCE: Samuel S. Kim, *The Quest for a Just World Order* (Boulder, Colo.: Westview Press, 1984).

platinum for military purposes surpasses the entire Third World's demand for these materials.[35]

Leading the way in high-tech weaponry, the United States accounts for by far the largest share of military consumption of such valuable raw materials. The Pentagon's portion of total U.S. use of non-fuel minerals ranges generally from 5 to 15 percent, but rises to 25–40 percent for beryllium, cobalt, germanium, thorium, thallium, and titanium. Soviet military consumption of "strategic" raw materials is thought to be comparable in relative terms, but is no doubt lower in absolute amounts. For China and Europe, the share is estimated in the 3–7 percent range.[36]

Mining operations to extract these minerals entail significant environmental burdens, and many materials are highly toxic. (See Chapter 3.) Some of these materials are heavily used for civilian purposes but others, such as tita-

nium, are so expensive that they are mined primarily with military applications in mind.

The end of the cold war suggests that the armed forces may begin at last to make less of a claim on the world's scarce resources. This is certainly true to the extent that the number of weapons declines. At the same time, however, there are no indications that the quest for technological sophistication will slow, let alone come to a halt. This trend will offset at least part of any lower demand for materials that results from smaller quantities of arms.

TOXIC MENACE

"We can no longer grow our gardens, we can no longer safely bathe, and we have no water to drink." For Lorraine Hufstutler and her fellow residents of Mountainview, New Mexico, living in the shadow of nearby Kirtland Air Force Base exacts a heavy price: hazardous wastes migrating off base are contaminating the community's water supply. Mountainview's fate is shared by thousands of towns and cities across the United States (see Table 8–6) and untold numbers of communities in other countries.[37]

In their incessant pursuit of prowess and preparedness, the armed forces are poisoning the land and people they are supposed to protect. Military toxics are contaminating water used for drinking or irrigation, killing fish, befouling the air, and rendering vast tracts of land unusable for generations to come. Having been dumping grounds for a lethal soup of hazardous materials for decades, military bases have become health time bombs detonating in slow motion.

The production, maintenance, and storage of conventional, chemical, and

Table 8-6. United States: Selected Military Hazardous Waste Sites

Location	Observation
Otis Air Force Base, Mass.	Groundwater contaminated with trichloroethylene (TCE), a known carcinogen, and other toxins. In adjacent towns, lung cancer and leukemia rates 80 percent above state average.
Picatinny Arsenal, N.J.	Groundwater at the site shows TCE levels at 5,000 times Environmental Protection Agency (EPA) standards; polluted with lead, cadmium, polychlorinated biphenyls (used in radar installations and to insulate electrical equipment), phenols, furans, chromium, selenium, toluene, and cyanide. Region's major aquifer contaminated.
Aberdeen Proving Ground, Md.	Water pollution could threaten a national wildlife refuge and habitats critical to endangered species.
Norfolk Naval Shipyard, Va.	High levels of copper, zinc, and chromium discharges. Contamination of Elizabeth River, and of Willoughby and Chesapeake bays.
Tinker Air Force Base, Okla.	Concentrations of tetrachloroethylene and methylene chloride in drinking water at levels far exceeding EPA limits. TCE concentration highest ever recorded in U.S. surface waters.
Rocky Mountain Arsenal, Colo.	125 chemicals dumped over 30 years of nerve gas and pesticide production. The largest of all seriously contaminated sites, called "the most contaminated square mile on earth" by the Army Corps of Engineers.
Hill Air Force Base, Utah	Heavy on-base groundwater contamination, including volatile organic compounds up to 27,000 parts per billion (ppb); TCE up to 1.7 million ppb; chromium up to 1,900 ppb; lead up to 3,000 ppb.
McClellan Air Force Base, Calif.	Unacceptable levels of TCE, arsenic, barium, cadmium, chromium, and lead found in municipal well system serving 23,000 people.
McChord Air Force Base, Wash.	Benzene, a carcinogen, found on-base in concentrations as high as 503 ppb, nearly 1,000 times the state's limit of 0.6 ppb.

SOURCE: Worldwatch Institute, based on sources documented in endnote 37.

nuclear weapons and other pieces of military equipment generates vast amounts of materials inimical to human health and environmental quality. These wastes include fuels, paints, solvents, heavy metals, pesticides, poly-chlorinated biphenyls (PCBs), cyanides, phenols, acids, alkalies, propellants, and explosives.[38]

Knowledge about the health effects of these substances remains limited, but it is suspected that human exposure through drinking, skin absorption, or in-halation may cause cancer, birth defects, and chromosome damage or may seri-ously impair the function of a person's liver, kidneys, blood, and central ner-vous system. According to a study by the National Cancer Institute, 14,500 civil-ian employees at Hill Air Force Base in Utah exposed to carbon tetrachloride, trichloroethylene (TCE), and other sol-vents during the mid-fifties suffered a higher death rate from multiple myelo-mas and non-Hodgkins lymphoma than other civilians in their age group.[39]

The military is quite likely the largest generator of hazardous wastes in the United States and, rivaled only by the Soviet armed forces, the world. In recent years, the Pentagon generated between 400,000 and 500,000 tons of toxics an-nually, more than the top five U.S. chem-ical companies combined. Its contrac-tors produced tens if not hundreds of thousands of tons more. And these fig-ures do not even include the large amounts of toxics spewing from the De-partment of Energy's nuclear weapons complex.[40]

Assessing the extent of toxic contami-nation is akin to opening Pandora's box: the number of U.S. sites on which prob-lems have been spotted mushroomed from 3,526 on 529 military bases in 1986 to 14,401 on 1,579 installations in 1989. In addition, more than 7,000 former military properties are being investi-gated. Some 96 bases are so badly pol-luted that they are already on the Super-fund National Priorities List. But Gordon Davidson, deputy director of the Federal Facilities Compliance Task Force of the Environmental Protection Agency (EPA), believes as many as 1,000 military sites may eventually be added to the Priorities List. "Cleanup" is pro-ceeding at a snail's pace, and appears designed primarily to preclude any fur-ther deterioration. Meanwhile, new wastes are generated each day, though the Pentagon has said it wants to cut the volume in half by 1992.[41]

In recent years, the Pentagon generated more toxics annually than the top five U.S. chemical companies combined.

The extent of pollution at the Depart-ment of Defense's 375 bases outside the United States remains shrouded in se-crecy. In violation of a 1978 presidential order, the Pentagon has neither a pro-gram nor a budget for cleaning up over-seas bases. Publication of a 1986 Gen-eral Accounting Office (GAO) study that identified significant contamination at U.S. bases in Italy, the United Kingdom, and West Germany was suppressed by the Pentagon and the State Department. A second GAO report, completed in the fall of 1990, is expected to be classified as well because it could prove embar-rassing and might fuel demands for a U.S. withdrawal.[42]

U.S. military installations abroad are exempt from the U.S. National Environ-mental Policy Act and, under basing agreements, from pertinent host-nation laws as well. But host governments are beginning to demand compliance with their environmental rules. As the U.S. military prepares to withdraw from some of its European bases, the question of who will shoulder the cleanup costs will become more and more important.[43]

Half the U.S. bases abroad are located in the western part of the new Germany. An informal and quite likely incomplete survey revealed that the U.S. Army alone holds 300 contaminated sites there. But the Army plans to turn over vacated facilities without a major cleanup effort. The Air Force, meanwhile, acknowledges that it has polluted soil and groundwater at every one of its airfields in Europe. In Japan, too, what little is known about the U.S. military's toxic effects confirms the story. Heavy metals such as lead and mercury have been detected in a dump at Atsugi Naval Air Station near Tokyo. There is air and soil pollution from on-base industrial plants, and water pollution from American naval vessels.[44]

Even if nuclear arsenals were abolished tomorrow, their waste products cannot be.

Even less is known about conditions at U.S. installations in the Third World, though contamination is likely to be extensive. PCB pollution afflicts U.S. bases in Guam, South Korea, and the Philippines. On Guam, the U.S. Air Force and Navy dumped large quantities of the solvent TCE and untreated antifreeze solutions onto the ground and into storm drains, contaminating the aquifer that supplies drinking water for three quarters of the island's population. Tests showed TCE levels at some points in the aquifer to be six times the permissible limit.[45]

A veil of secrecy surrounds the situation at most other countries' military installations, though bits and pieces of information are available. The armed forces of the former West Germany, for example, incinerated some 100 million tons of solid waste each year, and used about 500 tons of toxic chemicals, including 50–90 tons of fungicides and herbicides. Some 12 million cubic meters of liquid wastes, out of an annual volume of 30 million, were released into local streams or the groundwater.[46]

As Soviet forces withdraw from Eastern Europe, it is becoming clear that the bases they occupied are in desperate need of cleanup. In addition, fuel, wastes, and unexploded ammunition were dumped in many unmarked off-base locations. The groundwater beneath Frenstat in northern Moravia, Czechoslovakia, is so contaminated, says Deputy Environment Minister Jaroslav Vlcek, that "you could practically drill for diesel there." In Vysoke Myto in central Bohemia, groundwater tests reveal toxics in concentrations 30–50 times allowable levels. Up to 8,000 square kilometers—6 percent of Czechoslovakia's territory—have been polluted or despoiled.[47]

In Hungary, parts of Kiskunsag National Park have been used as firing ranges and ammunition dumping grounds. In the former East Germany, at least 90 Soviet installations are severely polluted. At Lärz Air Base in Mecklenburg, for example, more than 50,000 tons of fuel leaked into the soil. An estimated 10 percent of East German territory has been despoiled by Soviet military operations. Polish environmental inspectors were given free access to Soviet bases in their country in August 1990: the first probes involve the Swinoujscie naval base near Szczecin, where the aquifer is suspected to be polluted from fuel dumping, and airfields near Chojno and Kluczewo.[48]

Even less is known about the toxics used in the arms industry and about workers' exposure to them. Military secrecy has hampered efforts to monitor and enforce safety at aerospace and other factories. It is indisputable, however, that the manufacture of explosives, composite materials, and electronic components can endanger human health. The production of explosives and propulsion systems, for example, entails potential exposure to such hazardous emissions as chlorine gas, dibenzodioxins, and dibenzofurans.[49]

Composite materials like carbon fiber and glass fiber that make military aircraft lighter, stronger, and less visible on radar screens are suspected of poisoning workers who handle them. Chemicals used to bond these materials, including phenol formaldehyde and methylene dianiline, are thought to cause cancer when inhaled or absorbed through the skin, while fiber fragments can damage the lungs and also cause cancer. Workers at plants involved in top-secret projects such as the F-117 Stealth jet fighter are not permitted to explain fully even to their own doctors the circumstances that may cause their illnesses. Inspectors of the Occupational Safety and Health Administration (OSHA) need special security clearances to visit some arms production facilities. Between 1985 and 1989, Lockheed workers in California who had fallen ill filed 352 claims against the company, charging that they were never informed of the hazards involved. In June 1989, management agreed to pay $1.4 million in penalties for 440 violations of workplace safety rules.[50]

The production of semiconductors and other electronic components involves many highly toxic materials. In the United States, 20 percent of that industry's output was purchased by the Pentagon in 1987. Workers may be exposed to solvents, alkalies, and metals used in electroplating, etching, stripping, soldering, and degreasing; to vapors from phosphine, arsine, and phosgene gases; and to ionizing and non-ionizing forms of radiation. Hazards derive mostly from long-term exposure to a multitude of substances that are suspected carcinogens, teratogens, or mutagens. But knowledge about the full range of effects is still in its infancy.[51]

What is publicly known about military toxics, particularly in the workplace, constitutes probably little more than the tip of the iceberg. As the residents of Mountainview, New Mexico, have discovered, acknowledgement of the problem is but a tiny first step on the long path toward coping with the inherent dangers.

NUCLEAR WASTELAND

Of all the different ways in which military operations have an impact on human health and the environment, nuclear weapons production and testing is the most severe and enduring. While the effect of toxic wastes is relatively localized, the spread of nuclear debris is global, and while hazardous substances will be with us for generations, plutonium has a half-life of 24,000 years. Even if nuclear arsenals were abolished tomorrow, their waste products cannot be.

In February 1955, Thomas E. Murray, a member of the Atomic Energy Commission (AEC), the government body in charge of the U.S. nuclear weapons program, asserted: "We must not let anything interfere with this series of [nuclear] tests—nothing." Made in closed session, it was a statement emblematic of the priorities of the time in both East and West: the brisk buildup of nuclear arsenals—from uranium mining, to warhead design and manufacture, to testing and deployment—won unambiguous precedence over the health and safety of workers, soldiers, and residents. For decades, officials knowingly subjected their own unsuspecting citizens to the dangers of radioactivity in the name of national security.[52]

The U.S. government only recently acknowledged that radiation doses emanating from its plutonium production facility in Hanford, Washington, in the forties and fifties were sufficient to cause cancer. Similarly, only in 1989 did Soviet authorities finally confirm a fatal accident had occurred at a plutonium processing plant 32 years before. As early as the sixties, local Soviet officials were aware of the health risks of nuclear weapons tests conducted on Siberia's Chukotka Peninsula, but failed to inform the public.[53]

Compensation for injuries is a distant dream for Soviet citizens. In the United States, government trust funds totalling a paltry $200 million were set up in 1985 and 1990 for specific groups of victims. But the government has long claimed that its "sovereign immunity" shields it from any additional liability (which could well run into the billions of dollars). And the corporate contractors operating the nuclear weapons facilities are protected from all liabilities and penalties, though efforts are being made to change this.[54]

Hundreds of workers at Hanford were absorbing every six months a quantity of plutonium equal to the current lifetime limit.

Like a nuclear reactor reaching critical mass, the past two years has seen a flood of front-page articles, official investigations, and hearings in the United States, showering the public with shocking new revelations about the nuclear weapons complex. Although many details remain to be uncovered, what has emerged is a story ranging from gross negligence and

excessive secrecy to pervasive deceit and outright criminal conduct. Despite all ideological differences, these are attributes shared by bomb makers in West and East. While some of the worst practices seem to belong to the past—a number of nuclear weapons plants in the United States and the Soviet Union are closed at least temporarily for safety or political reasons—the peril of highly radioactive wastes "may exist for centuries or millennia," in the words of an internal study by Du Pont, a U.S. government contractor.[55]

The size of the nuclear weapons industry is truly colossal. Since the forties, the United States alone has spent close to $300 billion (in 1990 dollars) on designing, testing, and manufacturing nuclear warheads. Over that time, approximately 60,000 warheads were produced in a complex of more than 100 facilities in 32 states, employing some 600,000 workers. Either stored or assembled in warheads are 90–100 tons of weapon-grade plutonium and 500 tons of highly enriched uranium. Stockpiles in the Soviet Union are believed to be roughly of the same magnitude, while those of the other self-acknowledged nuclear powers—China, France, and the United Kingdom—are much smaller.[56]

Every step in the bomb-making process involves severe environmental threats. At the Purex plant at the Hanford Reservation in Washington, which is now closed, the production of a single kilogram of plutonium generated about 1,300 liters of liquid high-level radioactive waste laced with hazardous chemicals, more than 200,000 kilograms of low- to intermediate-level waste, and almost 10 million liters of contaminated cooling water. Military nuclear reactors are responsible for an estimated 97 percent of all high-level nuclear waste and 78 percent of all low-level nuclear waste (both by volume) in the United States.

Measured in curies, however, the military portion comes to 6 and 74 percent, respectively. The military-related high-level waste inventory has been estimated at about 1.4 billion curies. (A curie measures the intensity of radiation and is equal to 3.7×10^{10} disintegrations per second; by comparison, about 50 million curies were released during the accident at Chernobyl.)[57]

By 1989, more than 3,200 sites in about 100 locations owned by the U.S. Department of Energy (which took over the work of AEC) had been identified as having tainted soil, groundwater, or both. Decades of deliberate and accidental releases of radioactive material and toxic substances make for a modern-day horror story. (See Table 8–7.) More than 50 Nagasaki-size bombs could be manufactured from the waste that has leaked just from Hanford's underground tanks. At Rocky Flats, enough plutonium has accumulated in ventilation ducts to make seven nuclear bombs. After a large 1969 fire there, investigators found the highest concentrations of plutonium ever measured near an urban area, including around Nagasaki.[58]

Additional danger looms from wastes that have not escaped into the environment—at least not yet. Some storage tanks at Savannah River and Hanford holding plutonium by-products such as cesium, strontium, and iodine are apparently in danger of exploding, according to a government advisory panel. Should such a detonation occur at Savannah River, residents nearby could contract up to 20,000 additional cancers.[59]

Radiation is known to cause cancer, leukemia, multiple myeloma, brain tumors, thyroid disorders, sterility, miscarriages, and birth defects. Damage to the human body depends on the size and type of the radiation dose and on how fast it is absorbed. It is difficult, however, to establish a causal link between a specific radiation exposure and adverse health effects because of latency periods that are sometimes long, the possibility that illness is caused by other factors, and the fact that most government records are still secret. Recent studies conclude that the risks of ionizing radiation are three times higher than previously thought, and many scientists believe there is no "safe" level of radiation exposure.[60]

Some 300,000 people, or half of those who ever worked in the U.S. nuclear weapons complex, are believed to have been affected by exposure to radiation. A study of almost 4,000 Rocky Flats workers found elevated incidence of brain tumors, malignant melanoma, respiratory cancer, and chromosome aberrations, even though they had been exposed to only billionths of a curie of radioactivity. Hundreds of workers at Hanford were absorbing every six months a quantity of plutonium equal to the current lifetime limit.[61]

DOE has begun to release data on worker health. The records are far from complete, however, and do not allow any firm conclusions about actual health effects. Furthermore, the Comprehensive Epidemiological Data Resource—DOE's planned system for disseminating health data to the Department of Health and Human Services and to independent researchers—is likely to continue to impede public access to essential data. DOE will also retain sole responsibility for collecting and releasing worker and community health records in the future.[62]

People living near the Hanford Reservation in the Pacific Northwest have received some of the largest amounts of radiation in the world over a long period. More than 400,000 curies of radioactive iodine—26,000 times the amount released at Three Mile Island in 1979—were emitted between 1944 and 1947

**Table 8-7. United States: Radioactive and Toxic Contamination at Major Nuclear
Weapons Production Facilities, 1990**

Facility (Task)	Observation
Feed Materials Production Center, Fernald, Ohio (converts uranium into metal ingots)	Since plant's opening, at least 250 tons of uranium oxide (and perhaps six times as much as that) released into the air. Off-site surface and groundwater contaminated with uranium, cesium, thorium. High levels of radon gas emitted.
Hanford Reservation, Wash. (recycles uranium and extracts plutonium)	Since 1944, 760 billion liters of contaminated water (enough to create a 12-meter-deep lake the size of Manhattan) have entered groundwater and Columbia River; 4.5 million liters of high-level radioactive waste leaked from underground tanks. Officials knowingly and sometimes deliberately exposed the public to large amounts of airborne radiation in 1943–56.
Savannah River, S.C. (produces plutonium and tritium)	Radioactive substances and chemicals found in the Tuscaloosa aquifer at levels 400 times greater than government considers safe. Released millions of curies of tritium gas into atmosphere since 1954.
Rocky Flats, Colo. (assembles plutonium triggers)	Since 1952, 200 fires have contaminated the Denver region with unknown amount of plutonium. Strontium, cesium, and cancer-causing chemicals leaked into underground water.
Oak Ridge Reservation, Tenn. (produces lithium-deuteride and highly enriched uranium)	Since 1943, thousands of pounds of uranium emitted into atmosphere. Radioactive and hazardous wastes have severely polluted local streams flowing into the Clinch River. Watts Bar Reservoir, a recreational lake, is contaminated with at least 175,000 tons of mercury and cesium.

SOURCES: "Status of Major Nuclear Weapons Production Facilities: 1990," *PSR Monitor*, September 1990; Robert Alvarez and Arjun Makhijani, "Hidden Legacy of the Arms Race: Radioactive Waste," *Technology Review*, August/September 1989; and other sources.

alone, exposing over a quarter-million unsuspecting people. Close to 14,000 residents, about 5 percent, received doses of 33 rads ("radiation absorbed dose," which measures the amount of radiation absorbed by the human body but not the biological damage). This is 1,200 times the level currently considered safe by the federal government. Some residents were even exposed to doses of up to 2,900 rads. People living near Hanford have an unusually high number of various cancers, miscarriages, and other ailments.[63]

Glasnost has given the world first insights into the consequences of the Soviet nuclear weapons program. Though still very limited in scope, the picture that emerges is one of enormous contamination. At Kyshtym in the eastern Urals (the Soviet counterpart to Hanford), perhaps over 6,000 workers were exposed to radiation doses of more than 100 rem. (This measure recognizes that different types of radiation have different biological effects. One rem is roughly equivalent to seven or eight x rays. A 500-rem dose is usually fatal, while 100–200 rem could produce cancer in the long run.) Cesium, strontium, and other liquid radioactive wastes were dumped from the late forties into the Techa river. The river became so polluted that traces of radioactivity showed up in the Arctic Ocean, nearly 1,000 miles away. Those living along the Techa had to be evacuated.[64]

From 1952 on, nuclear waste was dumped into nearby Lake Karachay; the heat of the radionuclides began to dry out the 10-square-kilometer body of water. By 1988, it contained 120 million curies of strontium-90, cesium-137, residual plutonium, and other long-lived isotopes, two-and-a-half times more than was released at Chernobyl. The lake is now covered by a thick layer of concrete.[65]

In September 1957, high-level nuclear waste stored at Kyshtym suffered a chemical explosion. The accident severely contaminated 15,000 square kilometers of land that was home to more than a quarter-million people, forcing the evacuation of 10,000. The explosion released about a third as much overall radiation as at Chernobyl.[66]

Warhead testing is the final phase in the development of nuclear arms, but it was the activity that elicited the earliest health concerns. From 1945 to 1989, more than 1,800 bombs were exploded at more than 35 sites around the world—virtually all of them on the land of colonized or otherwise subjected native peoples, including the western Shoshones, Kazakhs, Uygurs, Australian aborigines, and Pacific Islanders.[67]

Roughly a quarter of all tests, most of them before 1963, were conducted in the atmosphere, injecting far more radioactive debris into the atmosphere than the Chernobyl accident did. The fallout may have caused as many as 86,000 birth defects worldwide and, according to a 1977 U.N. estimate, some 150,000 premature deaths. Although underground testing has cut down on radiation, some still escapes into the atmosphere (known as "venting") and is also suspected of leaching into groundwater. More than a third of U.S. underground tests and an unknown number of Soviet blasts have vented.[68]

In the United States, individuals exposed to nuclear fallout include 400,000 "atomic veterans"—soldiers ordered to observe atmospheric testing, 100,000 test site workers, and a similar number of "downwinders" living in parts of Nevada, Arizona, and Utah. Yet millions more Americans are thought to bear trace amounts of plutonium in their tissues and organs. Since 1961, leukemia cases began to appear with increasing frequency in U.S. communities downwind from test sites. Today, thyroid and bone cancer in southwestern Utah are, respectively, 8 and 12 times the national average.[69]

High levels of radioactivity in the soil and food crops have rendered Bikini atoll in the Pacific uninhabitable since 1954. Many residents of neighboring Rongelap have developed thyroid tumors. The full extent of radioactive contamination from 160 French nuclear tests conducted since 1966 on two other Pacific atolls, Moruroa and Fangataufa, is unknown. A typhoon in 1981 dispersed huge amounts of nuclear waste, including 10–20 kilograms of plutonium, in the ocean. From the early eighties on, increases in the number of leukemia cases, brain tumors, and thyroid cancers have been registered in French Polynesia.[70]

The most severely poisoned areas may become "national sacrifice zones," ghastly monuments to the cold war.

The Soviet Academy of Medical Sciences determined in 1989 that residents of Semipalatinsk, near the main test site in Kazakhstan, had experienced excess cancers, genetic diseases, and child mortality because of radiation exposure from pre-1963 atmospheric tests. In 1988, the incidence of cancer was 70 percent above the national average. Kazakh activists claim that life expectancy in the republic has declined by four years over the past two decades, and that the number of people suffering from blood diseases has doubled since 1970. Bowing to strong grassroots pressure, the Soviet government canceled 11 tests in 1989 and decided in March 1990 to end nuclear testing near Semipalatinsk by 1993. (Tests, though fewer in number, may continue on Novaya Zemlya island in the Arctic.)[71]

MAKING PEACE WITH THE ENVIRONMENT

As the East-West confrontation has faded, the environmental legacy of the cold war is slowly being put on the agenda. The cost of repairing the damage wrought by permanent war preparation will be staggering.

For the United States, the General Accounting Office calculated in 1988 nuclear decontamination costs of $100–130 billion, or $2 million for every nuclear warhead the nation has produced. More recent assessments speak of $200 billion. Estimates for required outlays to deal with toxic wastes at U.S. military bases have skyrocketed from $500 million in 1983 to $20–40 billion today, and are certain to escalate further as additional toxic sites are identified and cleanup work progresses. In addition, U.S. forces stationed in Western Europe would need to spend at least $580 million to reduce air and water pollution at their bases.[72]

Cleaning up Soviet bases in Czechoslovakia has been estimated to cost $2 million per site, or close to $300 million for all 132 installations. In Hungary, the cleanup bill could cost several tens of millions of dollars. These amounts are hardly affordable in these financially strapped nations. It has been estimated that it may cost $250 million to rehabilitate one square kilometer of strafed and bombed land in the United States.[73]

Funding still badly trails assessed needs. The budget for environmental programs at U.S. military installations, for example, has risen from virtually nothing in the early eighties to about $600 million in 1990 and a projected $850 million in 1991. Yet the Pentagon's "Defense Environmental Restoration Program" constitutes only about 0.2 percent of the annual military budget. The U.S. Department of Energy's budget for coping with contamination of the nuclear weapons complex has more than quadrupled between 1986 and 1991, to $4.3 billion, but is still dwarfed by the department's spending for continued weapons production.[74]

Beyond the financial implications, however, are the less quantifiable though by no means insignificant social costs. Those who have been exposed to crippling or fatal pollution in the name of national security are already paying a heavy price for the geopolitical rivalry of the past half-century. And the time required for decontaminating sites polluted by toxic and radioactive wastes may have to be measured in decades and generations. The most severely poisoned areas could prove impossible to "clean up" or otherwise rehabilitate. Fenced-off and unsuitable for any use, they may become "national sacrifice zones," ghastly monuments to the cold war. Environmental destruction is certain to be a most lasting legacy of the East-West rivalry.

The military sector has long considered itself beyond the purview of existing environmental laws and regulations. Public awareness of environmental problems generated by military activities is important if the government agencies and their private contractors who inflicted the damage are to be held to greater accountability.

In 1978, President Carter signed an executive order demanding that all U.S. federal facilities comply with the government's environmental regulations. But the Reagan administration left the Pentagon to police itself, assigning it sole responsibility for base cleanups. Representative John Dingell of Michigan complained in 1988 that "the Defense Department's attitude varies between reluctant compliance and active disregard for the law."[75]

The Environmental Protection Agency's powers to enforce environmental laws on military bases, meanwhile, are severely circumscribed, as are those of OSHA. The Justice Department has prevented EPA from suing other federal agencies, from imposing cleanup orders on them without their consent, or from fining them. And it has gone to court several times to preclude state agencies from fining federal installations. In consequence, EPA has had to settle for negotiating "voluntary compliance agreements" of doubtful value with the military. Two bills pending in Congress would strengthen EPA's hand and allow states to penalize federal polluters.[76]

An assessment of environmentally relevant laws in Germany, including those regulating land use, waste disposal, and emissions of pollutants, found that virtually every one of them contained some loopholes that accorded the armed forces special privileges. And in a classic example of the fox guarding the henhouse, the *Bundeswehr* has had the sole right since 1986 to inspect its own compliance with federal air pollution emission laws. Similar conditions are likely to exist in other countries as well.[77]

The issue of military-related pollution and degradation can unite environmental and peace movements. In the United States, the National Toxics Campaign and the Citizen's Clearinghouse for Hazardous Wastes are assisting communities in confronting military pollution in their own backyards. On the national level, along with other groups, they are pushing for legislation making military facilities subject to the same environmental requirements and penalties as private polluters, and calling for an "Environmental Security Fund" that automatically provides monies for the investigation and cleanup of toxic contamination at military facilities. The Military Production Network, meanwhile, brings together groups across the nation concerned about the effects of nuclear weapons production.[78]

In West Germany, citizens outraged at the continuing stress from low-level flights demanded an end to the practice. In both parts of the newly unified Germany, toxic contamination, particularly at bases occupied by their former superpower patrons, is rapidly becoming a "hot" issue. In Kazakhstan, in the Soviet Union, a large and vocal grassroots movement opposed to all nuclear tests has arisen virtually overnight. Supported by the coal miners union, the "Nevada-Semipalatinsk" movement (as it calls itself, to underline the shared fate of Americans and Soviets) succeeded in forcing the cancellation of most tests planned for 1989 and an end to all tests by 1993.[79]

These examples show that strong public pressure can succeed in changing the military's attitude toward the environment. But to be more effective in their struggle, grassroots movements need adequate tools. One is "right-to-know" legislation as it is now being applied to U.S. companies' pollution in the civilian sphere. Piercing through the national security smokescreen, such legislation could require not only defense agencies but also military contractors to prepare detailed reports on hazardous substances handled and released by them, and to make the data available to the public. Environmental impact statements for any future military projects, already required for the U.S. and Canadian armed forces, are an important way to identify potential adverse impacts before they become a reality.[80]

Unlike in the civilian sphere, however, it makes little sense to demand stricter emission norms for bomb plants or more fuel-efficient tanks. The essence of all military operations is achieving a margin of superiority over real or perceived adversaries, at whatever environmental or other cost. The fundamental incompatibility of the military and the environment was brought home recently in a community hearing in Virginia by a U.S. military base commander: "We are in the business of protecting the nation, not the environment."[81]

A world that wants to make peace with the environment cannot continue to fight wars or to sacrifice human health and the earth's ecosystems preparing for them. Environmental quality joins a long list of solid reasons for moving toward disarmament. Despoiling and undermining vital natural support systems is a steep price to pay for freedom and national sovereignty.

9

Asking How Much Is Enough

Alan Durning

Early in the age of affluence that followed World War II, an American retailing analyst named Victor Lebow proclaimed, "Our enormously productive economy . . . demands that we make consumption our way of life, that we convert the buying and use of goods into rituals, that we seek our spiritual satisfaction, our ego satisfaction, in consumption . . . .We need things consumed, burned up, worn out, replaced, and discarded at an ever increasing rate." Americans have responded to Mr. Lebow's call, and much of the world has followed.[1]

Consumption has become a central pillar of life in industrial lands, and is even embedded in social values. Opinion surveys in the world's two largest economies—Japan and the United States—show consumerist definitions of success becoming ever more prevalent. In Taiwan, a billboard demands "Why Aren't You a Millionaire Yet?" The Japanese speak of the "new three sacred treasures": color television, air conditioning, and the automobile.[2]

The affluent life-style born in the United States is emulated by those who can afford it around the world. And many can: the average person today is four-and-a-half times richer than were his or her great-grandparents at the turn of the century. Needless to say, that new global wealth is not evenly spread among the earth's people. One billion live in unprecedented luxury; 1 billion live in destitution. Even American children have more pocket money—$230 a year—than the half-billion poorest people alive.[3]

Overconsumption by the world's fortunate is an environmental problem unmatched in severity by anything but perhaps population growth. Their surging exploitation of resources threatens to exhaust or unalterably disfigure forests, soils, water, air, and climate. Ironically, high consumption may be a mixed blessing in human terms too. The time-honored values of integrity of character, good work, friendship, family, and community have often been sacrificed in the rush to riches. Thus, many in the industrial lands have a sense that their world of plenty is somehow hollow—that, hoodwinked by a consumerist culture, they have been fruitlessly attempting to satisfy what are essentially social, psychological, and spiritual needs with material things.[4]

Of course, the opposite of overconsumption—poverty—is no solution to either environmental or human problems. It is infinitely worse for people and bad for the natural world too. Dispossessed peasants slash and burn their way into the rain forests of Latin America, and hungry nomads turn their herds out onto fragile African rangeland, reducing it to desert. If environmental destruction results when people have either too little or too much, we are left to wonder how much is enough. What level of consumption can the earth support? When does having more cease to add appreciably to human satisfaction?

Answering these questions definitively is impossible, but for each of us in the world's consuming class, asking is essential nonetheless. Unless we see that more is not always better, our efforts to forestall ecological decline will be overwhelmed by our appetites.

The Consuming Society

Skyrocketing consumption is the hallmark of our era. The headlong advance of technology, rising earnings, and consequently cheaper material goods have lifted overall consumption to levels never dreamed of a century ago. The trend is visible in statistics for almost any per capita indicator. Worldwide, since mid-century the intake of copper, energy, meat, steel, and wood has approximately doubled; car ownership and cement consumption have quadrupled; plastic use has quintupled; aluminum

consumption has grown sevenfold; and air travel has multiplied 32 times.[5]

Moneyed regions account for the largest waves of consumption since 1950. In the United States, the world's premier consuming society, on average people today own twice as many cars, drive two-and-a-half times as far, use 21 times as much plastic, and travel 25 times as far by air as did their parents in 1950. Air conditioning spread from 15 percent of households in 1960 to 64 percent in 1987, and color televisions from 1 to 93 percent. Microwave ovens and video cassette recorders found their way into almost two thirds of American homes during the eighties alone. (See Figure 9–1.)[6]

That decade was a period of marked extravagance in the United States; not since the roaring twenties had conspicuous consumption been so lauded. Between 1978 and 1987, sales of Jaguar automobiles increased eightfold, and the average age of first-time fur coat buyers fell from 50 to 26. The select club of American millionaires more than doubled its membership from 600,000 to 1.5 million over the decade, while the number of American billionaires reached 58 by 1990.[7]

Japan and Western Europe have dis-

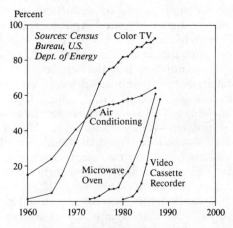

Figure 9-1. U.S. Household Ownership of Appliances, 1960–88

played parallel trends. Per person, the Japanese of today consume more than four times as much aluminum, almost five times as much energy, and 25 times as much steel as people in Japan did in 1950. They also own four times as many cars and eat nearly twice as much meat. In 1972, 1 million Japanese traveled abroad; in 1990, the number was expected to top 10 million. As in the United States, the eighties were a particularly consumerist decade in Japan, with sales of BMW automobiles rising tenfold over the decade. Ironically, in 1990 a *reja bumu* (leisure boom) combined with concern for nature to create two new status symbols: four-wheel drive Range Rovers from England and cabins made of imported American logs.[8]

Still, Japan has come to the high consumption ethos hesitantly. Many older Japanese still hold to their time-honored belief in frugality. Yorimoto Katsumi of Waseda University in Tokyo writes, "Members of the older generation . . . are careful to save every scrap of paper and bit of string for future use." A recent wave of stratospheric spending—cups of coffee that cost $350 and mink coats for dogs—has created a crisis of values in the society. Says one student, "Japanese people are materialistically well-off, but not inside . . . .We never have time to find ourselves, or what we should seek in life."[9]

Like the Japanese, West Europeans' consumption levels are only one notch below Americans'. Taken together, France, West Germany, and the United Kingdom almost doubled their per capita use of steel, more than doubled their intake of cement and aluminum, and tripled their paper consumption since mid-century. Just in the first half of the eighties, per capita consumption of frozen prepared meals—with their excessive packaging—rose more than 30 percent in every West European country except Finland; in Switzerland, the jump was 180 percent. As trade barriers come down in the move toward a single European market by 1992, prices will likely fall and product promotion grow more aggressive, boosting consumption higher.[10]

What level of consumption can the earth support?

The collapse of socialist governments in Eastern Europe, meanwhile, unleashed a tidal wave of consumer demand that had gone unsatisfied in the region's ossified state-controlled economies. A young man in a Budapest bar captured his country's mood when he told a western reporter: "People in the West think that we in Hungary don't know how they live. Well, we do know how they live, and we want to live like that, too." Says German banker Ulrich Ramm, "The East Germans want cars, videos and Marlboros." Seventy percent of those living in the former East Germany hope to enter the world's automobile class soon; they bought 200,000 used western cars in the first half of 1990 alone. Western carmakers' plans for Eastern Europe promise to give the region the largest number of new car factories in the world.[11]

The late eighties saw some poor societies begin the transition to consuming ways. In China, the sudden surge in spending on consumer durables shows up clearly in data from the State Statistical Bureau: between 1982 and 1987, color televisions spread from 1 percent to 35 percent of urban Chinese homes, the share with washing machines quadrupled from 16 to 67 percent, and refrigerators grew in prevalence from 1 percent to 20 percent of homes.[12]

Meanwhile, in India, the emergence of a middle class with perhaps 100 million members, along with liberalization of the consumer market and the introduction of buying on credit, has led to explosive growth in sales of everything from automobiles and motorbikes to televisions and frozen dinners. The *Wall Street Journal* gloats, "The traditional conservative Indian who believes in modesty and savings is gradually giving way to a new generation that thinks as freely as it spends."[13]

The world's 1 billion meat eaters and car drivers are responsible for the lion's share of the damage humans have caused to common global resources.

Few would begrudge anyone the simple advantages of cold food storage or mechanized clothes washing. The point, rather, is that even the non-western nations with the longest histories are increasingly emulating the high-consumption style of life. The lure of "modern" things is hard to resist: Coca-Cola soft drink is sold in more than 160 countries, and "Dallas," the television series that portrays the richest class of Americans, is avidly followed in many of the world's poorest nations.[14]

Long before all the world's people could achieve the American dream, however, the planet would be laid waste. The world's 1 billion meat eaters, car drivers, and throwaway consumers are responsible for the lion's share of the damage humans have caused to common global resources. For one thing, supporting the life-style of the affluent requires resources from far away. A Dutch person's consumption of food, wood, natural fibers, and other products of the soil involves exploitation of five times as much land outside the country as inside—much of it in the Third World. Industrial

nations account for close to two thirds of global use of steel, more than two thirds of aluminum, copper, lead, nickel, tin, and zinc, and three fourths of energy.[15]

Those in the wealthiest fifth of humanity have built more than 99 percent of the world's nuclear warheads. Their appetite for wood is a driving force behind destruction of the tropical rain forests, and the resulting extinction of countless species. (See Chapter 5.) Over the past century, their economies have pumped out two thirds of the greenhouse gases that threaten the earth's climate, and each year their energy use releases perhaps three fourths of the sulfur and nitrogen oxides that cause acid rain. Their industries generate most of the world's hazardous chemical wastes, and their air conditioners, aerosol sprays, and factories release almost 90 percent of the chlorofluorocarbons that destroy the earth's protective ozone layer. Clearly, even 1 billion profligate consumers is too much for the earth.[16]

Beyond the environmental costs of acquisitiveness, some perplexing findings of social scientists throw doubt on the wisdom of high consumption as a personal and national goal: rich societies have had little success in turning consumption into fulfillment. Regular surveys by the National Opinion Research Center of the University of Chicago reveal, for example, that no more Americans report they are "very happy" now than in 1957. The share has fluctuated around one third since then, despite a doubling of personal consumption expenditures per capita. Whatever Americans are buying, it does not seem to be enough.[17]

Likewise, a landmark study in 1974 revealed that Nigerians, Filipinos, Panamanians, Yugoslavians, Japanese, Israelis, and West Germans all ranked themselves near the middle of a happiness scale. Confounding any attempt to correlate affluence and happiness, poor

Cubans and rich Americans were both found to be considerably happier than the norm, and citizens of India and the Dominican Republic, less so. As Oxford psychologist Michael Argyle writes, "there is very little difference in the levels of reported happiness found in rich and very poor countries."[18]

Measured in constant dollars, the world's people have consumed as many goods and services since 1950 as all previous generations put together. As noted in Chapter 3, since 1940 Americans alone have used up as large a share of the earth's mineral resources as did everyone before them combined. If the effectiveness of that consumption in providing personal fulfillment is questionable, perhaps environmental concerns can help us redefine our goals.[19]

IN SEARCH OF SUFFICIENCY

In simplified terms, an economy's total burden on the ecological systems that undergird it is a function of three factors: the size of the population, average consumption, and the broad set of technologies—everything from mundane clotheslines to the most sophisticated satellite communications systems—the economy uses to provide goods and services.

Changing agricultural patterns, transportation systems, urban design, energy use, and the like could radically reduce the total environmental damage caused by the consuming societies, while allowing those at the bottom of the economic ladder to rise without producing such egregious effects. Japan, for example, uses a third as much energy as the Soviet Union to produce a dollar's worth of goods and services, and Norwegians use half as much paper and cardboard apiece

as their neighbors in Sweden, though they are equals in literacy and richer in monetary terms.[20]

Eventually, though, technological change will need its complement in the reduction of material wants. José Goldemberg of the University of São Paulo and an international team of researchers conducted a careful study of the potential to cut fossil fuel consumption through greater efficiency and use of renewable energy. The entire world population, Goldemberg concludes, could live with the quality of energy services now enjoyed by West Europeans—things like modest but comfortable homes, refrigeration for food, and ready access to public transit, augmented by limited auto use.[21]

The study's implicit conclusion, however, is that the entire world decidedly could *not* live in the style of Americans, with their larger homes, more numerous electrical gadgets, and auto-centered transportation systems. Technological change and the political forces that must drive it hold extraordinary potential, but are ultimately limited by the compulsion to consume. If money saved through frugal use of materials and energy is simply spent buying private jets for weekend excursions to Antarctica, what hope is there for the biosphere? In the end, the ability of the earth to support billions of human beings depends on whether we continue to equate consumption with fulfillment.

Some guidance on what the earth can sustain emerges from an examination of current consumption patterns around the world. For three of the most ecologically important types of consumption—transportation, diet, and use of raw materials—the world's people are distributed unevenly over a vast range. Those at the bottom clearly fall below the "too little" line, while those at the top, in what could be called the cars-meat-and-disposables class, clearly consume too much.

About 1 billion people do most of their traveling, aside from the occasional donkey or bus ride, on foot, many of them never going more than 100 kilometers from their birthplaces. Unable to get to jobs easily, attend school, or bring their complaints before government offices, they are severely hindered by the lack of transportation options.[22]

The massive middle class of the world, numbering some 3 billion, travels by bus and bicycle. Kilometer for kilometer, bikes are cheaper than any other vehicles, costing less than $100 new in most of the Third World and requiring no fuel. The world's automobile class is relatively small: only 8 percent of humans, about 400 million people, own cars. Their vehicles are directly responsible for an estimated 13 percent of carbon dioxide emissions from fossil fuels worldwide, along with air pollution, acid rain, and a quarter-million traffic fatalities a year.[23]

Car owners bear indirect responsibility for the far-reaching impacts of their chosen vehicle. The automobile makes itself indispensable: cities sprawl, public transit atrophies, shopping centers multiply, workplaces scatter. (See Chapter 4.) As suburbs spread, families start to need a car for each driver. One fifth of American households own three or more vehicles, more than half own at least two, and 65 percent of new American houses are built with two-car garages. Today, working Americans spend nine hours a week behind the wheel. To make these homes-away-from-home more comfortable, 90 percent of new cars have air-conditioning, doubling their contribution to climate change and adding emissions of ozone-depleting chlorofluorocarbons.[24]

Around the world, the great marketing achievement of the auto industry has been to turn its machines into cultural icons. As French philosopher Roland Barthes writes, "cars today are almost the exact equivalent of the great Gothic cathedrals . . . the supreme creation of an era, conceived with passion by unknown artists, and consumed in image if not in usage by a whole population which appropriates them as . . . purely magical object[s]."[25]

Some in the auto class are also members of a more select group: the global jet set. Although an estimated 1 billion people travel by air each year, the overwhelming majority of trips are taken by a small group. The 4 million Americans who account for 41 percent of domestic trips, for example, cover five times as many kilometers a year as average Americans. Furthermore, because each kilometer traveled by air uses more energy than one traveled by car, jet-setters consume six-and-a-half times as much energy for transportation as other car-class members.[26]

The global food consumption ladder has three rungs. At the bottom, the world's 630 million poorest people are unable to provide themselves with a healthy diet according to the latest World Bank estimates. On the next rung, the 3.4 billion grain eaters of the world's middle class get enough calories and plenty of plant-based protein, giving them the healthiest basic diet of the world's people. They typically receive less than 20 percent of their calories from fat, a level low enough to protect them from the consequences of excessive dietary fat.[27]

The top of the ladder is populated by the meat eaters, those who obtain close to 40 percent of their calories from fat. These 1.25 billion people eat three times as much fat per person as the remaining 4 billion, mostly because they eat so much red meat. (See Table 9–1.) The meat class pays the price of its diet in high death rates from the so-called dis-

Table 9-1. Consumption of Red Meat Per Capita, Selected Countries, 1989

Country	Red Meat[1]
	(kilograms)
East Germany	96
United States	76
Argentina	73
France	66
Soviet Union	57
Japan	27
Brazil	22
China	21
Egypt	12
India	1

[1]Beef, veal, pork, lamb, mutton, and goat, in carcass weight equivalents.
SOURCE: Foreign Agricultural Service, U.S. Department of Agriculture, "World Livestock Situation," Washington, D.C., March 1990.

eases of affluence—heart disease, stroke, and certain types of cancer.[28]

In 1990, the U.S. government officially endorsed recommendations that have long come from the medical profession, urging Americans to limit their fat intake to no more than 30 percent of their calories. Meanwhile, early results of the largest-ever study of diet and health, which has been monitoring thousands of Chinese villagers, provides compelling evidence that the healthiest diet for humans is nearly vegetarian, containing 10–15 percent of calories from fat.[29]

The earth also pays for the high-fat diet. Indirectly, the meat-eating quarter of humanity consumes nearly 40 percent of the world's grain—grain that fattens the livestock they eat. Meat production is behind a substantial share of the environmental strains induced by the present global agricultural system, from soil erosion to overpumping of underground water. In the extreme case of American beef, producing 1 kilogram of steak requires 5 kilograms of grain and the energy equivalent of 9 liters of gasoline, not to mention the associated soil erosion, water consumption, pesticide and fertilizer runoff, groundwater depletion, and emissions of the greenhouse gas methane.[30]

Beyond the effects of livestock production, the affluent diet rings up an ecological bill through its heavy dependence on long-distance transport. North Europeans eat lettuce trucked from Greece and decorate their tables with flowers flown in from Kenya. Japanese eat turkey from the United States and ostrich from Australia. One fourth of the grapes eaten in the United States are grown 11,000 kilometers away, in Chile, and the typical mouthful of American food travels 2,000 kilometers from farm field to dinner plate. This far-flung agribusiness food system is only partly a product of agronomic forces. It is also a result of farm policies and health standards that favor large producers, massive government subsidies for western irrigation water, and a national highway system that makes trucking economical by transferring the tax burden from truckers to other highway users.[31]

Processing and packaging add further resource costs to the way the affluent eat. Extensively packaged foods are energy gluttons, but even seemingly simple foods need a surprising amount of energy to prepare: gram for gram, getting canned corn to the consumer takes 10 times the energy of providing fresh corn in season. Frozen corn, if left in the freezer for much time, takes even more energy. To be sure, canned and frozen vegetables make a healthy diet easy even in the dead of winter; more of a concern are the new generation of microwave-ready instant meals. Loaded with disposable pans and multilayer packaging, their resource inputs are orders of magnitude larger than preparing the same dishes at home from scratch.[32]

Global beverage consumption reveals

a similar pattern. The 1.75 billion people at the bottom are clearly deprived: they have no option but to drink water that is often contaminated with human, animal, and chemical wastes. Those in the next group up, in this case nearly 2 billion people, take more than 80 percent of their liquid refreshment in the form of clean drinking water, with the remainder coming from commercial beverages such as tea, coffee, and, for children, milk. At the quantities consumed, these beverages pose few environmental problems; they are packaged minimally, and transport energy needs are low because they are moved only short distances or in a dry form.[33]

Americans now drink more soda pop than water from the kitchen sink.

In the top class once again are the billion people in industrial countries. At a growing rate, they imbibe soft drinks, bottled water, and other prepared commercial beverages packaged in single-use containers and transported over great distances—sometimes even across oceans. Ironically, where tap water is purest and most accessible, its use as a beverage is declining. It now typically accounts for only a quarter of drinks in industrial countries. In the extreme case of the United States, per capita consumption of soft drinks rose to 176 liters in 1989 (nearly seven times the global mean), compared with water intake of 141 liters. Americans now drink more soda pop than water from the kitchen sink.[34]

In raw material consumption, the same pattern emerges. About 1 billion rural people subsist on local biomass collected from the immediate environment. Most of what they use each day—

about a half-kilogram of grain, 1 kilogram of fuelwood, and fodder for their animals—could be self-replenishing renewable resources. Unfortunately, because these people are often pushed by landlessness and population growth into fragile, unproductive ecosystems, their minimal needs are not always met.[35]

These materially destitute billion are part of a larger group that lacks many of the benefits provided by modest use of nonrenewable resources—particularly durable things like radios, refrigerators, water pipes, high-quality tools, and carts with lightweight wheels and ball bearings. More than 2 billion people live in countries where per capita consumption of steel, the most basic modern material, falls below 50 kilograms a year. In those same countries, per capita energy use—a fairly good indirect indicator of overall use of materials—is lower than 20 gigajoules per year. (See Table 9–2.)[36]

Table 9-2. Steel and Energy Consumption Per Capita, Selected Countries, 1987

Country	Steel	Energy
	(kilograms)	(gigajoules)
United States	417	280
Soviet Union	582	194
West Germany	457	165
Japan	582	110
Mexico	93	50
Turkey	149	29
Brazil	99	22
China	64	22
Indonesia	21	8
India	20	8
Nigeria	8	5
Bangladesh	5	2

SOURCES: U.S. Bureau of the Census, *Statistical Abstract of the United States: 1990* (Washington, D.C.: U.S. Government Printing Office, 1990); World Resources Institute, *World Resources 1990–91* (New York: Oxford University Press, 1990).

Roughly 1.5 billion live in the middle class of materials use. Providing each of them with durable goods every year uses between 50 and 150 kilograms of steel and 20–50 gigajoules of energy. At the top of the heap is the throwaway class, which uses raw materials extravagantly. A typical resident of the industrialized fourth of the world uses 15 times as much paper, 10 times as much steel, and 12 times as much fuel as a Third World resident. The extreme case is again the United States, where the average person consumes most of his or her own weight in basic materials each day—18 kilograms of petroleum and coal, 13 kilograms of other minerals, 12 kilograms of agricultural products, and 9 kilograms of forest products.[37]

In the throwaway economy, packaging becomes an end in itself, disposables proliferate, and durability suffers. (See Chapter 3.) Four percent of consumer expenditures on goods in the United States goes for packaging—$225 a year. Likewise, the Japanese use 30 million "disposable" single-roll cameras each year, and the British dump 2.5 billion diapers. Americans toss away 180 million razors annually, enough paper and plastic plates and cups to feed the world a picnic six times a year, and enough aluminum cans to make 6,000 DC-10 airplanes.[38]

Where disposability and planned obsolescence fail to accelerate the trip from cash register to junk heap, fashion sometimes succeeds. Most clothing goes out of style long before it is worn out; lately, the realm of fashion has even colonized sports footwear. Kevin Ventrudo, chief financial officer of California-based L.A. Gear, which saw sales multiply 50 times over in four years, told the *Washington Post*, "If you talk about shoe performance, you only need one or two pairs. If you're talking fashion, you're talking endless pairs of shoes."[39]

In transportation, diet, and use of raw materials, as consumption rises on the economic scale so does waste—both of resources and of health. Bicycles and public transit are cheaper, more efficient, and healthier transport options than cars. A diet founded on the basics of grains and water is gentle to the earth and the body. And a lifestyle that makes full use of raw materials for durable goods without succumbing to the throwaway mentality is ecologically sound while still affording many of the comforts of modernity. Yet despite these arguments in favor of modest consumption, few people who can afford high consumption levels opt to live simply. What prompts us, then, to consume so much?

THE CULTIVATION OF NEEDS

"The avarice of mankind is insatiable," wrote Aristotle 23 centuries ago, describing the way that as each of our desires is satisfied a new one seems to appear in its place. That observation, on which all of economic theory is based, provides the most obvious answer to the question of why people never seem satisfied with what they have. If our wants are insatiable, there is simply no such thing as enough.[40]

Much confirms this view of human nature. The Roman philosopher Lucretius wrote a century before Christ: "We have lost our taste for acorns. So [too] we have abandoned those couches littered with herbage and heaped with leaves. So the wearing of wild beasts' skins has gone out of fashion . . . . Skins yesterday, purple and gold today—such are the baubles that embitter human life with resentment." Nearly 2,000 years later, Russian novelist Leo Tolstoy echoed Lucretius: "Seek among men, from beggar to millionaire, one who is contented with his lot, and you will not find one such in a thousand . . . .Today we must buy an overcoat and galoshes, tomorrow, a watch and a chain; the next day we must install ourselves in an apartment with a sofa and a bronze lamp; then we must have carpets and velvet gowns; then a house, horses and carriages, paintings and decorations."[41]

What distinguishes modern consuming habits from those of interest to Lucretius and Tolstoy, some would say, is simply that we are much richer than our ancestors, and consequently have more ruinous effects on nature. There is no doubt a great deal of truth in that view, but there is also reason to believe that certain forces in the modern world encourage people to act on their consumptive desires as rarely before. Five distinctly modern factors seem to play a role in cultivating particularly voracious appetites: the influence of social pressures in mass societies, advertising, the shopping culture, various government policies, and the expansion of the mass market into the traditional realm of household and local self-reliance.

Most psychological data show that the main determinants of happiness in life are not related to consumption at all.

In the anonymous mass societies of advanced industrial nations, daily interactions with the economy lack the face-to-face character that prevails in surviving local communities. Traditional virtues such as integrity, honesty, and skill are too hard to measure to serve as yardsticks of social worth. By default, they are gradually supplanted by a simple, single indicator—money. As one Wall Street Banker put it bluntly to the *New York Times*, "Net worth equals self-worth." Under this definition, consumption becomes a treadmill, with everyone judging their status by who is ahead and who is behind.[42]

Psychological data from several nations confirm that the satisfaction derived from money does not come from simply having it. It comes from having more of it than others do, and from having more this year than last. Thus, the bulk of survey data reveals that the upper classes in any society are more satisfied with their lives than the lower classes are, but they are no more satisfied than the upper classes of much poorer countries—nor than the upper classes were in the less-affluent past.[43]

More striking, perhaps, most psychological data show that the main determinants of happiness in life are not related to consumption at all: prominent among them are satisfaction with family life, especially marriage, followed by satisfaction with work, leisure, and friendships. Indeed, in a comprehensive inquiry into the relationship between affluence and satisfaction, social commentator Jonathan Freedman notes, "Above the poverty level, the relationship between income and happiness is remarkably small."[44]

Yet when alternative measures of success are not available, the deep human need to be valued and respected by others is acted out through consumption. Buying things becomes both a proof of self-esteem ("I'm worth it," chants one advertising slogan) and a means to social acceptance—as token of what turn-of-the-century economist Thorstein Veblen termed "pecuniary decency."[45]

Beyond social pressures, the affluent live completely enveloped in pro-consumption advertising messages. The sales pitch is everywhere. One analyst estimates that the typical American is exposed to 50–100 advertisements each morning before nine o'clock. Along with their weekly 22-hour diet of television, American teenagers are typically exposed to 3–4 hours of TV advertisements a week, adding up to at least 100,000 ads between birth and high school graduation.[46]

Marketers have found ever more ways to push their products. Advertisements are broadcast by over 10,000 television and radio stations in the United States, towed behind airplanes, plastered on billboards and in sports stadiums, bounced around the planet from satellites. They are posted on chair-lift poles on ski slopes, and played through closed circuit televisions at bus stops, in subway stations, and on wall-sized video screens at shopping malls.[47]

Ads are piped into classrooms and doctors' offices, woven into the plots of feature films, placed on board games, mounted in bathroom stalls, and played back between rings on public phones in the Kansas City airport. Even the food supply may soon go mass media: the Viskase company of Chicago now offers to print edible ad slogans on hot dogs, and Eggverts International is using a similar technique to advertise on thousands of eggs in Israel.[48]

Advertising has been one of the fastest growing industries during the past half-century. In the United States, ad expenditures rose from $198 per capita in 1950 to $498 in 1989. Total global advertising expenditures, meanwhile, rose from an estimated $39 billion in 1950 to $237 billion in 1988, growing far faster than economic output. Over the same period, per person advertising expenditures grew from $15 to $46. (See Figure 9–2.) In developing countries, the increases have been astonishing. Advertising billings in India jumped fivefold in the eighties, and South Korea's advertising industry has recently grown 35–40 percent annually.[49]

The proliferation of shopping centers has, in a roundabout way, also promoted the compulsion to consume. Mall design

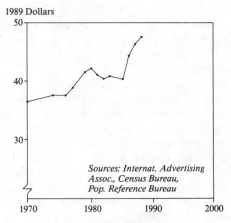

Figure 9-2. World Advertising Expenditures Per Capita, 1970–88

itself encourages acquisitive impulses, many critics believe. But perhaps more important, suburban malls and commercial strips suck commerce away from downtown and neighborhood merchants. Shopping by public transit or on foot becomes difficult, auto traffic increases, and sprawl accelerates. In the end, public places such as town squares and city streets are robbed of their vitality, leaving people fewer attractive places to go besides the malls that set the whole shopping process in motion. Perhaps by default, malls have even become popular spots to exercise. Avia, a leading sports footwear manufacturer, introduced a shoe designed for the rigors of mall walking.[50]

Particularly in the United States, shopping seems to have become a primary cultural activity. Americans spend 6 hours a week doing various types of shopping, and they go to shopping centers on average once a week—more often than they go to church or synagogue. Some 93 percent of American teenage girls surveyed in 1987 deemed shopping their favorite pastime. The 32,563 shopping centers in the country surpassed high schools in number in 1987. Just from 1986 to 1989, total retail space in these centers grew by 65 million square meters, or 20 percent. Shopping centers now garner 55 percent of retail sales in the United States, compared with 16 percent in France and 4 percent in Spain.[51]

Shopping centers are sprouting across the landscape in many industrial lands. Spain's 90-odd centers are expected to triple in number by 1992. Britain's bevy of one-stop superstores doubled to about 500 during the eighties. Italy, despite a strong tradition of community merchants, has recently relaxed controls on mall development, leading to predictions that its shopping centers will multiply from 35 to 100 in five years.[52]

The recycling ethos of the past was built upon a materials economy that valued things.

Countless government policies also play a role both in promoting high consumption and in worsening its ecological impact. Urban and transport planning favor private vehicles—and motorized ones—to the exclusion of cleaner modes. The British tax code encourages businesses to buy thousands of large company cars for employee use. (See Chapter 4.) Most governments in both North and South America subsidize beef production on a massive scale. Tax law in the United States allows virtually unlimited deductions for purchases of houses: the more homes a family buys, the more taxes they save. Partly as a consequence, 10 million Americans now have two or more homes, while at bare minimum 300,000 are homeless.[53]

Land use and materials policies in most of the world undervalue renewable resources, ignore natural services provided by ecosystems, and underprice raw materials extracted from the public domain. (See Chapters 3 and 5.) More

fundamentally, national economic goals are built squarely on the assumption that more is better. National statistics, for example, refer to people more frequently as consumers than as citizens. Economic policy, because it is based on modern economics' system of partial accounting, views as healthy growth what is often feverish and debilitating overconsumption. (See Chapter 1.)

Finally, the sweeping advance of the commercial mass market into realms once dominated by family members and local enterprise has made consumption far more wasteful than in the past, as American history illustrates. The modern consumer economy was born in the United States in the twenties, when brand names became household words, packaged foods made their large-scale debut, and the automobile assumed its place at the center of American culture.

After World War II, the consuming society came of age. In 1946, *Fortune* magazine heralded the arrival of a "dream era . . . The Great American Boom is on." Government subsidies for housing loans and highway construction helped unleash the suburbanization of the country: the urban-to-suburban migration of the fifties involved five times as many people as the unprecedented influx of European immigrants in the century's first decade. Human settlements spread across the countryside, locking people into wasteful ways of using energy and materials. In turn, status competition got a boost from the atomization of cities into unattached suburban bungalows, each housing a single family.[54]

Over the past century, the mass market has taken over an increasing number of the productive tasks once provided within the household. More and more, flush with cash but pressed for time, households opt for the questionable "conveniences" of prepared, packaged foods, miracle cleaning products, and disposable everythings—from napkins to shower curtains. All these things, while saving the householders time, cost the earth dearly, and change households from the primary unit of the economy to passive, consuming entities. Shifting one economic activity after another out of the home does boost the gross national product (GNP)—but that is largely a fiction of bookkeeping, an economic sleight of hand.[55]

Like the household, the community economy has atrophied—or been dismembered—under the blind force of the money economy. Shopping malls, superhighways, and "strips" have replaced corner stores, local restaurants, and neighborhood theaters—the very things that help to create a sense of common identity and community in an area. Traditional vegetable stands and fish shops in Japan are giving way to supermarkets and convenience stores; along the way styrofoam and plastic film have replaced yesterday's newspaper as fish wrap. Even in France, where the passion for fresh foods is legend, the microwave and the *grande surface* (shopping mall) are edging out bakeries, dairies, and farmers' markets.[56]

The recycling ethos of the past was built upon a materials economy that valued things, and it embodied that value in institutions. Not long ago in western lands—and to this day in nonindustrial regions—rag pickers, junkyard dealers, scrap collectors, and dairy deliverers kept used materials and containers flowing back into the economy. In the United States, where the demise of local economies is furthest advanced, many neighborhoods are little more than a place to sleep. Americans move, on average, every five years, and develop little attachment to those who live near them.[57]

The search for social status in massive and anonymous societies, omnipresent advertising messages, a shopping culture that edges out nonconsuming alternatives, government biases favoring consumption, and the spread of the commercial market into most aspects of private life—all these things nurture the acquisitive desires that everyone has. Can we, as individuals and as citizens, act to confront these forces?

A CULTURE OF PERMANENCE

When Moses came down from Mount Sinai he could count the rules of ethical behavior on the fingers of his two hands. In the complex global economy of the late twentieth century, in which the simple act of turning on an air conditioner sends greenhouse gases up into the atmosphere, the rules for ecologically sustainable living run into the hundreds. The basic value of a sustainable society, though, the ecological equivalent of the Golden Rule, is simple: each generation should meet its needs without jeopardizing the prospects of future generations to meet their own needs. What is lacking is the thorough practical knowledge—at each level of society—of what living by that principle means.[58]

Ethics, after all, exist only in practice, in the fine grain of everyday decisions. As Aristotle argued, "In ethics, the decision lies with perception." When most people see a large automobile and think first of the air pollution it causes, rather than the social status it conveys, environmental ethics will have arrived. In a fragile biosphere, the ultimate fate of humanity may depend on whether we can cultivate deeper sources of fulfillment, founded on a widespread ethic of limiting consumption and finding nonmaterial enrichment. An ethic becomes widespread enough to restrain antisocial behavior effectively, moreover, only when it is encoded in culture, in society's collective memory, experience, and wisdom.[59]

For individuals, the decision to live a life of sufficiency—to find their own answer to the question "How much is enough?"—is to begin a highly personal process. The goal is to put consumption in its proper place among the many sources of personal fulfillment, and to find ways of living within the means of the earth. One great inspiration in this quest is the body of human wisdom passed down over the ages.

Materialism was denounced by all the sages, from Buddha to Muhammad. (See Table 9–3.) "These religious founders," observed historian Arnold Toynbee, "disagreed with each other in the pictures of what is the nature of the universe, the nature of the spiritual life, the nature of ultimate reality. But they all agreed in their ethical precepts....They all said with one voice that if we made material wealth our paramount aim, this would lead to disaster." The Christian Bible echoes most of human wisdom when it asks "What shall it profit a man if he shall gain the whole world and lose his own soul?"[60]

The attempt to live by nonmaterialistic definitions of success is not new. Social researcher Duane Elgin estimated in 1981—perhaps optimistically—that 10 million adult Americans were experimenting "wholeheartedly" with voluntary simplicity. India, the Netherlands, Norway, the former West Germany, and the United Kingdom all have small seg-

Table 9-3. Teachings of World Religions and Major Cultures on Consumption

Religion or Culture	Teaching and Source
American Indian	"Miserable as we seem in thy eyes, we consider ourselves . . . much happier than thou, in this that we are very content with the little that we have." (Micmac chief)
Buddhist	"Whoever in this world overcomes his selfish cravings, his sorrows fall away from him, like drops of water from a lotus flower." (*Dhammapada*, 336)
Christian	It is "easier for a camel to go through the eye of a needle than for a rich man to enter into the kingdom of God." (*Matt.* 19:23–24)
Confucian	"Excess and deficiency are equally at fault." (Confucius, XI.15)
Ancient Greek	"Nothing in Excess." (Inscribed at Oracle of Delphi)
Hindu	"That person who lives completely free from desires, without longing . . . attains peace." (*Bhagavad-Gita*, II.71)
Islamic	"Poverty is my pride." (Muhammad)
Jewish	"Give me neither poverty nor riches." (*Proverbs* 30:8)
Taoist	"He who knows he has enough is rich." (*Tao Te Ching*)

SOURCES: Compiled by Worldwatch Institute.

ments of their populations who try to adhere to a nonconsuming philosophy. For these practitioners, motivated by the desire to live justly in an unjust world, to walk gently on the earth, and to avoid distraction, clutter, and pretense, the goal is not ascetic self-denial. What they are after is personal fulfillment; they just do not think consuming more is likely to provide it.[61]

Still, shifting emphasis from material to nonmaterial satisfaction is no mean feat: it means trying both to curb personal appetites and to resist the tide of external forces encouraging consumption. Mahatma Gandhi testified to the difficulty of living frugally: "I must confess to you that progress at first was slow. And now, as I recall those days of struggle, I remember that it was also painful in the beginning . . . .But as days went by, I saw that I had to throw overboard many other things which I used to consider as mine, and a time came when it became a matter of positive joy to give up those things."[62]

Many people find simpler living offers rewards all its own. They say life can become more deliberate as well as spontaneous, and even gain a sort of unadorned elegance. Vicki Robin, president of the Seattle-based New Road Map Foundation, which offers courses on getting off the more-is-better treadmill, notices that those who succeed in her program always have "a sense of purpose larger than their own needs, wants, and desires." Many find that sense of purpose in working to foster a more just, sustainable world. As French novelist Albert Camus wrote, "Without work, all life goes rotten, but when work is soulless, life stifles and dies."[63]

Others describe the way simpler technologies add unexpected qualities to life. Some come to feel, for example, that clotheslines, window shades, and bicycles have a utilitarian elegance that clothes dryers, air conditioners, and au-

tomobiles lack. These modest devices are silent, manually operated, fire-proof, ozone- and climate-friendly, easily repaired, and inexpensive. While certainly less "convenient," they require a degree of forethought and attention to the weather that grounds life in place and time.[64]

Realistically, voluntary simplicity is unlikely to gain ground rapidly against the onslaught of consumerist values. As historian David Shi of North Carolina's Davidson College chronicles, the call for a simpler life has been perennial through the history of North America, from the Puritans of Massachusetts Bay to the back-to-the-landers of the seventies. None of these movements ever gained more than a slim minority of adherents. Elsewhere, entire nations such as China and Vietnam have dedicated themselves to rebuilding human character—sometimes through brutal techniques—in a less self-centered mold, but nowhere have they succeeded with more than a token few of their citizens.[65]

It would be naive to believe that entire populations will suddenly experience a moral awakening, renouncing greed, envy, and avarice. What can be hoped for is a gradual weakening of the consumerist ethos of affluent societies. The challenge before humanity is to bring environmental matters under cultural controls, and the goal of creating a sustainable culture—a culture of permanence—is a task that will occupy several generations. Just as smoking has lost its social cachet in the United States in the space of a decade, conspicuous consumption of all types may be susceptible to social pressure over a longer period.

Ultimately, personal restraint will do little, though, if not wedded to bold political steps against the forces promoting consumption. In addition to the oft-repeated agenda of environmental and social reforms necessary to achieve sustainability, such as overhauling energy systems, stabilizing population, and ending poverty, action is needed to restrain the excesses of advertising, to curb the shopping culture, to abolish policies that push consumption, and to revitalize household and community economies as human-scale alternatives to the high-consumption life-style. Such changes promise to help both the environment, by reducing the burden of overconsumption, and our peace of mind, by taming the forces that keep us dissatisfied with our lot.

The advertising industry is a formidable foe and on the march around the world. But it is already vulnerable where it pushes products demonstrably dangerous to human health. Tobacco ads are or soon will be banished from television throughout the West, and alcohol advertising is under attack as never before. By limiting advertisers' access to the most vulnerable consumers, their influence can be further dulled. In late 1990, the U.S. Congress, for example, wisely hemmed in television commercials aimed at children, and the European Communities' standards on television for Europe after 1992 will put strict limits on some types of ads.[66]

At the grassroots level, the Vancouver-based Media Foundation has set out to build a movement boldly aimed at turning television to anti-consuming ends. The premiere spot in their High on the Hog campaign shows a gigantic animated pig frolicking on a map of North America while a narrator intones: "Five percent of the people in the world consume *one-third* of the planet's resources . . . those people are us." The pig belches.[67]

Irreverence aside, the Media Foundation is on target: commercial television will need fundamental reorientation in a culture of permanence. As religious historian Robert Bellah put it, "That happiness is to be attained through limitless material acquisition is denied by every religion and philosophy known to humankind, but is preached incessantly by every American television set."[68]

Some countries have resisted the advancing shopping culture, though only rarely is the motivation opposition to consumerism itself. England and Wales have restricted trading on Sundays for 400 years, and labor groups beat back the most recent proposal to lift those limits. Similarly, the protected green belts around British cities have slowed the pace of development of suburban malls there. As in much of Europe, German stores must close most evenings at 6:00 p.m. and have limited weekend hours as well. In Japan, most shopping continues to take place in neighborhood shopping lanes, which are closed to traffic during certain hours to become *hokoosha tengoku*, literally "pedestrian heavens."[69]

All these things help control the consumerist influence of marketing on the shape and spirit of public space. Shopping is less likely to become an end in itself if it takes place in stores thoroughly knit into the fabric of the community rather than in massive, insular agglomerations of retail outlets each planned in minute detail to stimulate spendthrift ways. The design of communities shapes human culture.

Direct incentives for overconsumption are also essential targets for reform. If goods' prices reflected something closer to the environmental cost of their production, through revised subsidies and tax systems, the market itself would guide consumers toward less damaging forms of consumption. Disposables and packaging would rise in price relative to durable, less-packaged goods; local unprocessed food would fall in price relative to prepared products trucked from far away.

The net effect might also be lower overall consumption as people's effective purchasing power declined. As currently constituted, unfortunately, economies penalize the poor when aggregate consumption contracts—unemployment skyrockets and inequalities grow. Thus arises one of the greatest challenges for sustainable economics in rich societies: finding ways to ensure basic employment opportunities for all without constantly having to stoke the fires of GNP growth.

Ultimately, efforts to revitalize household and community economies may prove the decisive element in the attempt to create a culture less prone to consumption. At a personal level, commitment to nonmaterial fulfillment is hard to sustain without reinforcement from family, friends, and neighbors. At a political level, vastly strengthened local institutions may be the only counterweight to the colossus of vested interests—ranging from gas stations to multinational marketing conglomerates—that currently benefit from profligate consumption.

Despite the ominous scale of the challenge, there could be many more people ready to begin saying "enough" than prevailing opinion suggests. After all, much of what we consume is wasted or unwanted in the first place. How much of the packaging that we put out with the household trash each year—78 kilograms apiece in the Netherlands—would we rather never see? How much of the rural land built up into housing developments, "industrial parks," and commercial strips—23 square kilometers a day in the United States—could be left alone if we insisted on well-planned land use inside city limits?[70]

How many of the unsolicited sales pitches each of us receives daily in the post—37 percent of all mail in the United States—are nothing but bothersome junk? How many of the 18 kilograms of nonrefillable beverage bottles each Japanese throws out each year could not just as easily be reused if the facilities existed? How much of the advertising in our morning newspapers—covering 65 percent of the newsprint in U.S. papers—would we not gladly see left out? How many of the kilometers we drive—6,160 a year apiece in the former West Germany—would we not gladly give up if livable neighborhoods were closer to work, a variety of local merchants closer to home, streets safe to walk and bike, and public transit easier and faster?[71]

In many ways, we might be happier with less. In the final analysis, accepting and living by sufficiency rather than excess offers a return to what is, culturally speaking, the human home: to the ancient order of family, community, good work, and good life; to a reverence for excellence of skilled handiwork; to a true materialism that does not just care *about* things but cares *for* them; to communities worth spending a lifetime in. Maybe Henry David Thoreau had it right when he scribbled in his notebook beside Walden Pond, "A man is rich in proportion to the things he can afford to let alone."[72]

For the luckiest among us, a human lifetime on earth encompasses perhaps a hundred trips around the sun. The sense of fulfillment received on that journey—regardless of a person's religious faith—has to do with the timeless virtues of discipline, hope, allegiance to principle, and character. Consumption itself has little part in the playful camaraderie that inspires the young, the bonds of love and friendship that nourish adults, the golden memories that sustain the elderly. The very things that make life worth living, that give depth and bounty to human existence, are infinitely sustainable.

10

Reshaping the Global Economy

Sandra Postel and Christopher Flavin

For much of this century, economic debates have focused on whether capitalism or socialism is the best way to organize a modern industrial economy. That argument now seems to be over, as the nations of eastern Europe move swiftly toward market mechanisms, and as the Soviet economy teeters on the brink of collapse. Yet even before the political dust settles from these transformations, a new, more fundamental question has arisen: How can we design a vibrant economy that does not destroy the natural resources and environmental systems on which it depends?

The vast scale and rapid growth of the $20-trillion global economy are hailed as great achievements of our time. But as the pace of environmental deterioration quickens, the consequences of failing to bridge the gap between the workings of economic systems and natural ones are becoming all too clear.[1]

Rising material consumption multiplied by unprecedented growth in human numbers has translated into mounting stress on local, regional, and global life-support systems. Atmospheric stability is among the major casualties. Powered by fossil fuels, the fivefold expansion of the world economy since 1950 caused the concentration of carbon dioxide (CO_2) to climb by 40 parts per million, whereas it took the previous two centuries to rise by 30 parts per million. Scientists now believe this rapid and continuing assault on the atmosphere will make the world warmer in the next few decades than it has been for thousands of years.[2]

Nearly 1 billion people will be added to the planet during the nineties, each of them striving for a materially satisfying life. Much of the increase will occur in parts of the developing world sliding toward ecological bankruptcy, including a good deal of Africa and parts of Latin America and the Indian subcontinent. The prospects are daunting, given that in 1989 some 1.2 billion people—23 percent of humanity—lived in the grim state called absolute poverty, where their most basic needs for food, clothing, and shelter were not being met. Per capita incomes in more than 40 poor countries declined during the eighties.[3]

Despite what leading economic indicators may imply, no economy can be called successful if its prosperity comes at the expense of future generations and if the ranks of the poor continue to grow. With mounting evidence that environmental deterioration and economic decline feed on each other, the fate of the poor and the fate of the planet have become tightly entwined.

Redirecting the global economy toward environmental sustainability requires fundamental reforms at both the international and national levels. In an age when deforestation in one country reduces the entire earth's biological richness, when chemicals released on one continent can lead to skin cancer on another, and when CO_2 emissions anywhere hasten climate change everywhere, economic policymaking is no longer exclusively a national concern.

Two of the primary forces shaping prospects in developing countries today are their heavy debt burdens and the tens of billions of dollars of development assistance they receive. By 1989, the Third World's external debt stood at $1.2 trillion, 44 percent of its collective gross national product (GNP). In some countries, the figure was far higher—140 percent in Egypt and Zaire, and a staggering 400 percent in Mozambique. Developing nations paid $77 billion in interest on their debts that year, and repaid $85 billion worth of principal. Since 1983, the traditional flow of capital from North to South has been reversed: the poor countries pay more to the rich than they receive in return, a net hemorrhage that now stands at more than $50 billion a year.[4]

Lack of capital has made it nearly impossible for developing countries to invest adequately in forest protection, soil conservation, irrigation improvements, more energy-efficient technologies, or pollution control devices. Even worse, growing debts have compelled them to sell off natural resources, often their only source of foreign currency. Like a consumer forced to hock the family heirlooms to pay credit card bills, developing countries are plundering forests, decimating fisheries, and depleting water supplies—regardless of the long-term consequences. Unfortunately, no global pawnbroker is holding on to this inheritance until the world can afford to buy it back. Greatly lessening the debt burden is thus a prerequisite for an environmentally sustainable world economy.

No economy can be called successful if prosperity comes at the expense of future generations and if the ranks of the poor continue to grow.

Very little of the aid money disbursed to developing countries by governments and international lending institutions supports ecologically sound development. The World Bank, the largest single funder, lacks a coherent vision of a sustainable economy, and thus its lending priorities often run counter to the goal of creating one. Bilateral aid agencies, with a few important exceptions, do little better. Moreover, the scale of total lending falls far short of that needed to help the Third World escape from the overlapping traps of poverty, overpopulation, and ecological decline.

At the heart of the dilemma at the national level is the failure of economies to incorporate environmental costs into private decisions, which results in society at large bearing them, often in unanticipated ways. Automobile drivers do not pay the full costs of local air pollution or long-term climate change when they fill their gas tanks, nor do farmers pick up the whole tab for the health and ecological risks of using pesticides. This blinkered view of societal expenses has burdened many nations with huge environmental cleanup bills. In the United States, for instance, cleaning up thousands of abandoned hazardous waste sites is expected to cost $500 billion. And the Soviet Union's total bill from the Chernobyl nuclear accident is now expected to reach $358 billion, 14 percent of the country's GNP in 1988.[5]

Many industrial nations now spend 1–2 percent of their total economic output on pollution control, and these figures will increase in the years ahead. Such large sums spent on capturing pollutants at the end of the pipe, while necessary, are to some extent a measure of the economy's failure to foster practices that curb pollution at its source. Governments mandate catalytic converters for cars, but neglect energy-efficient transport systems that would lessen automobile dependence. They require expensive methods of treating hazardous waste, while doing little to encourage industries to reduce their generation of waste.[6]

Of the many tools governments can use to reorient economic behavior, environmental taxes are among the most promising. Designed to make prices better reflect true costs, they would help ensure that those causing environmental harm pay the price, rather than society as a whole. In addition, eliminating government incentives that unwittingly foster resource destruction and establishing ones that encourage environmentally sound practices is essential to moving national economies quickly onto a stable path.

Many of these changes will only come about if policymakers replace growth with sustainability as their central goal. As long as GNP expands through massive releases of greenhouse gases into the atmosphere, rampant deforestation,

and health-threatening air pollution, it no longer makes sense to equate this common measure with progress, as noted in Chapter 1. With sustainability as the yardstick, what counts is not whether the economy grows but whether needs and wants are met without destroying the resource base. Examined in this light, it becomes clear that sustainability can only be achieved by slowing and then stopping population growth and by reducing the material consumption of the world's fortunate.

Not only do global environmental threats now constrain economic activity, they raise the wrenching question of whether the world our children inherit will provide for their needs as well as it does our own. Never before have economic policymakers had to be so concerned about future generations. A wholly new set of goals have been added to the traditional ones of creating jobs, spurring growth, and allocating resources efficiently.

AID FOR SUSTAINABLE DEVELOPMENT

After a decade of economic and environmental decline, many developing countries are at a dangerous crossroads. Unless poor nations are able to invest sufficient resources in such things as conserving soil, improving energy efficiency, and providing family planning to the impoverished majority, their life-support systems will be irreparably damaged. And as environmental problems become global in scale, the world as a whole has a growing stake in the ability to marshal an ecologically sound development effort in the Third World.

Bilateral nonmilitary aid provided by rich nations to poor ones in 1989 reached a net total of $41 billion. Loans from the World Bank and the regional development banks totaled $28 billion in 1989, most of it borrowed on commercial markets. For 50 nations, annual net receipts exceed 10 percent of their individual GNPs.[7]

U.S. aid has actually declined in real terms, to $7.7 billion in 1989, while Japan has emerged as the world's largest donor, contributing nearly $9 billion that year. (See Table 10–1.) Measured as a share of GNP, the differences among aid levels are notable—from less than 0.2 percent in the United States to more than 1 percent in Norway.[8]

The Organisation for Economic Co-operation and Development (OECD) has set a goal of boosting annual aid levels to 0.7 percent of each member's GNP, which would double current assistance to over $80 billion a year. Unfortunately, in many donor countries aid levels are actually declining. Moreover, the shift of aid toward such sustainable development priorities as reforestation,

Table 10-1: Development Assistance from Selected Industrial Nations, 1989

Country	Development Aid	Share of GNP
	(billion dollars)	(percent)
Norway	0.92	1.04
Netherlands	2.09	0.94
France	7.45	0.78
Canada	2.32	0.44
Italy	3.61	0.42
Germany	4.95	0.41
Australia	1.02	0.38
Japan	8.95	0.32
United Kingdom	2.59	0.31
United States	7.66	0.15

SOURCE: Organisation for Economic Co-operation and Development, *Development Co-operation* (Paris: in press).

family planning, or energy efficiency is proceeding slowly if at all. Just 7 percent of bilateral aid funds go to population and health, for example.[9]

As much as two thirds of some countries' aid is tied to the domestic purchase of goods and services, essentially a form of export promotion. Furthermore, the Soviet Union and the United States give most of their assistance to just a handful of nations deemed strategically important. Soviet aid is now dwindling rapidly, and Washington provides 39 percent of its nonmilitary aid to Israel, Egypt, and El Salvador, which together have only 1.2 percent of the world's population. Fortunately, other donor nations in Europe and elsewhere tend to spread their development assistance more widely.[10]

Aid programs are therefore badly in need of an overhaul. Norway, in many ways the world leader in development assistance, might serve as a model. Not only does this small nation provide more aid as a share of its GNP than any other country, it is increasingly focused on sustainable development, as mandated by Parliament in 1987. Agriculture and fisheries receive 19 percent of Norwegian development assistance, and education gets 8 percent. In addition, a special environment fund disbursed more than $10 million to developing countries in 1990. The leading recipients of Norwegian aid are the neediest countries—including, for example, Tanzania, Bangladesh, and India. If the world as a whole had the priorities reflected in Norway's aid budget, Third World environmental reforms would be much further along.[11]

The World Bank and the three regional development banks are well situated to help the Third World develop sustainably. Their influence is even greater than the $28 billion they lent in 1989 suggests, since their prejudices are reflected in the lending patterns of commercial banks and in the investment priorities of many poor nations. A clearly articulated sustainable development strategy by the World Bank would provide badly needed intellectual leadership for the world.[12]

At the moment, the World Bank continues its traditional bread and butter lending for large capital-intensive projects such as road building, dam construction, and irrigation projects, making it an accomplice to the pollution of rivers, the burning of rain forests, and the strip-mining of vast areas, often in countries that cannot even monitor the damage. In several cases, Bank-supported projects are now the object of vehement opposition by local people—usually the rural poor, who are most affected.[13]

A clearly articulated sustainable development strategy by the World Bank would provide badly needed intellectual leadership.

Serious efforts to reform the Bank began slowly in the early eighties under pressure from environmental groups worldwide. In a 1987 speech, Bank president Barber Conable acknowledged the institution's problems and pledged new initiatives. This was followed by the creation of a central Environment Department as well as four regional environment divisions. Yet today, the professional environmental staff numbers just 54, assisted by 23 consultants—out of a total World Bank professional staff of more than 4,000.[14]

Among the accomplishments touted by World Bank officials are 11 "freestanding" environmental loans in 1990. Some are indeed laudable, such as $237 million given for sewerage, drainage, and water supply improvements in several Indonesian cities. Included, however, is a "sustainable forestry" project in Côte d'Ivoire that is likely to result in accelerated logging and deforestation. Even more suspect is the Bank's claim that half its loans now include "environmental components." This classification is often little more than a new label on old projects.[15]

Barber Conable has found it easy to get inspiring reports written, but harder to motivate the people who continue to churn out loans for dams and roads. Bank staffers are rewarded for the quantity of loans they process, not their quality. The Bank is also plagued by a culture of secrecy and arrogance that makes it resistant both to its own internal reformers and to pressures exerted from the outside by governments and nongovernmental organizations (NGOs). Staff who push for faster and more fundamental reforms have sometimes been reassigned to less influential posts.[16]

Although new priorities, such as improved energy efficiency, are recommended in World Bank policy papers, they are still badly underfunded. Energy supply projects such as coal plants and hydro dams are the largest area of Bank lending, receiving 16–18 percent of the loans in recent years. Energy efficiency loans, however, still represent less than 3 percent of the Bank's lending to energy and industry.[17]

An environmental assessment process has also been set up to review the potential impact of proposed projects. But its effectiveness is undermined by the fact that the borrowing countries, eager to obtain loans, are responsible for the assessment; often they have neither the staff nor the skills to do the job. As a result, destructive projects are still going forward with only minor restrictions.[18]

Part of the problem is that within this huge bureaucracy, the new Environment Department is weak—appended to the Policy, Research, and External Affairs complex, with no direct involvement in lending operations. The department will need to be strengthened and the environmental review process more carefully controlled by in-house staff if the list of environmental disasters supported by the World Bank is to be shortened.[19]

It is time for a second generation of fundamental reforms at the World Bank—ones that address the institutional resistance to change and set genuinely new priorities. Even a strengthened Environment Department is not enough. Without a coherent vision of ecologically sound development, the Bank will continue to stumble from one environmental confrontation to another.

Restructuring lending programs will involve tackling some thorny issues. The World Bank's current portfolio of large, capital-intensive project loans requires less staff time to design and oversee than a program of smaller loans would. This allows the institution to finance its lending using the small margin between its own borrowing costs and the rate it charges developing countries—which is lower than comparable commercial lending rates. To support smaller, more labor-intensive projects such as community woodlots, integrated pest management for small farmers, rural cookstove industries, or urban bicycle factories, new financing mechanisms are needed.

One possibility is to shift the balance between project and policy lending. This latter category now accounts for 20–30 percent of the Bank's loan portfolio and is used to meet government funding needs, including structural adjustment lending that has been used recently to reduce subsidies and otherwise streamline Third World governments. Policy loans involve lower overhead costs than project loans do; if their share were increased, the project loans could be made at lower interest rates, making it possible to support smaller, more labor-intensive development efforts. At the same time,

however, it is essential that policy loans be reoriented to encourage environmentally sound development, in effect using structural adjustment lending to foster environmental as well as economic reforms. Levying pollution taxes, for example, or cutting pesticide subsidies would improve the fiscal health of Third World governments and reduce their environmental problems.[20]

On the project lending side, an environmentally responsible development bank might, at least in the initial years, be one that provided more loans but less money. The Bank needs to emphasize the nature and effect of its loans rather than the dollars disbursed. It could support such projects as raising irrigation efficiency, building factories that turn out efficient light bulbs, and training workers in everything from planting trees to installing solar collectors. Directing even a small portion of loans to facilities such as Bangladesh's Grameen Bank, which makes "micro loans" to the rural poor, could spur myriad grassroots projects.[21]

For sustainable development to become the priority, it is essential that the development banks do more to involve local people in decision making. This would require easing the oppressive secrecy that now prevents both the affected public and even the Bank's directors from learning essential details of proposed projects. Ideally, the World Bank would become a force for openness and provide avenues for public participation. Many groups in the Third World are ready and willing to get involved in this process.[22]

Beyond the reform of aid and lending, debt reduction is essential to sustainable economic progress in many developing countries. Although the first step out of the morass is for the poor nations to continue their fundamental economic reforms, richer countries have their own responsibility to help reduce Third World debts, many of them accrued with their encouragement. Unfortunately, efforts to date have only nibbled at the problem. Neither the Baker plan of the mid-eighties nor the Brady plan that followed has appreciably reduced the debt burden, though they did give the commercial banks enough breathing room to reduce their risk of default.[23]

Turning the debt crisis around will require more than rescheduling payments or issuing new loans. The international financial institutions and commercial banks that hold most of the outstanding notes will almost certainly need to write down many debts and entirely forgive others. The governments of Canada, Germany, the United Kingdom, and the United States have between them already forgiven over $5 billion worth of public loans to sub-Saharan African countries. This is the right approach, but commercial loans will also need to be written off.[24]

The world community is making only halting progress in mobilizing the financial resources to stop global environmental decline.

A number of imaginative proposals to reduce Third World debt have been floated, but so far the leadership needed to implement them has been lacking. By definition, any successful debt-reduction strategy is one that brings Third World debt down to a level that allows environmentally sound development to be restored. Achieving this may require debt reduction on the order of 60 percent, a cut from $1.2 trillion to $500 billion. As several economists have suggested, it is logical to build incentives for environmental protection into a debt-reduction strategy.[25]

On a more limited scale, U.S. biologist Thomas Lovejoy has introduced an environmental financing concept known as "debt-for-nature swaps." Under his proposal, a conservation organization buys a portion of a debtor's obligation from a commercial bank on the open market, usually at just 15–30 percent of its face value. The developing country's central bank then issues bonds in local currency, at something less than the value of the original debt, which are used by an indigenous environmental group for conservation purposes.[26]

By August 1990, 15 such debt-for-nature swaps had been arranged in eight countries, including Bolivia, Madagascar, and Poland. One of the largest and most far-reaching is the Dutch government's purchase of $33 million worth of Costa Rica's debt in exchange for $10 million of local investments in reforestation, watershed management, and soil conservation. The face value of all debt eliminated in this way so far amounts to less than $100 million, or one ten-thousandth of the total. This is clearly not a solution to the debt problem, but it is an important source of funds for environmental NGOs and for a broader array of sustainable development programs. If other governments or even private banks were to follow the Dutch approach, the far larger sums involved could meaningfully reduce debt as well as help more countries onto a sustainable development path.[27]

Another financing idea whose time may have come is that of establishing one or more international environmental funds to provide resources to address global concerns such as climate change and ozone depletion that individual nations do not have sufficient incentive to tackle on their own. The bulk of the money raised would go to poor nations that are short of capital for needed investments.

The notion of an international environmental fund was proposed by former Indian prime minister Rajiv Gandhi in 1989, and has been endorsed by the French government and the Executive Director of the United Nations Environment Programme (UNEP), Mostafa Tolba. Such a fund could either be paid for through government donations, such as those used to replenish the World Bank and U.N. agencies, or by levying a new environmental tax, possibly on carbon emitted by burning fossil fuels. The creation of a new financing mechanism of this kind will be high on the agenda for the U.N. Conference on Environment and Development in Brazil in 1992.[28]

In September 1989, the international community agreed to set up an environmental fund—to be managed by the World Bank in cooperation with the U.N. Development Programme and UNEP and to be in place by early 1991. Although the Bank's reputation for efficiency led governments to place the fund there, some environmental NGOs have opposed this, given the Bank's poor environmental record.[29]

The new fund is to be dedicated to four key priorities: protecting the ozone layer, limiting greenhouse gas emissions, preserving biodiversity, and protecting international water resources. Initial financing of the ozone portion was set at $240 million at a June 1990 conference on revising the Montreal Protocol held in London. Additional government commitments are still being discussed—reportedly aiming at a total fund of more than $1 billion for the first three years. The U.S. government opposed establishing such a fund, but finally agreed in November 1990 to provide financing if certain conditions were met.[30]

So far, the world community is making only halting progress in mobilizing the financial resources to stop the process of global environmental decline. The cen-tral issues are how to reduce the debt burden, how to increase and rechannel development aid, and how to overcome the institutional biases and inertia of the World Bank and other multilateral lenders. Unless nations address the twin problems of growing Third World poverty and increasing international inequity, global economic and environmental decline are certain to accelerate.

REDIRECTING GOVERNMENT INCENTIVES

At the national level, governments employ a wide variety of tools to shape economic and social activity. Unfortunately, and rather surprisingly, many deliberate government policies are stacked squarely against sustainability. Road building, biased utility regulation, subsidized irrigation services, and below-cost timber sales are but a sampling of the numerous public programs that result in environmental damage. Often just where taxes are justified to reduce a harmful activity, a public subsidy instead promotes it. Collectively, governments spend tens of billions of dollars a year supporting environmentally unsound economic practices.

Government subsidies for pesticides, which take such forms as tax exemptions and below-cost sales by government-controlled distributors, provide one example of these perverse incentives. In examining policies among nine developing countries—three each in Asia, Africa, and Latin America—Robert Repetto of the World Resources Institute in Washington, D.C., found pesticide subsidies in the early eighties ranging from 19 percent of the unsubsidized retail cost (in China) to 89 percent (in Senegal). The median subsidy was Colombia's 44 percent. In Egypt, subsidies equal to 83 percent of full retail costs drained the treasury of more than $200 million per year. The Egyptian government spent more per capita on pesticide subsidies in 1982 than it currently spends on health.[31]

Many governments are in effect subsidizing wholesale forest destruction, a practice that costs public treasuries vast sums each year.

By keeping pesticide costs low, governments aim to help farmers reduce pest damage and thereby increase crop yields. But it also encourages them to use pesticides excessively, increasing the myriad risks associated with toxic farm chemicals. And subsidies undermine the development and use of integrated pest management (IPM), a package of measures designed to control pests in a safer, more ecologically sound way. To name but a few successes, IPM has proved effective with soybeans in Brazil, with cotton in China, Nicaragua, and Texas, with cassava in equatorial Africa, and with rice in Indonesia—often reducing pesticide use by more than half. Heavy subsidies for chemicals prevent these promising methods from taking hold.[32]

Similarly, forests have suffered in rich and poor countries alike from government efforts to "develop" their economies and promote growth. Many governments are in effect subsidizing wholesale forest destruction, a practice that costs public treasuries vast sums each year. Laden with debt and looking for quick revenues, many tropical-country governments—often aided by international donors—have instituted tax credits and other fiscal incentives to encourage the conversion of forests to pas-

ture, cash crops, and other land uses that may earn short-term profits but rarely prove sustainable on poor tropical soils. Harvesting contracts excessively favorable to loggers have fueled "timber booms" that not only deplete and degrade forests but give colonizing farmers access to lands with soils that often will not sustain agriculture. (See Chapter 5.)[33]

Brazil, Indonesia, and the Philippines are among the countries losing from $500 million to more than $1 billion annually through such economic policies. Much of the deforestation of the Brazilian Legal Amazon, totaling by 1989 some 40 million hectares (an area larger than Japan), can be linked to government road building, resettlement schemes, and various fiscal and land tenure policies. One particularly powerful incentive was hefty income tax credits—up to 50 percent in some cases—if the resulting savings were invested in the Amazon region. A good deal of this money went into clearing land to plant pasture for livestock ranches, many of which now yield only a small fraction of planned production; some no longer produce anything at all.[34]

Recent deforestation trends in Brazil suggest how rapidly change can occur once subsidies are removed. Former president José Sarney suspended most tax credits that encouraged forest clearing in 1988 and the new administration of Fernando Collor de Mello has curtailed them further. Satellite data show that deforestation in the Amazon peaked in 1987 at 8 million hectares, dropping to 4.8 million in 1988 and to 3 million in 1989. An unusually rainy dry season, when most of the burning takes place, coupled with stepped-up enforcement against illegal burning, helped stem the loss in 1989. But the elimination of financial incentives appears to have played a major role.[35]

In addition to the immediate environmental benefits, reducing such subsidies often lessens a source of social inequity and frees up funds for programs that benefit the poor. Those in place today often enrich the politically powerful and relatively well-off, who can successfully lobby for economic favors. Pesticide and irrigation subsidies, for instance, do nothing for the cash-poor, dryland farmer who has no access to these inputs. Likewise, subsidies for cattle ranching and logging bypass those on the lower economic rungs.[36]

Eliminating environmentally destructive incentives helps ensure that people and industries pay the full costs of their activities. Reshaping economies rapidly enough to avoid the breakdown of critical environmental systems requires a distinctly different set of incentives, however—ones that reward ecologically sound practices, and thus makes them attractive. Such incentives would not remain in place indefinitely, but would jump-start the economy, moving it quickly onto a sustainable track.

There is almost no limit to the innovative ways of marshaling private investment to work for the good of the environment. It demands, however, a systematic look at how current rules, regulations, and incentives shape behavior, and how they can be changed to foster sound decisions.

In the United States, for example, the Conservation Reserve Program gives farmers an economic reason to conserve soil. By agreeing to plant their most erodible land in trees or grass for 10 years, farmers receive about $120 per hectare in annual rental payments. As of 1990, almost 14 million hectares had entered the five-year-old program, and excessive soil erosion nationwide had been cut by nearly a third, from 1.6 billion tons to 1.1 billion.[37]

Reforming the way utilities are regulated could unleash the vast money-saving potential of energy efficiency while slowing global warming, reducing acid rain, and curbing urban air pollution. Under most current regulations, utility profits rise in tandem with electricity sales. Even though utilities could save energy—for example, through consumer service programs that install efficient lighting, low-flow showerheads, and insulation in homes and offices—at far less cost than supplying more, they have little incentive to do so.[38]

In the United States, new programs in California, New York, Oregon, and five New England states are "decoupling" profits from power sales, and giving utilities a direct financial incentive to invest in efficiency. In California, a proposal by the three largest electric utilities, approved in August 1990 by the Public Utilities Commission, ties earnings to energy savings. If conservation targets are met, one utility will be allowed electricity rates that yield an annual return of 14.6 percent on its conservation investments, substantially higher than the 10.7 percent the company would get from investing those funds in a new power plant. The other two will receive in profits 15–17 percent of the value of the energy savings they undertake for customers. Together, the efficiency programs will cost an estimated $500 million over the next two years, but are expected to save more than twice that in reduced power bills.[39]

Per capita energy use in developing countries is far lower than in industrial ones; in many cases, increased supplies are essential to raising living standards. But efficiency improvements have an enormous untapped potential here as well. Energy analyst Howard Geller has found, for instance, that over the next two decades Brazil could cut its growth in electricity use in half, from 5.2 percent per year to 2.6 percent, by promoting efficient technologies. Indeed, by using economic incentives to encourage conservation and efficiency investments—

instead of subsidizing energy use—developing countries could avoid more than $1.4 trillion in energy supply costs over the next 20 years, saving scarce capital and improving the environment at the same time.[40]

Creative incentives could also give a much-needed boost to family planning efforts in the Third World, which unfortunately have been neglected during the eighties. (See Chapter 1.) Setting up education savings accounts for the children of couples who limit their family size, allowing higher income tax deductions for couples with no more than two children, and providing free family planning services are but a few of the incentives possible.[41]

Well-designed incentive programs are cost-effective, since expenditures to reduce fertility levels avoid larger social service costs later on. In Mexico, for example, every peso spent on family planning by the urban social security system between 1972 and 1984 saved nine pesos that would have been spent on maternal and infant health care. By providing nearly 800,000 women with contraceptives, the program averted 3.6 million unwanted births and resulted in a net savings of some 318 billion pesos ($2 billion).[42]

Freer trade would not necessarily help the poorest people in the Third World, nor be a net benefit to the environment.

Relatively little attention has been given to the environmental effects of trade policies, but they are undoubtedly as serious as they are difficult to untangle. Trade rules and agreements are a major determinant of how natural resources are used, what pressures are placed on the environment, and who

benefits from the huge money flows—now $3 trillion annually—that cross borders with the exchange of goods.[43]

From the standpoint of economic efficiency alone, trade distortions—including import quotas, tariffs, export subsidies, and domestic price supports—are undesirable, since they restrict competition in the global marketplace. It was a pre-world-war trading system plagued by such measures that spurred the creation of the General Agreement on Tariffs and Trade (GATT), which began operating in 1948 and now covers nearly 90 percent of world merchandise trade. Seven rounds of negotiations to amend the GATT have left many restrictions in place, particularly in politically sensitive areas such as agriculture. In recent years, the rich nations' trade barriers and domestic farm price supports for commodities such as sugar have cost the Third World an estimated $30 billion annually in lost agricultural income, and industrial-country consumers some $245 billion in higher prices and taxes.[44]

Freer trade, however, would not necessarily help the poorest people in the Third World, nor be a net benefit to the environment. Much depends, for instance, on who gains from the added export revenue—peasant farmers or wealthy landowners. Much depends, too, on whether opening world markets would cause scarce land and water to be diverted from subsistence to export crops, at the expense of the poor and of food self-sufficiency.[45]

Moreover, freer trade could draw countries to the least common denominator in environmental protection and undermine conservation efforts. A U.S. proposal to "harmonize" international food safety standards under the GATT could force countries that have strict limits on pesticide residues in food to lower them to the established international standard. Removing a country's prerogative to set restrictions could eliminate important conservation tools, such as the import ban placed on ivory to help protect the African elephant, or the bans on raw log exports instituted by Indonesia, the Philippines, and Thailand to help preserve their forests.[46]

When the Danish government decided that all beer and soft drinks, whether produced domestically or imported, should be sold in refillable bottles, it was taken to the European Community's Court of Justice on the grounds that the requirement restricted free trade. Setting what may be a key precedent, the Court upheld Denmark's right to refuse imports of canned beverages on environmental grounds. That the Danish initiative even was challenged, however, underscores the need to ensure that trade rules explicitly permit countries to set high standards and to freely pursue their environmental goals. Unfortunately, as of November 1990, with the Uruguay Round slated to end in December, the GATT negotiators had not seriously considered the environmental implications of their proposals.[47]

In establishing a comprehensive incentive structure to promote sustainability, governments might now consider one overarching guideline: no net environmental damage. This would preclude projects that destroy forests, add carbon to the atmosphere, or pave over croplands unless additional investments were made to compensate for the damage done. Enforcing such a policy would be politically difficult, to say the least, yet one or two modest steps in this direction have been suggested.

The Netherlands has launched a project to plant 125,000 hectares of trees in five Latin American countries over the next 25 years to offset the estimated carbon emissions from a Dutch coal-fired power plant to be completed during the nineties. Ideally, of course, the coal plant would not be built in the first place, and the Dutch would instead meet new energy demands through improved efficiency and renewable sources. But since trees absorb carbon from the atmosphere through photosynthesis, planting more of them can counteract emissions from fossil fuels and help lessen the risk of greenhouse warming.[48]

Making such compensating investments mandatory, for both public and private investors, would ensure that those who profit from "development" plow some of their expected proceeds back into safeguarding the natural systems they place in jeopardy. It is no more radical a notion than that of requiring investors to pay back their creditors. In this case, the creditor is the global ecosystem.

GREEN TAXES

Perhaps the single most powerful instrument for redirecting national economies toward environmental sustainability is taxation. Taxing products and activities that pollute, deplete, or otherwise degrade natural systems is a way of ensuring that environmental costs are taken into account in private decisions—whether to commute by car or bicycle, for example, or to generate electricity from coal or sunlight. Each individual producer or consumer decides how to adjust to the higher costs: a tax on air emissions would lead some factories to add pollution controls, some to change their production processes, and others to redesign products so as to generate less waste. By raising a large proportion of revenue from such "green taxes" and reducing income taxes or others to compensate, governments can help move economies swiftly onto a sustainable track.

Taxes are appealing because they offer an efficient way of correcting for the market's failure to value environmental services. If the atmosphere is a free repository for waste products, industries will pollute heavily, and society at large will bear the costs in terms of health care, lost agricultural output, and climate change. Similarly, if farmers pay nothing for using nearby waterways to carry off pesticide residues, they will use more of these chemicals than society would want, and rural people will pay the price in contaminated drinking water.[49]

So far, most governments trying to correct such market failures have turned to regulatory standards, dictating what measures must be taken to meet environmental goals. This approach has measurably improved the environment in many cases, and is especially important where there is little room for error, such as in disposing of high-level radioactive waste or safeguarding an endangered species. But it has often turned out to be a costly and cumbersome way of bringing about widespread change. Taxes can help meet broad environmental goals efficiently, since they adjust prices and then let the market do the rest.[50]

Many countries have already established green taxes. A survey of OECD members turned up more than 50 environmental charges, including levies on air and water pollution, waste, and noise, as well as various product charges, such as fees on fertilizers and batteries. In most cases, however, these fees have been set too low to motivate major changes in behavior, and have been used instead to raise a modest amount of revenue for an environmental program or other specific purpose. Norway's surcharge on fertilizers and pesticides, for instance, raises funds for programs in sustainable agriculture—certainly a worthy cause—but is too low to reduce greatly the amount of chemicals farmers use in the short term.[51]

There are, however, some notable exceptions. In the United Kingdom, a higher tax on leaded gasoline increased the market share of unleaded gas from 4 percent in April 1989 to 30 percent in March 1990. And in late 1989, the U.S. Congress passed a tax on the sale of ozone-depleting chlorofluorocarbons (CFCs) in order to hasten their phase-out, which the nation has agreed to do by the end of the decade, and to capture the expected windfall profits as the chemicals' prices rise. The most widely used CFCs are initially being taxed at $3.02 per kilogram ($1.37 per pound), roughly twice the current price; the tax will rise to $6.83 per kilogram by 1995 and to $10.80 per kilogram by 1999. During the first five years, this is expected to generate $4.3 billion in revenues.[52]

A comprehensive set of environmental taxes, designed as part of a broader restructuring of fiscal policy, could do much more to steer the economy toward sustainability. Most governments raise the bulk of their revenues by taxing income, profits, and the value added to goods and services. This has the perverse effect of discouraging work, savings, and investment—things that are generally good for an economy. If governments substituted taxes on pollution, waste, and resource depletion for a large portion of current levies, both the environment and the economy could benefit.

Completely shifting the tax base would not be desirable, since income taxes can be designed to ensure that the wealthy pay a proportionately higher share; green taxes, on balance, would not serve this equity goal. Indeed, to offset any regressive effect, income tax rates would need to be lowered for poorer people, who would suffer, for example, from higher heating fuel prices. Government payments could compensate the very poor, who may not pay any income taxes at all now but who might experience higher living costs under an environmental tax code. Moreover, since green-tax revenues would diminish as production and consumption patterns shift away from the taxed activity, they would not be as constant a source of revenue as income taxes are. For all these reasons, some blend of taxes seems best.

A tax on carbon emissions from fossil fuels, urgently needed to slow the pace of global warming, is the one likely to raise the most revenue. Levied on the carbon content of coal, oil, and natural gas, an effective charge must be high enough to reduce emissions of carbon dioxide, now the official goal of more than a dozen industrial nations. Carbon taxes went into effect in Finland and the Netherlands in early 1990; Sweden is expected to begin collecting carbon taxes in January 1991. Unfortunately, none of these levies seems high enough to spur major changes in energy use.[53]

In late September 1990, the 12 environment ministers from the European Community (EC) gathered in Rome to discuss the possibility of community-wide green taxes. Though they failed to reach agreement, the meeting placed environmental taxes squarely on Europe's political agenda. The European Commission itself supports a common EC tax on carbon emissions, as do Belgium, Denmark, France, and Germany. The less wealthy EC members fear, however, that a harmonized tax would be too high, jeopardizing their growth, while the Netherlands worries that it might be too low. Even if community-wide taxes are not set, however, it seems likely that many countries will introduce them individually over the next few years.[54]

In the United States, several energy taxes have been proposed, including higher levies on gasoline, new fees on imported oil, and taxes on the carbon content of fossil fuels. Among these, the carbon tax—levied on coal at the mine, on oil at the wellfield or dock, and on

natural gas at the wellhead—would most efficiently and effectively reduce CO_2 emissions. An August 1990 study by the U.S. Congressional Budget Office (CBO) examined the effect of phasing in a carbon tax over the next decade, beginning with $11 per ton of carbon in 1991 and rising to $110 per ton in 2000 (in 1988 dollars). When fully implemented, the tax would generate an estimated $120 billion in annual revenues, equal to 30 percent of federal receipts from individual income taxes in 1988.[55]

A tax on carbon emissions from fossil fuels, urgently needed to slow the pace of global warming, is likely to raise the most revenue.

The CBO estimates that the fee of $110 per ton of carbon would raise oil and natural gas prices by about half over the levels currently projected for 2000, and the expected price of coal—the most carbon-rich of the fossil fuels—by 256 percent. This would encourage industries and consumers to invest in efficiency measures, and to switch to non-carbon energy sources.[56]

The model used by CBO that best reflects business and consumer responses to changed energy prices shows that carbon emissions would be 37 percent lower than now projected in the year 2000, while the nation's energy efficiency would improve by 23 percent. (See Table 10–2.) The nation would also meet the much discussed international target of cutting CO_2 emissions 20 percent from the 1988 level by the year 2005. The model projects a drop of $45 billion in the GNP in 2000, a modest 0.6 percent, which could likely be avoided by pairing the carbon tax with reductions in income or other taxes.[57]

A comprehensive environmental tax

Table 10-2. United States: Estimated Effects of a $110-Per-Ton Carbon Tax in the Year 2000[1]

Options	Energy Consumption	Energy Intensity	Carbon Emissions	Real GNP[2]
	(quadrillion Btus)	(1,000 Btus per 1988 dollar of GNP)	(billion tons)	(billion 1988 dollars)
Year 2000 Without Tax	90	13	1.6	7,137
Year 2000 With Tax	69	10	1.0	7,092
		(percent)		
Change	−23	−23	−37	−0.6

[1]Assumes tax is phased in, starting at $11 per ton in 1991. Since these carbon figures are all metric, they differ from those in the source, which also gives emissions of carbon dioxide rather than carbon. [2]Does not assume any offsetting reductions in income taxes.
SOURCE: U.S. Congressional Budget Office, *Carbon Charges as a Response to Global Warming: The Effects of Taxing Fossil Fuels* (Washington, D.C.: U.S. Government Printing Office, 1990).

code would alter economic activity in many other areas. It could penalize the use of virgin materials, the generation of toxic waste, emissions of acid rain-forming pollutants, and the overpumping of groundwater. A team of researchers at the Umwelt und Prognose Institut (Environmental Assessment Institute) in Heidelberg proposed a varied set of taxes for the former West Germany that would have collectively raised more than 210 billion deutsche marks ($136 billion). The researchers analyzed more than 30 possible "eco-taxes," and determined tax levels that would markedly shift consumption patterns for each item. In some cases, a doubling or tripling of prices was needed to cut consumption substantially. For example, halving pesticide use would require a tax on the order of 200 percent of current pesticide prices.[58]

No study as comprehensive has been done yet for the United States. But a list of just eight possible green taxes suggests they have substantial revenue-raising potential while working to protect the environment. (See Table 10–3.) Determining the appropriate tax levels—ones that reduce harm to human health and the environment without damaging the economy—is complicated; the ones shown here are simply for illustration. Moreover, data on all the activities that would be taxed are not up to date. The estimate for groundwater depletion, for example, is for 1980; pesticide sales are for 1988. It is impossible to say what level of activity would exist when the taxes were fully in force.[59]

Because some taxes have multiple effects (a carbon tax, for example, would reduce emissions of sulfur dioxide by lowering fossil fuel consumption), and because levels of the taxed activity will decline even before the tax is completely in place, revenues shown in Table 10–3 cannot be totaled. But it seems likely that more than $100 billion could be raised just from the eight listed here.

Phasing in each tax over, say, 5 or 10 years would ease the economic effects and allow for a gradual adjustment. Countries wishing to keep the total tax

Table 10-3. United States: Potential Green Taxes

Tax Description	Quantity of Taxed Activity	Assumed Charge[1]	Resulting Annual Revenue[2]
			(billion dollars)
Carbon content of fossil fuels	1.3 billion tons	$100 per ton	130.0
Hazardous wastes generated	266 million tons	$100 per ton	26.6
Paper and paperboard produced from virgin pulp	61.5 million tons	$64 per ton	3.9
Pesticide sales	$7.38 billion	half of total sales	3.7
Sulfur dioxide emissions[3]	21 million tons	$150 per ton	3.2
Nitrogen oxides emissions[3]	20 million tons	$100 per ton	2.0
Chlorofluorocarbon sales[4]	225 million kilograms	$5.83 per kilogram	1.3
Groundwater depletion	20.4 million acre-feet	$50 per acre-foot	1.0

[1]Charges shown here are for illustration only, and are based simply on what seems reasonable given existing costs and prices. In some cases several taxes would exist in a given category to reflect differing degrees of harm; the hazardous waste tax shown, for instance, would be the average charge. [2]Since revenue would diminish as the tax shifted production and consumption patterns, and since some taxes have multiple effects, the revenue column cannot be added to get a total revenue estimate. [3]The Clean Air Act passed in October 1990 requires utility sulfur dioxide emissions to drop by 9 million tons and nitrogen oxide emissions by 1.8 million tons by the end of the decade. [4]This tax already exists. Revenues shown here are expected for 1994.
SOURCE: Worldwatch Institute. See endnote 59 for sources on the quantity of taxed activity.

burden the same so as to avoid slowing their economies could reduce income and other taxes in proportion to the added revenues. Others might choose to use some of the green-tax revenues for unmet fiscal needs—in the United States, for instance, to reduce the federal budget deficit. Virtually anywhere environmental taxes are applied, other taxes would need to be adjusted to ensure a progressive overall tax structure.

Beyond their role in reshaping national economies, green taxes can raise funds for global initiatives that require transfers from rich countries to poorer ones, transfers that would begin to pay back the ecological debt industrial countries have incurred by causing most of the damage to the global environment thus far. An extra tax of $10 per ton of carbon emitted in industrial countries (excluding Eastern Europe and the Soviet Union) would initially generate $25 billion per year for a global fund.[60]

Fiscal policy is a highly sensitive political issue. Opinion polls show that a good share of the public thinks more should be spent on protecting the environment, but most people harbor strong aversions to higher taxes. By shifting the tax base away from income and toward environmentally damaging activities, governments can reflect new priorities without increasing the total tax burden.[61]

FROM GROWTH TO SUSTAINABLE PROGRESS

Even if development aid is rechanneled, government incentives are restructured, and green taxes are instituted—all to encourage environmentally sound economic activity—there remains the vexing problem of scale. Listening to most economists and politicians, unlimited expansion of the economy seems not only possible but desirable. Political leaders tout growth as the answer to unemployment, poverty, ailing industries, fiscal crises, and myriad other societal ills. To question the wisdom of growth seems almost blasphemous, so ingrained is it in popular thinking about how the world works.

Yet to agree that creating an environmentally sustainable economy is necessary is to acknowledge that limits on some forms of growth are inevitable—in particular the consumption of physical resources. Textbook models often portray the economy as a self-contained system, with money flowing between consumers and businesses in a closed loop. In reality, however, the economy is not isolated. It operates within the boundaries of a global ecosystem with finite capacities to produce fresh water, form new topsoil, and absorb pollution. As a subset of the biosphere, the economy cannot outgrow its physical limits and still remain intact.[62]

With an annual output of $20 trillion, the global economy now produces in 17 days what it took an entire year to generate in 1900. Already, economic activity has breached numerous local, regional, and global thresholds, resulting in the spread of deserts, acidification of lakes and forests, and the buildup of greenhouse gases. If growth proceeds along the lines of recent decades, it is only a matter of time before global systems collapse under the pressure.[63]

One useful measure of the economy's size relative to the earth's life-supporting capacity is the share of the planet's photosynthetic product now devoted to human activity. "Net primary production" is the amount of solar energy fixed by green plants through photosynthesis minus the energy used by those plants themselves. It is, in essence, the planet's total food resource, the biochemical energy that supports all forms of animal life, from earthworms to humans.

Biologist Peter Vitousek at Stanford University and his colleagues estimate that 40 percent of the earth's annual net primary production on land now goes directly to meet human needs or is indirectly used or destroyed by human activity—leaving 60 percent for the millions of other land-based species with which humans share the planet. While it took all of human history to reach this point, the share could double to 80 percent by 2030 if current rates of population growth and consumption continue; rising per capita consumption could shorten the doubling time considerably. Along the way, with people usurping an ever larger share of the earth's life-sustaining energy, natural systems will unravel faster. Exactly when vital thresholds will be crossed irreversibly is impossible to say. But as Vitousek and his colleagues state, those "who believe that limits to growth are so distant as to be of no consequence for today's decision makers appear unaware of these biological realities."[64]

For humanity to avoid the wholesale breakdown of natural systems requires not just a slowing in the expansion of our numbers but a shift from the pursuit of growth to that of sustainable progress—human betterment that does not come at the expense of future generations. The first and easiest phase in the transition is to increase greatly the efficiency with which water, energy, and materials are used, which will allow people's needs to be satisfied with fewer resources and less environmental harm. This shift is already under way, but is proceeding at a glacial pace compared with what is needed.

One example of the necessary approach is in California. Pioneering energy policies there have fostered utility investments in efficiency, causing electricity use per person to decline 0.3 percent between 1978 and 1988, compared with an 11-percent increase in the rest of the United States. Californians suffered no drop in living standards as a result; indeed, their overall welfare improved since their electricity bills were reduced and their cooking, lighting, and other electrical needs were met with less sacrifice of air quality.[65]

Producing goods and services as efficiently as possible and with the most environmentally benign technologies available will move societies a long way toward sustainability, but it will not allow them to achieve it. Continuing growth in material consumption—the number of cars and air conditioners, the amount of paper used, and the like—will eventually overwhelm gains from efficiency, causing total resource use (and all the corresponding environmental damage) to rise. A halving of pollution emissions from individual cars, for example, will not result in much improvement in air quality if the total distance driven doubles, as it has in the United States since 1965.[66]

This aspect of the transition from growth to sustainability is thus far more difficult, as it goes to the heart of people's consumption patterns. (See also Chapter 9.) In poorer countries, simply meeting the basic needs of growing human numbers will require that consumption of water, energy, and forest products increases, even if these resources are used with the utmost efficiency. But the wealthier industrial countries—especially the dozen that

have stabilized their population size, including Austria, Germany, Italy, Norway, Sweden, and Switzerland—are in the best position to begin satisfying their needs with no net degradation of the natural resource base. These countries could be the first to benefit from realizing that some growth costs more than it is worth, and that an economy's optimum size is not its maximum size.[67]

Avoiding the wholesale breakdown of natural systems requires a shift from the pursuit of growth to that of sustainable progress.

GNP becomes an obsolete measure of progress in a society striving to meet people's needs as efficiently as possible and with the least damage to the environment. What counts is not growth in output, but the quality of services rendered. Bicycles and light rail, for instance, are less resource-intensive forms of transportation than automobiles are, and contribute less to GNP. But a shift to mass transit and cycling for most passenger trips would enhance urban life by eliminating traffic jams, reducing smog, and making cities safer for pedestrians. GNP would go down, but overall well-being would increase—underscoring the need for new indicators of progress. (See Chapter 1.)[68]

Likewise, investing in water-efficient appliances and irrigation systems instead of building more dams and diversion canals would meet water needs with less harm to the environment. Since massive water projects consume more resources than efficiency investments do, GNP would tend to decline. But quality of life would improve. It becomes clear that striving to boost GNP is often inappropriate and counterproductive.

As ecologist and philosopher Garrett Hardin puts it, "For a statesman to try to maximize the GNP is about as sensible as for a composer of music to try to maximize the number of notes in a symphony."[69]

Abandoning growth as an overriding goal does not mean forsaking the poor. Rising incomes and material consumption are essential to improving well-being in much of the Third World. But contrary to what political leaders imply, global economic growth as currently pursued is not the solution to poverty. Despite the fivefold rise in world economic output since 1950, 1.2 billion people—more than ever—live in absolute poverty today. More growth of the sort engineered in recent decades will not save the poor; only a new set of priorities can.[70]

Formidable barriers stand in the way of shifting from growth to real progress as the central goal of economic policy. The vision that growth conjures up of an expanding pie of riches is a powerful and convenient political tool because it allows the tough issues of income inequality and skewed wealth distribution to be avoided. People assume that as long as there is growth, there is hope that the lives of the poor can be bettered without sacrifices from the rich. The reality, however, is that achieving an environmentally sustainable global economy is not possible without the fortunate limiting their consumption in order to leave room for the poor to increase theirs.

With the ending of the cold war and the fading of ideological barriers, an opportunity has opened to build a new world upon the foundations of peace. A sustainable economy represents nothing less than a higher social order—one as concerned with future generations as with our own, and more focused on the health of the planet and the poor than on material acquisitions and military might. While it is a fundamentally new endeavor, with many uncertainties, it is far less risky than continuing with business as usual.

The basic elements involved in getting there are no mystery; all the needed technologies, tools, and instruments of change exist. The real hurdle is deciding to commit ourselves to a new path. That commitment needs to come from each of us individually. And from all of us together.

Notes

Chapter 1. The New World Order

1. For a more detailed discussion of this time of change, see Charles William Maynes, "America Without the Cold War," *Foreign Policy*, Spring 1990, and Paul H. Nitze, "America: An Honest Broker," and Robert Tucker, "1989 and All That," both in *Foreign Affairs*, Fall 1990.

2. Jean-Paul Lanly, *Tropical Forest Resources* (Rome: U.N. Food and Agriculture Organization (FAO), 1982); H.E. Dregne, *Desertification of Arid Land* (New York: Harwood Academic Publishers, 1983); U.N. Environment Programme, *General Assessment of Progress in the Implementation of the Plan of Action to Combat Desertification 1978–1984* (Nairobi: 1984); species loss from E.O. Wilson, ed., *Biodiversity* (Washington, D.C.: National Academy Press, 1988); U.N. Department of International Economic and Social Affairs (DIESA), *World Population Prospects 1988* (New York: 1989); Lester R. Brown and Edward C. Wolf, *Soil Erosion: The Quiet Crisis in the World Economy*, Worldwatch Paper 60 (Washington, D.C.: Worldwatch Institute, September 1984).

3. Denis Hayes, "Earth Day 1990: Threshold of the Green Decade," *Natural History*, April 1990.

4. For a more detailed discussion of the differences between economists and ecologists, see the writings of Hazel Henderson, one of the pioneers in this field, especially *The Politics of the Solar Age: Alternatives to Economics* (Indianapolis, Ind.: Knowledge Systems, Inc., rev. ed., 1988).

5. Earth Day 1990 participants and countries based on Christina L. Dresser, Earth Day 1990 Executive Director, San Francisco, Calif., private communication, October 1, 1990.

6. Data in Table 1–1 based on the following: gross world economic output in 1990 from the 1988 gross world product from Central Intelligence Agency (CIA), *Handbook of Economic Statistics, 1989* (Washington, D.C.: 1989), with Soviet and Eastern Europe gross national products extrapolated from Paul Marer, *Dollar GNP's of the USSR and Eastern Europe* (Baltimore: Johns Hopkins University Press, 1985), with adjustments to 1990 based on growth rates from International Monetary Fund (IMF), *World Economic Outlook* (Washington, D.C.: October 1990), and CIA, *Handbook of Economic Statistics*, and with the composite deflator from Office of Management and Budget, *Historical Tables, Budget of the United States Government, Fiscal Year 1990* (Washington, D.C.: U.S. Government Printing Office, 1989); historical estimates based on Angus Maddison, *The World Economy in the 20th Century* (Paris: Organisation for Economic Co-operation and Development, 1989); international trade increase is Worldwatch Institute estimate based on IMF, *International Financial Statistics*, October 1990, and *Yearbook* (Washington, D.C.: 1990); U.S. Department of Commerce, Bureau of Economic Analysis, "Standard and Poor Index of 500 Widely Held Stocks," Washington, D.C., 1990; Tokyo Stock Exchange, *Monthly Statistics Report*, June 1990; deforestation figure from FAO, which is in the midst of preparing

a new global forest assessment, according to "New Deforestation Rate Figures Announced," *Tropical Forest Programme* (IUCN Newsletter), August 1990; Brown and Wolf, *Soil Erosion*; Dregne, *Desertification of Arid Land*; carbon dioxide estimate based on Gregg Marland et al., *Estimates of CO$_2$ Emissions from Fossil Fuel Burning and Cement Manufacturing, Based on the United Nations Energy Statistics and the U.S. Bureau of Mines Cement Manufacturing Data* (Oak Ridge, Tenn.: Oak Ridge National Laboratory, 1989), on Gregg Marland, private communication and printout, Oak Ridge National Laboratory, Oak Ridge, Tenn., July 6, 1989, and on British Petroleum (BP), *BP Statistical Review of World Energy* (London: 1990).

7. IMF, *International Financial Statistics*.

8. International Labour Organization, *Economically Active Population Estimates, 1950–80, and Projections, 1985–2025, Vol. 5* (Geneva: 1986).

9. U.S. Department of Commerce, "Standard and Poor Index of 500 Widely Held Stocks;" Tokyo Stock Exchange, *Monthly Statistics Report*.

10. FAO, "New Deforestation Rate Figures Announced"; Erik P. Eckholm, *Losing Ground: Environmental Stress and World Food Prospects* (New York: W.W. Norton & Co., 1976); World Resources Institute, *World Resources, 1990–91* (New York: Oxford University Press, 1990); FAO, *Production Yearbook* (Rome: various years).

11. Dregne, *Desertification of Arid Land*.

12. Worldwatch Institute estimate based on Marland et al., *Estimates of CO$_2$ Emissions*, on Marland, private communication and printout, and on BP, *BP Statistical Review*; James E. Hansen, Goddard Institute for Space Studies, National Aeronautics and Space Administration (NASA), "The Green House Effect: Impacts on Current Global Temperature and Regional Heat Waves," Testimony before the Committee on Energy and Natural Resources, U.S. Senate, Washington, D.C., June 23, 1988; James E. Hansen et al., "Comparison of Solar and Other Influences on Long-Term Climate," Proceedings of Goddard conference, NASA, 1990; P.D. Jones, Climatic Research Unit, University of East Anglia, Norwich, U.K., "Testimony to the U.S. Senate on Global Temperatures," before the Commerce Committee, U.S. Senate, Washington, D.C., October 11, 1990.

13. U.N. Environment Programme and World Health Organization, *Assessment of Urban Air Quality* (Nairobi: Global Environment Monitoring System, 1988); W. Martin Williams et al., Office of Pesticide Programs, U.S. Environmental Protection Agency (EPA), *Pesticides in Ground Water Data Base: 1988 Interim Report* (Washington, D.C.: 1988); Stanley J. Kabala, "Poland: Facing the Hidden Costs of Development," *Environment*, November 1985.

14. Ariel E. Lugo, "Estimating Reductions in the Diversity of Tropical Forest Species," in Wilson, *Biodiversity*.

15. Herman E. Daly, "Sustainable Development: From Concept and Theory Towards Operational Principles," *Population and Development Review* (Proceedings of Hoover Institution Conference on Population and Development), forthcoming special issue.

16. U.N. Development Programme (UNDP), *Human Development Report 1990* (New York: Oxford University Press, 1990); Herman E. Daly and John B. Cobb, Jr., *For the Common Good: Redirecting the Economy Toward Community, the Environment, and a Sustainable Future* (Boston: Beacon Press, 1989).

17. UNDP, *Human Development Report 1990*.

18. Ibid.; adjusted per capita gross domestic product is in 1987 U.S. dollars; note that income figures that are not adjusted for purchasing power can differ significantly—in Sri

Lanka, for example, the unadjusted figure is $400.

19. Daly and Cobb, *For the Common Good*.

20. Ibid.; Figure 1–2 is based on Clifford W. Cobb and John B. Cobb, Jr., revised Index of Sustainable Economic Development, according to C.W. Cobb, Sacramento, Calif., private communication, September 28, 1990.

21. World Bank, *World Development Report 1990* (New York: Oxford University Press, 1990); U.S. Department of Agriculture (USDA), Economic Research Service (ERS), *World Grain Database* (unpublished printouts) (Washington, D.C.: 1990). Based on the author's personal experience, to avoid starvation a person needs roughly 1 pound of grain per day, while 13 ounces is enough for survival with minimum physical activity.

22. FAO, *Produce and Protect: Soil Conservation for Development* (Rome: 1983); FAO, *Production Yearbook*.

23. Joyce R. Starr and Daniel C. Stoll, *U.S. Foreign Policy on Water Resources in the Middle East* (Washington, D.C.: Center for Strategic & International Studies, 1987); Joyce R. Starr and Daniel C. Stoll, eds., *The Politics of Scarcity: Water in the Middle East* (Boulder, Colo.: Westview Press, 1988); Philip P. Micklin, "The Water Management Crisis in Soviet Central Asia," final report to the National Council for Soviet and East European Research, Washington, D.C., February 1989; Carl Widstrand, ed., *Water Conflicts and Research Priorities* (Elmsford, N.Y.: Pergamon Press, 1980); Raj Chengappa, "India's Water Crisis," *India Today*, May 31, 1986, excerpted in *World Press Review*, August 1986; James Nickum and John Dixon, "Environmental Problems and Economic Modernization," in Charles E. Morrison and Robert F. Dernberger, *Focus: China in the Reform Era*, Asia-Pacific Report 1989 (Honolulu: East-West Center, 1989); Edwin D. Gutentag et al., *Geohydrology of the High Plains Aquifer in Parts of Colorado, Kansas, Nebraska, New Mexico, Okla-*

homa, South Dakota, Texas, and Wyoming, U.S. Geological Survey Paper 1400-B (Washington, D.C.: U.S. Government Printing Office, 1984); *Water Market Update, Vols. 2–3* (Santa Fe, N.M.: Shupe & Associates, 1988–1989); Elizabeth Checchio, *Water Farming: The Promise and Problems of Water Transfers in Arizona* (Tucson: University of Arizona, 1988).

24. James J. MacKenzie and Mohamed T. El-Ashry, *Ill Winds: Airborne Pollution's Toll on Trees and Crops* (Washington, D.C.: World Resources Institute, 1988); EPA, Environmental Research Laboratory, *The Economic Effects of Ozone on Agriculture* (Washington, D.C.: 1984); USDA, Foreign Agricultural Service (FAS), *World Grain Situation and Outlook*, Washington, D.C., various issues.

25. Duane Chapman and Randy Barker, *Resource Depletion, Agricultural Research, and Development* (Ithaca, N.Y.: Cornell University, 1987); International Rice Research Institute, *Work Plan for 1990–1994* (Manila, Philippines: 1989).

26. FAO, *Fertilizer Yearbook* (Rome: various years); FAO, *Production Yearbook*.

27. FAO, *Fertilizer Yearbook*, various years, and The Fertilizer Institute, *Fertilizer Facts and Figures, 1990* (Washington, D.C.: 1990), with Worldwatch Institute estimates for 1990; USDA, ERS, *World Grain Database*.

28. K.F. Isherwood and L.M. Maene, "The Medium Term Outlook for the Supply and Demand of Fertilizer and Raw Materials," International Fertilizer Industry Association Annual Conference, Vancouver, May 1990.

29. USDA, ERS, *World Grain Database*.

30. Ibid., with updates for 1990 harvest.

31. Ibid.

32. USDA, ERS, "CRP up to 34 Million Acres," *Agricultural Outlook*, Washington, D.C., March 1990; USDA, ERS, *Agricultural Resources: Cropland, Water and Conservation Situ-*

ation and Outlook Report, Washington, D.C., September 1990; USDA, ERS, *World Grain Database*.

33. USDA, ERS, *World Grain Database*.

34. Francis Urban and Michael Trueblood, *World Population by Country and Region, 1950–2050* (Washington, D.C.: USDA, ERS, 1990); USDA, ERS, *World Grain Database*.

35. USDA, ERS, *World Grain Database*; Urban and Trueblood, *World Population*.

36. USDA, FAS, *World Grain Situation and Outlook*, Washington, D.C., October 1990.

37. Ibid.

38. Ibid.

39. Timothy C. Weiskel, Harvard Divinity School, "Cultural Values and Their Environmental Implications: An Essay on Knowledge, Belief, and Global Survival," The North American Conference on Religion and Ecology, Washington, D.C., May 15–17, 1990.

40. U.N. DIESA, *World Population Prospects*; Population Reference Bureau, *World Population Data Sheet* (Washington, D.C.: 1990).

41. Thomas R. Malthus, "An Essay on the Principle of Population" (1798), in Garrett Hardin, ed., *Population, Evolution & Birth Control: A Collage of Controversial Readings* (San Francisco: W.H. Freeman and Company, 1964).

42. For further information on firewood scarcity, see Sandra Postel and Lori Heise, *Reforesting the Earth*, Worldwatch Paper 83 (Washington, D.C.: Worldwatch Institute, April 1988).

43. Based on FAO, *Production Yearbook*, and on U.N. DIESA, *World Population Prospects*.

44. National Family Planning and Reproductive Health Association, "The 1980s: Decade of Disaster for Family Planning," Washington, D.C., April 1990.

45. Mary Kent, Population Reference Bureau, Washington, D.C., private communication, October 23, 1990.

46. Malcolm W. Browne, "93 Nations Agree to Ban Chemicals That Harm Ozone," *New York Times*, June 30, 1990.

47. "Germany and the Greenhouse: A Closer Look," *Global Environmental Change Report*, August 17, 1990.

Chapter 2. Designing a Sustainable Energy System

1. "Cost of Change Could Be Great," *Financial Times*, October 13, 1989.

2. Worldwatch Institute estimates based on U.S. Department of Energy (DOE), Energy Information Administration (EIA), *International Energy Outlook 1990* (Washington, D.C.: 1990); Frank Barnaby, "World Energy Prospects," *Ambio*, Vol. 18, No. 8, 1989.

3. British Petroleum (BP), *BP Statistical Review of World Energy* (London: 1990).

4. Estimate for 1990 world economic output based on 1988 gross world product from Central Intelligence Agency (CIA), *Handbook of Economic Statistics, 1989* (Washington, D.C.: 1989), with Soviet and East European gross national product extrapolated from Paul Marer, *Dollar GNP's of the USSR and Eastern Europe* (Baltimore: Johns Hopkins University Press, 1985), with adjustment to 1990 based on growth rates from International Monetary Fund, *World Economic Outlook* (Washington, D.C.: October 1990), and CIA, *Handbook of Economic Statistics*, and with the composite deflator from Office of Management and Budget, *Historical Tables, Budget of the United States Government, Fiscal Year 1990* (Washington, D.C.: U.S. Government Printing Office, 1989); carbon emissions estimate from Worldwatch Institute, based on Gregg Marland et al., *Estimates of CO_2 Emissions from Fossil Fuel Burning and Cement Manufacturing, Based on the United Nations Energy Statistics and the*

U.S. Bureau of Mines Cement Manufacturing Data (Oak Ridge, Tenn.: Oak Ridge National Laboratory, 1989), and on BP, *BP Statistical Review*.

5. Christopher Flavin, *Reassessing Nuclear Power: The Fallout from Chernobyl*, Worldwatch Paper 75 (Washington, D.C.: Worldwatch Institute, March 1987); "Wackersdorf Finally Dies," *Nature*, June 8, 1989; Radio Liberty, "Ban on Nuclear Construction in RSFSR," June 29, 1990; "Soviet Nuclear Power Plant Programme Marks Time," *Nature*, January 26, 1989; Marie Leone, "New Powerplant Projects," *Power*, August, 1990; Usha Rai, "Unique Protest Against Big Dams, *Times of India*, September 29, 1989; Kavita Singh, "Harsud Says No!" *Times of India*, October 8, 1989.

6. United Nations, *World Energy Supplies 1950–1974* (New York: 1976); United Nations, *1988 Energy Statistics Yearbook* (New York: 1990).

7. DOE, EIA, "Weekly Petroleum Status Report," Washington, D.C., October 12, 1990; BP, *BP Statistical Review*; American Petroleum Institute (API), *Basic Petroleum Data Book, Vol. 5* (Washington, D.C.: 1985); DOE, EIA, *Monthly Energy Review* (Washington, D.C.: various issues); 1990 oil price from DOE, EIA, "Weekly Petroleum Status Report," Washington, D.C., November 9, 1990.

8. International Energy Agency (IEA), *Energy Policies and Programmes of IEA Countries, 1989 Review* (Paris: Organisation for Economic Co-operation and Development (OECD), 1990); DOE, EIA, *International Energy Annual 1989* (Washington, D.C.: 1990); BP, *BP Statistical Review*.

9. Thomas W. Lippman, "Saudis Come Up with Major Oil Find," *Washington Post*, October 15, 1990; BP, *BP Statistical Review* (various years). "Proven reserves" are those quantities of oil in known reservoirs that can be extracted under existing economic and operating conditions; these rise as new oil is discovered via exploratory drilling and fall as oil is extracted.

10. BP, *BP Statistical Review*; DOE, EIA, *Monthly Energy Review, May 1990* (Washington, D.C.: August 1990); oil well production is Worldwatch Institute estimate based on BP, *BP Statistical Review*, and on API, *Basic Petroleum Data Book, Vol. 10* (Washington, D.C.: 1990); Matthew L. Wald, "Effect of Fall in Soviet Oil Output," *New York Times*, September 6, 1990; A.L. Johnson, "Soviet Oil Outlook Less Promising in 1990s," *Oil & Gas Journal*, September 17, 1990.

11. Indian data from Philip K. Verleger, "The Energy Crisis of 1990," Testimony before the Committee on the Budget, U.S. House of Representatives, Washington, D.C., October 24, 1990.

12. BP, *BP Statistical Review*; United Nations, Department of International Economic and Social Affairs, *Global Estimates and Projections of Population by Sex and Age*, 1988 Edition (New York: 1989).

13. Worldwatch Institute estimates based on Marland et al., *Estimates of CO_2 Emissions*, and on BP, *BP Statistical Review*; Intergovernmental Panel on Climate Change (IPCC), "Policymakers' Summary of the Potential Impacts of Climate Change," Report from Working Group II, undated.

14. Worldwatch Institute estimates based on Marland et al., *Estimates of CO_2 Emissions*, and on BP, *BP Statistical Review*.

15. IPCC, "Policymakers' Summary of the Scientific Assessment of Climate Change," Report from Working Group I, June 1990; Roger Milne, "Pressure Grows for US to Act on Global Warming," *New Scientist*, June 2, 1990.

16. "Germany and the Greenhouse: A Closer Look," *Global Environmental Change Report*, August 17, 1990; "East Germany: Country will Comply with CFC Ordinance of West Germany, Seeks Smaller CO_2 Cut," *International Environment Reporter*, July 1990; "Japan

to Stabilize Greenhouse Gas Emissions by 2000," *Global Environmental Change Report*, July 20, 1990; "Switzerland to Announce Stabilization Goal at Second World Climate Conference," *Global Environmental Change Report*, August 3, 1990; "The Netherlands Sets CO_2 Emissions Tax for 1990," *Global Environmental Change Report*, December 22, 1989; "Country Profiles: Denmark," *European Energy Report*, May 1990; The Ministry of Environment and Energy, *Action for a Common Future: Swedish National Report for Bergen Conference, May 1990* (Stockholm: 1989); U.K. plan from U.K. Department of the Environment, *This Common Inheritance: Britain's Environmental Strategy* (London: 1990); "New Zealand Announces CO_2 Reduction Target," *Global Environmental Change Report*, August 17, 1990; "Canada to Stabilize CO_2 Emissions at 1990 Levels by 2000," *Global Environmental Change Report*, June 22, 1990; Gunnrr Mathisen, Secretariate for Climate Affairs, Ministry of the Environment, Oslo, Norway, private communication, January 30, 1990; "Austria to Reduce CO_2 Emissions 20% by 2005," *Global Environmental Change Report*, September 14, 1990; Emmanuele D'Achon, First Secretary, Embassy of France, Washington, D.C., private communication, October 10, 1990; Ron Scherer, "Australia to Press for Worldwide Gas-Emissions Limits," *Christian Science Monitor*, October 18, 1990; IPCC, "Policymakers' Summary of the Scientific Assessment of Climate Change; "Ministerial Declaration of the Second World Climate Conference," Geneva, November 7, 1990.

17. Christopher Flavin, *Slowing Global Warming: A Worldwide Strategy*, Worldwatch Paper 91 (Washington, D.C.: Worldwatch Institute, October 1989); Worldwatch Institute estimates based on J.M.O. Scurlock and D.O. Hall, "The Contribution of Biomass to Global Energy Use," *Biomass*, No. 21, 1990, on BP, *BP Statistical Review*, on Marland et al., *Estimates of CO_2 Emissions*, and on Nigel Mortimer, "Proposed Nuclear Power Station Hinckley Point C," Proof of Evidence, Friends of the Earth U.K., London, undated.

18. Gregg Marland, "Carbon Dioxide Emission Rates for Conventional and Synthetic Fuels," *Energy*, Vol. 8, No. 12, 1983; BP, *BP Statistical Review*.

19. Marland, "Carbon Dioxide Emission Rates"; BP, *BP Statistical Review*.

20. Christopher Flavin, "Decline of Nuclear Power: The Worldwide Prospect" (draft), Worldwatch Institute, August 1990.

21. IEA, *Energy Policies and Programmes, 1989*; William U. Chandler et al., "Energy for the Soviet Union, Eastern Europe and China," *Scientific American*, September 1990.

22. Christopher Flavin and Alan Durning, *Building on Success: The Age of Energy Efficiency*, Worldwatch Paper 82 (Washington, D.C.: Worldwatch Institute, March 1988); Arnold P. Fickett et al., "Efficient Use of Electricity," *Scientific American*, September 1990; California Energy Commission, *Conservation Report, 1990*, Staff Draft (Sacramento, Calif.: 1990); Rick Bevington and Arthur H. Rosenfeld, "Energy for Buildings and Homes," *Scientific American*, September 1990.

23. José Goldemberg et al., *Energy for a Sustainable World* (Washington, D.C.: World Resources Institute, 1987); Amulya K.N. Reddy et al., "Comparative Costs of Electricity Conservation: Centralised and Decentralised Electricity Generation," *Economic and Political Weekly*, June 2, 1990.

24. Meridian Corporation, "Characterization of U.S. Energy Resources and Reserves," prepared for Deputy Assistant Secretary for Renewable Energy, DOE, Alexandria, Va., June 1989; Idaho National Engineering Laboratory (INEL) et al., *The Potential of Renewable Energy: An Interlaboratory White Paper*, prepared for the Office of Policy, Planning and Analysis, DOE, in support of the National Energy Strategy (Golden, Colo.: Solar Energy Research Institute (SERI), 1990); DOE, EIA, *Annual Energy Review 1989* (Washington, D.C.: 1990).

25. Scurlock and Hall, "The Contribution of Biomass to Global Energy Use"; Norwegian figure is based on Norwegian Central Bureau of Statistics, *Natural Resources and the Environment, 1989* (Oslo: 1990), wherein more than 45 percent of total supply is from hydroelectric power and 5 percent from biomass.

26. INEL et al., *The Potential of Renewable Energy*; Christopher Flavin and Rick Piltz, *Sustainable Energy* (Washington, D.C.: Renew America, 1989); DOE, *Energy Technologies & the Environment* (Washington, D.C.: 1988); Peggy Sheldon, Luz International Limited, Los Angeles, Calif., private communication and printout, August 28, 1990; Susan Williams and Kevin Porter, *Power Plays* (Washington, D.C.: Investor Responsibility Research Center, 1989); Nancy Rader et al., *Power Surge* (Washington, D.C.: Public Citizen, 1989); "Country Profiles: Denmark"; "Spain Resurrects Funding Programme," *European Energy Report*, July 13, 1990; "West Germany Announces $3bn Plan for Research and Technology," *European Energy Report*, March 9, 1990.

27. Low-temperature heat is Worldwatch Institute estimate based on Amory B. Lovins, *Soft Energy Paths: Toward A Durable Peace* (Cambridge, Mass.: Ballinger Publishing Company, 1977), on John Hebo Nielsen, "Denmark's Energy Future," *Energy Policy*, January/February 1990, and on DOE, EIA, *Annual Energy Review 1989*; Bevington and Rosenfeld, "Energy for Buildings and Homes"; Solar Technical Information Program, *Energy for Today: Renewable Energy* (Golden, Colo.: SERI, 1990).

28. Cynthia Pollock Shea, *Renewable Energy: Today's Contribution, Tomorrow's Promise*, Worldwatch Paper 81 (Washington, D.C.: Worldwatch Institute, January 1988); Joyce Whitman, *The Environment in Israel* (Jerusalem: Environmental Protection Service, Ministry of the Interior, 1988); Mark Newham, "Jordan's Solution Circles the Sky," *Energy Economist*, June 1989; Eric Young, "Aussies to Test Novel Solar Energy Collector," *Energy Daily*, May 3, 1990; Solar Technical Information Program, *Energy for Today: Renewable Energy*.

29. Sheldon, private communication and printout; Don Logan, Luz International Limited, Los Angeles, Calif., private communication, September 26, 1990; U.S. Bureau of the Census, *Statistical Abstract of the United States: 1990* (Washington, D.C.: U.S. Government Printing Office, 1990).

30. INEL et al., *The Potential of Renewable Energy*.

31. Steven Dickman, "The Sunny Side of the Street . . .," *Nature*, May 3, 1990; "Sanyo Develops Solar Cell Shingles," *Independent Energy*, April 1989.

32. DOE, *Energy Technologies and the Environment* (Washington, D.C.: 1988); DOE, *Photovoltaic Energy Program Summary* (Washington, D.C.: 1990); Ken Zweibel, *Harnessing Solar Power: The Photovoltaics Challenge* (New York: Plenum Publishing, 1990); Meridian Corporation and IT Power Limited, "Learning from Success: Photovoltaic-Power Water Pumping in Mali," prepared for U.S. Committee on Renewable Energy Commerce and Trade, Alexandria, Va., February 20, 1990; Maheshwar Dayal, Secretary, Department of Non-Conventional Energy Sources, New Delhi, India, private communication, July 13, 1989; "Indonesia Installs First Solar Village, Schedules Total of 2,000," *International Solar Energy Intelligence Report*, February 9, 1990; Sri Lanka from "A New Group of Sun Worshippers," *Asiaweek*, October 12, 1990.

33. Zweibel, *Harnessing Solar Power*; INEL et al., *The Potential of Renewable Energy*.

34. Flavin and Piltz, *Sustainable Energy*; INEL et al., *The Potential of Renewable Energy*; Danish experience from Paul Gipe, "Wind Energy Comes of Age," Gipe & Assoc., Tehachapi, Calif., May 13, 1990.

35. U.S. Windpower, Inc., "The Design Specifications for a Wind Power Plant in

Patagonia Using U.S. Wind Turbines,'' Livermore, Calif., January 1989; ''Minnesota Resource Greater than Previously Reported,'' *Wind Energy Weekly* (American Wind Energy Association), July 5, 1990.

36. P.J. de Groot and D.O. Hall, ''Biomass Energy: A New Perspective,'' prepared for the African Energy Policy Research Network, University of Botswana, Gaborone, January 8, 1990.

37. Lester R. Brown, *The Changing World Food Prospect: The Nineties and Beyond*, Worldwatch Paper 85 (Washington, D.C.: Worldwatch Institute, October 1988); Sandra Postel, *Water for Agriculture: Facing the Limits*, Worldwatch Paper 93 (Washington, D.C.: Worldwatch Institute, December 1989).

38. Biofuels and Municipal Waste Technology Program, Office of Renewable Energy Technologies, DOE, *Five Year Research Plan: 1988–1992, Biofuels: Renewable Fuels for the Future* (Springfield, Va.: National Technical Information Service, 1988); Norman Hinman, SERI, Golden, Colo., private communication, August 25, 1989.

39. P.P.S. Gusain, *Cooking Energy in India* (Delhi: Vikas Publishing House, 1990); Eric D. Larson et al., ''Biomass Gasification for Gas Turbine Power Generation,'' in T.B. Johansson et al., *Electricity: Efficient End-Use and New Generation Technologies, and Their Planning Implications* (Lund, Sweden: Lund University Press, 1989); Eric D. Larson et al., ''Biomass-Gasifier Steam-Injected Gas Turbine Cogeneration for the Cane Sugar Industry,'' presented at Energy from Biomass and Wastes XIV, Lake Buena Vista, Fla., January 29-February 2, 1990; United Nations, *1988 Energy Statistics Yearbook*.

40. United Nations, *1988 Energy Statistics Yearbook*; Satyajit K. Singh, ''Evaluating Large Dams in India,'' *Economic and Political Weekly*, March 17, 1990.

41. Donald Finn, Geothermal Energy Institute, New York, private communication

and printout, March 16, 1990; United Nations, *1988 Energy Statistics Yearbook*; Phillip Michael Wright, ''Developments in Geothermal Resources, 1983–1988,'' *The American Association of Petroleum Geologist Bulletin*, October 1989.

42. INEL, *The Potential of Renewable Energy*; ''Solar Showers in Massachusetts,'' *Science*, September 7, 1990; J. Edward Sunderland and Dwayne S. Breger, ''The Development of a Central Solar Heating Plants with Seasonal Storage at the University of Massachusetts/Amherst,'' University of Massachusetts, Amherst, undated.

43. Christopher Hocker, ''The Miniboom in Pumped Storage,'' *Independent Energy*, March 1990; Greg Paula, ''Load Management through Energy Storage,'' *Electrical World*, August 1990; David Bautacoff, ''Emerging Strategies for Energy Storage,'' *EPRI Journal*, July/August 1989; Zweibel, *Harnessing Solar Power*.

44. Bautacoff, ''Emerging Strategies for Energy Storage''; DOE, EIA, *Annual Energy Review 1989*; Electric Power Research Institute (EPRI), ''Electric Van and Gasoline Van Emissions: A Comparison,'' Technical Brief, Palo Alto, Calif., 1989.

45. Mark A. DeLuchi et al., ''Electric Vehicles: Performance, Life-Cycle Costs, Emissions, and Recharging Requirements,'' *Transportation Research*, Vol. 22A, No. 5, 1989; Zweibel, *Harnessing Solar Power*.

46. German Aerospace Research Establishment and King Abdulaziz City for Science and Technology, ''Hysolar: Solar Hydrogen Energy,'' Stuttgart, Germany, 1989.

47. Mark A. DeLuchi, ''Hydrogen Vehicles,'' in Daniel Sperling, ed., *Alternative Transportation Fuels: An Environmental and Energy Solution* (Westport, Conn.: Quorum Books, 1989); Joan Ogden and Robert Williams, *Solar Hydrogen* (Washington, D.C.: World Resources Institute, 1989).

48. DeLuchi, "Hydrogen Vehicles."

49. DOE, *Fuel Cell Systems Program Plan, Fiscal Year 1989* (Washington, D.C.: 1989); John Schmitt, Director of Marketing, "The Future of Fuel Cells," ONSI Corporation, South Windsor, Conn., May 29, 1990; Paul J. Werbos, *Oil Dependency and the Potential for Fuel Cell Vehicles*, Technical Paper Series (Warrendale, Pa.: Society of Automotive Engineers, 1987).

50. IEA, *Energy Policies and Programmes, 1989*; "World Status Report; Fusion Power," *Energy Economist*, June 1988.

51. As international statistics include energy production along with other non-energy mining activities, country energy employment totals are high. International Labour Organization (ILO), *Yearbook of Labour Statistics 1988* (Geneva: 1988).

52. Ibid.; Bureau of the Census, *Statistical Abstract of the United States: 1990*; DOE, EIA, *Monthly Energy Review February 1990* (Washington, D.C.: May 1990); Edison Electric Institute, *Statistical Yearbook of the Electric Utility Industry/1988* (Washington, D.C.: 1989).

53. Robert L. Mansell, "Economic Development, Growth and Land Use Planning in Oil and Gas Producing Regions," in J. Barry Cullingworth, ed., *Energy, Land and Public Policy* (New Brunswick, N.J.: Transaction Publishers, 1990); Robert L. Mansell, University of Calgary, Alberta, Canada, private communication, September 21, 1990; all amounts are in U.S. dollars.

54. Michael Philips, "Energy Conservation Activities in Latin America and the Caribbean," International Institute for Energy Conservation, Washington, D.C., undated; Howard Geller, "Electricity Conservation in Brazil: Status Report and Analysis," American Council for an Energy-Efficient Economy, Washington, D.C., August 1990; William Chandler, Pacific Northwest Laboratories, Washington, D.C., private communication, August 14, 1990; Chandler et al., "Energy for the Soviet Union"; S. Sitnicki et al., "Poland: Opportunities For Carbon Emissions Control," prepared for the U.S. Environmental Protection Agency (EPA), Pacific Northwest Laboratories, Richland, Wash., May 1990.

55. ILO, *Yearbook of Labour Statistics 1988*; "Germany to End Coal Subsidy?" *Business Europe*, London, April 6, 1990; William Chandler, Pacific Northwest Laboratories, Washington, D.C., private communication, July 26, 1990; "Reduced Use of Brown Coal and Its Products Called Top East German Environmental Goals," *International Environment Reporter*, March 1990; World Bank, *China: Socialist Economic Development, Vol. II* (Washington, D.C.: 1983); World Bank, *China: The Energy Sector* (Washington, D.C.: 1985).

56. Steven Buchsbaum and James W. Benson, *Jobs and Energy: The Employment and Economic Impacts of Nuclear Power, Conservation, and Other Energy Options* (New York: Council on Economic Priorities, 1979).

57. Olav Hohmeyer et al., *Employment Effects of Energy Conservation Investments in EC Countries* (Luxembourg: Office for Official Publications of the European Communities, 1985); Steve Colt, University of Alaska-Anchorage, "Income and Employment Impacts of Alaska's Low Income Weatherization Program," ISER Working Paper 89.2, prepared for Second Annual Rural Energy Conference, Anchorage, Ak., October 12, 1989; Meridian Corporation, *Iowa Weatherization Assistance Program Evaluation* (Alexandria, Va.: 1988); State of Connecticut, Office of Policy and Management, Energy Division, *An Initial Analysis of Low Income Weatherization Issues in Connecticut* (Hartford, Conn.: Office of Policy and Management, Energy Division, 1988).

58. Michelle Yesney, "Sustainable City Project Annual Report and Recommendation," City of San Jose, Calif., Memorandum, February 22, 1990; Skip Laitner, "Fiscal and Economic Analysis of the Proposed 1990 Energy Management Program for San Jose,"

prepared for the city of San Jose, Calif., Economic Research Associates, Eugene, Oreg., January 30, 1990.

59. Worldwatch Institute, based on DOE, EIA, *Electric Plant Cost and Power Production Expenses 1988* (Washington, D.C.: 1990); DOE, EIA, *Coal Production Statistics 1988* (Washington, D.C.: 1989); Mark Sisinyak, Vice President, California Energy Company, Coso Junction, Calif., private communication, June 19, 1990; Kathleen Flanagan, Director of Government Relations and Public Affairs, Luz International Limited, Los Angeles, Calif., private communication, June 18, 1990; Paul Gipe, Gipe & Assoc., Tehachapi, Calif., private communication, April 12, 1990; "Solarex Posts Multi-Junction PV Record, Moving to Automated Line," *International Solar Energy Intelligence Report*, June 1, 1990.

60. Neill and Gunter Limited, "A Study of the Socio-Economic Impact of Wood Energy 1988–2008 in New Brunswick," prepared for the New Brunswick Department of Natural Resources and Energy, Fredericton, N.B., October 1989; Robert Chamberlin and Colin High, "Economic Impacts of Wood Energy in the Northeast 1985," Northeast Regional Biomass Program, Policy Research Center, Coalition of Northeastern Governors, Washington, D.C., May 1986; Employment Research Associates, "Biomass Resources: Generating Jobs and Energy," Great Lakes Regional Biomass Energy Program, Council of Great Lakes Governors, Madison, Wisc., November 1985.

61. Amory B. Lovins, "Energy Strategy: The Road Not Taken?" *Foreign Affairs*, October 1976.

62. Ibid.; Energy Policy Project of the Ford Foundation, *A Time to Choose: America's Energy Future* (Cambridge, Mass: Ballinger, 1974); DOE, EIA, *Annual Energy Review 1989*; U.S. energy consumption for 1990 is a Worldwatch Institute estimate based on DOE, EIA, *Monthly Energy Review May 1990*.

63. Lovins, "Energy Strategy"; DOE, EIA, *Annual Energy Review 1989*; INEL et al., *The Potential for Renewable Energy*.

64. Lovins, "Energy Strategy"; INEL et al., *The Potential of Renewable Energy*; Carl J. Weinberg and Robert H. Williams, "Energy from the Sun," *Scientific American*, September 1990.

65. Ogden and Williams, *Solar Hydrogen*.

66. Meridian Corporation, "Energy System Emissions and Materiel Requirements," prepared for DOE, Alexandria, Va., February 1989; Kevin DeGroat, Meridian Corporation, private communication, October 15, 1990; Paul Savoldelli, Luz International Limited, Los Angeles, Calif., private communication and printout, July 11, 1989; Paula Blaydes, California Energy Company, San Francisco, Calif., private communication, June 19, 1990; Gipe, "Wind Energy Comes of Age."

67. Gipe, "Wind Energy Comes of Age."

68. The photovoltaic panels would actually cover just 15 percent of this land area; John Schaefer and Edgar DeMeo, Electric Power Research Institute, "An Update on U.S. Experiences with Photovoltaic Power Generation," Proceedings of the American Power Conference, April 23, 1990; Timothy Egan, "Land-Buying Drive by Pentagon Runs into Stiff Resistance in West," *New York Times*, July 5, 1990; Randall Swisher, Executive Director, American Wind Energy Association, Washington, D.C., press release, September 25, 1990, based on D.L. Elliott et al., Pacific Northwest Laboratories, Richland, Wash., "U.S. Areal Wind Resource Estimates Considering Environmental and Land-Use Exclusions," presented at the American Wind Energy Association Windpower '90 Conference, Washington, D.C., September 28, 1990.

69. J. Davidson, "Bioenergy Tree Plantations in the Tropics: Ecological Implications and Impacts," Commission on Ecology Paper No. 12, International Union for Con-

servation of Nature and Natural Resources, Gland, Switzerland, 1987; Zweibel, *Harnessing Solar Power*; ethanol and electric car comparison is a Worldwatch Institute estimate based on Jim MacKenzie, "Powering Transportation in the Future: Methanol from Trees or Electricity from Solar Cells?" World Resources Institute, Washington, D.C., March 26, 1987, on EPA, Office of Mobile Source, *Analysis of the Economic and Environmental Effects of Ethanol as an Automotive Fuel* (Ann Arbor, Mich.: April, 1990), and on Savoldelli, private communication and printout; William Babbitt, Associated Appraisers, Cheyenne, Wyo., private communication, October 11, 1990; U.S. Department of Agriculture, Economic Research Service, *Agricultural Resources: Agricultural Land Values and Markets Situation and Outlook Report*, Washington, D.C., June 1990.

70. Lena Gustafsson, "Plant Conservation Aspects of Energy Forestry—A New Type of Land Use in Sweden," *Forest Ecology and Management*, No. 21, 1987; Lawrence S. Hamilton, East-West Center, "Some Soil and Water Concerns Associated with Commercial Biofuels Operation," presented at Third Pacific Basin Biofuels Workshop, Honolulu, Hi., March 27–28, 1989; Timothy Egan, "Energy Project Imperils a Rain Forest," *New York Times*, January 26, 1990; Susan Meeker-Lowry, "Shattering the Geothermal Myth," *Catalyst*, Vol. 8, Nos. 1&2; California Energy Commission, "Avian Mortality at Large Wind Energy Facilities in California: Identification of a Problem," Sacramento, Calif., August 1989; Jos van Beek, "Developers Strike Deal with Bird Societies," *Windpower Monthly*, December 1989.

71. Susan E. Owens, "Land Use Planning for Energy Efficiency," in Cullingworth, *Energy, Land, and Public Policy*.

72. Peter Newman and Jeffrey Kenworthy, *Cities and Automobile Dependence: An International Sourcebook* (Aldershot, U.K.: Gower, 1989).

73. Owens, "Land Use Planning for Energy Efficiency"; Michael B. Brough, "Density and Dimensional Regulations, Article XII," *A Unified Development Ordinance* (Washington, D.C.: American Planning Association, Planners Press, 1985).

74. Owens, "Land Use Planning for Energy Efficiency"; "Country Profiles: Denmark."

75. Owens, "Land Use Planning for Energy Efficiency."

76. José Goldemberg and Amulya Reddy, "Energy for Development," *Scientific American*, September 1990; United Nations, *Global Estimates and Projections of Population*.

Chapter 3. Reducing Waste, Saving Materials

1. Amory B. Lovins, *Soft Energy Paths: Toward A Durable Peace* (Cambridge, Mass.: Ballinger Publishing Company, 1977).

2. Materials use trends from C.K. Leith, "Exploitation and World Progress," *Foreign Affairs*, October 1927; Marc H. Ross and Robert H. Williams, *Our Energy: Regaining Control* (New York: McGraw-Hill, 1981); Eric D. Larson et al., "Materials, Affluence, and Industrial Energy Use," *Annual Review of Energy, Vol. 12* (Palo Alto, Calif.: 1987); Eric D. Larson, Center for Energy and Environmental Studies, Princeton University, Princeton, N.J., unpublished data, 1990.

3. Larson, unpublished data; Larson et al., "Materials, Affluence, and Industrial Energy Use"; for a discussion of the second point, see Peter F. Drucker, "The Changed World Economy," *Foreign Affairs*, Spring 1986.

4. Larson et al., "Materials, Affluence, and Industrial Energy Use"; Drucker, "The Changed World Economy."

5. Steel consumption from U.S. Bureau of the Census, *Statistical Abstract of the United States: 1990* (Washington, D.C.: U.S. Govern-

ment Printing Office, 1990); zinc and copper consumption from U.N. Environment Programme (UNEP), *Environmental Data Report 1989–90* (Oxford: Basil Blackwell, 1990).

6. Steel consumption from Bureau of the Census, *Statistical Abstract*; aluminum consumption from Aluminum Association, *Aluminum Statistical Review for 1988* (Washington, D.C.: 1989); paper consumption from Greenpeace, *The Greenpeace Guide to Paper* (Vancouver, Canada: 1990); nickel consumption from UNEP, *Environmental Data Report*.

7. Larson, unpublished data; Ralph C. Kirby and Andrew S. Prokopovitsh, "Technological Insurance Against Shortages in Minerals and Metals," *Science*, February 20, 1976.

8. U.N. Food and Agriculture Organization, *Forest Products Yearbook 1988* (Rome: 1990).

9. U.S. mined area from Philip M. Hocker, President, Mineral Policy Center, Washington, D.C., private communication, September 21, 1990; U.S. paved area based on Richard Register, "What is an Ecocity," *Earth Island Journal*, Fall 1987.

10. U.S. Department of State, Council on Environmental Quality, *The Global 2000 Report to the President: Entering the Twenty-First Century* (New York: Penguin Books, 1982).

11. John A. Wolfe, *Mineral Resources: A World Review* (New York: Chapman and Hall, 1984); U.S. Environmental Protection Agency (EPA), Office of Solid Waste and Emergency Response (OSWER), *Report to Congress: Wastes from the Extraction and Beneficiation of Metallic Ores, Phosphate Rock, Asbestos, Overburden from Uranium Mining, and Oil Shale* (Washington, D.C.: U.S. Government Printing Office, 1985); municipal solid waste from EPA, OSWER, *Characterization of Municipal Solid Waste in the United States: 1990 Update* (Washington, D.C.: 1990).

12. EPA, OSWER, *Report to Congress*. In the United States in 1988, for every ton of ore yielded, surface mining produced 11 times as much waste as underground mining; U.S. Department of the Interior, Bureau of Mines, *1988 Minerals Yearbook* (Washington, D.C.: U.S. Government Printing Office, 1989).

13. EPA, OSWER, *Report to Congress*; stream damage from Hocker, private communication.

14. EPA and Montana Department of Health and Environmental Sciences, *Clark Fork Superfund Master Plan* (Helena, Mont.: 1988); Timothy Egan, "Some Say Mining Company's Move Could Thwart U.S. Plan for Cleanup," *New York Times*, October 2, 1990.

15. Marc H. Ross, "Improving the Efficiency of Electricity Use in Manufacturing," *Science*, April 21, 1989; see also U.S. Congress, Office of Technology Assessment (OTA), *Background Paper: Energy Use and the U.S. Economy* (Washington, D.C.: U.S. Government Printing Office, 1990).

16. Vance Packard, *The Waste Makers* (New York: David McKay, 1960).

17. For trends in materials intensity, see Ross and Williams, *Our Energy*; Larson et al., "Materials, Affluence, and Industrial Energy Use"; and Robert Herman et al., "Dematerialization," in Jesse H. Ausubel and Hedy E. Sladovich, eds., *Technology and Environment* (Washington, D.C.: National Academy Press, 1989).

18. EPA, OSWER, *The Solid Waste Dilemma: An Agenda for Action* (Washington, D.C.: 1989); EPA, OSWER, *Characterization of Municipal Solid Waste*.

19. Waste generation in Tokyo grew by 12 percent between 1987 and 1989; see Yorimoto Katsumi, "Tokyo's Serious Waste Problem," *Japan Quarterly*, July/September 1990, and "Japan's Trash Monster," *Asiaweek*, July 27, 1990; Bernd Franke, Institute for Energy and Environmental Research, Heidelberg, Germany, private communication, October 19, 1990.

20. D.J. Peterson, "The State of the Environment: Solid Wastes," *Report on the USSR*, Radio Liberty, May 11, 1990; East German waste output from Franke, private communication, and from Marlise Simons, "In Leninallee, Cans, Bottles and Papers: It's the West's Waste!" *New York Times*, July 5, 1990.

21. Organisation for Economic Co-operation and Development (OECD), *OECD Environmental Data Compendium 1989* (Paris: 1989); EPA, OSWER, *Characterization of Municipal Solid Waste*.

22. OECD, *OECD Environmental Data 1989*; EPA, OSWER, *The Solid Waste Dilemma: Agenda for Action*; EPA, OSWER, *Characterization of Municipal Solid Waste*. Inconsistent data collection and differences in what counts as garbage make it extremely difficult to compare national generation and recycling rates; Japan and several European countries, for example, do not consider recycled or reused materials as solid waste. This rather sensible distinction nonetheless complicates statistical comparisons. For more information, see U.S. Congress, OTA, *Facing America's Trash: What Next for Municipal Solid Waste?* (Washington, D.C.: U.S. Government Printing Office, 1989).

23. Cynthia Pollock, *Mining Urban Wastes: The Potential for Recycling*, Worldwatch Paper 76 (Washington, D.C.: Worldwatch Institute, April 1987).

24. Municipal landfills on Superfund National Priority List from Richard A. Denison and John Ruston, eds., *Recycling and Incineration: Evaluating the Choices* (Washington, D.C.: Island Press, 1990); chemicals in leachate and methane emissions from OTA, *Facing America's Trash*.

25. Japanese incineration figure is a Worldwatch Institute estimate derived from recycling estimate in OTA, *Facing America's Trash*, and from incineration figure for 1985 in Government of Japan, Environment Agency, *Quality of the Environment in Japan 1988* (Tokyo: undated); Japanese recycling estimate from OTA, *Facing America's Trash*; West German incineration figure is for 1987, from Franke, private communication; West German plans to increase incineration from Adrian Peracchio, "West Germany Combines Recycling and Burning," in Newsday, *Rush to Burn: Solving America's Garbage Crisis?* (Washington, D.C.: Island Press, 1989); West German recycling from UNEP, *Environmental Data Report*; landfilling in Western Europe estimated from post-recycling data in OTA, *Facing America's Trash*.

26. U.S. landfilling from EPA, OSWER, *Characterization of Municipal Solid Waste*; U.K. landfilling from Julie Johnson, "Waste That No One Wants," *New Scientist*, September 8, 1990.

27. Noel J. Brown, "Waste: Resource of the Future—Developing the Municipal Agenda," speech to the World Congress of Local Governments for a Sustainable Future, New York, September 5, 1990; for other endorsements, see, for example, National Governors' Association, Task Force on Solid Waste Management, *Curbing Waste in a Throwaway World* (Washington, D.C.: 1990).

28. Survey cited in Alvin E. Bessent and William Bunch, "The Promise of Recycling," in Newsday, *Rush to Burn*; Stephen J. LeBlanc, *Up in Smoke: Will Massachusetts Gamble on Incineration and Forfeit a Recycling/Composting Future?* (Boston: Massachusetts Public Interest Research Group, 1988); Denison and Ruston, *Recycling and Incineration*.

29. Denison and Ruston, *Recycling and Incineration*.

30. Comparison of paper recycling with energy recovery through incineration from Jeff Morris, Sound Resource Management Group, Seattle, Wash., private communication, October 5, 1990; energy savings from high-density polyethylene recycling from Gary Chamberlain, "Recycled Plastics: Building Blocks of Tomorrow," *Design News*, May 4, 1987.

31. Denison and Ruston, *Recycling and Incineration*.

32. Incinerator subsidies from Janine L. Migden, "State Policies on Waste-to-Energy Facilities," *Public Utilities Fortnightly*, September 13, 1990; for a full discussion of the relative costs of recycling and incineration, see Denison and Ruston, *Recycling and Incineration*; waste-handling capacity from investment in incineration or recycling/composting is a Worldwatch Institute estimate based on capital cost estimates from Institute for Local Self-Reliance (ILSR), "Estimated Solid Waste Management Costs," mimeographed table, September 12, 1990, from Scott Chaplin, ILSR, Washington, D.C., private communication, September 24, 1990, and from current recycling and incineration rates and waste generation projections in EPA, OSWER, *Characterization of Municipal Solid Waste*.

33. Barry Commoner, *Making Peace With the Planet* (New York: Pantheon Books, 1990).

34. Ibid.; Robert Hanley, "Lacking Garbage, a New Jersey Incinerator Is Losing Money," *New York Times*, January 25, 1989; "New Jersey: Blount Gets $1.8 Million from Warren County Incinerator Authority for Lost Revenues Due to Garbage Shortfall," *Waste Not* (Work on Waste USA, Canton, N.Y.), January 17, 1989.

35. Packard, *The Waste Makers*.

36. According to the Office of Technology Assessment, it costs more in the United States to repair most items than to replace them; see OTA, *Facing America's Trash*.

37. Packaging in U.S. waste from EPA, OSWER, *Characterization of Municipal Solid Waste*; Netherlands figure (though not directly comparable to U.S. number, because it includes only domestic (household) waste) from J. M. Joosten et al., *Informative Document: Packaging Waste* (Bilthoven, The Netherlands: National Institute of Public Health and Environmental Protection, 1989); West German

packaging waste from "Environment Minister Proposes Ordinance on Re-Use, Recycling of Packaging Materials," *International Environment Reporter*, September 1990.

38. Refillable bottles from Sue Robson, "Harmony in Abundance," *New Internationalist*, January 1990; OECD, *Economic Instruments for Environmental Protection* (Paris: 1989); Hans-Juergen Oels, Federal Environment Agency, Federal Republic of Germany, lecture, Bath, U.K., March 1990; Jennifer S. Gitlitz, "The Decline of Returnables," *Resource Recycling*, July 1990; Louis Blumberg and Robert Gottlieb, *War on Waste* (Washington, D.C.: Island Press, 1989); OECD, *Beverage Containers: Reuse or Recycling* (Paris: 1978).

39. L.L. Gaines, *Energy and Materials Use in the Production and Recycling of Consumer-Goods Packaging* (Argonne, Ill.: Argonne National Laboratory, 1981); Veronica R. Sellers and Jere D. Sellers, *Comparative Energy and Environmental Impacts for Soft Drink Delivery Systems* (Prairie Village, Kans.: Franklin Associates, 1989); for additional comparisons of energy use for different types of beverage containers, see OECD, *Beverage Containers: Reuse or Recycling*; Bruce M. Hannon, "Bottles, Cans, Energy," *Environment*, March 1972.

40. "Germany Steps Up Antiwaste Campaign," *Business Europe*, June 1, 1990; "Environment Minister Proposes Ordinance," *International Environment Reporter*; "German Business Responds on Packaging," *Business Europe*, August 31, 1990.

41. Tellus Institute, *CSG/Tellus Packaging Study: Literature and Public Policy Review* (Boston: 1990); Government of the Netherlands, Ministry of Housing, Physical Planning, and Environment, *Memorandum on the Prevention and Recycling of Waste* (The Hague: 1988); William G. Mahoney, "Swiss Slap Tight New Restrictions on Packaging Materials for Drinks," *Multinational Environmental Outlook*, October 2, 1990.

42. Tracey Totten, Coalition of Northeastern Governors, Source Reduction Coun-

cil, Washington, D.C., private communication, October 23, 1990; Denison and Ruston, *Recycling and Incineration*; Allen Hershkowitz and Eugene Salerni, *Garbage Management in Japan: Leading the Way* (New York: INFORM, 1987).

43. There were about 500 new curbside recycling programs in the United States in 1989, an increase of more than one fourth over the previous year, according to Jim Glenn, "Curbside Recycling Reaches 40 Million," *BioCycle*, July 1990.

44. Pollock, *Mining Urban Wastes: The Potential for Recycling*; energy savings of metals recycling from Marc H. Ross, University of Michigan, Ann Arbor, Mich., private communication, September 11, 1990.

45. Barry Commoner et al., *Development and Pilot Test of an Intensive Municipal Solid Waste Recycling System for the Town of East Hampton* (Flushing, N.Y.: Center for the Biology of Natural Systems, Queens College, 1987); see also Commoner, *Making Peace With the Planet*.

46. Commoner et al., *Intensive Municipal Solid Waste Recycling System for East Hampton*.

47. Ibid.; see also Jerry Powell, "Intensive Recycling: What It Is All About . . .," *Resource Recycling*, September 1990; Theresa Allen et al., *Beyond 25 Percent: Materials Recovery Comes of Age* (Washington, D.C.: ILSR, 1988).

48. City of Seattle, *On the Road to Recovery: Seattle's Integrated Solid Waste Plan* (Seattle, Wash.: 1989); Diana Gale, Director, Seattle Solid Waste Utility, Seattle, Wash., private communication, July 8, 1990; see also Randolph B. Smith, "Cleaning Up: Aided by Volunteers, Seattle Shows How Recycling Can Work," *Wall Street Journal*, July 19, 1990; Jerome Richard, "Better Homes and Garbage," *Amicus Journal*, Summer 1990.

49. Brenda Platt et al., *Beyond 40 Percent: Record-Setting Recycling and Composting Programs* (Washington, D.C.: ILSR, 1990).

50. Franke, private communication; population of Heidelberg is a 1983 figure from David Munro, ed., *Chambers World Gazetteer: An A-Z of Geographical Information* (Cambridge: Cambridge University Press, 1988).

51. EPA, OSWER, *Characterization of Municipal Solid Waste*; Carl Woestendiek, Seattle Solid Waste Utility, Seattle, Wash., private communication, July 8, 1990; Platt et al., *Beyond 40 Percent*.

52. Jonathan Yardley, "Awakening to an Environmental Alarm," *Washington Post*, January 22, 1990.

53. Wendell Berry, *Home Economics* (San Francisco: North Point Press, 1987).

54. Depletion allowances for various minerals are listed in U.S. Department of the Interior, Bureau of Mines, *Mineral Commodity Summaries 1990* (Washington, D.C.: U.S. Government Printing Office, 1990).

55. For General Mining Act, see "Mining Reform Alternatives Compared: Point-by-Point," *Clementine* (Mineral Policy Center, Washington, D.C.), Spring/Summer 1990, and U.S. General Accounting Office (GAO), *Federal Land Management: The Mining Law of 1872 Needs Revision* (Washington, D.C.: 1989); lack of revenue and value of mineral production on federal land from James Duffus III, Director, Natural Resources Management Issues, GAO, testimony before the Subcommittee on Mining and Natural Resources, Committee on Interior and Insular Affairs, U.S. House of Representatives, Washington, D.C., September 6, 1990.

56. "House RCRA Bill Hearings to Begin," *Environmental and Energy Study Institute Weekly Bulletin*, January 22, 1990; John Holusha, "Old Newspapers Hit a Logjam," *New York Times*, September 10, 1989.

57. Walden Bello, *Brave New Third World? Strategies for Survival in the Global Economy* (San Francisco: Institute for Food and Development Policy, 1989).

58. Letter from Michael M. Wolfe, Director, Industry and Consumer Affairs, Anheuser-Busch Companies, St. Louis, Mo., to Scott Chaplin, ILSR, Washington, D.C., August 27, 1990; Rainier Brewing Company, Seattle, Wash., press release, April 24, 1990.

59. Knapp quoted in Paul Connett, "Waste Management: As If the Future Mattered," Frank P. Piskor Faculty Lecture, St. Lawrence University, Canton, N.Y., May 5, 1988; tires from Keith Schneider, "Worst Tire Inferno Has Put Focus on Disposal Problem," *New York Times*, March 2, 1990.

60. Law on U.S. government procurement of secondary materials from Rich Braddock, OSWER, EPA, Washington, D.C., private communication, October 23, 1990.

61. Lisa A. Skumatz and Cabell Breckinridge, *Variable Rates in Solid Waste: Handbook for Solid Waste Officials* (Seattle, Wash.: EPA, 1990).

62. King County Solid Waste Division, *King County Home Waste Guide* (Seattle, Wash.: 1990).

63. Petra Lösch, "Green Consumerism and Eco-Labels," *Earth Island Journal*, Spring 1990; Environmental Data Services Ltd., *Eco-Labels: Product Management in a Greener Europe* (London: 1989); "Cross Fire," *The Green Consumer Letter* (Tilden Press, Washington, D.C.), October 1990.

64. Environmental Data Services, *Eco-Labels*; "Cross Fire."

65. E.F. Schumacher, *Small Is Beautiful* (New York: Harper & Row, 1973).

Chapter 4. Rethinking Urban Transport

1. Technology remark from Jacques Ellul, *The Technological Society* (New York: Knopf, 1964), as mentioned in Peter Newman, "Building Cities for People Not Cars," paper presented at the Consumers' Association of Penang Seminar on Economics, Development and the Consumer, Penang, Malaysia, November 17–22, 1980; "Floating Parking Lot Launched in Yokohama," *Public Innovation Abroad*, December 1989.

2. Motor Vehicle Manufacturers Association (MVMA), *Facts and Figures* (Detroit, Mich.: various editions). For a thorough discussion of the automobile's role and its consequences, see Michael Renner, *Rethinking the Role of the Automobile*, Worldwatch Paper 84 (Washington, D.C.: Worldwatch Institute, June 1988).

3. Asian Development Bank, *Review of the Scope For Bank Assistance to Urban Transport* (Manila: October 1989); Ricardo Neves, "Changing Car-Oriented Paradigms of Urban Transportation Planning," *Alternative Transportation Network*, March/April 1990; Chris Cragg and Debra Johnson, "No Particular Place to Go," *Energy Economist*, August 1989; Alan Cowell, "Constant Din is Getting Cairo Residents Down," *New York Times*, March 25, 1990; U.S. General Accounting Office, *Traffic Congestion: Trends, Measures, and Effects* (Washington, D.C.: 1989).

4. Michael P. Walsh, "The Global Importance of Motor Vehicles in the Climate Modification Problem," *International Environmental Reporter*, May 1989; Melinda Warren and Kenneth Chilton, "Clearing the Air of Ozone," *Society*, March/April 1989; United Nations, *1988 Energy Statistics Yearbook* (New York: 1990); Gregg Marland, "Carbon Dioxide Emission Rates for Conventional and Synthetic Fuels," *Energy*, Vol. 8, No. 12, 1983; Christopher Flavin, *Slowing Global Warming: A Worldwide Strategy*, Worldwatch Paper 91 (Washington, D.C.: Worldwatch Institute, October 1989).

5. Department of Energy (DOE), Energy Information Administration (EIA), *Monthly Energy Review, May 1990* (Washington, D.C.: August 1990); Matthew L. Wald, "U.S. Imports Record 49.9 Percent of Oil," *New York Times*, July 19, 1990; British Petroleum, *BP*

Statistical Review of World Energy (London: June 1990).

6. MVMA, *Facts and Figures 90* (Detroit, Mich.: 1990); U.S. Environmental Protection Agency, *Environmental News*, August 16, 1990.

7. National Safety Council, *Accident Facts 1989 Edition* (Chicago: 1989); International Road Federation, *World Road Statistics 1984–1988* (Geneva: 1989); World Bank, *Urban Transport: A World Bank Policy Study* (Washington, D.C.: 1986).

8. Xu Yuan Chao, "Auto Sales Slow in Domestic Market," *China Daily*, January 26, 1990.

9. United Nations, *Urban Transport Development with Particular Reference to Developing Countries* (New York: 1989).

10. Peter Newman and Jeffrey Kenworthy, *Cities and Automobile Dependence: An International Sourcebook* (Aldershot, U.K.: Gower, 1989).

11. Vukan R. Vuchic, *Urban Public Transportation Systems and Technology* (Englewood Cliffs, N.J.: Prentice-Hall, 1981); Mary C. Holcomb et al., *Transportation Energy Data Book: Edition 9* (Oak Ridge, Tenn.: Oak Ridge National Laboratory, 1987).

12. Michael Walsh, international technical consultant on vehicular emissions, private communication, Arlington, Va., August 22, 1990; "Butterfly Buses," *Transport Retort*, April 1990.

13. Metro, surface rapid rail, trolley, and bus figures from Alan Armstrong-Wright, *Urban Transit Systems: Guidelines for Examining Options* (Washington, D.C.: World Bank, 1986); automobile figure from Transportation Research Board, "Highway Capacity Manual," Special Report No. 209, National Research Council, Washington, D.C., 1985.

14. Cost of driving calculated from average for intermediate-sized cars of model years 1985 through 1990, in MVMA, *Facts and Figures 90*; average public transport fare calculated from figures in American Public Transit Association (APTA), *1989 Transit Fact Book* (Washington, D.C.: 1989).

15. J. Michael Thomson, *Great Cities and Their Traffic* (London: Victor Gollancz Ltd, 1977); Chris Bushell and Peter Stonham, ed., *Jane's Urban Transport Systems: Fourth Edition* (London: Jane's Publishing, 1985); Newman and Kenworthy, *Cities and Automobile Dependence*.

16. John Pucher, "Capitalism, Socialism, and Urban Transportation: Policies and Travel Behavior in the East and West," *APA Journal*, Summer 1990; Bushell and Stonham, *Jane's Urban Transport Systems*.

17. Newman and Kenworthy, *Cities and Automobile Dependence*; Organisation for Economic Co-operation and Development (OECD), *Cities and Transport* (Paris: 1988).

18. Michael A. Replogle, *Bicycles and Public Transportation: New Links to Suburban Transit Markets*, 2nd ed. (Washington, D.C.: The Bicycle Federation, 1988); OECD, *Cities and Transport*; World Bank, *Urban Transport: A World Bank Policy Study*.

19. United Nations, *Urban Transport Development with Particular Reference to Developing Countries*.

20. World Bank, *Urban Transport: A World Bank Policy Study*; Asian Development Bank, *Review of the Scope For Bank Assistance to Urban Transport*.

21. Development Bank Associates, "Urban Transport Plans in Developing Countries 1986–2000," survey prepared for the International Mass Transit Association, Washington, D.C., 1987; J.M. Thomson et al., "Rail Mass Transit in Developing Cities: The Transport and Road Research Laboratory Study," in *Rail Mass Transit* (London: Thomas Telford, 1989).

22. APTA, *1989 Transit Fact Book*; George M. Smerk, *The Federal Role in Urban Mass*

Transportation (pre-publication manuscript) (Bloomington, Ind.: Indiana University Press, 1991).

23. Smerk, *The Federal Role in Urban Mass Transportation*; Jay Mathews, "Los Angeles Hails Rebirth of Rail Mass Transit," *Washington Post*, July 14, 1990.

24. Armstrong-Wright, *Urban Transit Systems: Guidelines for Examining Options*.

25. Ibid.; Bushell and Stonham, *Jane's Urban Transport Systems*.

26. Transport and Environmental Studies of London (TEST), *Quality Streets: How Traditional Urban Centres Benefit from Traffic-calming* (London: 1988); Friends of the Earth, *An Illustrated Guide to Traffic Calming: The Future Way of Managing Traffic* (London: 1990).

27. Friends of the Earth, *An Illustrated Guide to Traffic Calming*; TEST, *Quality Streets*.

28. TEST, *Quality Streets*.

29. "Sidewalks in the Sky," *The Futurist*, January/February 1989; John Whitelegg, "Traffic Calming: A Green Smokescreen?" paper presented at London Borough of Ealing conference "Traffic Calming: Ways Forward," January 24, 1990; Dirk H. ten Grotenhuis, "The Delft Cycle Plan: Characteristics of the Concept," in *Velo City 87 International Congress: Planning for the Urban Cyclist*, proceedings of the Third International Velo City Congress, Groningen, the Netherlands, September 22–26, 1987.

30. Tom Godefrooij, "The Importance of the Bicycle in an Environmental Transport Policy," paper prepared for the Dutch Cyclists' Union, January 1989; "Population Control Comes in the 'Kingdom of Bikes'," *China Daily*, January 9, 1989; "Gridlock Weary, Some Turn to Pedal Power," *The Urban Edge: Issues and Innovations*, World Bank newsletter, March 1990.

31. John Roberts, *User-friendly Cities: What Britain Can Learn from Mainland Europe*, Rees Jeffreys Discussion Paper (London: TEST, 1989).

32. TEST, *Quality Streets*.

33. Jens Rorbech, "Eliminating Cars from City Centers," *Alternative Transportation Network*, March/April 1990; "Zimbabwe is Bicycle Friendly," *International Bicycle Fund News*, Winter 1990; Replogle, *Bicycles and Public Transportation*.

34. John Pucher, "Urban Travel Behavior as the Outcome of Public Policy: The Example of Modal-split in Western Europe and North America," *APA Journal*, Autumn 1988; World Bank, *Urban Transport: A World Bank Policy Study*.

35. Replogle, *Bicycles and Public Transportation*.

36. Ibid.

37. Asian Development Bank, *Review of the Scope For Bank Assistance to Urban Transport*.

38. "Gridlock Weary, Some Turn to Pedal Power"; Wang Zhi Hao, "Bicycles in Large Cities in China," *Transport Reviews*, Vol. 9, No. 2, 1989; "Zimbabwe is Bicycle Friendly."

39. Renner, *Rethinking the Role of the Automobile*.

40. Newman and Kenworthy, *Cities and Automobile Dependence*; Pucher, "Urban Travel Behavior as the Outcome of Public Policy."

41. Newman and Kenworthy, *Cities and Automobile Dependence*.

42. Kenneth T. Jackson, *Crabgrass Frontier: The Suburbanization of the United States* (New York: Oxford University Press, 1985); Pucher, "Urban Travel Behavior as the Outcome of Public Policy."

43. Newman and Kenworthy, *Cities and Automobile Dependence*; study cited is Real Estate Research Corporation, "The Costs of Sprawl: Environmental and Economic Cost of Alternative Residential Patterns at the

Fringe," prepared for the U.S. Environmental Protection Agency, Washington, D.C., 1974.

44. Robert Cervero, *Transportation and Urban Development: Perspectives for the Nineties*, Working Paper 470 (University of California, Berkeley: 1987).

45. Ibid.; Wilfred Owen, "Moving in the Metropolis: The Demand Side," paper prepared for the Center for Advanced Research in Transportation, Arizona State University, Tempe, September 1988.

46. Cervero, *Transportation and Urban Development: Perspectives for the Nineties*.

47. Southern California Association of Governments, "Regional Mobility Plan," Los Angeles, February 1989.

48. Michael A. Goldberg and John Mercer, *The Myth of the North American City: Continentalism Challenged* (Vancouver: University of British Columbia Press, 1986); Juri Pill, "Land Development: The Latest Panacea for Transit," paper prepared for the International Public Works Congress and Equipment Show, Toronto, September 1988; Juri Pill, "Land Use and Transit: Recent Metro Toronto Experience," presented at the APTA Rapid Transit Conference, Washington, D.C., June 1990. Unfortunately, spending on Toronto's rapid rail system has dropped to roughly one fourth the level of the sixties and seventies, threatening to set back the city's widely acclaimed progress in transport service.

49. Pill, "Land Development: The Latest Panacea for Transit"; Juri Pill, "Metro's Future: Vienna Surrounded by Phoenix?" *Toronto Star*, February 5, 1990; Cervero, *Transportation and Urban Development: Perspectives for the Nineties*; Peter Hall and Carmen Hass-Klau, *Can Rail Save the City? The Impacts of Rail Rapid Transit and Pedestrianization on British and German Cities* (Aldershot, U.K.: Gower, 1985); Vuchic, *Urban Public Transportation Systems and Technology*.

50. Newman and Kenworthy, *Cities and Automobile Dependence*.

51. Opinion poll in Robert Fishman, "America's New City: Megalopolis Unbound," *Wilson Quarterly*, Winter 1990; Michael Replogle, "Sustainability: A Vital Concept for Transportation Planning and Development," paper presented at the Conference on the Development and Planning of Urban Transport in Developing Countries, São Paulo, Brazil, September 1990.

52. Pucher, "Urban Travel Behavior as the Outcome of Public Policy."

53. World Bank, *Urban Transport: A World Bank Policy Study*; Wilfred Owen, *Transportation and World Development* (Baltimore: Johns Hopkins University Press, 1987).

54. Owen, *Transportation and World Development*.

55. Stanley Hart, "Huge City Subsidies for Autos, Trucks," *California Transit*, July/September 1986.

56. U.S. Department of Transportation, Urban Mass Transportation Administration, "Transit and Parking Public Policy," Washington, D.C., March 1989; Pucher, "Capitalism, Socialism, and Urban Transportation: Policies and Travel Behavior in the East and West."

57. Malcolm Fergusson, "Subsidized Pollution: Company Cars and the Greenhouse Effect," report prepared for Greenpeace U.K., London, January 1990; David Waller, "The Attraction of a Free Ride," *The Times* (London), February 21, 1990; "No Major Advance," *Transport Retort*, April 1990.

58. Department of Transportation, "Transit and Parking Public Policy."

59. DOE, EIA, *International Energy Annual 1988* (Washington, D.C.: 1989).

60. "West Germany Plans Exhaust Gas Tax," *European Energy Report*, March 23, 1990.

61. "Potential for Improving End-use Efficiency in Developing Countries," *Energy Policy*, January/February 1990.

62. Urban Land Institute, "Myths and Facts about Transportation and Growth," pamphlet, Washington, D.C., 1989.

63. Pill, "Land Development: The Latest Panacea for Transit"; Bushell and Stonham, *Jane's Urban Transport Systems*.

64. Cervero, *Transportation and Urban Development: Perspectives for the Nineties*.

65. In *Transportation and World Development*, Owen proposes a world tax to raise revenues for such a global fund, although there is no precedent for a truly international tax; levies within individual nations appear to be more feasible.

66. OECD, *Cities and Transport*; Jeffry J. Erickson et al., "An Analysis of Transportation Energy Conservation Projects in Developing Countries," *Transportation*, Vol. 1, No. 5, 1988.

67. Fines can be imposed under current regulations, but no enforcement mechanism now exists; the group intends to establish such a mechanism when funds become available, according to Fernando Del Rio, principal of public communications of the Southern California Association of Governments, private communication, September 19, 1990.

68. Newman and Kenworthy, *Cities and Automobile Dependence*.

69. Fishman, "America's New City: Megalopolis Unbound."

70. Newman and Kenworthy, *Cities and Automobile Dependence*.

Chapter 5. Reforming Forestry

1. Historical forest shrinkage from Sandra Postel and Lori Heise, *Reforesting the Earth*, Worldwatch Paper 83 (Washington, D.C.: Worldwatch Institute, April 1988); 17 million hectares figure from U.N. Food and Agriculture Organization (FAO), which is in the midst of preparing a new global forest assessment, according to "New Deforestation Rate Figures Announced," *Tropical Forest Programme* (IUCN Newsletter), August 1990. In World Resources Institute (WRI), *World Resources 1990–91* (New York: Oxford University Press, 1990), closed tropical forest clearing is estimated at up to 20.4 million hectares annually, which is probably high since it includes the peak deforestation in Brazil, 8 million hectares in 1987. Changes in government policies and programs, along with a rainy dry season, brought deforestation of the Brazilian Amazon down to 4.8 million hectares in 1988 and to 3 million hectares in 1989; "Brazil: Latest Deforestation Figures," *Nature*, June 28, 1990.

2. Tropical estimate from Norman Myers, *Deforestation Rates in Tropical Forests and Their Climatic Implications* (London: Friends of the Earth, 1989). Data in Table 5–1 based on the following: present forest cover from FAO, *Production Yearbook 1988* (Rome: 1990), from Myers, *Deforestation Rates*, from Forestry Canada, *Canada's Forest Inventory 1986* (Ottawa: 1988), from Karen L. Waddell et al., *Forest Statistics of the United States 1987* (Portland, Oreg.: U.S. Department of Agriculture (USDA) Forest Service (USFS), Pacific Northwest Research Station, 1989), and from K.F. Wells et al., *Loss of Forests and Woodlands in Australia: A Summary by State Based on Rural and Local Government Areas* (Canberra: Commonwealth Scientific and Industrial Research Organisation, 1984); Soviet primary forest estimate from J. Michael McCloskey and Heather Spalding, "A Reconnaissance-Level Inventory of the Amount of Wilderness Remaining in the World," *Ambio*, Vol. 18, No. 4, 1989; Canadian primary forest estimate derived from Christie McLaren, "Heartwood," *Equinox*, September/October 1990, from Keith Moore, "Where Is It and How Much Is Left? The State of the Temperate Rainforest in British Columbia," *Forest Planning Canada*, July-August 1990, and from Joe

Lowe, Forestry Canada, Chalk River, Ontario, private communication, August 15, 1990; original extent of Canadian forest from Harry Hirvonen, Environment Canada, Ottawa, private communication, October 10, 1990; U.S. figures for Alaska from Willem W. S. van Hees, USFS Forest Sciences Laboratory, Anchorage, Alaska, private communication, September 27, 1990; figure for lower 48 states from Reed Noss, Corvallis, Oreg., private communication, September 27, 1990; U.S. preagricultural forest area from Postel and Heise, *Reforesting the Earth*; Bill Hare, Australian Conservation Foundation (ACF), Fitzroy, Australia, private communications, October 22 and 24, 1990; Rolf Löfgren, "Importance and Value of A Network of Large Protected Woodlands," National Swedish Environment Protection Board, Solna, Sweden, 1986; China figures from Yin Runsheng, University of Georgia, Athens, Ga., private communication, September 10, 1990; Peter S. Grant, Maruia Society, Nelson, New Zealand, private communication, September 17, 1990; "other" category includes 157 million hectares of tropical moist forest from Myers, *Deforestation Rates*, 172 million hectares of tropical dry forest and woodlands from McCloskey and Spalding, "A Reconnaissance-Level Inventory," and 2.4 million hectares of Chilean forest from A. Jèlvez et al., *A Profile of the Chilean Forestry Sector* (Seattle: University of Washington Center for International Trade in Forest Products (CINTRAFOR), 1988); total preagricultural forest and woodland area from Elaine Matthews, "Global Vegetation and Land Use: New High-Resolution Data Bases for Climate Studies," *Journal of Climate and Applied Meteorology*, March 1983.

3. Richard Plochmann, "The Forests of Central Europe: A Changing View," 1989 Starker Lecture, Oregon State University, Corvallis, October 12, 1989.

4. Catherine Caufield, "The Ancient Forest," *The New Yorker*, May 14, 1990.

5. R. Goodland et al., "Tropical Moist Forest Management: The Urgent Transition to Sustainability," *Environmental Conservation*, forthcoming; Jeffrey T. Olson, *Pacific Northwest Lumber and Wood Products: An Industry in Transition*, Vol. 4 of *National Forests: Policies for the Future* (Washington, D.C.: The Wilderness Society and National Wildlife Federation, 1988).

6. FAO, *Forest Products Yearbook 1988* (Rome: 1990); see Postel and Heise, *Reforesting the Earth*, for discussion of fuelwood issues.

7. Tropical logging figure from Goodland et al., "Tropical Moist Forest Management."

8. Clark Binkley et al., International Institute of Applied Systems Analysis, *The Global Forest Sector: An Analytical Perspective* (New York: John Wiley & Sons, 1987); Roger A. Sedjo and Kenneth S. Lyon, *The Long-Term Adequacy of World Timber Supply* (Washington, D.C.: Resources for the Future, 1990).

9. "Forests Plundered Despite NPC Laws," *Beijing Review*, September 11–17, 1989; "Tree Shortage Still A Problem," *China Daily*, December 25, 1989; Gao Anming, "Demand for Timber Outpacing Growth," *China Daily*, April 3, 1990; Yin Runsheng, in "An Overview of China's Forests," USDA, Economic Research Service (ERS), *China: Agriculture & Trade Report*, Washington, D.C., July 1990, reports prediction that all mature and over-mature production forests will be gone within decade; both "China's Slowdown Expected To Cut Into Its Wood Imports," *Journal of Commerce*, July 16, 1990, and DBC Associates, Inc., "China Timber Market Prospects," Portland, Oreg., 1990, discuss imports.

10. Indian deforestation rate from WRI, *World Resources 1990–91*; U.S. consumption from Alice H. Ulrich, *U.S. Timber Production, Trade, Consumption, and Price Statistics 1950–87* (Washington, D.C.: USFS, 1989); other figures from "India: Forestry Situation," in USDA, Foreign Agricultural Service, *World*

Agricultural Production, Washington, D.C., July 1990.

11. New plantation supplies and growth rates from Sedjo and Lyon, *Long-Term Adequacy*. For discussion of greater risks associated with plantations, see David A. Perry and Jumanne Maghembe, "Ecosystem Concepts and Current Trends in Forest Management: Time for Reappraisal," *Forest Ecology and Management*, Vol. 26, 1989; John I. Cameron and Ian W. Penna, *The Wood and the Trees: A Preliminary Economic Analysis of a Conservation-Oriented Forest Industry Strategy* (Hawthorn, Australia: ACF, 1988); Julian Evans, *Plantation Forestry in the Tropics* (New York: Oxford University Press, 1984); and William M. Ciesla, "Pine Bark Beetles: A New Pest Management Challenge for Chilean Foresters," *Journal of Forestry*, December 1988.

12. Latin America figures from Sedjo and Lyon, *Long-Term Adequacy*; Arnaldo Jèlvez et al., "Chile's Evolving Forest Products Industry," *Forest Products Journal*, October 1989; Jèlvez et al., *A Profile of the Chilean Forestry Sector*; native forest destruction described in Antonio Lara, Comite Nacional Pro Defensa de la Fauna y Flora, "Notes on the Proposals About Forest Conservation in Chile," unpublished, 1988; export values from FAO, *Forest Products Yearbook 1988*.

13. Laura E. Cottle and Gerard F. Schreuder, *Brazil: A Country Profile of the Forests and Forest Industries* (Seattle, Wash.: CINTRAFOR, 1990).

14. Forest area and growing stock from Brenton M. Barr, "Perspectives on Deforestation in the U.S.S.R.," in John F. Richards and Richard P. Tucker, eds., *World Deforestation in the Twentieth Century* (Durham, N.C.: Duke University Press, 1988); Economic Commission for Europe (ECE) and FAO, *Outlook for the Forest and Forest Products Sector of the USSR* (New York: United Nations, 1989); Peter A. Cardellichio et al., *Potential Expansion of Soviet Far East Log Exports to the Pacific Rim* (Seattle, Wash.: CINTRAFOR, 1989).

15. François Nectoux and Yoichi Kuroda, *Timber from the South Seas: An Analysis of Japan's Tropical Timber Trade and Its Environmental Impact* (Gland, Switzerland: World Wide Fund for Nature International, 1989).

16. Estimates of sustained yield vary, depending on assumptions of how fast cutover forests can grow wood and how much forest is to be opened to logging; timber production exceeds sustained yield in Malaysia by 71–228 percent, according to Nectoux and Kuroda, *Timber from the South Seas*. Export figure from "The Industry Strikes Back," *Asiaweek*, May 6, 1990; "Timber Traders Fail to Quell Fears Over Rainforests," *New Scientist*, June 9, 1990; Robert Repetto, "Deforestation in the Tropics," *Scientific American*, April 1990. Net importer prediction from Sahabat Alam Malaysia, *Solving Sarawak's Forest and Native Problem* (Penang: 1990).

17. FAO, *Forest Products Yearbook 1988*.

18. Simon Rietbergen, "Africa," in Duncan Poore, *No Timber Without Trees: Sustainability in the Tropical Forest* (London: Earthscan Publications, 1989); FAO, *Forest Products Yearbook 1988*.

19. Old-growth logging from Sharon Chow, Sierra Club of Western Canada, Victoria, B.C., private communication, September 27, 1990; sustained yield figure from British Columbia Ministry of Forests, *Annual Report 1988–89* (Victoria, B.C.: Queen's Printer, 1990); Moore, "The State of the Temperate Rainforest in British Columbia."

20. Olson, *Pacific Northwest Lumber and Wood Products*.

21. U.S. General Accounting Office (GAO), *Forest Service Timber Harvesting, Planting, Assistance Programs and Tax Provisions* (Washington, D.C.: 1990).

22. U.S. depletion in Olson, *Pacific Northwest Lumber and Wood Products*; John Davies, "Another US Firm Eyes Siberian Log Prospects," *Journal of Commerce*, July 25, 1990;

Brenton M. Barr, "Regional Alternatives in Soviet Timber Management," in Fred Singleton, ed., *Environmental Problems in the Soviet Union & Eastern Europe* (Boulder, Colo.: Lynne Rienner Publishers, 1986); Thai role in regional deforestation discussed in Philip Smucker, "Southeast Asia Devours Its Rain Forests," *San Francisco Examiner*, July 15, 1990; Hamish McDonald, "Partners in Plunder," *Far Eastern Economic Review*, February 22, 1990; and James Pringle, "Thais Lending a Big Hand in the Rape of Teak Forests," *Bangkok Post*, May 19, 1990.

23. Poore, *No Timber Without Trees*; Chris Maser, *The Redesigned Forest* (San Pedro, Calif.: R. & E. Miles, 1988).

24. Southeast Asia figure based on Nectoux and Kuroda, *Timber from the South Seas*; Gregor Hodgson and John A. Dixon, *Logging Versus Fisheries and Tourism in Palawan: An Environmental and Economic Analysis* (Honolulu: East-West Environment and Policy Institute, 1988); U.S. road length from Richard E. Rice, *The Uncounted Costs of Logging* (Washington, D.C.: The Wilderness Society, 1989); area figure based on 10 acres per mile of road estimate in Elliott A. Norse, *Ancient Forests of the Pacific Northwest* (Washington, D.C.: Island Press, 1990).

25. Norse, *Ancient Forests*; D.A. Perry, "Landscape Pattern and Forest Pests," *Northwest Environmental Journal*, Vol. 4, No. 2, 1988; Rice, *The Uncounted Costs of Logging*; Hodgson and Dixon, *Logging Versus Fisheries and Tourism.*

26. Robert J. Buschbacher, "Ecological Analysis of Natural Forest Management in the Humid Tropics," in Robert Goodland, ed., *Race to Save the Tropics: Ecology & Economics for a Sustainable Future* (Washington, D.C.: Island Press, 1990); Norman Myers, "Finding Ways to Stem the Tide of Deforestation," *People* (International Planned Parenthood Federation), Vol. 17, No. 1, 1990.

27. James Brooke, "Saving Scraps of the Rain Forest May Be Pointless, Naturalists Say," *New York Times*, November 14, 1989;

Norse, *Ancient Forests*; Löfgren, "Importance and Value of a Network of Large Protected Woodlands"; Peter H. Morrison, *Old Growth in the Pacific Northwest: A Status Report* (Washington, D.C.: The Wilderness Society, 1988).

28. Perry and Maghembe, "Ecosystem Concepts"; D. A. Perry et al., "Bootstrapping in Ecosystems," *BioScience*, April 1989; S. S. Zyabchenko et al., "Dynamics of Ecological Processes on Extensive Clear Fellings in Northern Karelia," *Lesovedenie* [Soviet Forest Sciences], No. 3, 1988; L. B. Kholopova, "Soil Cover After Clear Cutting of a Hardwood Stand in the Southern Moscow Region," *Lesovedenie* [Soviet Forest Sciences], No. 6, 1988.

29. Christopher Uhl et al., "Disturbance and Regeneration in Amazonia: Lessons for Sustainable Land-Use," *The Ecologist*, November/December 1989; Christopher Uhl, "Amazon Forest Fires: Strategies for Forest Conservation," Proposal to World Wildlife Fund, Washington, D.C., 1989; Hira P. Jhamtani, "An Overview of Forestry Policies and Commercialization in Indonesia," presented to the Rainforest Alliance Workshop on the U.S. Tropical Timber Trade: Conservation Options and Impacts, New York, April 14–15, 1989.

30. See Richard Houghton, "Emissions of Greenhouse Gases," in Myers, *Deforestation Rates in Tropical Forests*. Mark E. Harmon et al., "Effects on Carbon Storage of Conversion of Old-Growth Forests to Young Forests," *Science*, February 9, 1990, find that less than half the forests' carbon actually ends up in durable wood products after logging; decomposition—of wood left in the forest, bark, sawdust created in milling, and paper products—releases most of the carbon to the atmosphere. They conclude that similar results are likely in most forests in which trees are harvested before the age at which they reach the old-growth stage of succession. P.B. Alaback, "Logging of Temperate Rainforests and the Greenhouse Effect: Ecological Factors to Consider," in E. Alexander,

ed., *Stewardship of Soil, Air and Water Resources*, Proceedings of Watershed '89 (Juneau, Alaska: USFS, 1989) reached similar conclusions for forests in Alaska and Chile.

31. Martin C.D. Speight, "Life in Dead Trees: A Neglected Part of Europe's Wildlife Heritage," *Environmental Conservation*, Winter 1989; Richard K. Hermann, "North American Tree Species in Europe," *Journal of Forestry*, December 1987, states that Norway spruce, Scotch pine, and beech cover 97 percent of German woodlands; Pacific yew from Norse, *Ancient Forests*.

32. Charles M. Peters et al., "Valuation of an Amazonian Rainforest," *Nature*, June 29, 1989; in British Columbia, overfishing has also played a role in reduced catches, but with more than half the coastal salmon habitat lost, logging has clearly been the primary factor, per Chow, private communication; on British Columbia pulp mill pollution, see West Coast Environmental Law Research Foundation, "Newsletter, Special Pulp Pollution Edition," Vancouver, B.C., Spring 1990.

33. Rice, *Uncounted Costs of Logging*; Hodgson and Dixon, *Logging Versus Fisheries and Tourism*; *Virola* from Buschbacher, "Ecological Analysis of Natural Forest Management"; Masson pine from S. D. Richardson, *Forests and Forestry in China: Changing Patterns of Resource Development* (Washington, D.C.: Island Press, 1990); Sara Oldfield, *Rare Tropical Timbers* (Gland, Switzerland: International Union for Conservation of Nature and Natural Resources (IUCN), 1988).

34. "Research Begins on Tree Pests," *China Daily*, March 20, 1990; "pests" of various kinds, including fire, attack 6–10 million hectares of woodland annually, according to "Demand for Timber Outpacing Growth," *China Daily*, April 3, 1990; Maser, *Redesigned Forest*; Jerry F. Franklin et al., "Importance of Ecological Diversity in Maintaining Long-Term Site Productivity," in D. A. Perry et al., eds., *Maintaining the Long-Term Productivity of Pacific Northwest Forest Ecosystems* (Portland,

Oreg.: Timber Press, 1989); T.D. Schowalter, "Pest Response to Simplification of Forest Landscapes," *Northwest Environmental Journal*, Fall/Winter 1988; Perry and Maghembe, "Ecosystem Concepts."

35. Franklin et al., "Importance of Ecological Diversity"; Plochmann, "The Forests of Central Europe"; Perry, "Landscape Pattern and Forest Pests"; Stefan Godzik and Jadwiga Sienkiewicz, "Air Pollution and Forest Health in Central Europe: Poland, Czechoslovakia, and the German Democratic Republic," in Wladyslaw Grodzinski et al., eds., *Ecological Risks: Perspectives from Poland and the United States* (Washington, D.C.: National Academy Press, 1990).

36. Even less intact rain forest remains on the British Columbia mainland, Moore, "Where Is It and How Much Is Left?"; ninety percent figure from Vicky Husband, Conservation Chair, Sierra Club of Western Canada, private communication, Vancouver, March 6, 1990; Shirley Christian, "Ecologists Act to Save Ancient Forest in Chile From Industry," *New York Times*, April 3, 1990.

37. Timothy D. Schowalter, "Forest Pest Management: A Synopsis," *Northwest Environmental Journal*, Fall/Winter 1988; Perry, "Landscape Pattern and Forest Pests"; Franklin et al., "Importance of Ecological Diversity."

38. Seri G. Rudolph, "Ancient Forests as Genetic Reserves for Forestry," in Norse, *Ancient Forests*; Jerry Franklin, "Toward a New Forestry," *American Forests*, November/December 1989; Franklin et al., "Importance of Ecological Diversity."

39. Carl Goldstein, "The Planters Are Back," *Far Eastern Economic Review*, April 13, 1989; Maser, *The Redesigned Forest*; 90 percent figure from Perry et al., "Bootstrapping"; D.A. Perry et al., "Mycorrhizae, Mycorrhizospheres, and Reforestation: Current Knowledge and Research Needs," *Canadian Journal of Forest Research*, Vol. 17, No. 8, 1987; Franklin et al., "Importance of Ecological Diver-

sity"; M.P. Amaranthus et al., "Decaying Logs as Moisture Reservoirs After Drought and Wildfire," in Alexander, ed., *Stewardship of Soil, Air and Water Resources*.

40. While many of the individual techniques are not new, their application in an integrated fashion, based on recent findings on the ecology of Northwest forests, is. Franklin, "Toward A New Forestry"; Anna Maria Gillis, "The New Forestry: An Ecosystem Approach to Land Management," *BioScience*, September 1990; Paul Roberts, "A 'Kinder, Gentler Forestry'," *Seattle Weekly*, September 12, 1990.

41. John C. Ryan, "Oregon's Ancient Laboratory," *World Watch*, November/December 1990; USFS, *Draft Environmental Impact Statement, Shasta Costa Timber Sales and Integrated Resource Projects, Siskiyou National Forest* (Gold Beach, Oreg.: 1990).

42. Buschbacher, "Ecological Analysis"; Gary S. Hartshorn, "Application of Gap Theory to Tropical Forest Management: Natural Regeneration on Strip Clear-Cuts in the Peruvian Amazon," *Ecology*, Vol. 70, No. 3, 1989; Gary S. Hartshorn et al., "Sustained Yield Management of Tropical Forests: A Synopsis of the Palcazu Development Project in the Central Selva of the Peruvian Amazon," in J.C. Figueroa C. et al., eds., *Management of the Forests of Tropical America: Prospects and Technologies* (Rio Piedras, P.R.: Institute of Tropical Forestry, 1987); Mario Pariona and Roberto Simeone, "Management of Natural Forests in the Palcazu Valley," no location, 1990.

43. For debate on possibility of sustainable tropical logging, see Poore, *No Timber Without Trees*; FAO, *Review of Forest Management Systems of Tropical Asia: Case-studies of Natural Forest Management for Timber Production in India, Malaysia and the Philippines*, Forestry Paper 89 (Rome: 1989); Alex S. Moad, "Sustainable Forestry in the Tropics: The Elusive Goal," presented to Rainforest Alliance Workshop on the U.S. Tropical Timber Trade, New York, April 14–15, 1989; Marcus Colchester, "Guilty Until Proven Innocent," *The Ecologist*, May/June 1990; Patrick Anderson, "The Myth of Sustainable Logging: The Case for a Ban on Tropical Timber Imports," *The Ecologist*, September 1989. For role of disturbance in natural systems, see Norse, *Ancient Forests*; Perry, "Landscape Pattern and Forest Pests"; William K. Stevens, "Research in 'Virgin' Amazon Uncovers Complex Farming," *The New York Times*, April 3, 1990; Uhl et al., "Disturbance and Regeneration in Amazonia."

44. Wadsworth cited in Roger A. Sedjo, "Can Tropical Forest Management Systems Be Economic?" *Journal of Business Administration*, forthcoming.

45. Postel and Heise, *Reforesting the Earth*; China example from Runsheng, "An Overview of China's Forests." Goodland et al., "Tropical Moist Forest Management," note that natural forest logging is so profitable partly because it is not sustainable; the lower yields (and therefore higher relative costs) afforded by sustainable logging would make plantation establishment more attractive economically.

46. Robert J. Seidl, "Plantation Grown Douglas Fir: A Perspective," *Pilchuck Tree Farm Notes*, Vol. 6, 1987 (CINTRAFOR Reprint Series No. 8); Mark Wigg and Anae Boulton, "Quality Wood, Sustainable Forests: A New Agenda For Managed Forests in the Northwest," *Forest Watch*, January/February 1989; Maser, *Redesigned Forest*; Alan Grainger, "Future Supplies of High-Grade Tropical Hardwoods From Intensive Plantations," *Journal of World Forest Resource Management*, Vol. 3, 1988.

47. Jerry F. Franklin et al., "Modifying Douglas-Fir Management Regimes for Nontimber Objectives," in C.D. Oliver et al., eds., *Douglas-fir: Stand Management for the Future* (Seattle: College of Forest Resources, University of Washington, 1986).

48. R.R.B. Leakey, "Clonal Forestry in the Tropics—A Review of Developments, Strate-

gies and Opportunities," *Commonwealth Forestry Review*, Vol. 66, No. 1, 1987; Julian Evans, *Plantation Forestry in the Tropics* (Oxford: Oxford University Press, 1982).

49. S.N. Trivedi and Colin Price, "The Incidence of Illicit Felling in Afforestation Project Appraisal: Some Models Illustrated for Eucalyptus Plantations in India," *Journal of World Forest Resource Management*, Vol. 3, 1988.

50. The remainder of the industrial wood harvest is turned into miscellaneous products such as poles, fence posts, etc. FAO, *Forest Product Yearbook 1988*; Richard W. Haynes, *An Analysis of the Timber Situation in the United States: 1989–2040, Part I: The Current Resource and Use Situation, A Technical Document Supporting the 1989 RPA Assessment* (draft) (Washington, D.C.: USFS, 1988); ECE and FAO, *European Timber Trends and Prospects to the Year 2000 and Beyond* (New York: United Nations, 1986). In Japan and the Soviet Union, construction is the main end-use for timber products, but it is not clear what role housing plays versus other types of construction.

51. Nectoux and Kuroda, *Timber from the South Seas*; FAO, *Forest Products Yearbook 1988*; ECE and FAO, *European Timber Trends and Prospects*; Temagami Wilderness Society, "Wilderness Report," Toronto, Ontario, Summer 1990; Canadian per capita paper consumption from Greenpeace, *The Greenpeace Guide to Paper* (Vancouver: 1990), assuming a family of four.

52. Richard W. Haynes, *An Analysis of the Timber Situation in the United States: 1989–2040, Part II: The Future Resource Situation, A Technical Document Supporting the 1989 RPA Assessment* (draft) (Washington, D.C.: USFS, 1988). USFS estimate of savings is 10–15 percent of "dimension lumber," such as two-by-fours, which is the great majority of lumber used in construction.

53. One major Japanese manufacturer, Daiken, claims to have achieved 80 percent conversion efficiency. Nectoux and Kuroda,

Timber from the South Seas; Robert Repetto and Malcolm Gillis, eds., *Public Policies and the Misuse of Forest Resources* (Cambridge: Cambridge University Press, 1988); Japanese mill labor-intensity from David Brooks, U.S. Forest Service, Corvallis, Oreg., private communication, August 20, 1990.

54. Haynes, *Analysis, Part II*; Clark Row and Robert B. Phelps, "Carbon Cycle Impacts of Improving Forest Products Utilization and Recycling," presented to North American Conference on Forestry Responses to Climate Change, Climate Institute, Washington, D.C., May 15–17, 1990.

55. A. V. Yablokov, "State of Nature in the USSR," presented to the East European Environmental Challenge seminar at the Ecology 89 International Congress, Gothenburg, Sweden, August 28–31, 1989.

56. Hideo Ono, "Battle Rages Over Throw-away Chopsticks," *The Japan Economic Journal*, July 14, 1990.

57. Haynes, *Analysis, Part I*; ECE and FAO, *European Timber Trends and Prospects*; Jonathan Friedland, "Paper Money: Indonesia's Pulp Industry Joins Top League," *Far Eastern Economic Review*, June 28, 1990.

58. John Lancaster, "Logging the Last Rain Forest: Exploitation of Unique Woods Divides Alaskans," *Washington Post*, September 5, 1989; Joe Rinkevich, "Destruction of an Internationally Important Wetland in Irian Jaya, Indonesia for Woodchipping Exports to Japan," *Japan Environment Monitor*, June 30, 1990; Lisa Tweten, "Guatemalan Pulp Plant Threatens Forest," *EPOCA Update*, Summer 1990; FAO, *Forest Products Yearbook 1988*. For example of destructive Canadian pulpwood logging, see The Valhalla Society, "Position Paper on Pulpwood Agreement No. 9 and Other Pulpwood Agreements in the Province," New Denver, British Columbia, July 1990.

59. Haynes, *Analysis, Part II*; ECE and FAO, *European Timber Trends and Prospects*.

60. Greenpeace, *The Greenpeace Guide to Paper*; FAO, *Forest Products Yearbook 1988*.

61. Temagami Wilderness Society, *Wilderness Report*.

62. Table 5–4 estimates based on FAO, *Forest Products Yearbook 1988*; manufacturing efficiency from Haynes, *An Analysis, Part I*; efficiency increases from Row and Phelps, "Carbon Cycle Impacts"; construction waste from Haynes, *An Analysis, Part II*, and from ECE and FAO, *European Timber Trends and Prospects*; Norwegian consumption from Greenpeace, *The Greenpeace Guide to Paper*; wood savings from recycling derived from A. Clark Wiseman, "U.S. Wastepaper Recycling Policies: Issues and Effects," Resources for the Future, Energy and Natural Resources Division, discussion paper, Washington, D.C., August 1990; U.S. industrial roundwood consumption in 1988 from Alice H. Ulrich, USFS, Forest Inventory, Economics, and Recreation Research Staff, Washington, D.C., private communication, October 15, 1990.

63. Energy and Environmental Study Institute (EESI), "Many Proposals for Ancient Forests," *Weekly Bulletin*, July 23, 1990; timber harvest reduction from "Forest Service Estimates Effects of Spotted Owl Strategy," *Forest Planning Canada*, July/August 1990; "Pact Limits Timber Cutting in Alaska Forest," *New York Times*, October 21, 1990; EESI, "Tongass, Howls Over Owls Dominate Second Session," Special Report, August 7, 1990.

64. Sierra Club of Western Canada, "Canada's Vanishing Temperate Rainforest: Are We Foreclosing On Our Future?" Victoria, B.C., 1989; Timothy Egan, "Struggles Over the Ancient Trees Shift to British Columbia," *New York Times*, April 15, 1990; British Columbia Ministry of Forests, Integrated Resources Branch, "Towards An Old Growth Strategy," Victoria, B.C., Spring 1990.

65. 200 million figure from Mark Poffenberger, ed., *Keepers of the Forest: Land Manage-ment Alternatives in Southeast Asia* (West Hartford, Conn.: Kumarian Press, 1990); Peter Bunyard, "Guardians of the Amazon," *New Scientist*, December 16, 1989; James Brooke, "Tribes Get Right to 50% of Colombian Amazon," *New York Times*, February 4, 1990.

66. The Nature Conservancy, "Officially Sanctioned Debt-for-Nature Swaps to Date," Washington, D.C., August 1990; Robert Repetto and Frederik van Bolhuis, *Natural Endowments: Financing Resource Conservation for Development* (Washington, D.C.: WRI, 1989).

67. Fred Pearce, "Bolivian Indians March to Save their Homeland," *New Scientist*, August 25, 1990; James Painter, "Bolivian Indians Protest Wrecking of Rain Forest," *Christian Science Monitor*, September 18, 1990; Edward C. Wolf, Conservation International, Washington, D.C., private communications, October 12 and 23, 1990.

68. 15 percent figure from Jeff DeBonis, "Timber Industry's Claims," *Journal of Forestry*, July 1989, which notes that the timber cut on federal lands in Oregon increased 18.5 percent in the eighties. Even with a projected 55-percent increase in the U.S. timber harvest by 2040, employment in the increasingly mechanized timber industry is expected to decline by 27 percent; GAO, *Forest Service Timber Harvesting*.

69. Jobs bypassing local communities from FAO, *Review of Forest Management Systems of Tropical Asia*; community-oriented management discussed in Poffenberger, *Keepers of the Forest*; John O. Browder, "Development Alternatives for Tropical Rain Forests," in H. Jeffrey Leonard et al., *Environment and the Poor: Development Strategies for a Common Agenda* (New Brunswick, N.J.: Transaction Books, 1989); Jenne H. De Beer and Melanie J. McDermott, *The Economic Value of Non-Timber Forest Products in Southeast Asia* (Amsterdam: Netherlands Committee for IUCN, 1989); Larry Lohmann, "Commercial Tree Plantations in Thailand: Deforestation by Any

Other Name," *The Ecologist*, January/February 1990.

70. Richard Rice, "Budgetary Savings From Phasing Out Subsidized Logging," unpublished paper, The Wilderness Society, Washington, D.C., June 5, 1990; Tongass figures are averages for 1982–89 from Susan Warner, Southeast Alaska Conservation Council, Washington, D.C., private communication, September 25, 1990.

71. Repetto and Gillis, *Public Policies and the Misuse of Forest Resources*.

72. Repetto, "Deforestation in the Tropics."

73. Marcus Colchester and Larry Lohmann, *The Tropical Forestry Action Plan: What Progress?* (Penang, Malaysia: World Rainforest Movement and *The Ecologist*, 1990).

74. Robert Winterbottom, *Taking Stock: The Tropical Forestry Action Plan After Five Years* (Washington, D.C.: WRI, 1990).

75. Terence Hpay, *The International Tropical Timber Agreement: Its Prospects for Tropical Timber Trade, Development and Forest Management* (London: IUCN/International Institute for Environment and Development, 1986); action at Bali meeting from Marcus Colchester, "The International Tropical Timber Organization: Kill or Cure for the Rainforests?" *The Ecologist*, September/October 1990.

76. GAO, *Forest Service Timber Harvesting*; Tongass timber expenditures in 1989 were approximately $40 million, according to Warner, private communication.

77. "China's Slowdown Expected to Cut into its Wood Imports," *Journal of Commerce*, July 16, 1990; "India: Forestry Situation"; past efforts described in Postel and Heise, *Reforesting the Earth*.

78. Office of the Press Secretary, The White House, "Proposed Global Forests Convention," fact sheet, Houston, Tex., July 11, 1990.

Chapter 6. Restoring the East European and Soviet Environments

1. Mark Schapiro, "The New Danube," *Mother Jones*, May 1990.

2. For a discussion of the role the environment played in the political changes in the region, see János Vargha, "Green Revolutions in East Europe," *Panoscope*, May 1990, and Larry Tye, "Rallies Against Pollution Paced Other Protests," *Boston Globe*, December 18, 1989. The region discussed in this chapter encompasses Bulgaria, Czechoslovakia, the former East Germany, Hungary, Poland, Romania, and the Soviet Union; Yugoslavia and Albania, as they were never members of the Warsaw Pact and as information about them is scarce, are not included.

3. Andrzej Kassenberg, "Environmental Situation in Poland," unpublished background paper, 1989; Josef Vavroušek et al., *The Environment in Czechoslovakia* (Prague: Department of the Environment, State Commission for Science, Technology, and Investments, 1990); Murray Feshbach and Ann Rubin, "Why Ivan Can't Breathe," *Washington Post*, January 28, 1990.

4. Carbon dioxide emissions data from Gregg Marland et al., Oak Ridge National Laboratory, *Estimates of CO_2 Emissions from Fossil Fuel Burning and Cement Manufacturing, Based on the United Nations Energy Statistics and the U.S. Bureau of Mines Cement Manufacturing Data* (Oak Ridge, Tenn.: Oak Ridge National Laboratory, 1989); on the cost-effectiveness of emissions-reduction investments in Eastern Europe, see, for example, "Pooled Aid Proposed," *Acid News*, July 1989, and Joseph Alcamo et al., "A Simulation Model for Evaluating Control Strategies," *Ambio*, Vol. 16 No. 5, 1987.

5. United Nations, *Energy Statistics Yearbook, 1988* (New York: 1990).

6. For statistics on the use of open-hearth technology, see William U. Chandler, *The Changing Role of the Market in National Econo-*

mies, Worldwatch Paper 72 (Washington, D.C.: Worldwatch Institute, September 1986). Gross domestic product measures a country's domestically produced economic output; for Eastern Europe and the Soviet Union, it is essentially equivalent to gross national product. The most recent year for which reliable data are available for all countries shown in Figure 6–1 is 1985; reliable data are not available for Bulgaria. Ranges shown in the figure reflect differing estimates of economic output, corrected for purchasing power and currency fluctuations.

7. Dr. Volker Beer, East German environmentalist, unpublished data, February 1990.

8. U.N. Economic Commission for Europe (ECE), *The State of Transboundary Air Pollution: 1989 Update* (Geneva: 1990); Christer Ågren, "Tracking Air Pollutants," *Acid News*, January 1, 1990; unofficial translation of Statistical Supplement to USSR State Committee for the Protection of Nature, *Report on the State of the Environemnt in USSR* (Moscow: 1989); population data from Population Reference Bureau, *1988 World Population Data Sheet* (Washington, D.C.: 1988); GNP extrapolated from adjusted 1980 levels in Paul Marer, *Dollar GNP's of the USSR and Eastern Europe* (Baltimore: Johns Hopkins University Press, 1985), using growth rates from U.S. Central Intelligence Agency, *Handbook of Economic Statistics* (Washington, D.C.: 1989).

9. Michael P. Walsh, "Motor Vehicle Pollution in Hungary: A Strategy for Progress," prepared for the World Bank, Arlington, Va., June 1990; Michael P. Walsh, Arlington, Va., private communication, October 19, 1990.

10. György Vukovich, "Trends in Economic and Urban Development and Their Environmental Implications," in Don Hinrichsen and György Enyedi, eds., *State of the Hungarian Environment* (Budapest: Hungarian Academy of Sciences, 1990); industrial base figures from World Bank, *World Development Report 1982* (New York: Oxford University

Press, 1982). A similar breakdown has not been provided in subsequent reports.

11. Vera Gavrilov, "Environmental Damage Creates Serious Problem for Government," *Report on Eastern Europe*, Radio Free Europe, May 25, 1990.

12. Import and export are 1988 numbers from *Acid News*, January 1, 1990, based on ECE data; Ruse information from Ecoglasnost, "The Rise of the Independent Movements for the Ecological Protection of the Environment in Bulgaria," Sofia, Bulgaria, undated; "Lukanov Meets with Ruse Delegation," *Sofia BTA*, June 29, 1990, and "Diplomatic Protest to Romania Issued," *Sofia BTA*, June 29, 1990, translated in Foreign Broadcast Information Service (FBIS) Daily Report/East Europe, Rosslyn, Va., July 2, 1990; "Environmental Protection Talks with Bulgaria," *Bucharest Rompres*, July 27, 1990, translated in FBIS Daily Report/East Europe, Rosslyn, Va., July 30, 1990.

13. Beer, unpublished data.

14. Vavroušek et al., *The Environment in Czechoslovakia*; Béla Hock and László Somlyódy, "Freshwater Resources and Water Quality," in Hinrichsen and Enyedi, *The State of the Hungarian Environment*; Poland figure from World Bank report cited in Larry Tye, "Poland is Left Choking on its Wastes," *Boston Globe*, December 18, 1989; D.J. Peterson, "The State of the Environment: The Water," *Report on the USSR*, Radio Liberty, March 16, 1990.

15. Hungarian data from Hock and Somlyódy, "Freshwater Resources"; Vavroušek et al., *Environment in Czechoslovakia*; Naďa Johanisová, Information Center, Czech Union of Nature Protectors, private communication, June 23, 1990; Poland figure based on newly released government statistics cited in Tye, "Poland is Left Choking"; Peterson, "State of the Environment: The Water."

16. D.J. Peterson, "Baikal: A Status Report," *Report on the USSR*, Radio Liberty, January 12, 1990; John Massey Stewart, "The

Great Lake is in Great Peril," *New Scientist*, June 30, 1990.

17. Tisza information from U.K. Foreign and Commonwealth Office, "Environmental Pollution in the USSR and Eastern Europe," October 1989; "Czechoslovakia/Poland," *Multinational Environmental Outlook*, April 28, 1988; Marlise Simons, "Befouled to Its Romantic Depths, Danube Reaches a Turning Point," *New York Times*, May 7, 1990.

18. On the Elbe, see U. Adler, "Umweltschutz in der DDR: Ökologische Modernisierung und Entsorgung unerlässlich," *Ifo schnell-dienst*, June 18, 1990; Caspian and Black Seas data from Peterson, "The State of the Environment: Water"; Baltic information from Bertil Hagerhall, "Saving the Baltic: A Race Against Mankind," *Our Planet*, Vol. 2, No. 2, 1990, and from Arthur H. Westing, *Comprehensive Security for the Baltic: An Environmental Approach* (London: Sage Publishing, 1989).

19. Peterson, "The State of the Environment: The Water"; Alexei Yablokov, Deputy Chairman of the Ecological Committee, the USSR Supreme Soviet, "State of Nature in the USSR," presented to The East European Environmental Challenge seminar at the Ecology '89 International Congress, Gothenburg, Sweden, August 28–31, 1989; "Pollution Forces Closing of Dagestan Beaches," *Izvestiya*, June 23, 1990, translated in FBIS Daily Report/Soviet Union, Rosslyn, Va., June 29, 1990; "Black Sea Resorts Face Overcrowding, Pollution," *Izvestiya*, June 22, 1990, translated in FBIS Daily Report/Soviet Union, Rosslyn, Va., July 6, 1990; Environmental Protection Club of Latvia, USA Chapter, "Latvia: Environmental Crisis/Environmental Activism," Vienna, Va., 1990.

20. Marlise Simons, "West Germans Get Ready to Scrub the East's Tarnished Environment," *New York Times*, June 27, 1990; Prague number from Richard A. Liroff, "Eastern Europe: Restoring a Damaged Environment," *EPA Journal*, July/August 1990; Jiri Pehe, "A Record of Catastrophic Environmental Damage," *Report on Eastern Europe*, Radio Free Europe, March 23, 1990, based upon Radio Czechoslovakia report, February 22, 1990.

21. D.J. Peterson, "The State of the Environment: Solid Wastes," *Report on the USSR*, Radio Liberty, May 11, 1990.

22. "Burial money" from Ruth E. Gruber, "Word is Out: East Europe is a Disaster Area," *Christian Science Monitor*, April 18, 1990.

23. Nicholas Eberstadt, "Health and Mortality in Eastern Europe, 1965 to 1985," in *Pressures for Reform in the East European Economies, Vol. 1*, submitted to the Joint Economic Committee, U.S. Congress, October 20, 1989; Alina Potrykowska, "Recent Trends and Spatial Patterns of Mortality in Poland," presented to the International Geographical Union Commission on Population Geography symposium on the Geographical Inequalities of Mortality, Lille, France, April 24–28, 1990; Dagmar Dzúrova et al., "Environment and Health in Czechoslovakia," presented to the Woodrow Wilson International Center for Scholars conference on Public Health and the Environmental Crisis in Eastern Europe, Washington, D.C., April 30-May 2, 1990.

24. USSR State Committee for the Protection of Nature, *Report on the State of the Environment*, translated for the U.S. Environmental Protection Agency; Yablokov, "State of Nature."

25. Marnie Stetson, "Chernobyl's Deadly Legacy Revealed," *World Watch*, November/December 1990; "Wider Chernobyl Evacuation Ordered," *Washington Post*, April 24, 1990; Felicity Barringer, "Four Years Later, Kremlin Speaks Candidly of Chernobyl's Horrors," *New York Times*, April 28, 1990; David Marples, "A Retrospective of a Nuclear Accident," *Report on the USSR*, Radio Liberty, April 20, 1990; Robert Peter Gale,

"Chernobyl: Answers Slipping Away," *Bulletin of the Atomic Scientists*, September 1990.

26. Vavroušek et al., *The Environment in Czechoslovakia*; Poland data from Eugeniusz Pudlis, "Who Will Pay for the Clean-Up?" *Panoscope*, May 1990, and from Marlise Simons, "Rising Iron Curtain Exposes Haunting Veil of Polluted Air," *New York Times*, April 8, 1990; Jeffrey Gedmin, "Polluted East Germany," *Christian Science Monitor*, March 16, 1990; Bedřich Moldan et al., *Environment of the Czech Republic: Development and Situation up to the End of 1989* (Prague: Ministry of Environment of the Czech Republic, 1990), translated by Naďa Johanisová.

27. Josh Friedman,"Bulgaria's Deadly Secret" and "Silent Killers in Kuklen," *Newsday*, April 22, 1990.

28. Moldan et al., *Environment of the Czech Republic*; see also Bohumil Ticháček and Miroslav Cikrt, Institute of Hygiene and Epidemiology, Prague, "Czechoslovak Health System and its Capacity of Coping with Environmental Crises," presented to the Woodrow Wilson International Center for Scholars conference on Public Health and the Environmental Crisis in Eastern Europe, Washington, D.C., April 30-May 2, 1990.

29. Vukovich, "Trends in Economic and Urban Development"; National Institute of Public Health study cited in Don Hinrichsen, "Blue Danube," *Amicus Journal*, Winter 1989.

30. Report cited in Stanley J. Kabala, Center for Hazardous Materials Research, University of Pittsburgh, "Environmental Deterioration in Poland and the Impact on Public Health: Difficulties in Assessment," presented to the Woodrow Wilson International Center for Scholars conference on Public Health and the Environmental Crisis in Eastern Europe, Washington, D.C., April 30-May 2, 1990; Potrykowska, "Recent Trends."

31. Soil erosion data and doubling of salinized land figure from D.J. Peterson (citing Goskompriroda), "The State of the Environment: The Land," *Report on the USSR*, Radio Liberty, June 1, 1990; lost fertility from Yuri Markish, "Soviet Environmental Problems Mount," *Centrally Planned Economies Agriculture Report*, Economic Research Service, May-June 1989; economic costs from Herman Cesar, "Environmental Issues in the Soviet Union: Description and Annotated Bibliography," World Bank, Washington, D.C., unpublished, September 1990; irrigated land salinization from Philip P. Micklin, Western Michigan University, Kalamazoo, cited in Sandra Postel, *Water for Irrigation: Facing the Limits*, Worldwatch Paper 93 (Washington, D.C.: Worldwatch Institute, December 1989).

32. William S. Ellis, "A Soviet Sea Lies Dying," *National Geographic*, February 1990; Philip P. Micklin, "Desiccation of the Aral Sea: A Water Management Disaster in the Soviet Union," *Science*, September 2, 1988; Martin Walker, "Sea Turning into Desert," *Manchester Guardian Weekly*, April 24, 1988; Philip P. Micklin, "The Water Management Crisis in Soviet Central Asia," final report to the National Council for Soviet and East European Research, Washington, D.C., February 1989.

33. World Conservation Monitoring Centre, "The Environment in Eastern Europe, 1990: A Summary" (draft), Cambridge, U.K., 1990; Vavroušek et al., *The Environment in Czechoslovakia*; Hungarian data from Vukovich, "Trends in Economic and Urban Development"; Romanian information from Peter Jenkins, "New Romania: A Preliminary Assessment of High Priority Problems in Environmental Policy and Natural Resources Management and a Proposal to Prepare an Action Plan" (draft), Yale School of Forestry and Environmental Studies, New Haven, Conn., March 28, 1990.

34. Peterson, "The State of the Environment: The Land"; Yablokov, "State of Nature."

35. USSR State Committee for the Protection of Nature, *Report on the State of the Envi-*

ronment; Dr. Jan Cerovsky, "Environmental Status Report 1988/89: Czechoslovakia," in International Union for Conservation and Natural Resources (IUCN), *Environmental Status Reports: 1988/1989, Vol. 1: Czechoslovakia, Hungary, Poland* (Thatcham, U.K.: Thatcham Printers, 1990).

36. ECE, "Air Pollution and Forest Damage in Europe: Still Critical but Some Improvements," press release, Geneva, August 29, 1990.

37. USSR State Committee for the Protection of Nature, *Report on the State of the Environment*.

38. Yablokov, "State of Nature"; Zoltan Szilassy, "Environmental Status Reports 1988/89: Hungary," in IUCN, *Environmental Status Reports*; Bulgaria data from Friedman, "Bulgaria's Deadly Secret"; on nature reserves, see IUCN, *Environmental Status Reports*, and Douglas R. Weiner, *Models of Nature: Ecology, Conservation, and Cultural Revolution in Soviet Russia* (Bloomington: Indiana University Press, 1988).

39. Data in Table 6–2 based on the following: Duncan Fisher, "Report on Visit to Bulgaria," February 18–24, 1990, "Report on Visit to Czechoslovakia," December 5–9, 1989, and "Report on Two Visits to Romania," March 10–12 and March 28-April 8, 1990, all from The Ecological Studies Institute, London; Jiri Pehe, "The Green Movements in Eastern Europe," *Report on Eastern Europe*, Radio Free Europe, March 16, 1990; World Conservation Monitoring Centre, "The Environment in Eastern Europe, 1990: A Summary"; Eric Green, *Ecology and Perestroika: Environmental Protection in the Soviet Union* (Washington, D.C.: American Committee on U.S.-Soviet Relations, 1990); and private communications.

40. A.L Yanshin, "Reviving Vernadsky's Legacy," *Environment*, December 1988; *On The Road to the Noosphere* (Moscow: Novosti Press Agency, 1989); Igor Altshuler and Ruben Mnatsakanyan, "Excerpts from a Roundtable at Moscow State University," *Environment*, December 1988; Weiner, *Models of Nature*.

41. "The State of Soviet Ecology: An Interview with Maria V. Cherkasova," *Multinational Monitor*, March 1990; "The Changing Face of Environmentalism in the Soviet Union," interview with Igor Altshuler and Ruben Mnatsakanyan, *Environment*, March 1990; Altshuler, private communications, March 1990; Robert G. Darst, Jr., "Environmentalism in the USSR: The Opposition to the River Diversion Projects," *Soviet Economy*, Vol. 4, No. 3, 1988.

42. Darst, "Environmentalism"; Yourina quoted in Elizabeth Darby Junkin, "Green Cries from Red Square," *Buzzworm*, March/April 1990; Ann Sheehy and Sergei Voronitsyn, "Ecological Protest in the USSR, 1986–88," Radio Liberty Research Report, May 11, 1988; Green, *Ecology and Perestroika*.

43. Staff of U.S. Commission on Security and Cooperation in Europe, U.S. Congress, *Renewal and Challenge: The Baltic States 1988–1989* (Washington, D.C.: U.S. Government Printing Office, 1990); private communications with members of the Estonian Green Party, March 1990; David Marples, "The Ecological Situation in the Ukraine," *Report on the USSR*, Radio Liberty, January 19, 1990; Green, *Ecology and Perestroika*.

44. "The Social Ecological Union," brochure, 1990; Eliza Klose, Institute of Soviet-American Relations, Washington, D.C., private communication, October 24, 1990; Green, *Ecology and Perestroika*.

45. Eva Kruzikova, Czech Ministry of Environment, Prague, private communication, June 22, 1990; Johanisová, private communication, October 2, 1990. For a description of Charter 77's environmental activities, see Catherine Fitzpatrick and Janet Fleischman, *From Below: Independent Peace and Environmental Movements in Eastern Europe and the Soviet Union* (New York: Helsinki Watch Committee, 1987).

46. Zygmunt Fura, "The Polish Ecological Club," *Environment*, November 1985; Pehe, "The Green Movements in Eastern Europe."

47. Green, *Ecology and Perestroika*; number of Green members of parliament from "The Green Party of Sweden," informational brochure, March 11, 1990.

48. Duncan Fisher, The Ecological Studies Institute, London, private communication, October 2, 1990; Johanisová, private communication, October 2, 1990.

49. Eric S. Johnson with Murray Feshbach, "The Greenhouse Effect: Energy and the Environment in the Soviet Union and Eastern Bloc," prepared for the Office of Technology Assessment, U.S. Congress, Washington, D.C., unpublished, May 1, 1989.

50. Green, *Ecology and Perestroika*.

51. Ibid.; "Vorontsov Defends Goskompriroda Progress," interview with Nikolai Vorontsov, November 9–15, 1989, *Moscow Poisk*, translated by FBIS, unpublished; Dinah Bear and Jonathan Elkind, "Soviet-U.S. Cooperation," *Environment*, April 1990.

52. Eric S. Johnson, "The Politics of Local Environmental Movements in the USSR," unpublished, May 3, 1990; "The Changing Face of Environmentalism in the Soviet Union"; for a listing of members of the Supreme Soviet Ecology Committee, see Green, *Ecology and Perestroika*.

53. "Vorontsov Defends Goskompriroda Progress"; Bear and Elkind, "Soviet-U.S. Cooperation"; Green, *Ecology and Perestroika*; "USSR Supreme Soviet Resolution on Urgent Measures to Promote the Country's Ecological Recovery," *Pravda*, December 3, 1989, translated by FBIS, unpublished.

54. Plant closing information from World Conservation Monitoring Centre, "The Environment in Eastern Europe"; D.J. Peterson, "Medicines, Newspapers, and Protecting the Environment," *Report on the USSR*, Radio Liberty, March 23, 1990.

55. Marlise Simons, "Eastern Bloc's Nuclear Plants Stir West's Safety Concerns," *New York Times*, June 7, 1990; Marnie Stetson, "Auf Wiedersehen to East German Nukes?" *World Watch*, September/October 1990; Fritz Pesata, "Secret Report on Nuclear Commission Detailed," Vienna Domestic Service, July 20, 1990, translated in FBIS Daily Report/East Europe, Rosslyn, Va., July 20, 1990; David Marples, "Growing Influence of Antinuclear Movement in Ukraine," *Report on the USSR*, Radio Liberty, June 22, 1990; "Nuclear Notes," *WISE News Communique*, February 9, 1990; Steve Dickman, "Campaign to Shut Plant," *Nature*, March 22, 1990; "Bulgaria Suspends Nuclear Unit Building," *WISE News Communique*, March 9, 1990; "Hungary Cancels Nuclear Expansion," *European Energy Report*, December 1, 1989; "Czechs Halt Construction at Temelin," *European Energy Report*, January 26, 1990; Gerhardt Schmidt, OKO Institute, Bonn, West Germany, private communication, May 7, 1990; Jeffrey Michel, consulting engineer, Schuttertal/Dörlinbach, West Germany, private communication, May 5, 1990; "Poland Cancels Nuclear Energy Program," Reuters, September 4, 1990.

56. Simons, "West Germans Get Ready to Scrub the East's Tarnished Environment"; "East, West German Environment Ministers Call for Unification of Laws, Practices," *International Environment Reporter*, May 1990.

57. Dr. Bronislaw Kaminski, "Poland's Environmental Problems and Priorities," presented to International Environment Forum meeting, World Environment Center, New York, March 13, 1990.

58. Vaclav Havel, "Our Freedom," *Washington Post*, January 3, 1990. Bedřich Moldan heads the Czech Ministry, Vladimir Ondrus the Slovak Commission on the Environment, and Josef Vavroušek the Federal Ministry. Moldan and Vavroušek were both active in the Czech Academy of Sciences' ecological section before the revolution. Ondrus is a respected scientist who was part of the panel

of experts that reviewed the Bratislava Aloud report, thereby lending it legitimacy.

59. Cynthia Whitehead, "Czechoslovakia Launches a Great Clean Up," *New Scientist*, July 28, 1990; Johanisová, private communication, October 3, 1990.

60. János Vargha, ISTER (East European Environmental Research), Budapest, Hungary, private communication, September 27, 1990; Blaine Harden, "Key Bulgarian Industry is Poisoning Children," *Washington Post*, August 13, 1990; Gavrilov, "Environmental Damage Creates Serious Problem for Government"; Dan Ionescu, "Ecology and Politics after the Revolution," *Report on Eastern Europe*, Radio Free Europe, May 11, 1990.

61. Ulrich Petschow et al., Instituts für Ökologische Wirtschaftsforschung, *Umweltreport DDR* (Frankfurt am Main: Fischer Verlag, 1990); Kaminski, "Poland's Environmental Problems"; "Prague to Spend $23.7 Billion To Clean Up Devastated Economy," *International Environment Reporter*, July 1990; Zhores Medvedev, "The Environmental Destruction of the Soviet Union," *The Ecologist*, January/February 1990; David Goodhart, "Two Germanys Tackle One Environment," *Financial Times*, February 21, 1990.

62. The American Council for an Energy-Efficient Economy has estimated that sulfur dioxide emissions from power plants in the Midwest could be halved at a net savings of $4–8 billion if pollution control and energy efficiency were pursued simultaneously; "Statement of Howard S. Geller," in Subcommittee on Health and the Environment, Committee on Energy and Commerce, U.S. House of Representatives, *Acid Rain Control Proposals*, Hearings, Washington, D.C., April 6, 1989; Howard S. Geller et al., *Acid Rain and Electricity Conservation* (Washington, D.C.: American Council for an Energy-Efficient Economy/Energy Conservation Coalition, 1987).

63. William U. Chandler et al., "Energy for the Soviet Union, Eastern Europe and

China," *Scientific American*, September 1990; Alexei A. Makarov, Institute of Energy Research, USSR Academy of Sciences, and Igor A. Bashmakov, State Committee for Science and Technology, "The Soviet Union: A Strategy of Energy Development with Minimum Emission of Greenhouse Gases," and S. Sitnicki et al., "Poland: Opportunities for Carbon Emissions Control," both in William Chandler, ed., *Carbon Emissions Control Strategies: Case Studies in International Cooperation* (Washington, D.C.: World Wildlife Fund and Conservation Foundation, forthcoming).

64. Michael Totten, Legislative Assistant, Office of Representative Claudine Schneider, "Efficient Lighting Facts," unpublished data, Washington, D.C., 1990. Estimate assumes that it costs $7.5 million to build a compact fluorescent plant, and that each plant produces 1.8 million lamps per year, based upon analysis in Ashok Gadgil and Arthur Rosenfeld, "Conserving Energy with Compact Fluorescent Lamps," Lawrence Berkeley Laboratories, Berkeley, Calif., May 1, 1990.

65. See, for example, Erik Hagerman, "California's Drive to Mass Transit," *World Watch*, September/October 1990.

66. Peterson, "State of the Environment: Solid Wastes"; on waste reduction, see U.S. Congress, Office of Technology Assessment, *From Pollution to Prevention: A Progress Report on Waste Reduction* (Washington, D.C.: U.S. Government Printing Office, 1987), and Sandra Postel, *Defusing the Toxics Threat: Controlling Pesticides and Industrial Waste*, Worldwatch Paper 79 (Washington, D.C.: Worldwatch Institute, September 1987).

67. Vaclav Havel et al., *The Power of the Powerless: Citizens Against the State in Central-Eastern Europe* (London: Hutchinson, 1985), quoted in Andrew Nagorski, "The Intellectual Roots of Eastern Europe's Upheavals," *SAIS Review*, Summer/Fall 1990.

68. "Various Environmental Taxes May be Introduced by End of 1990," *International Environment Reporter*, June 1990; Howard

Gleckman and Vicky Cahan, "Will 'Eco-Tax' Fervor Sweep Congress Off Its Feet?" *Business Week*, April 30, 1990.

69. *Balto-Scandian Bulletin*, No. 1, 1989; Hanns Langer, "Ecological Bricks for our Common House Europe," Global Challenges Network, Munich, West Germany, May 15, 1990.

70. "Hungary, Poland Said at Top of List for U.S. Aid to Stem Environmental Damage," *International Environment Reporter*, June 1990; Steve Lintner, World Bank, address at the Conservation Foundation, Washington, D.C., May 30, 1990; information about Nordic Investment Bank from "First Environmental Investments in Eastern Europe May Be Approved By Fall," *International Environment Reporter*, July 1990; John Hontelez and Alex Hittle, "Letter to the Drafters of the By-laws of the European Bank for Reconstruction and Development," Friends of the Earth International, Brussels and Washington, D.C., May 29, 1990; David Reed, *The European Bank for Reconstruction and Development: An Environmental Opportunity* (Washington, D.C.: World Wild Fund for Nature-International, 1990); "WWF Offers Environmental Strategy for New European Reconstruction Bank," *International Environment Reporter*, September 1990.

71. Philippe Bourel de la Roucière, Commission of the European Communities, Brussels, private communication, September 26, 1990; David Thomas, "East and West to Cooperate on Environment," *Financial Times*, June 18, 1990; "Environment Ministers Agree on Plan to Set Up European Environment Agency," *International Environment Reporter*, December 1989; "Eastern, Central Europe to Get Help from New Center on Environmental Clean Up," *International Environment Reporter*, September 1990.

72. "Eastern Europe: New Initiatives," *Weekly Bulletin*, Energy and Environment Study Institute, U.S. Congress, July 16, 1990; "SEED II Moves in Foreign Relations,"

Weekly Bulletin, Energy and Environment Study Institute, U.S. Congress, March 19, 1990; German aid figures from Alex Hittle, Friends of the Earth, Washington, D.C., private communication, August 16, 1990; Hagerhall, "Saving the Baltic."

73. Craig Whitney, "Europeans to Consider Proposal on Economic Help for the Soviet Union," *New York Times*, June 20, 1990; USSR State Committee for the Protection of Nature, *Report on the State of the Environment*; "EC to Assist USSR Industry," *European Energy Report*, July 27, 1990; "Soviet Union Gives Finnish Metal Company Go-Ahead to Modernize Two Nickel Smelters," *International Environment Reporter*, October 10, 1990.

74. William Freeman, "Environmental Opposition to Foreign Investment in the USSR," U.S. Information Agency, research memorandum, Washington, D.C., November 22, 1989; Thomas, "East and West to Cooperate"; Liroff, "Eastern Europe."

75. ECE, "Acid Rain: Protocol on Emissions Enters into Force," press release, Geneva, August 25, 1987; "25 ECE Members Sign Protocol to Limit Emissions of Nitrogen Oxides," *International Environment Reporter*, November 1988; "Probability Seen as Highly Desirable for Volatile Organic Compound Protocol," *International Environment Reporter*, August 1989; "Proposal Submitted by the Delegations of Austria, Finland, Sweden, and Switzerland," meeting on the protection of the environment, Commission on Security and Cooperation in Europe, Sofia, Bulgaria, October 16-November 3, 1989; Håkan Alm, "Emissions are Falling . . . but is it Enough," *Acid News*, September 1989.

76. World Bank, *World Debt Tables: 1989–90* (Washington, D.C., 1989); Czechoslovakia and Bulgaria debt material from Ulrich Hewer and John Wilton, World Bank, private communications, September 20, 1990; Hittle, private communication; "Poland Debt-for-Nature Swap Term Sheet," World Wildlife Fund, Washington, D.C., un-

dated; "The Vistula Program—An International Attempt to Rescue Polish Water Resources from Total Collapse," Vistula Auxiliary Services AB, Stockholm, Sweden, October 16, 1989.

Chapter 7. Coming to Grips With Abortion

1. Henry David, Director, Transnational Family Research Institute, Bethesda, Md., private communication, February 28, 1990.

2. Since January 1990, several other countries have liberalized their abortion laws, including Belgium, Bulgaria (which made abortion available on request in the first trimester), and Malaysia; Stanley K. Henshaw, Deputy Director of Research, Alan Guttmacher Institute, New York, private communication, June 7, 1990.

3. Stanley K. Henshaw, "Induced Abortion: A World Review, 1990," *Family Planning Perspectives*, March/April 1990.

4. Abortion-related mortality rates in the United States from W. Cates et al., "Legalized Abortion: Effect on National Trends of Maternal and Abortion-Related Mortality," *American Journal of Obstetricians and Gynecologists*, Vol. 132, 1978; Marek Okolski, "Abortion and Contraception in Poland," *Studies in Family Planning*, November 1983.

5. Henshaw, private communication.

6. A comprehensive discussion of abortion laws and trends worldwide can be found in Henshaw, "Induced Abortion," and in Rebecca J. Cook, "Abortion Laws and Policies: Challenges and Opportunities," *International Journal of Gynecology and Obstetrics*, Supplement 3, 1989; see also Rebecca J. Cook and Bernard M. Dickens, "International Developments in Abortion Laws: 1977–88," *American Journal of Public Health*, October 1988.

7. Ruth Dixon-Mueller, "Abortion Policy and Women's Health in Developing Countries," *International Journal of Health Services*, Vol. 20, No. 2, 1990.

8. Cook, "Abortion Laws and Policies."

9. Ibid.; Henshaw, "Induced Abortion."

10. Cook, "Abortion Laws and Policies"; Henshaw, "Induced Abortion."

11. Cook, "Abortion Laws and Policies"; Henshaw, "Induced Abortion"; India's population from Population Reference Bureau, *1990 World Population Data Sheet* (Washington, D.C.: 1990).

12. Henshaw, "Induced Abortion."

13. Ibid.

14. Cook, "Abortion Laws and Policies"; National Abortion Rights Action League, "Post-*Webster* Anti-Choice Legislative Activity," Washington, D.C., memorandums, March 29 and July 31, 1990.

15. D.K. Piragoff, Canadian Department of Justice, Ottawa, Canada, private communication, June 7, 1990.

16. Dixon-Mueller, "Abortion Policy and Women's Health in Developing Countries"; "Deaths from Abortion," in Erica Royston and Sue Armstrong, eds., *Preventing Maternal Deaths* (Geneva: World Health Organization (WHO), 1989).

17. "Deaths from Abortion," in Royston and Armstrong, *Preventing Maternal Deaths*.

18. Katie McLaurin, "Issues of Access to Abortion: Policy, Law and Reality," presentation at the American Public Health Association Annual Meeting, Chicago, October 22–26, 1989.

19. Ibid.; Renee Holt, "Abortion: Law, Practice, and Project Possibilities in Zambia," prepared for Columbia University Center for Population and Family Health, New York, September 25, 1989.

20. Holt, "Abortion in Zambia."

21. Julie DeClerque, "Unsafe Abortion Practices in Subsaharan Africa and Latin America: A Call to Policymakers," presentation at Panel on Culture, Public Policy, and Reproductive Health, Association for Women in Development Conference, Washington, D.C., November 17–19, 1989; Holt, "Abortion in Zambia."

22. Tomas Frejka, Senior Representative, Population Council Latin America Region, private communication, March 12, 1990; Dixon-Mueller, "Abortion Policy and Women's Health in Developing Countries"; DeClerque, "Unsafe Abortion Practices."

23. Royston and Armstrong, *Preventing Maternal Deaths*.

24. Mary O'Keefe, "Abortion: Law, Practice, and Project Possibilities in Mexico," prepared for Columbia University Center for Population and Family Health, New York, September 25, 1989.

25. Cook, "Abortion Laws and Policies"; Henshaw, private communication.

26. Al Kamen, "5–4 Ruling Stops Short of Overturning Roe," *Washington Post*, July 4, 1989; for in-depth analyses of the Webster decision, see "The Fight Over *Roe v. Wade*: The *Webster* Briefs," *Family Planning Perspectives*, May/June 1989, and Jeannie I. Rosoff, "The *Webster* Decision: A Giant Step Backwards," *Family Planning Perspectives*, July/August 1989.

27. Howard LaFranchi, "Wind From the West: Europe Gears for Abortion Battle," *Christian Science Monitor*, August 17, 1989.

28. For a discussion of these trends, see Tomas Frejka, "Induced Abortion and Fertility," *International Family Planning Perspectives*, December 1985.

29. Henshaw, "Induced Abortion"; Frejka, "Induced Abortion and Fertility."

30. Henshaw, "Induced Abortion."

31. John Paxman, "Abortion in Latin America" (draft), prepared for Population

Council meeting in Bogotá, Colombia, October 1988.

32. Adrienne Germain, *Reproductive Health and Dignity: Choices By Third World Women* (New York: International Women's Health Coalition, 1987).

33. Henshaw, "Induced Abortion"; Frejka, "Induced Abortion and Fertility."

34. Tomas Frejka, *Induced Abortion and Fertility: A Quarter Century of Experience in Eastern Europe*, Center for Policy Studies, Working Paper No. 99 (New York: Population Council, 1983); Henry P. David, *Abortion Research Notes* (Transnational Family Research Institute, Bethesda, Md.), various issues.

35. Frejka, *Induced Abortion and Fertility: Eastern Europe*; Henshaw, "Induced Abortion."

36. "Poland's Hard Life Finds More Women Choosing Abortion," *New York Times*, May 23, 1983; John Tagliabue, "Abortion Issue in Poland Splits the Opposition," *New York Times*, May 29, 1989.

37. Frejka, *Induced Abortion and Fertility: Eastern Europe*; Popov as quoted in Michael Dobbs, "90% of 1st Pregnancies Said Aborted in USSR," *Washington Post*, January 20, 1989.

38. Henshaw, "Induced Abortion"; Frejka, *Induced Abortion and Fertility: Eastern Europe*.

39. Frejka, *Induced Abortion and Fertility: Eastern Europe*; Statisticheskiy Spornik, *Naseleniye SSR*, Moscow, 1987; Feshbach quoted in Dobbs, "90% of 1st Pregnancies Said Aborted in USSR."

40. Frejka, *Induced Abortion and Fertility: Eastern Europe*; David, private communication.

41. Tomas Frejka and Lucille Atkin, "The Role of Induced Abortion in the Fertility Transition of Latin America," prepared for

IUSSP/CELADE/CENEP Seminar on the Fertility Transition, Buenos Aires, Argentina, April 3, 1990.

42. IPPF cited in Tomas Frejka et al., *Program Document: Research Program for the Prevention of Unsafe Induced Abortion and Its Adverse Consequences in Latin America and the Caribbean*, Center for Policy Studies, Working Paper No. 23 (Mexico City: Population Council, 1989).

43. Frejka and Atkin, "The Role of Induced Abortion in the Fertility Transition of Latin America."

44. Paxman, "Abortion in Latin America"; Mary O'Keefe, "Abortion: Law, Practice, and Project Possibilities in Brazil," prepared for Columbia University Center for Population and Family Health, September 25, 1989.

45. Frejka et al., *Program Document: Research Program for the Prevention of Unsafe Induced Abortion*; O'Keefe, "Abortion in Brazil."

46. Frejka and Atkin, "The Role of Induced Abortion in the Fertility Transition of Latin America."

47. Khama Rogo, "Induced Abortion in Africa" (unpublished draft), prepared for Population Association of America Annual Meeting, Toronto, Canada, May 2–3, 1990.

48. N.N. Mashalaba, "Commentary on the Causes and Consequences of Unwanted Pregnancy from an African Perspective," *International Journal of Gynecology and Obstetrics*, Supplement 3, 1989.

49. Ibid.

50. Ninuk Widyantoro et al., "Induced Abortion: The Indonesian Experience," prepared for the Population Association of America Annual Meeting, Toronto, Canada, May 3, 1990.

51. Ibid.; Renee Holt, "Abortion: Law, Practice, and Project Possibilities in Indonesia," paper prepared for Columbia University Center for Population and Family Health, September 25, 1989.

52. Widyantoro et al., "Induced Abortion: The Indonesian Experience"; Holt, "Abortion in Indonesia."

53. Henry P. David et al., "United States and Denmark: Different Approaches to Health Care and Family Planning," *Studies in Family Planning*, January/February 1990.

54. Ibid.

55. Ibid.

56. Ibid.

57. Ibid.

58. Germain, *Reproductive Health and Dignity*.

59. "Deaths from Abortion," in Royston and Armstrong, *Preventing Maternal Deaths*; Holt, "Abortion in Indonesia."

60. Rogo, "Induced Abortion in Africa."

61. Ibid.; Francine M. Coeytaux, "Induced Abortion in sub-Saharan Africa: What We Do and Do Not Know," *Studies in Family Planning*, May/June 1988.

62. Rogo, "Induced Abortion in Africa."

63. DeClerque, "Unsafe Abortion Practices"; Royston and Armstrong, *Preventing Maternal Deaths*; Henshaw, "Induced Abortion"; data on numbers of women whose health is impaired as a result of illegal abortion from DeClerque, "Unsafe Abortion Practices."

64. DeClerque, "Unsafe Abortion Practices."

65. Fred T. Sai and Janet Nassim, "The Need for a Reproductive Health Approach," *International Journal of Gynecology and Obstetrics*, Supplement 3, 1989; Royston and Armstrong, *Preventing Maternal Deaths*; Frejka and Atkin, "The Role of Induced Abortion in the Fertility Transition of Latin America."

66. Rogo, "Induced Abortion in Africa."

67. Ibid.

68. Irene Figa-Talamanca et al., "Illegal Abortion: An Attempt to Assess its Cost to the Health Services and Its Incidence in the Community," *International Journal of Health Services*, Vol. 16, No. 3, 1986; Rogo, "Induced Abortion in Africa"; Royston and Armstrong, *Preventing Maternal Deaths*.

69. Ann Leonard and Francine Coeytaux, "Abortion Complications in Subsaharan Africa" (internal document), International Projects Assistance Services, Chapel Hill, N.C., undated.

70. "Determinants and Consequences of Pregnancy Wastage in Zaire: A Study of Patients with Complications Requiring Hospital Treatment in Kinshasa, Matadi and Bukavu" (draft), prepared by Family Health International, Research Triangle Park, N.C., and Comite National des Naissances Desirables, Kinshasa, Zaire, undated.

71. Jacqueline Darroch Forrest and Susheela Singh, "Public Sector Savings Resulting from Expenditures for Contraceptive Services," *Family Planning Perspectives*, January/February 1990.

72. Stephen D. Mumford and Elton Kessel, "Is Wide Availability of Abortion Essential to National Population Growth Control Programs? Experiences of 116 Countries," *American Journal of Obstetrics and Gynecology*, July 15, 1984.

73. Cook, "Abortion Laws and Policies."

74. Ibid.

Chapter 8. Assessing the Military's War on the Environment

1. Quoted in "Defending the Environment? The Record of the U.S. Military," *The Defense Monitor*, Vol. 18, No. 6, 1989.

2. Philip Shabecoff, "Senator Urges Military Resources Be Turned to Environmental Battle," *New York Times*, June 29, 1990.

3. Ralph Ostermann, "Umwelt als Waffe—Das Zerstörungspotential ökologischer Kriegsführung," in Arnim Bechmann, ed., *Umwelt Braucht Frieden* (Fischer Verlag: Frankfurt, 1983).

4. Third World share of global military spending from U.S. Arms Control and Disarmament Agency (ACDA), *World Military Expenditures and Arms Transfers* (Washington, D.C.: U.S. Government Printing Office, various editions).

5. Center for Disarmament, *The Relationship Between Disarmament and Development*, Disarmament Study Series No. 5 (New York: United Nations, 1982).

6. Battalion and fighter plane examples from Molly Moore, "Land Squeeze Hampers U.S. Military," *Washington Post*, December 31, 1988.

7. Industrial nations from Nicolai N. Smirnov, "The Impact of Conventional War on Natural Areas of the USSR," *Environmental Conservation*, Winter 1989; global estimate from Wolfgang Schwegler-Rohmeis, "Rüstungskonversion als Sicherheitspolitik," in Marcus Breitschwerdt, ed., *Rüstungskonversion. Facetten einer Strukturfrage* (Stuttgart: Wissenschaftsedition SPD Baden-Württemberg, 1988), and from Samuel S. Kim, *The Quest for a Just World Order* (Boulder, Colo.: Westview Press, 1984).

8. Paul J.M. Vertegaal, "Environmental Impact of Dutch Military Activities," *Environmental Conservation*, Spring 1989.

9. Total land area controlled by Pentagon from U.S. Department of Defense (DOD), *Our Nation's Defense and the Environment. A Department of Defense Initiative* (Washington, D.C.: 1990); additional land acquisition from Michael Satchell, "Operation Land-Grab," *U.S. News and World Report*, May 14, 1990; Timothy Egan, "Pentagon, Facing Opposi-

tion, Suspends Land-Buying Plans," *New York Times*, September 18, 1990.

10. Edward McGlinn, "The Military Land Grab," *The Riverwatch* (Anglers of the Au Sable River, Grayling, Mich.), Winter 1990; total U.S. military land holdings abroad from DOD, *Our Nation's Defense and the Environment*; Department of Energy holdings from Thomas B. Cochran et al., *Nuclear Weapons Databook, Vol. II: U.S. Nuclear Warhead Production* (Cambridge, Mass.: Ballinger, 1987); Philippines from Joseph Collins, "Cory's Broken Promise," *The Nation*, November 14, 1987.

11. Paul Quinn-Judge, "Soviet Writers Blast Nuclear Testing," *Christian Science Monitor*, March 14, 1989; size of test site from Thomas B. Cochran et al., *Nuclear Weapons Databook, Vol. IV: Soviet Nuclear Weapons* (New York: Harper & Row, Ballinger Division, 1989).

12. Vertegaal, "Environmental Impact of Dutch Military Activities."

13. Olaf Achilles, "Der Preis der Freiheit," in Olaf Achilles, ed., *Natur Ohne Frieden* (Munich: Knaur, 1988); maneuver space from Schwegler-Rohmeis, "Rüstungskonversion als Sicherheitspolitik"; East Germany from "Alles Zerwühlt und Kaputt," *Der Spiegel*, October 1, 1990, and from Frank Marczinek, "Conversion of the Armed Forces in the GDR," paper presented at U.N. conference on "Economic Adjustments in an Era of Arms Reduction," Moscow, August 13–17, 1990.

14. Bruno Jerlitschka, "Umweltzerstörung durch Truppenstandorte und Manöver," in Bechmann, *Umwelt Braucht Frieden*; Olaf Achilles, "Bodenbelastung und Flächenverbrauch durch Militär," *Forum Wissenschaft*, No. 1, 1989; Peter Grier, "Defense Contractors Go for 'Green' Look," *Christian Science Monitor*, May 22, 1990.

15. Timothy Egan, "Land-Buying Drive by Pentagon Runs into Stiff Resistance in West," *New York Times*, July 5, 1990; J.L. Cloudsley-Thompson, "The Destructive Effects of Warfare on the Desert Environment," *Environmental Awareness* (India), Vol. 13, No. 2, 1990.

16. Nevada example from Bert Lindler, "Foes Unite to Fight Military Proposal," *High Country News*, February 12, 1990; Satchell, "Operation Land-Grab"; Robert Stone from Andrew Melnykovich, "Torn Between Cows and Jets," *High Country News*, February 12, 1990.

17. Olaf Achilles and Jochen Lange, *Tiefflieger. Vom Täglichen Angriff auf die Bürger* (Reinbek bei Hamburg: Rowohlt Verlag, 1989).

18. Mojave from Robert Reinhold, "Military and Conservationists Clash over Mojave's Future," *New York Times*, June 25, 1988; Grace Bukowski, "The Militarization of Nevada," *Earth Island Journal*, Spring 1990; range of military use of total U.S. airspace from Stephen Stuebner, "Homing in on the Range," *Earth Island Journal*, Spring 1990; Grace Bukowski, Citizen Alert, Reno, Nev., private communication, September 18, 1990.

19. Bill Robinson, "Games Air Forces Play," *Ploughshares Monitor*, December 1989; Canada National Defence, *Goose Bay EIS: An Environmental Impact Statement on Military Flying Activities in Labrador and Quebec* (Ottawa: 1989).

20. Achilles and Lange, *Tiefflieger*; Petra Lösch, "When the Sun Shines, We Have War in the Skies," *Earth Island Journal*, Summer 1989; Grace Bukowski and Fielding M. McGehee III, "The Military Invasion of America's Skies," Skyguard, Reno, Nev., June 1989.

21. Achilles and Lange, *Tiefflieger*; U.S. situation from Bukowski and McGehee, "The Military Invasion of America's Skies."

22. Average F-16 fuel consumption from "Defending the Environment? The Record of the U.S. Military"; afterburner from Tom

Cutler, "Myths of Military Oil Supply Vulnerability," *Armed Forces Journal International*, July 1989.

23. Share of petroleum products from Gunar Seitz, "Ressourcenvergeudung durch Rüstung," in Bechmann, *Umwelt Braucht Frieden*; global share of military jet fuel use from Olaf Achilles, "Militär, Rüstung und Klima," MÖP Studie VII, Arbeits- und Forschungsstelle Militär, Ökologie und Planung, Bonn, West Germany, June 1990; U.S. and Soviet shares from Cutler, "Myths of Military Oil Supply Vulnerability"; West German figure from Schwegler-Rohmeis, "Rüstungskonversion als Sicherheitspolitik."

24. DOD share of total U.S. oil and energy consumption calculated from Department of Energy (DOE), Energy Information Administration (EIA), *Annual Energy Review 1988* (Washington, D.C.: U.S. Government Printing Office, 1989); comparison with urban mass transit is a Worldwatch Institute calculation based on American Public Transit Association, *1989 Transit Fact Book* (Washington, D.C.: 1989); status as largest domestic consumer from Seitz, "Ressourcenvergeudung durch Rüstung"; DOD, *Our Nation's Defense and the Environment*; wartime estimates from Cutler, "Myths of Military Oil Supply Vulnerability."

25. West German government data are reprinted in Achilles, *Natur Ohne Frieden*; other estimate is by AG Energiebilanzen, in Achilles, "Militär, Rüstung und Klima"; Dutch data from Vertegaal, "Environmental Impact of Dutch Military Activities"; U.K. Central Statistical Office, *Input-Output Tables for the United Kingdom* (London: Her Majesty's Stationery Office, 1985).

26. 1971 figure from Helge Hveem, "Militarization of Nature: Conflict and Control over Strategic Resources and Some Implications for Peace Policies," *Journal of Peace Research*, Vol. 16, No. 1, 1979; 1989 figure is a Worldwatch Institute estimate, based on data in Stockholm International Peace Research Institute (SIPRI), *SIPRI Yearbook 1990: World Armaments and Disarmament* (Oxford: Oxford University Press, 1990), and in Paul Quigley, "Arms Exports: The Stop-Gap Alternative to Pentagon Contracts?" *Bulletin of Peace Proposals*, Vol. 19, No. 1, 1988.

27. Estimates for armed forces' energy use from Center for Disarmament, *The Relationship Between Disarmament and Development*; Achilles, "Militär, Rüstung und Klima"; comparison with Japanese oil consumption from British Petroleum (BP), *BP Statistical Review of World Energy* (London: 1990).

28. Global air pollution estimate from Seitz, "Ressourcenvergeudung durch Rüstung"; Starnberg Institute estimate from Achilles, "Militär, Rüstung und Klima"; West German estimate from Achilles, "Der Preis der Freiheit"; West German jets' pollution is a Worldwatch Institute estimate based on data provided in Achilles, "Militär, Rüstung und Klima."

29. U.S. military carbon emission is a Worldwatch Institute estimate, based on DOE, EIA, *Annual Energy Review 1988*.

30. Carbon emissions from military jet fuel use from Achilles, "Militär, Rüstung und Klima"; global military carbon emission is a Worldwatch Institute estimate based on Gregg Marland et al., *Estimates of CO_2 Emissions from Fossil Fuel Burning and Cement Manufacturing, Based on the United Nations Energy Statistics and the U.S. Bureau of Mines Cement Manufacturing Data* (Oak Ridge, Tenn.: Oak Ridge National Laboratory, 1989), and on BP, *BP Statistical Review*.

31. Casey Bukro, "Military Faces Difficult Task in Ending 'War' on Environment," *Journal of Commerce*, March 22, 1989; depletion potential of CFC-113 and Halon 1211 from Cynthia Pollock Shea, *Protecting Life on Earth: Steps to Save the Ozone Layer*, Worldwatch Paper 87 (Washington, D.C.: Worldwatch Institute, December 1988).

32. B-2 fuel additive from Ulrich Blumenschein, "Tarnsystem des B-2-Bombers Baut

Ozon ab," *Die Welt*, January 5, 1989; Lenny Siegel, "No Free Launch," *Mother Jones*, September/October 1990.

33. Iron consumption from Seitz, "Ressourcenvergeudung durch Rüstung"; missile materials consumption from Center for Disarmament, *The Relationship Between Disarmament and Development*; number of missiles in superpower arsenals from "Nuclear Notebook," *Bulletin of the Atomic Scientists*, May 1988.

34. Titanium from "Resource Wars: The Myth of American Mineral Vulnerability," *The Defense Monitor*, Vol. 14, No. 9, 1985, and from Center for Disarmament, *The Relationship Between Disarmament and Development*; components of F-16 engine from Ewan W. Anderson, "Strategic Materials," *Journal of Defense and Diplomacy*, November/December 1985; M-1 tank engine from "The U.S. Strategic Minerals Position—The 1980's and Beyond," Strategic Studies Institute, U.S. Army War College, Carlisle Barracks, Pa., November 15, 1981.

35. Center for Disarmament, *The Relationship Between Disarmament and Development*.

36. Seitz, "Ressourcenvergeudung durch Rüstung"; Vertegaal, "Environmental Impact of Dutch Military Activities"; "Resource Wars: The Myth of American Mineral Vulnerability."

37. Hufstutler quoted in Lenny Siegel, "Communities Organize Against Military Toxics," *Nuclear Times*, Autumn 1990. Data in Table 8–6 based on the following: Seth Shulman, "The US Military's Environmental Record Under Fire from Congress," *Nature*, June 16, 1988; Philip Shabecoff, "Military Is Accused of Ignoring Rules on Hazardous Waste," *New York Times*, June 14, 1988; Anthony Kimery, "Base Maneuvers: The Air Force Serves Up Toxic Soup," *The Progressive*, December 1986; Thane Grauel, "Dishonorable Discharges," *E Magazine*, July/August 1990; *Uncle Sam's Hidden Poisons*, reprint from a *Sacramento Bee* series published September

30-October 5, 1984; D'Vera Cohn, "Some Federal Facilities Flout Environmental Laws," *Washington Post*, May 22, 1989; "Defending the Environment? The Record of the U.S. Military"; Seth Shulman, "Toxic Travels: Inside the Military's Environmental Nightmare," *Nuclear Times*, Autumn 1990; DOD, *Defense Environmental Restoration Program. Annual Report to Congress for Fiscal Year 1989* (Washington, D.C.: 1990).

38. Heavy metals include beryllium, cadmium, chromium, mercury, lead, copper, zinc, iron, and others. They attack and weaken the cellular tissues of most living things. Solvents include tri- and di-chloro ethylenes, ethanes and ethenes, carbon tetrachloride, methyl chloride, and trichlorofluoromethane (Freon). Tom Harris and Jim Morris, "Military's Awash in Toxic Waste," in *Uncle Sam's Hidden Poisons*.

39. Ibid.; Jim Morris, "How Serious is the Peril to Public Health?" and Tom Harris, "Air Force Bases Leave Toxic Trail," both in *Uncle Sam's Hidden Poisons*; Utah study from "Cancer Deaths High Among Aircraft Workers," *Federal Times*, November 23, 1987.

40. Waste generation data for recent years from Lenny Siegel, "The Growing Nightmare of Military Toxics," *Nuclear Times*, Spring 1990; "Turning the Wastes of War into a War on Waste," *Toxic Times*, Summer 1990; Will Collette, *Dealing with Military Toxics* (Arlington, Va.: Citizen's Clearinghouse for Hazardous Wastes, Inc., 1987); emissions of top five chemical firms in 1988 from John Holusha, "Ed Woolard Walks Du Pont's Tightrope," *New York Times*, October 14, 1990.

41. Number of sites and bases and Superfund listing from DOD, *Defense Environmental Restoration Program*; former military sites and slow cleanup pace from Shulman, "Toxic Travels: Inside the Military's Environmental Nightmare"; Davidson statement from Shabecoff, "Military is Accused of Ignoring Rules on Hazardous Waste."

42. GAO studies in John M. Broder, "U.S. Military Leaves Toxic Trail Overseas," *Los Angeles Times*, June 18, 1990; Presidential order from Travis Brown, "Program Ignores Bases Abroad," in *Uncle Sam's Hidden Poisons*.

43. Exemption from host-country laws from Brown, "Program Ignores Bases Abroad."

44. West German sites from Broder, "U.S. Military Leaves Toxic Trail Overseas"; Army plan from John G. Roos, "US Army Plans to Turn Over Facilities in Germany in 'As Is' Condition," *Armed Forces Journal International*, September 1990; Atsugi base from "Japanese Group Plans to Sue U.S. Navy for Violating NEPA," *Multinational Environmental Outlook*, October 31, 1989.

45. Broder, "U.S. Military Leaves Toxic Trail Overseas"; Jorge Emmanuel, "Environmental Destruction Caused by U.S. Military Bases and the Serious Implications for the Philippines," paper presented at Crossroad 1991: Towards a Nuclear Free, Bases Free Philippines, Manila, May 14–16, 1990; Guam from "U.S. Defense Department Lax in Environmental Protection at Overseas Bases, Official Charges," *World Environment Report*, July 23, 1987.

46. Achilles, "Der Preis der Freiheit."

47. Henry Kamm, "Americans Help Czechs Clean Up After the Soviets," *New York Times*, July 24, 1990; Peter S. Green, "Cleaning up After the Soviet Army," *U.S. News and World Report*, May 28, 1990; Vera Rich, "Departing Red Army Leaves its Rubbish Behind," *New Scientist*, June 2, 1990.

48. Rich, "Departing Red Army Leaves its Rubbish Behind"; Celestine Bohlen, "As Soviets Leave Hungary, Dispute Arises Over the Bill," *New York Times*, July 4, 1990; East Germany from "Alles Zerwühlt und Kaputt," and from "Die Fliegen als Erste Raus," *Der Spiegel*, July 16, 1990; Polish developments from "Environmental Inspectors to Visit So-

viet Bases," Foreign Broadcast Information Service (FBIS) Daily Report/Soviet Union, Rosslyn, Va., August 30, 1990; "Pollution Problems in Soviet Army Units Viewed," FBIS Daily Report/Soviet Union, Rosslyn, Va., September 5, 1990.

49. Vertegaal, "Environmental Impact of Dutch Military Activities."

50. "Secrecy Hides the Hazards of Working in the Aerospace Industry," *New Scientist*, April 8, 1989; Kenneth B. Noble, "Health Troubles at Military Plant Add Mystery to Top-Secret Project," *New York Times*, September 18, 1988; "Defending the Environment? The Record of the U.S. Military."

51. Military share of electronics components industry from Ann Markusen, "The Military Remapping of the United States," in Michael J. Breheny, ed., *Defence Expenditure and Regional Development* (London: Mansell Publishing, 1988); K. Geiser, "Health Hazards in the Micro-Electronics Industry," *International Journal of Health Services*, Vol. 16, No. 1, 1986.

52. Murray quote from Howard Ball, "Downwind from the Bomb," *New York Times Magazine*, February 9, 1986; Keith Schneider, "Atom Tests' Legacy of Grief: Workers See Betrayal on Peril," *New York Times*, December 14, 1989.

53. Schneider, "Atom Tests' Legacy of Grief"; Keith Schneider, "U.S. Admits Peril of 40's Emissions at A-Bomb Plant," *New York Times*, July 12, 1990; Soviet situation from Francis X. Clines, "Soviets Now Admit '57 Nuclear Blast," *New York Times*, June 18, 1989; "Defending the Environment? The Record of the U.S. Military."

54. U.S. trust funds from Keith Schneider, "U.S. Fund Set Up to Pay Civilians Injured by Atomic Arms Program," *New York Times*, October 16, 1990; DOE, Office of Inspector General, "Report on Indemnification of the Department of Energy's Management and

Operating Contractors," Washington, D.C., September 1989.

55. U.S. plants from "Status of Major Nuclear Weapons Production Facilities: 1990," *PSR Monitor*, September 1990; Matthew L. Wald, "U.S. Decides Not to Reopen Plant that Makes Plutonium for Bombs," *New York Times*, October 17, 1990; Soviet plants from R. Jeffrey Smith, "Soviets Vow to Close 5 Reactors," *Washington Post*, June 9, 1989; Du Pont study quoted by Robert Alvarez and Arjun Makhijani, "The Hidden Legacy of the Arms Race," *Technology Review*, August/September 1988.

56. Cochran et al., *Nuclear Weapons Databook, Vol. II*; Cochran et al., *Nuclear Weapons Databook, Vol. IV*; "Status of Major Nuclear Weapons Production Facilities: 1990."

57. Waste products of 1 kilogram of plutonium from Karen Dorn Steele, "Hanford: America's Nuclear Graveyard," *Bulletin of the Atomic Scientists*, October 1989; military portion by volume from "Defending the Environment? The Record of the U.S. Military"; military portion by curies from Scott Saleska et al., *Nuclear Legacy: An Overview of the Places, Problems and Politics of Radioactive Waste in the United States* (Washington, D.C.: Public Citizen Critical Mass Energy Project, 1989); U.S. high-level inventory from Radioactive Waste Campaign, *Deadly Defense* (New York: 1988).

58. Number of contaminated sites from Committee to Provide Interim Oversight of the DOE Nuclear Weapons Complex, Commission on Physical Sciences, Mathematics, and Resources, National Research Council, *The Nuclear Weapons Complex: Management for Health, Safety, and the Environment* (Washington, D.C.: National Academy Press, 1989); locations from Keith Schneider, "In the Trail of the Nuclear Arms Industry," *New York Times*, August 26, 1990; Nagasaki bomb comparison from Michael Satchell, "Uncle Sam's Toxic Folly," *U.S. News and World Report*, March, 27, 1989; plutonium in Rocky Flats ventilation ducts from Matthew L. Wald, "Doubt on Safety at Weapon Plant," *New York Times*, June 21, 1990; 1969 fire from Fox Butterfield, "Dispute on Wastes Poses Threat to Weapons Plant," *New York Times*, October 21, 1988.

59. Matthew L. Wald, "Hanford's Atom Waste Tanks Could Explode, Panel Warns," *New York Times*, July 31, 1990; Alvarez and Makhijani, "Hidden Legacy of the Arms Race."

60. Larry Thompson, "Scientists Reassess the Long-Term Impact of Radiation," *Washington Post*, August 15, 1990; "ICRP to Recommend More Stringent Human Radiation Exposure Limits," *Multinational Environmental Outlook*, October 16, 1990.

61. Total number of workers from Martin Tolchin, "U.S. to Release Health Data on Nuclear Plant Workers," *New York Times*, May 24, 1989; Rocky Flats from Carl Johnson, "Cancer Incidence Patterns in the Denver Metropolitan Area in Relation to the Rocky Flats Plant," *American Journal of Epidemiology*, Vol. 126, No. 1; Hanford from Matthew L. Wald, "Risks to A-Plant Workers Were Ignored, Study Says," *New York Times*, December 19, 1989; Keith Schneider, "U.S. Releases Radiation Records of 44,000 Nuclear Workers," *New York Times*, July 18, 1990.

62. "New Agreement Could Continue Department of Energy's Monopoly Over Radiation Health Research," *News Alert*, Physicians for Social Responsibility (PSR), Washington, D.C., October 26, 1990; Daryl Kimball, PSR, Washington, D.C., private communication, November 2, 1990.

63. Schneider, "U.S. Admits Peril of 40's Emissions at A-Bomb Plant"; Keith Schneider, "Radiation Peril at Hanford is Detailed," *New York Times*, July 13, 1990; Alvarez and Makhijani, "Hidden Legacy of the Arms Race"; Leslie Fraser, "Victims of National Security," *Nuclear Times*, Autumn 1990.

64. Matthew L. Wald, "High Radiation Doses Seen for Soviet Arms Workers," *New*

York Times, August 16, 1990; Bill Keller, "Soviet City, Home of the A-Bomb, is Haunted by its Past and Future," *New York Times*, July 10, 1989.

65. Zhores A. Medvedev, "The Environmental Destruction of the Soviet Union," *The Ecologist*, January/February 1990.

66. Ibid.; Clines, "Soviets Now Admit '57 Nuclear Blast"; Vera Rich, "Thirty-Year Secret Revealed," *Nature*, June 22, 1989; David Dickson, "Kyshtym 'Almost as Bad as Chernobyl'," *New Scientist*, December 23/30, 1989; Arjun Makhijani, Institute for Energy and Environmental Research, Takoma Park, Md., private communication, October 23, 1990.

67. Numbers of tests from SIPRI, *SIPRI Yearbook 1990: World Armaments and Disarmament*; Bernard Neitschmann and William Le Bon, "Nuclear Weapons States and Fourth World Nations," *Earth Island Journal*, Winter 1988.

68. The United States, the Soviet Union, and the United Kingdom stopped atmospheric tests in 1963 but France and China continued until 1974 and 1980, respectively; SIPRI, *SIPRI Yearbook 1990: World Armaments and Disarmament*. Birth defects from Barry Commoner, "Do Nuclear Plants Make Deadly Neighbors?" *Congressional Record*, March 23, 1972. U.N. estimate from Bernd W. Kubbig, "Atomtests: Gefährdung für Mensch und Umwelt," in Bechmann, *Umwelt Braucht Frieden*. The largest U.S. "venting" occurred in December 1970, when 6.7 million curies of radioactive materials were released; John Hanrahan, "Testing Ground," *Common Cause Magazine*, January/February 1989. Soviet venting from "A Nuclear Unthreat," *Economist*, March 29, 1986.

69. Soldiers from Kubbig, "Atomtests: Gefährdung für Mensch und Umwelt"; Kim, *The Quest for a Just World Order*, reports a number of 250,000 soldiers; workers from Schneider, "U.S. Fund Set Up to Pay Civilians Injured by Atomic Arms Program"; downwinders and their health effects from Ball, "Downwind from the Bomb"; Richard L. Miller, "Let's Not Forget Radiation in the U.S." (op ed), *New York Times*, June 27, 1986; Americans' exposure from Keith Schneider, "Senate Panel Describes Data on Nuclear Risks," *New York Times*, August 3, 1989.

70. Ian Anderson, "Potassium Could Cover Up Bikini's Radioactivity," *New Scientist*, December 10, 1988; Eliot Marshall, "Fallout from Pacific Tests Reaches Congress," *Science*, July 14, 1989; Bengt Danielsson, "Poisoned Pacific: The Legacy of French Nuclear Testing," *Bulletin of the Atomic Scientists*, March 1990.

71. Quinn-Judge, "Soviet Writers Blast Nuclear Testing"; Olzhas Suleymenov, "We Cannot Be Silent," *Earth Island Journal*, Summer 1989; Judith Perera, "Soviet Environmentalists Cite Health Problems Around Nuclear Testing Ground," *Multinational Environmental Outlook*, September 5, 1989; Vladimir Lysenkov, "Campaign to Close Semipalatinsk," *Nature*, September 7, 1989; R. Jeffrey Smith, "Soviets to Close Major Site of Underground Atomic Tests," *Washington Post*, March 11, 1990.

72. GAO from "Defending the Environment? The Record of the U.S. Military"; more recent estimate from "Problems Persist at Weapons Plants," *PSR Monitor*, September 1990; 1983 toxics estimate from Tom Harris, "Sky's the Limit on Cleanup Cost," in *Uncle Sam's Hidden Poisons*; $20–40 billion estimate from Siegel, "The Growing Nightmare of Military Toxics"; European cost estimate from Achilles, "Der Preis der Freiheit."

73. Czechoslovak per-base costs from Kamm, "Americans Help Czechs Clean Up After the Soviets"; Hungary from Rich, "Departing Red Army Leaves its Rubbish Behind"; U.S. rehabilitation cost from Edward McGlinn, Anglers of the Au Sable River, Grayling, Mich., private communication, February 18, 1990.

74. Defense Environmental Restoration Program spending from "Turning the Wastes of War into a War on Waste"; DOD, *Defense Environmental Restoration Program*; Robert Gough, Arms Control Research Center, San Francisco, Calif., private communication, October 16, 1990; DOE budget from Keith Schneider, "New Mission at Energy Department: Bomb Makers Turn to Cleanup," *New York Times*, August 17, 1990; "Problems Persist at Weapons Plants."

75. Carter Executive Order from Grauel, "Dishonorable Discharges"; Reagan policy from John Johnson, "Congress Slow to Awaken to Peril," in *Uncle Sam's Hidden Poisons*; Dingell quoted in Shabecoff, "Military is Accused of Ignoring Rules on Hazardous Waste."

76. Justice Department policy from Cohn, "Some Federal Facilities Flout Environmental Laws"; voluntary agreements from "Defending the Environment? The Record of the U.S. Military"; proposed legislation from Bill Turque and John McCormick, "The Military's Toxic Legacy," *Newsweek*, August 6, 1990.

77. Iciar Oquinena, "Das Militär Hat das Recht—die Umwelt Hat den Schaden," in Bechmann, *Umwelt Braucht Frieden*.

78. Siegel, "The Growing Nightmare of Military Toxics"; Lenny Siegel, "Coping With Toxic Cleanup," *Plowshare Press*, Spring 1990; "Turning the Wastes of War into a War on Waste"; Military Production Network from David Lewis, PSR, Washington, D.C., private communication, October 19, 1990.

79. West Germany from Achilles and Lange, *Tiefflieger*; Kazakhstan from James Lerager, "Kazakhs Stop Soviet Testing," *Nuclear Times*, Autumn 1990.

80. In the United States, Congress enacted the "Emergency Planning and Community Right-to-Know Act" in 1986; see U.S. Environmental Protection Agency, *The Toxics-Release Inventory. A National Perspective* (Washington, D.C.: U.S. Government Printing Office, 1989).

81. Base commander quoted by Shulman, "Toxic Travels."

Chapter 9. Asking How Much is Enough

1. Victor Lebow in *Journal of Retailing*, quoted in Vance Packard, *The Waste Makers* (New York: David McKay, 1960).

2. Sepp Linhart, "From Industrial to Post-industrial Society: Changes in Japanese Leisure-Related Values and Behavior," *Journal of Japanese Studies*, Summer 1988; Richard A. Easterlin and Eileen M. Crimmins, "Recent Social Trends: Changes in Personal Aspirations of American Youth," *Sociology and Social Research*, July 1988; Taiwan from "Asian Century," *Newsweek*, February 22, 1988.

3. Per capita income from Angus Maddison, *The World Economy in the 20th Century* (Paris: Organisation for Economic Co-operation and Development, 1989); income of American children, defined as 4- to 12-year-olds, from James McNeal, "Children as Customers," *American Demographics*, September 1990; poorest 500 million people based on Alan B. Durning, *Poverty and the Environment: Reversing the Downward Spiral*, Worldwatch Paper 92 (Washington, D.C.: Worldwatch Institute, November 1989), and on World Bank, *World Development Report 1990* (New York: Oxford University Press, 1990).

4. Paul Wachtel, *The Poverty of Affluence* (Philadelphia: New Society Publishers, 1989); Amy Saltzman, "The New Meaning of Success," *U.S. News & World Report*, September 17, 1990; Joseph T. Plummer, "Changing Values," *The Futurist*, January/February 1989; Ronald Henkoff, "Is Greed Dead?" *Fortune*, August 14, 1989.

5. Worldwatch Institute estimates, based on the following: copper and aluminum from United Nations (UN), *Statistical Yearbook*,

1953 (New York: 1954), and from UN, *Statistical Yearbook, 1985/86* (New York: 1988); energy from UN, *World Energy Supplies 1950–1974* (New York: 1976), and from UN, *1987 Energy Statistics Yearbook* (New York: 1989); meat from UN, *Statistical Yearbook, 1953,* and from Linda M. Bailey, agricultural economist, U.S. Department of Agriculture (USDA), Washington, D.C., private communication, September 11, 1990; steel, wood, cement, and air travel from UN, *Statistical Yearbook, 1953,* and from U.S. Bureau of the Census, *Statistical Abstract of the United States: 1990* (Washington, D.C.: U.S. Government Printing Office, 1990); car ownership from UN, *Statistical Yearbook, 1953,* and from Motor Vehicle Manufacturers Association (MVMA), *Facts and Figures '90* (Detroit, Mich.: 1990); plastic from UN, *Statistical Yearbook, 1970* (New York: 1971), and from UN, *Statistical Yearbook, 1983/84* (New York: 1985). Throughout this chapter, population data used to calculate per capita consumption are from UN, *Statistical Yearbook, 1975* (New York: 1975), from UN, *Statistical Yearbook, 1983/84* (New York: 1985), and from UN, *Statistical Yearbook, 1985/86,* with two exceptions: most recent years from Population Reference Bureau, *1988 Population Data Sheet* and *1990 Population Data Sheet* (Washington, D.C.: 1988 and 1990), and data for United States from U.S. Bureau of the Census, *Statistical Abstract of the United States: 1979* (Washington, D.C.: U.S. Government Printing Office, 1979), and from Bureau of the Census, *Statistical Abstract of the United States: 1990.*

6. Cars from MVMA, *Facts and Figures '90,* and from MVMA, Detroit, Mich., private communication, July 10, 1990; car-miles from U.S. Department of Energy (DOE), Energy Information Administration (EIA), *Annual Energy Review 1988* (Washington, D.C.: 1989), and from Paul Svercl, Federal Highway Administration, Washington, D.C., private communication, August 21, 1990; plastics from Sara Spivey, Society for the Plastics Industry, Washington D.C., private communication, August 23, 1990; air travel from Mary C. Holcomb et al., *Transportation Energy Data Book: Edition 9* (Oak Ridge, Tenn.: Oak Ridge National Laboratory, 1987), and from Federal Aviation Administration, Washington, D.C., private communication, August 17, 1990; air conditioning, color TVs, and microwaves from Bureau of the Census, *Statistical Abstract of the United States: 1979,* and from DOE, EIA, *Annual Energy Review 1988;* VCRs from Bureau of the Census, *Statistical Abstract of the United States: 1990.*

7. Jaguars and fur coats from Myron Magnet, "The Money Society," *Fortune,* July 6, 1987; millionaires in 1980 and 1990 from Kevin P. Phillips, "Reagan's America: A Capital Offense," *New York Times Magazine,* June 18, 1990; billionaires from Andrew Erdman, "The Billionaires," *Fortune,* September 10, 1990.

8. Japanese travel in 1972 from Linhart, "From Industrial to Postindustrial Society"; 1990 travel from "Rich Girls with Wanderlust," *Japan Economic Journal,* March 3, 1990; consumer spending surge from "Japan's Baby Boomers Spending Lavishly in Single-minded Pursuit of the Good Life," *Japan Economic Journal,* April 11, 1990; "Retail Sales Up 7 Percent; Capital Outlays Raised," *Japan Economic Journal,* July 14, 1990; BMW sales from *Japan Economic Journal,* September 8, 1990; Range Rovers from T.R. Reid, "U.S. Automakers Grind Gears in Japan," *Washington Post,* September 23, 1990; "With Permit Rules Relaxed, Log Cabin Sales Are Soaring," *Japan Economic Journal,* August 4, 1990.

9. Yorimoto Katsumi, "Tokyo's Serious Waste Problem," *Japan Quarterly,* July/September 1990; spending and student quote from Fred Hiatt and Margaret Shapiro, "Sudden Riches Creating Conflict and Self-Doubt," *Washington Post,* February 11, 1990.

10. Steel, cement, aluminum, and paper from Eric Larsen, Center for Energy and Environmental Studies, Princeton University, Princeton, N.J., unpublished data, 1990; fro-

zen meals from Euromonitor Publications Ltd., *Consumer Europe 1985* (London: 1985).

11. Budapest from Timothy Harper, "In Budapest, the Lines are at McDonald's," *Shopping Centers Today*, May 1989; Ramm quote, auto demand, and used car sales from Marc Fisher, "East Germany and the Wheels of Fortune," *Washington Post*, June 3, 1990; auto plant projection from "Motor Industry Banks on Eastern Promise," *Business Europe* (London), May 18, 1990.

12. State Statistical Bureau, cited in "TV Now in 50% of Homes," *China Daily*, February 15, 1988.

13. Prakash Chandra, "India: Middle-Class Spending," *Third World Week* (Institute for Current World Affairs, Hanover, N.H.), March 2, 1990; Anthony Spaeth, "A Thriving Middle Class Is Changing the Face of India," *Wall Street Journal*, May 19, 1988.

14. Coca-Cola from Matthew Cooper et al., "Global Goliath: Coke Conquers the World," *U.S. News and World Report*, August 13, 1990.

15. Netherlands study from the University of Amsterdam cited in Anil Agarwal, "The North-South Perspective: Alienation or Interdependence?" *Ambio*, April 1990; minerals consumption based on World Resources Institute (WRI), *World Resources 1990–91* (New York: Oxford University Press, 1990).

16. Nuclear warheads from Swedish International Peace Research Institute, *SIPRI Yearbook 1990: World Armaments and Disarmament* (Oxford: Oxford University Press, 1990); global warming, acid rain, hazardous chemicals, and chlorofluorocarbons are Worldwatch Institute estimates based on WRI, *World Resources 1990–91*.

17. Michael Worley, National Opinion Research Center, University of Chicago, Chicago, Ill., private communication, September 19, 1990; personal consumption expenditures from U.S. Bureau of the Census, *Statisti-cal Abstract of the United States: 1989* (Washington, D.C: U.S. Government Printing Office, 1989).

18. International comparison from R.A. Easterlin, "Does Economic Growth Improve the Human Lot? Some Empirical Evidence," cited in Michael Argyle, *The Psychology of Happiness* (London: Methuen, 1987); similar arguments are found in Angus Campbell, *The Sense of Well-being in America: Recent Patterns and Trends* (New York: McGraw-Hill, 1981), in Wachtel, *Poverty of Affluence*, and in F.E. Trainer, *Abandon Affluence* (Atlantic Highlands, N.J.: Zed Books, 1985).

19. Worldwatch Institute estimate of consumption since 1950 based on gross world product data from Maddison, *World Economy in the 20th Century*.

20. Japan and Soviet Union from Christopher Flavin and Alan B. Durning, *Building on Success: The Age of Energy Efficiency*, Worldwatch Paper 82 (Washington, D.C.: Worldwatch Institute, March 1988); Norway and Sweden paper use from Greenpeace, *The Greenpeace Guide to Paper* (Vancouver: 1990); literacy and income from World Bank, *World Development Report 1990*.

21. José Goldemberg et al., *Energy for a Sustainable World* (Washington, D.C.: WRI, 1987).

22. Marcia D. Lowe, *Alternatives to the Automobile: Transport for Livable Cities*, Worldwatch Paper 98 (Washington, D.C.: Worldwatch Institute, October 1990); Marcia D. Lowe, *The Bicycle: Vehicle for A Small Planet*, Worldwatch Paper 90 (Washington, D.C.: Worldwatch Institute, September 1989).

23. Auto fleet from MVMA, *Facts and Figures '90*; carbon emissions and traffic fatalities from Lowe, *Alternatives to the Automobile*.

24. Car ownership from Stacy C. Davis et al., *Transportation Energy Data Book: Edition 10* (Oak Ridge, Tenn.: Oak Ridge National Laboratory, 1989); two-car garages from "Motor

Motels," *American Demographics*, April 1989; driving hours from John P. Robinson, "Americans on the Road," *American Demographics*, September 1989; air-conditioned cars from MVMA, Detroit, Mich., private communication, September 10, 1990; impact of CFCs on climate change from Mark A. DeLuchi, "Emissions of Greenhouse Gases from the Use of Gasoline, Methanol, and Other Alternative Transportation Fuels" (draft), Transportation Research Group, University of California, Davis, Calif., 1990.

25. Quoted in Wachtel, *Poverty of Affluence*.

26. One billion air travellers from "High Hopes and Expectations," *Europe*, September 1990; 4 million and 41 percent from Air Transport Association, Washington, D.C., private communication, September 12, 1990; jet set's extra distance and energy consumption are Worldwatch Institute estimates based on average trip lengths and energy use of air travel from Davis et al., *Transportation Energy Data Book, Edition 10*.

27. World Bank, *World Development Report 1990*; dietary fat is Worldwatch Institute estimate based on World Commission on Environment and Development (WCED), *Our Common Future* (Oxford: Oxford University Press, 1987).

28. Gina Kolata, "Report Urges Low-Fat Diet for Everyone," *New York Times*, February 28, 1990; WCED, *Our Common Future*.

29. Kolata, "Report Urges Low-Fat Diet for Everyone"; China from Jane E. Brody, "Huge Study of Diet Indicts Fat and Meat," *New York Times*, May 8, 1990.

30. Share of world grain from Peter Riley, grains analyst, Economic Research Service, USDA, Washington, D.C., private communication, September 13, 1990; grain input per beef produced is Worldwatch Institute estimate based on Economic Research Service, USDA, Washington, D.C., various private communications; energy based on David Pimentel et al., "The Potential for Grass-Fed Livestock: Resource Constraints," *Science*, February 22, 1980, and on David Pimentel, Professor, Cornell University, Ithaca, N.Y., private communication, August 29, 1990; other environmental effects from Molly O'Neill, "An Icon of the Good Life Ends Up On a Crowded Planet's Hit Lists," *New York Times*, May 6, 1990.

31. Chile grapes from Bradley Graham, "South American Grapes: Tale of Two Countries," *Washington Post*, February 2, 1988; travel of average mouthful of food from U.S. Department of Defense, *U.S. Agriculture: Potential Vulnerabilities*, cited in Cornucopia Project, *Empty Breadbasket?* (Emmaus, Pa.: Rodale Press, 1981); farm policies favor large producers from Marty Strange, *Family Farming: A New Economic Vision* (Lincoln, Neb.: University of Nebraska Press, 1989); health standards from Wendell Berry, "Sanitation and the Small Farm," in *The Gift of Good Land* (San Francisco: North Point Press, 1981); irrigation subsidies from E. Phillip LeVeen and Laura B. King, *Turning Off the Tap on Federal Water Subsidies*, Vol. 1 (San Francisco: Natural Resources Defense Council and California Rural Legal Assistance Foundation, 1985); truck subsidies from Harriet Parcells, "Big Trucks Getting a Free Ride," National Association of Railroad Passengers, Washington, D.C., April 1990.

32. David Pimentel, "Energy Flow in the Food System," in David Pimentel and Carl W. Hall, eds., *Food and Energy Resources* (Orlando, Fla.: Academic Press, 1984).

33. Population without safe water from U.N. Development Program, *Human Development Report 1990* (New York: Oxford University Press, 1990); drinking classes from Frederick Clairmonte and John Cavanagh, *Merchants of Drink* (Penang, Malaysia: Third World Network, 1988).

34. Global mean soft drink consumption from Clairmonte and Cavanagh, *Merchants of Drink*; 1989 soft drinks and water consumption from *Beverage Industry*, Cleveland, Ohio, private communication, September 14, 1990.

35. Durning, *Poverty and the Environment*.

36. Worldwatch Inststute estimates based on steel figures from Bureau of the Census, *Statistical Abstract of the United States: 1990*, and on energy consumption (excludes subsistence use of fuelwood) from WRI, *World Resources 1990–91*.

37. Comparisons of industrial and developing countries from WCED, *Our Common Future*; U.S. per capita consumption of materials is Worldwatch Institute estimate based on petroleum and coal from DOE, EIA, *Annual Energy Review 1988*, on other minerals and agricultural products from Bureau of the Census, *Statistical Abstract of the United States: 1990*, and on forest products from Alice Ulrich, *U.S. Timber Production, Trade, Consumption, and Price Statistics 1950–87* (Washington, D.C.: USDA Forest Service, 1989).

38. Expenditures for packaging from U.S. Congress, Office of Technology Assessment, *Facing America's Trash: What Next for Municipal Solid Waste?* (Washington, D.C.: U.S. Government Printing Office, 1989); Steve Usdin, "Snap Happy: Throwaway Cameras Are an Instant Hit," *Intersect*, June 1990; diapers from Karen Christensen, independent researcher, Boulder, Colo., private communication, October 18, 1990; razors from Cheryl Russell, "Guilty as Charged," *American Demographics*, February 1989; plates, cups, and cans are Worldwatch Institute estimates based on Environmental Protection Agency, Office of Solid Waste and Emergency Response, "Characterization of Municipal Solid Waste in the United States: 1990 Update," Washington, D.C., June 1990; aluminum in DC-10 from Elaine Bendell, McDonnell Douglas, Long Beach, Calif., private communication, September 20, 1990.

39. Spencer S. Hsu, "The Sneaker Steps Out," *Washington Post*, July 22, 1990.

40. Aristotle, *Politics*, quoted in Goldian VandenBroeck, ed., *Less Is More: The Art of Voluntary Poverty* (New York: Harper & Row, 1978).

41. Lucretius, *On the Nature of the Universe*, and Tolstoy, *My Religion*, both quoted in VandenBroeck, *Less is More*.

42. Brooke Kroeger, "Feeling Poor on $600,000 a Year," *New York Times*, April 26, 1987.

43. Argyle, *Psychology of Happiness*.

44. Determinants of happiness from ibid.; Freedman quoted in Wachtel, *Poverty of Affluence*.

45. Veblen quoted in Lewis H. Lapham, *Money and Class in America* (New York: Weidenfeld & Nicolson, 1988).

46. Ads in the morning from Andrew Sullivan, "Buying and Nothingness," *The New Republic*, May 8, 1989; teenagers, defined as aged 12 to 17, from John Schwartz, "Stalking the Youth Market," *Newsweek Special Issue*, June 1990; childhood total is Worldwatch Institute estimate based on Action for Children's Television, Boston, Mass., private communication, October 17, 1990.

47. TV and radio stations from Bureau of the Census, *Statistical Abstract of the United States: 1990*; chair lifts, bus stops, and subway stations from Paula Span, "Ads: They're Everywhere!" *Washington Post*, April 28, 1990; Paula J. Silbey, "Merchants Star on Mall's Video Wall," *Shopping Centers Today*, August 1989.

48. Classrooms and doctors' offices from Randall Rothenberg, "Two Views on Whittle's TV Reports," *New York Times*, June 1, 1990; feature films from Randall Rothenberg, "Messages From Sponsors Become Harder to Detect," *New York Times*, November 19, 1989; Randall Rothenberg, "$30,000 Lands Product on Game Board," *New York Times*, February 6, 1989; bathrooms from Robert Geiger and Larry Teitelbaum, "Restaurants, Airlines Privy to New Medium," *Advertising Age*, October 24, 1988; phones from "Commercials Invade Ma Bell," *Family Circle*, April 24, 1990; hot dogs from Span, "Ads:

They're Everywhere!"; eggs from "Which Came First? Adman or Egg?" *Fortune*, April 9, 1990.

49. Monetary figures are adjusted for inflation and expressed in 1989 dollars. U.S. per capita from U.S. Department of Commerce, *Historical Statistics of the United States, Colonial Times to 1970, Bicentennial Edition, Part 2* (Washington, D.C.: 1975), and from Bureau of the Census, *Statistical Abstract of the United States: 1990*; world per capita from Robert J. Coen, *International Herald Tribune*, October 10, 1984, and from Tracy Poltie, International Advertising Association, New York, private communication, August 29, 1990; advertising growth faster than economic output based on Maddison, *World Economy in the 20th Century*; India from Chandra, "India: Middle-Class Spending"; Korea from "Asia's Network Boom," *Asiaweek*, July 6, 1990.

50. Roberta Brandes Gratz, "Malling the Northeast," *New York Times Magazine*, April 1, 1990; mall walkers from Mark J. Schoifet, "To AVIA, Mall Walking Is No Joke," *Shopping Centers Today*, January 1989; Bill Mintiens, Product Marketing Director for Walking, Avia, Portland, Oreg., private communication, July 3, 1990.

51. Time spent shopping from John P. Robinson, "When the Going Gets Tough," *American Demographics*, February 1989; shopping and church from Robert Fishman, "Megalopolis Unbound," *Wilson Quarterly*, Winter 1990; teenage girls from Magnet, "Money Society"; number of malls from Bureau of the Census, *Statistical Abstract of the United States: 1990*; high schools from Herbert I. Schiller, *Culture, Inc.* (New York: Oxford University Press, 1989); retail space growth (figures exclude automotive outlets) from International Council of Shopping Centers, "The Scope of the Shopping Center Industry in the U.S.," New York, 1989; U.S. sales from Donald L. Pendley, Director of Public Relations, International Council of Shopping Centers, New York, in "Malls Still

Dominant" (letter), *American Demographics*, September 1990; France and Spain from Paula J. Silbey, "Spain Leads European Growth," *Shopping Centers Today*, March 1989.

52. Silbey, "Spain Leads European Growth"; Britain from Carl Gardner and Julie Sheppard, *Consuming Passion: The Rise of Retail Culture* (London: Unwin Hyman, 1990); Paula J. Silbey, "Italian Centers Expected To Triple in Number Soon," *Shopping Centers Today*, May 1989.

53. Malcolm Fergusson, "Subsidized Pollution: Company Cars and the Greenhouse Effect," report prepared for Greenpeace U.K., London, January 1990; subsidized beef from Keith Schneider, "Come What May, Congress Stays True to the Critters," *New York Times*, May 6, 1990, and from George Ledec, "New Directions for Livestock Policy in Latin America," Department of Forestry and Resource Management, University of California, Berkeley, October 1988; taxes on homes from Peter Dreier and John Atlas, "Deductio Ad Absurdam," *Washington Monthly*, February 1990, and from Peter Dreier, Director of Housing, Boston Redevelopment Authority, Boston, Mass., private communication, October 12, 1990; multiple home owners from American Housing Survey, U.S. Bureau of the Census, Suitland, Md., private communication, October 16, 1990; homelessness estimate from "Examining Homelessness," *Science*, March 23, 1990.

54. *Fortune* quoted in David E. Shi, *Simple Life: Plain Living and High Thinking in American Culture* (New York: Oxford University Press, 1985); urban-to-suburban migrations from Stuart Ewen, *Captains of Consciousness* (New York: McGraw-Hill, 1976), and from Delores Hayden, *Redesigning the American Dream: The Future of Housing, Work, and Family Life* (New York: W.W. Norton & Co., 1984).

55. Scott Burns, *Home, Inc.* (Garden City, N.Y.: Doubleday, 1975).

56. Katsumi, "Tokyo's Serious Waste Problem"; "France: Aging but Dynamic,"

Market: Europe (Ithaca, N.Y.), September 1990.

57. History from Susan Strasser, *Satisfaction Guaranteed: The Making of the American Mass Market* (New York: Pantheon Books, 1989); American neighborhoods from Robert Reich, "A Question of Geography," *New Republic*, May 9, 1988.

58. Basic value of sustainable society from WCED, *Our Common Future*.

59. Aristotle, *Nicomachean Ethics* 1109b23.

60. Toynbee quoted in Wachtel, *Poverty of Affluence*.

61. Duane Elgin, *Voluntary Simplicity* (New York: William Morrow and Company, 1981); India from Mark Shepard, *Gandhi Today: A Report on Mahatma Gandhi's Successors* (Arcata, Calif.: Simple Productions, 1987); Netherlands and Norway from Elgin, *Voluntary Simplicity*; United Kingdom and West Germany from Pierre Pradervand, independent researcher, Geneva, Switzerland, private communication, July 14, 1990, and from Groupe de Beaulieu, *Construire L'Esperance* (Lausanne: Editions de l'Aire, 1990).

62. Quoted in VandenBroeck, *Less Is More*.

63. Vicki Robin, "How Much Is Enough?" *In Context* (Bainbridge Island, Wash.), Summer 1990; Camus quoted in E.F. Schumacher, *Good Work* (New York: Harper & Row, 1979).

64. Berry, *The Gift of Good Land;* "What Is Enough?" *In Context* (Bainbridge Island, Wash.), Summer 1990; Katy Butler, "Paté Poverty: Downwardly Mobile Baby Boomers Lust After Luxury," *Utne Reader*, September/ October 1989.

65. Shi, *Simple Life*.

66. Children's television restriction from Howard Kurtz, "Bush May Let Children's TV Measure Become Law," *Washington Post*, October 3, 1990, and from Action for Children's Television, private communication; Jeannine Johnson, "In Search of . . . the European T.V. Show," *Europe*, November 1989.

67. "American Excess," *Adbusters* (Vancouver), Summer 1990.

68. Robert Bellah, *The Broken Covenant* (New York: Seabury Press, 1975).

69. Timothy Harper, "British Sunday Law Intact—for Now," *Shopping Centers Today*, May 1989; green belts from Timothy Harper, "Rulings Slow U.K. Mall Development," *Shopping Centers Today*, May 1989; Japan from Arthur Getz, "Small Town Economics, West and East," letter to Peter Martin, Institute of Current World Affairs, Hanover, N.H., December 26, 1989.

70. Dutch household packaging waste is Worldwatch Institute estimate based on J.M. Joosten et al., *Informative Document: Packaging Waste* (Bilthoven, Netherlands: National Institute of Public Health and Environmental Protection, 1989); land developed from Jim Riggle, Director of Operations, American Farmland Trust, Washington, D.C., private communication, October 17, 1990.

71. Mail from Blayne Cutler, "Meet Jane Doe," *American Demographics*, June 1989; Japanese bottles figure is Worldwatch Institute estimate based on Hidefumi Kurasaka, Chief of Planning Section, Environmental Agency, Government of Japan, private communication, August 7, 1990; newspaper advertising from Sullivan, "Buying and Nothingness"; car travel is 1988 vehicle-kilometers per capita based on International Roads Federation, *World Road Statistics 1984–88* (Washington, D.C.: 1989).

72. Henry David Thoreau, *Walden* (1854; reprint, Boston: Houghton Mifflin, 1957).

Chapter 10. Reshaping the Global Economy

1. Throughout this chapter, the $20-trillion dollar world economy is a Worldwatch

Institute estimate based on 1988 gross world product from Central Intelligence Agency (CIA), *Handbook of Economic Statistics, 1989* (Washington, D.C.: 1989), with Soviet and Eastern Europe gross national products extrapolated from Paul Marer, *Dollar GNP's of the USSR and Eastern Europe* (Baltimore: Johns Hopkins University Press, 1985), with adjustments to 1990 based on growth rates from International Monetary Fund (IMF), *World Economic Outlook* (Washington, D.C.: October 1990), and CIA, *Handbook of Economic Statistics*, and with the composite deflator from Office of Management and Budget, *Historical Tables, Budget of the United States Government, Fiscal Year 1990* (Washington, D.C.: U.S. Government Printing Office, 1989)

2. Fivefold global expansion from Angus Maddison, *The World Economy in the 20th Century* (Paris: Organisation of Economic Co-operation and Development (OECD), 1989), and from IMF, *World Economic Outlook*; carbon emissions from "Mauna Loa, 30 Years of Continuous CO_2 Measurements," *CDIAC Communications*, Carbon Dioxide Information Analysis Center, Oak Ridge National Laboratory, Oak Ridge, Tenn., Summer 1988; Charles D. Keeling, "Measurements of the Concentration of Atmospheric Carbon Dioxide at Mauna Loa Observatory, Hawaii, 1958–1986," Final Report for the Carbon Dioxide Information and Analysis Center, Martin-Marietta Energy Systems Inc., Oak Ridge, Tenn., April 1987; Neftel et al., "Evidence from Polar Ice Cores for the Increase in Atmospheric CO_2 in the Last Two Centuries," *Nature*, May 2, 1985; Intergovernmental Panel on Climate Change, "Policymakers' Summary of the Scientific Assessment of Climate Change," Report from Working Group I, June 1990.

3. Population estimates from Population Reference Bureau (PRB), *1989* and *1990 World Population Data Sheet* (Washington, D.C.: 1989 and 1990); poverty figures from Alan B. Durning, *Poverty and the Environment: Reversing the Downward Spiral*, Worldwatch Paper 92 (Washington, D.C.: Worldwatch Institute, November 1989).

4. World Bank, *World Debt Tables 1989–1990: External Debt of Developing Countries, Vols. I and II* (Washington, D.C.: 1989).

5. Office of Technology Assessment, *Assessing Contractor Use in Superfund* (Washington, D.C.: 1989); WISE (World Information Service on Energy), "State of the Soviet Nuclear Industry," Paris, May 18, 1990; Soviet GNP from CIA, *Handbook of Economic Statistics, 1989*.

6. OECD, *OECD In Figures* (Paris: 1990); Kit D. Farber and Gary L. Rutledge, "Pollution Abatement and Control Expenditures, 1984–87," *Survey of Current Business*, U.S. Department of Commerce, June 1989.

7. OECD, *Development Co-operation: Efforts and Policies of the Members of the Development Assistance Committee* (Paris: in press); OECD, *Development Co-operation in the 1990s: Efforts and Policies of the Members of the Development Assistance Committee* (Paris: 1989).

8. OECD, *Development Co-operation in the 1990s*; OECD, *Development Co-operation* (in press).

9. OECD, *Development Co-operation* (in press).

10. OECD, *Development Co-operation in the 1990s*; Agency for International Development, *Agency for International Development Fiscal Year 1991 Summary Tables* (Washington, D.C.: 1990); PRB, *1990 World Population Data Sheet*.

11. OECD, *Developing Co-operation* (in prees); Sigismund Niebel, Reporting System Division, OECD, Paris, private communication, November 18, 1990.

12. OECD, *Development Co-operation* (in press); World Bank, *The World Bank Annual Report 1990* (Washington, D.C.: 1990).

13. World Bank, *The World Bank Annual Report 1990*; Bruce Rich, Environmental De-

fense Fund, "The Environmental Performance of the Public International Financial Institutions and Other Related Issues," Testimony before the Committee on Appropriations, U.S. Senate, Washington, D.C., July 25, 1990; Stephan Schwartzman, *Bankrolling Disasters: International Development Banks and the Global Environment* (Washington, D.C.: Sierra Club, 1986).

14. Barber B. Conable, President, World Bank, "The World Bank and International Finance Corporation," presented to the World Resources Institute, Washington, D.C., May 5, 1987; World Bank, *The World Bank and the Environment: First Annual Report Fiscal 1990* (Washington, D.C.: 1990); Personnel Office, World Bank, Washington D.C., private communication, November 1, 1990.

15. World Bank, *The World Bank and the Environment*; Bruce Rich, "The Emperor's New Clothes: The World Bank and Environmental Reform," *World Policy Journal*, Spring 1990.

16. Michael Irwin, "Why I've Had It with the World Bank," *Wall Street Journal*, March 30, 1990; World Bank staff, private communications, October 1990.

17. Howard Geller, "End-Use Electricity Conservation: Options for Developing Countries," Energy Department Paper No. 32, World Bank, Washington, D.C., 1986; World Bank, *The World Bank Annual Report 1990*; Rich, "The Environmental Performance of the Public International Financial Institutions and Other Related Issues."

18. Environmental assessment process detailed in World Bank, *The World Bank and the Environment*; Rich, "The Environmental Performance of the Public International Financial Institutions and Other Related Issues."

19. Location of the Environment Department in World Bank, *The World Bank and the Environment*.

20. World Bank staff, private communications.

21. Mahabub Hossain, *Credit for Alleviation of Rural Poverty: The Grameen Bank in Bangladesh*, Research Report 65 (Washington, D.C.: International Food Policy Research Institute, 1988).

22. NGO Working Group on the World Bank, "Position Paper of the NGO Working Group on the World Bank," Geneva, December 1989; Irwin, "Why I've Had It with the World Bank."

23. Overseas Development Council, "The Brady Plan: An Interim Assessment," Washington, D.C., 1990; *Securing Our Global Future: Canada's Stake in the Unfinished Business of Third World Debt*, Minutes of Proceedings and Evidence of the Standing Committee on External Affairs and International Affairs, Canadian House of Commons, June 7, 1990.

24. World Bank, *World Debt Tables*; Canadian House of Commons, *Securing Our Global Future*; Jane Perlez, "U.S. Forgives Loans to 12 African Countries," *New York Times*, January 10, 1990.

25. Robert Repetto and Frederik van Bolhuis, *Natural Endowments: Financing Resource Conservation for Development* (Washington, D.C.: World Resources Institute, 1989); David Bigman, "A Plan to End LDC Debt and Save the Environment Too," *Challenge*, July/August 1990.

26. Thomas E. Lovejoy, "Aid Debtor Nations' Ecology," *New York Times*, October 4, 1984; Diana Page, "Debt-for-Nature Swaps: Experience Gained, Lessons Learned," *International Environmental Affairs*, January 1990.

27. The Nature Conservancy, "Officially Sanctioned Debt-for-Nature Swaps to Date," Washington, D.C., August 1990; Roque Sevilla Larrea and Alvaro Umaña, "Por qué Canjear Deuda por Naturaleza?" World Wildlife Fund, World Resources Institute, and Nature Conservancy, Washington, D.C., 1989.

28. Address by Rajiv Gandhi, Prime Minister of India, at the Ninth Conference of Heads of State or Government of Non-Aligned Countries, Belgrade, Yugoslavia, September 5, 1989; France's endorsement was delivered at the World Bank's annual meeting, "French Proposal on the Environment," Press Communique from the Development Committee Meeting, September 25, 1989, Washington, D.C.; "Tolba Advocates World Environment Fund," *Our Planet*, Vol. 1, No. 2/3, 1989; funding mechanism as a centerpiece of the Brazil Conference from Mostafa Tolba quoted in Linda Starke, *Signs of Hope: Working Towards Our Common Future* (Oxford: Oxford University Press, 1990).

29. World Bank, *The World Bank and the Environment*; World Bank, "Funding for the Global Environment," Discussion Paper, Washington, D.C., February 1990; Steven Mufson, "World Bank Wants Fund to Protect Environment," *Washington Post*, May 3, 1990; Letter to Barber Conable, president, World Bank, from David A. Wirth et al., National Resources Defense Council (NRDC), on behalf of NRDC and six other national environmental groups, Washington, D.C., March 9, 1990.

30. World Bank, *The World Bank and the Environment*; "Parties to Montreal Protocol Agree to Phase Out CFCs, Help Developing Nations," *International Environment Reporter*, July 11, 1990; Philip Shabecoff, "U.S. Backs World Bank Environment Unit," *New York Times*, November 30, 1990.

31. Robert Repetto, *Paying the Price: Pesticide Subsidies in Developing Countries* (Washington, D.C.: World Resources Institute, 1985); Egyptian gross domestic product from World Bank, *World Development Report 1990* (New York: Oxford University Press, 1990); Egyptian health spending based on various Egyptian ministry reports provided by the World Bank.

32. Sandra Postel, *Defusing the Toxics Threat: Controlling Pesticides and Industrial Waste*, Worldwatch Paper 79 (Washington, D.C.: Worldwatch Institute, September 1987).

33. See Robert Repetto, *The Forest for the Trees? Government Policies and the Misuse of Forest Resources* (Washington, D.C.: World Resources Institute, 1988); Robert Repetto, "Deforestation in the Tropics," *Scientific American*, April 1990.

34. Estimate of $500 million to $1 billion from Repetto and van Bolhuis, *Natural Endowments*; Philip M. Fearnside et al., *Deforestation Rate in Brazilian Amazonia* (São Paulo, Brazil: Instituto de Pesquisas Espaciais and Instituto Nacional de Pesquisas da Amazônia, 1990).

35. "Brazil: Latest Deforestation Figures," *Nature*, June 28, 1990; Vera Machado, Head of the Environment Sector, Embassy of Brazil, Washington, D.C., private communication, October 30, 1990.

36. Repetto, *Paying the Price*; Robert Repetto, *Skimming the Water: Rent-Seeking and the Performance of Public Irrigation Systems* (Washington, D.C.: World Resources Institute, 1986); Repetto, *The Forest for the Trees?*

37. U.S. Department of Agriculture (USDA), Economic Research Service, *Agricultural Resources: Cropland, Water and Conservation: Situation and Outlook Report*, Washington, D.C., September 1990.

38. David Moskovitz, *Profits & Progress Through Least-Cost Planning* (Washington, D.C.: National Association of Regulatory Utility Commissioners, 1989).

39. California Public Utilities Commission (CPUC), "CPUC, Major Utilities Promote Energy Efficiency and Conservation Programs," press release, San Francisco, Calif., August 29, 1990; Elizabeth Kolbert, "Utility's Rates Tied to Saving of Electricity," *New York Times*, September 1, 1990; "NEES to 'Mine' Customers' kWh," *Electrical World*, October 1989; Oregon Public Utility Com-

mission, "PUC Lauds PP&L's Conservation Program as an Oregon 'First'," press release, Salem, Oreg., July 19, 1990; Armond Cohen, Conservation Law Foundation, Boston, Mass., private communication, October 29, 1990.

40. Howard S. Geller, "Electricity Conservation in Brazil: Status Report and Analysis," American Council for an Energy-Efficient Economy, Washington, D.C., August, 1990; David A. Wirth, "Climate Chaos," *Foreign Policy*, Spring 1989.

41. Judith Jacobsen, *Promoting Population Stabilization: Incentives for Small Families*, Worldwatch Paper 54 (Washington, D.C.: Worldwatch Institute, June 1983).

42. D.L. Nortman et al., "A Cost Benefit Analysis of Family Planning Program of Mexican Social Security Administration," paper presented at the general conference of the International Union for the Scientific Study of Population, Florence, Italy, June 5–12, 1985, cited in Jodi L. Jacobson, *Planning the Global Family*, Worldwatch Paper 80 (Washington, D.C.: Worldwatch Institute, December 1987).

43. IMF, *International Financial Statistics* (Washington, D.C.: various years).

44. Information and Media Relations Division, "General Agreement on Tariffs and Trade (GATT): What it is, What it Does," (Geneva: General Agreement on Tariffs and Trade, 1990); Third World lost income estimate from Paul Shaw, "Rapid Population Growth and Environmental Degradation: Ultimate versus Proximate Factors," *Environmental Conservation*, Autumn 1989; Steven Shrybman, "International Trade and the Environment: An Environmental Assessment of Present GATT Negotiations," *Alternatives*, Vol. 17, No. 2, 1990; Jeffrey J. Schott, "Uruguay Round: What Can Be Achieved," in Jeffrey J. Schott, ed., *Completing the Uruguay Round* (Washington, D.C.: Institute for International Economics, 1990); Dale E. Hathaway, "Agriculture," in ibid.

45. Ann Davison, "Developing Country Concerns," in *IOCU (International Organization of Consumers Unions) Newsletter*, No. 5, 1990; Herman E. Daly and John B. Cobb, *For the Common Good: Redirecting the Economy Toward Community, the Environment, and a Sustainable Future* (Boston: Beacon Press, 1989).

46. Stewart Hudson, "Trade, Environment, and the Negotiations on the General Agreement on Trade and Tariffs (GATT)," National Wildlife Federation, Washington, D.C., September 24, 1990.

47. Ebba Dohlman, "The Trade Effects of Environmental Regulation," *The OECD Observer*, February/March 1990; Court decision from Evy Jordan, Embassy of Denmark, Washington, D.C., private communication, October 29, 1990; Shrybman, "International Trade and the Environment."

48. Dutch Electricity Generating Board, "Dutch Plan for Reforestation in Latin America," press release, Arnhem, The Netherlands, March 30, 1990; Irene Carsouw, Dutch Electricity Generating Board, private communication, October 29, 1990.

49. David Pearce et al., *Blueprint for a Green Economy* (London: Earthscan Ltd., 1989).

50. Allen V. Kneese, *The United States in the 1980s* (Stanford: The Hoover Institution, 1980); Pearce et al., *Blueprint for a Green Economy*.

51. OECD, *Economic Instruments for Environmental Protection* (Paris: 1989).

52. U.K example from European Community Commission, "Report of the Working Group of Experts from the Member States on the Use of Economic and Fiscal Instruments in EC Environmental Policy," Brussels, May 1990; CFC figures from U.S. House of Representatives, "Omnibus Budget Reconciliation Act of 1989, Conference Report to Accompany H.R. 3299," Washington, D.C., November 21, 1989; Joint Committee on Taxation, "Estimated Revenue Effects of

Conference Agreement on Revenue Provisions of H.R. 3299," Washington, D.C., November 21, 1989; Michael Weisskopf, "A Clever Solution for Pollution: Taxes," *Washington Post*, December 12, 1989.

53. Carbon dioxide emissions goals from "Ministerial Declaration of the Second World Climate Conference," Geneva, November 7, 1990, from "Germany and the Greenhouse: A Closer Look," *Global Environmental Change Report*, August 17, 1990, from "East Germany: Country Will Comply with CFC Ordinance of West Germany, Seeks Smaller CO_2 Cut," *International Environment Reporter*, July 1990, from "Japan to Stabilize Greenhouse Gas Emissions by 2000," *Global Environmental Change Report*, July 20, 1990, from "Switzerland to Announce Stabilization Goal at Second World Climate Conference," *Global Environmental Change Report*, July 20, 1990, from "The Netherlands Sets CO_2 Emissions Tax for 1990," *Global Environmental Change Report*, December 22, 1989, from "Country Profiles: Denmark," *European Energy Report*, May 1990, from The Ministry of Environment and Energy, *Action for a Common Future: Swedish National Report for Bergen Conference, May 1990* (Stockholm: 1989), from U.K. Department of the Environment, *This Common Inheritance: Britain's Environmental Strategy* (London: 1990), from Gunnrr Mathisen, Secretariate for Climate Affairs, Ministry of the Environment, Oslo, Norway, private communication, January 30, 1990, from "Austria to Reduce CO_2 Emissions 20% by 2005," *Global Environmental Change Report*, September 14, 1990, from Emmanuele D'Achon, First Secretary, Embassy of France, Washington, D.C., private communication, October 10, 1990, and from Ron Scherer, "Australia to Press for Worldwide Gas-Emissions Limits," *Christian Science Monitor,* October 18, 1990: carbon taxes from Geraldine C. Kay, "Global Climate Change Timeline," *Global Environmental Change Report*, July 28, 1990, from "Nation Adopts Carbon Dioxide Tax; Measure to be Higher on Coal than Gas," *International Environment Report*, March

1990, and from Anders Boeryd, Fuel Market Division, National Energy Administration, Sweden, private communication, August 10, 1990.

54. Debora MacKenzie, " . . . as Europe's Ministers Fail to Agree on Framework for Green Taxes," *New Scientist*, September 29, 1990.

55. Kennedy Maize, "Budget Summit Looking at Carbon Tax," *Energy Daily*, June 1, 1990; U.S. Congressional Budget Office (CBO), *Carbon Charges as a Response to Global Warming: the Effects of Taxing Fossil Fuels* (Washington, D.C.: August 1990); income tax receipts from U.S. Bureau of the Census, *Statistical Abstract of the United States: 1990* (Washington, D.C.: U.S. Government Printing Office, 1990).

56. CBO, *Carbon Charges as a Response to Global Warming*.

57. Ibid.; CBO estimates are based on pre-Iraqi invasion oil price projections.

58. Dieter Teufel et al., "Kosteuern als marktwirtschaftliches Instrument im Umweltschutz: Vorschläge für eine ökologische Steuerreform," Umwelt und Prognose Institut, Heidelberg, April 1988.

59. Estimated tax revenues based on Gregg Marland et al., *Estimates of CO₂ Emissions from Fossil Fuel Burning and Cement Manufacturing, Based on the United Nations Energy Statistics and the U.S. Bureau of Mines Cement Manufacturing Data* (Oak Ridge, Tenn.: Oak Ridge National Laboratory, 1989), and on British Petroleum (BP), *BP Statistical Review of World Energy* (London: 1990); hazardous waste estimates are 1985 figures from World Resources Institute, *World Resources 1990–1991* (New York: Oxford University Press, 1990); virgin pulp estimate based on 1987 figures in Alice H. Ulrich, *U.S. Timber Production, Trade, Consumption, and Price Statistics 1950–87* (Washington, D.C.: USDA, December 1989); pesticide sales are 1988 figures in U.S. Environmental Protection Agency

(EPA), *Pesticides Industry Sales and Usage* (Washington, D.C.: 1990); sulfur dioxide and nitrogen oxide emission estimates are for 1988 in EPA, *National Air Quality Emissions and Trends Report, 1988* (Research Triangle Park, N.C.: 1990); CFC tax and revenue estimates for 1994 from U.S. House of Representatives, "Omnibus Budget Reconciliation Act of 1989," and from Joint Committee on Taxation, "Estimated Revenue Effects"; groundwater depletion estimates are for 1980 in U.S. Geological Survey, *National Water Summary 1983—Hydrologic Events and Issues* (Washington, D.C.: U.S. Government Printing Office, 1983).

60. Estimate for climate fund revenues based on Marland et al., *Estimates of CO₂ Emmisions,* and on BP, *BP Statistical Review.*

61. Louis Harris & Associates et al., *The Rising Tide: Public Opinion, Policy & Politics* (Washington, D.C.: Americans for the Environment, 1989).

62. See Herman Daly, "Towards an Environmental Macroeconomics," presented at "The Ecological Economics of Sustainability: Making Local and Short-Term Goals Consistent with Global and Long-Term Goals," the International Society for Ecological Economics, Washington, D.C., May 1990; see also Paul R. Ehrlich, "The Limits to Substitution: Meta-Resource Depletion and a New Economic-Ecological Paradigm," *Ecological Economics,* No. 1, 1989.

63. 1900 global world output from Lester R. Brown and Sandra Postel, "Thresholds of Change," in Lester Brown et al., *State of the World 1987* (Washington, D.C.: W.W. Norton & Company, 1987).

64. Peter M. Vitousek et al., "Human Appropriation of the Products of Photosynthesis," *BioScience,* June 1986; PRB, *1990 World Population Data Sheet.*

65. U.S. Department of Energy (DOE), Energy Information Agency (EIA), *State Energy Data Report, Consumption Estimates, 1960–1988* (Washington, D.C.: 1990); DOE, EIA, *Annual Energy Review 1989* (Washington, D.C.: 1990); Bureau of the Census, *Statistical Abstract of the United States: 1990.*

66. Total vehicle kilometers for 1965–70 from U.S. Department of Commerce, *Historical Statistics of the United States, Colonial Times to 1970, Bicentennial Edition* (Washington, D.C., 1975); 1970–88 from DOE, EIA, *Annual Energy Review 1989.*

67. PRB, *1990 World Population Data Sheet.*

68. See Hazel Henderson, "Moving Beyond Economism: New Indicators for Culturally Specific, Sustainable Development," in The Caracas Report on Alternative Development Indicators, *Redefining Wealth and Progress: New Ways to Measure Economic, Social and Environmental Change* (New York: The Bootstrap Press, 1989); Daly and Cobb, *For the Common Good.*

69. Garrett Hardin, "Paramount Positions in Ecological Economics," presented at "The Ecological Economics of Sustainability."

70. Durning, *Poverty and the Environment.*

Index